Muirhead Library of Philosophy

CONTEMPORARY PSYCHOLOGY

MUIRHEAD

Muirhead Library of Philosophy

PHILOSOPHY OF MIND AND PSYCHOLOGY
In 17 Volumes

I	The Nature of Thought (Vol I)	*Blanshard*
II	The Nature of Thought (Vol II)	*Blanshard*
III	A History of Psychology (Vol I)	*Brett*
IV	A History of Psychology (Vol II)	*Brett*
V	A History of Psychology (Vol III)	*Brett*
VI	The Subject of Consciousness	*Evans*
VII	Imagination	*Furlong*
VIII	Mental Images	*Hannay*
IX	Nature, Mind and Modern Science	*Harris*
X	Hypothesis and Perception	*Harris*
XI	The Problems of Perception	*Hirst*
XII	Memory	*Smith*
XIII	Analytic Psychology (Vol I)	*Stout*
XIV	Analytic Psychology (Vol II)	*Stout*
XV	Philosophy and Psychical Research	*Thakur*
XVI	Enigmas of Agency	*Thalberg*
XVII	Contemporary Psychology	*Villa*

CONTEMPORARY PSYCHOLOGY

GUIDO VILLA

LONDON AND NEW YORK

First published 1903 by
Swan Sonnenschein & Co. Ltd

Published 2013 by Routledge
2 Park Square, Milton Park, Abingdon, Oxfordshire OX14 4RN
711 Third Avenue, New York, NY 10017

First issued in paperback 2014

*Routledge is an imprint of the Taylor and Francis Group,
an informa business*

All rights reserved. No part of this book may be reprinted or reproduced or utilized in any form or by any electronic, mechanical, or other means, now known or hereafter invented, including photocopying and recording, or in any information storage or retrieval system, without permission in writing from the publishers.

The publishers have made every effort to contact authors/copyright holders of the works reprinted in the *Muirhead Library of Philosophy*. This has not been possible in every case, however, and we would welcome correspondence from those individuals/companies we have been unable to trace.

These reprints are taken from original copies of each book. In many cases the condition of these originals is not perfect. The publisher has gone to great lengths to ensure the quality of these reprints, but wishes to point out that certain characteristics of the original copies will, of necessity, be apparent in reprints thereof.

British Library Cataloguing in Publication Data
A CIP catalogue record for this book
is available from the British Library

Contemporary Psychology
ISBN 978-0-415-29622-9 (hbk)
ISBN 978-1-138-87121-2 (pbk)
Philosophy of Mind and Psychology: 17 Volumes
ISBN 978-0-415-29533-8
Muirhead Library of Philosophy: 95 Volumes
ISBN 978-0-415-27897-3

CONTEMPORARY PSYCHOLOGY

BY

GUIDO VILLA

LECTURER ON PHILOSOPHY IN THE UNIVERSITY OF ROME

REVISED BY THE AUTHOR, AND TRANSLATED WITH
HIS PERMISSION

BY

HAROLD MANACORDA

ATTACHÉ TO THE ITALIAN EMBASSY IN PARIS

London
SWAN SONNENSCHEIN & CO Ltd
New York: THE MACMILLAN CO
1903

TO THE MEMORY OF
MY FATHER
TO
MY MOTHER

G. V.

EDITOR'S NOTE

THE translation of the Italian into English has been done by Mr. Harold Manacorda, Attaché to the Italian Embassy in Paris. I ought, however, to explain that I have myself gone over the whole, both in MS. and in proof, and am responsible for many changes in phraseology and some condensations, which, while departing from the form of a literal translation, seem better fitted to represent the sense to English readers. In further deference to English taste, I have taken the liberty of dividing some of the chapters of the original. A few references to important contributions to English Psychology which have recently appeared have been added. Where there are English translations of the works alluded to in the text, I have quoted them in the notes under their English titles, and with references to the pages in the last English editions.

J. H. MUIRHEAD,
GENERAL EDITOR OF THE LIBRARY OF PHILOSOPHY.

BIRMINGHAM, *March 5th*, 1903.

PREFACE TO THE ENGLISH EDITION

THE present edition, which I have the honour to bring before the British public, differs considerably both in form and substance from the original Italian edition (Turin : Bocca, 1899). My own judgment and the observations of my critics are responsible for this. The principal difference consists in greater brevity and conciseness, obtained by the elimination of a number of repetitions, which were one of the chief defects of the original work. I have, however, attempted to introduce some even more important changes. Thus the different questions have been severally investigated with greater care; the references have been extended to a greater number of authors; and, lastly, the second part of Chapter IV. (on Method) has been suppressed, and has given place to a chapter (Chapter VI.) on the Composition and Development of Mental Life. I venture, therefore, to express the hope that my work, thus modified, may serve as a critical and historical introduction to the study of modern Psychology. The origin of the problems of contemporary Psychology, their genetic relation to general philosophy, natural science, and the social and moral sciences, and the different aspects they assume in the various scientific systems of the present day, make up the subject-matter of my work. In an age like the present, in which the historico-genetic method is justly considered the best adapted to the solution of scientific problems, it seems advisable to apply it also to psychological questions which, owing to their great complexity and original diversity, continue to present many points of extreme difficulty and uncertainty.

I owe a debt of infinite gratitude to all those who have kindly facilitated my labour with their help and their advice; and, amongst them, I wish especially to mention Mrs. C. A. F. Rhys Davids, so well known in England through her philosophical studies. I feel also deeply indebted to Mr. Manacorda, who has taken upon himself the laborious task of translation. I must finally acknowledge the help afforded the translator by the first volume of Professor Baldwin's *Dictionary of Philosophy and Psychology*, and can only regret that the second volume was published too late to be available.

GUIDO VILLA.

ROME, *December*, 1902.

CONTENTS

	PAGE
EDITOR'S NOTE	vii
PREFACE TO THE ENGLISH EDITION	ix
INTRODUCTION	1

CHAPTER I.—HISTORICAL DEVELOPMENT OF PSYCHOLOGY

1. *The Seventeenth and Eighteenth Centuries:* Three periods of the history of Psychology—Descartes—Spinoza—Locke—Leibnitz—Wolff—Tetens—Berkeley—Hume—Zanotti—Hartley—Priestley—E. Darwin—Reid—Stewart—Brown—Condillac—French materialism—La Mettrie—J. J. Rousseau—Bonnet
2. *The Early Part of the Nineteenth Century:* Kant—Hegel—Herbart—Schopenhauer—Beneke—Cabanis—De Biran—Other French psychologists—Jouffroy—Galluppi—Rosmini—Comte—Hamilton—J. S. Mill .
3. *Modern Psychology:* Modern Psychology—Materialists of the nineteenth century—Lotze—Weber—Fechner—Wundt—Horwicz—Spencer — Bain —Bailey — Lewes — Maudsley — Charles Darwin—Laicock and other English psychologists—Psychology of Peoples—Lubbock—Waitz—Bastian — Müller — Lazarus and Steinthal — Brentano and others — German psychophysics—Pathological Psychology—Psychology of childhood—Animal Psychology—Sully and other English psychologists—American psychologists—French psychologists of the nineteenth century—Taine—Ribot and others—Psychology in Italy—Ardigò—Sergi—Mosso—Criminal anthropology in Italy—Russian psychologists—Psychological laboratories—Periodicals 8

CHAPTER II.—OBJECT AND SCOPE OF PSYCHOLOGY

Object of Psychology—Scientific character of Psychology—Various definitions of Psychology—Fundamental characteristic of Psychology—Psychology and natural science—Fundamental characteristics of psychical phenomena—Relations between physical and mental phenomena—Recent discussions on the subjective character of mental phenomena—Aim and position of Psychology as a science—Psychology and the moral sciences—Psychology and the natural sciences—Psychology and the philosophical sciences—Psychology and logic—Psychology and epistemology—Psychology and ethics and æsthetics—Philosophy and positive science—Psychology and dynamics—Psychology and the special sciences—Limitations of scientific Psychology 63

Chapter III.—Mind and Body

Various conceptions of the relation between mind and body—Ancient philosophers—Descartes and the Cartesians—Spinoza and Leibnitz—Wolff—Gall and phrenology—Anatomical and physiological theory of Flourens—Broca—Modern physiological research—Ferrier, Munk, Goltz, etc.—Discussions on the functions of the brain—Modern histological research—Golgi, Waldeyer, Kölliker and others—Structure and functions of the cerebro-spinal nervous system—Co-ordination of the nervous centres—Physiological mechanism of speech—The relations between mind and body in modern philosophy—Theories regarding vital phenomena—Animism and vitalism—The mechanical conception of vital phenomena—Neo-vitalism—Modern spiritualism and materialism—Modern theories on the relations between mind and body—Theory of dualism—Physical and psychical causality—Monistic theories—The spiritualistic theory—The materialistic theory—Reality of psychical facts—Confutation of materialism—Theory of psychophysical parallelism—Theory of identity—Interpretation of the concept of parallelism . 91

Chapter IV.—The Methods of Psychology

Uncertainty of psychological methods—Psychological research has an inherent character of generality—Historical survey of psychological methods—The introspective method—Recent criticisms—Kant's criticism upon the introspective method—Herbart's criticism—Influence of Positivism and of the Natural Sciences—The ideas of Comte—Rise of experimental Psychology—Weber—Fechner—The new English Psychology—Bain's analytical Psychology—Experimental research in Germany—Wundt—Philosophical vindication of the experimental method in Psychology—Various experimental methods—Psychophysical method—Psychometrical methods—Measurement of the span of consciousness and of attention—Mnemonic and associative experiments—Criticisms on the experimental methods—The value of Weber's law discussed—Various interpretations of Weber's law—Psychological character of the experimental method—Psychophysical materialism discussed—The genetic methods—The Psychology of infancy—Psychology of Peoples—Anthropological and linguistic research—The theories of Lazarus and Steinthal—Objections to ethnographical Psychology—Specific character of social psychical processes—Difference between Psychology and the moral sciences—Difference between the Psychology of peoples and the history of philosophy—The Psychology of Animals—Pathological Psychology: its recent progress—Criticism of the various psychological methods—Direct and indirect methods—Value and limitations of the experimental methods—Relation between the experimental and other psychological methods—Unity of the various psychological methods—Recent attempts at blending the psychological methods—Preponderating value of the introspective method 128

Chapter V.—Psychical Functions

The fundamental functions of the mind according to ancient ideas—Wolff and the theory of faculties—Kant—English and French sensationalists

Contents xiii

—Gall's phrenology—Herbart's criticism of the theory of faculties—
Herbart's intellectualism—Herbart and Schopenhauer—Schopenhauer
against intellectualism—Beneke, Lotze, Volkmann—Intellectualism
critically examined—Sensation and feeling—Higher and lower faculties
—The Herbartian theories concerning feeling—The theories of the
psychophysical materialistic school on feeling—Feeling as a primitive
activity—Horwicz—Physiological theory of feeling—Ribot—Criticism
of Ribot's theory—James's and C. Lange's theory on the emotions—The
physiological theory and the unity of the psychical functions—Theories
concerning the Will—Intellectualistic theories—The will considered as
a derivative function—Spencer's theory—The theory of Horwicz—
Physiological theories—Münsterberg—Bain's theory—Ribot's theory—
Beneke's theory—Wundt's theory—Active character of the will—Will
and presentation—Impulsive acts and acts of choice—Inner acts of
volition—Attention a fundamental fact—Unity of the psychical functions
—Spencer's theory of evolution—Simultaneous evolution of the
psychical faculties—Intellect and character—Schopenhauer's theory—
Morality and progress 173

CHAPTER VI.—ON THE COMPOSITION AND DEVELOPMENT OF
MENTAL LIFE

Psychological analysis—Various kinds of sensations—Psychical elements—
The sensations possess an essentially qualitative character—Intensive
and extensive presentations—Space- and time-presentations—Emotions
and acts of volition—Consciousness, attention, and apperception—
Association—Similarity and contiguity—Is there one fundamental law
of association?—Materialistic explanation—Association takes place
between elements—Simultaneous association and perception—Assimilation
and complication—Recognition and memory—Affinity of psychical
elements — Apperceptive association — Attendant physiological
phenomena—Pyschological explanation of the "concept"—Psychical
evolution of animals—Instinct—The play of animals—The origin and
development of language—Importance of imitation in the mental
development of the child—Invention—Genius 224

CHAPTER VII.—CONSCIOUSNESS

Various meanings of the term "consciousness"—The physical and the psychical
world—Various theories concerning consciousness—Rationalistic
theories—Spiritualistic theories—Modern empirical theories—Natural
genesis of consciousness—Origin of the mental life—Ancient and
modern hylozoism—Biological and mental evolution—Materialist
theories concerning the origin of consciousness—Psychophysical
parallelism and consciousness—Primitive psychical elements—Psychical
life of micro-organisms—Progressive evolution of mental life—Importance
of attention—Theory of Maudsley and Ribot—The theory of
biological determinism—The concept of an unconscious psychic life—
Descartes—Leibnitz—Wolff—The modern evolutionist school—Criticism
of the arguments in favour of unconscious cerebration—The theory
of "mental dispositions"—Höffding—Subconsciousness of the lower
centres—The seat of the consciousness—Association and combination
of mental elements—Instinct—Reflex movements—Character . . 258

Contents

CHAPTER VIII.—CONSCIOUSNESS (*Continued*)

The continuity of consciousness—The characteristics of consciousness according to James—Attention or apperception—Various modes of considering the unity and multiplicity of consciousness—The relativity of mental processes — Psychical atomism — Rosmini's criticism of intellectualistic theories 296

CHAPTER IX.—THE LAWS OF PSYCHOLOGY

Meaning of the term "law"—Two phases of philosophical activity—Primitive naturalism — Democritus — Descartes — Spinoza — Leibnitz — Locke—Berkeley—Hume—Hartley—The two dominant schools at the close of the eighteenth century—Kant—Kant's successors—F. Herbart—Schopenhauer—Comte—Mill—Spencer—Taine—Rümelin—The concept of "soul"—The "substantiality" and "actuality" theories—Theory of the "unity of consciousness" 313

CHAPTER X.—THE LAWS OF PSYCHOLOGY (*Continued*)

Modern notions concerning the "psychic substance"—Spencer's explanation of the development of the intelligence—The law of relativity—The stream of consciousness: conception and discrimination—Leibnitz and the principle of "sufficient reason"—"Free will"—"Determinism"—Discussions as to the possibility of measuring mental processes—Wundt's fundamental psychological principles—Law of relation—The law of resultants—The law of relations—The law of contrasts—Laws of evolution—The law of the "increase of energy"—The law of "heterogony of ends"—The law of "evolution by contrast" . . . 336

CHAPTER XI.—THE LAWS OF PSYCHOLOGY (*Concluded*)

Teleological character of psychological principles—Value of psychological laws 373

CHAPTER XII.—CONCLUSION 385

INDEX 393

ERRATA

Page 17, line 4, *for* "*Delle forze attrattive delle cose*" *read* "*Della forza attratitva delle idee.*"
" 56, note [1], line 1, *for* "Ralier" *read* "Rabier."
" 59, line 18, *for* "Garofolo" *read* "Garofalo."
" " " 19, " "Paolo Lombroso" *read* "Paola Lombroso."
" " " 23, " "Boratelli" *read* "Bonatelli."
" " note [1], line 7, *for* "*La coscienza nell' uomo*" *read* "*La coscienza nel sonno.*"
" " " " " 12, " "*Genio naturale dell' istinto*" *read* "*Origine naturale dell' istinto.*"
" " " " " 14, " "Benatelli" *read* "Bonatelli."
" 60, line 27, *for* "Betchtesen" *read* "Betcherew."
" 61, " 1, " "Akiakow" *read* "Aksakow."
" " note, line 5, *for* "Alcam" *read* "Alcan."
" 177, line 7, *for* "Frederick" *read* "Frederic."
" 193, note [2], line 4, *for* "*L'expression des émotions*" *read* "*L'exposition des emotions.*"
" 227, " [2], *for* "Part I., chap. ii." *read* "Bk. I., chap. i."
" 247, " [1], line 2, *for* "No. X., chap. ii." *read* "Vol. X."
" 270, " [3], " 2, " "Torina" *read* "Torino."
" " " " " 4, " "Guiguo" *read* "Giugno."
" 359, line 33, *for* "psychological laws development" *read* "psychological laws of development."
" 367, note [1], line 1, *for* "*L'évolution des idées forces*" *read* "*L'évolutionisme des idées forces.*"
" 375, line 2, *for* "greatest advantage" *read* "greatest interest."
" 381, " 12, " "particular choice" *read* "particular chain."
" 382, note [3], line 6, *for* "1901" *read* "1891."
" 383, " [2], " 8, " "1878" *read* "1898."

Page 59, *for* paragraph about Bonatelli, *read* "Notwithstanding the favour shown to Positive Psychology in Italy, there are several psychologists with different views, like Bonatelli, professor at Padua University, who, in following Lotze, accentuates the latter's spiritualistic views, and Cantoni, professor at the University of Pavia, the gifted author of a celebrated work on Kant, in which he follows the Kantian theories tempered with ideas borrowed from Lotze. Other eminent philosophers, on the other hand, such as Tocco and Chiappelli, have accepted the teachings of modern scientific Psychology and have been the first to demonstrate its importance in their works, which, though not dealing exclusively with Psychology, reveal a highly developed critical sense coupled with extensive and profound learning."

CONTEMPORARY PSYCHOLOGY

INTRODUCTION

THE word Psychology is nowadays on every one's lips. Not only are there special treatises on the subject, but you cannot take up an essay on Law, Economics, or History, or even glance at a newspaper article, political or literary, without finding some allusion to psychological principles and laws, and these occur with such frequency as to lead a reader to suppose that such principles and laws have a common usage and acceptance. Of late, too, we have the so-called psychological novel, which, as opposed to the naturalistic, selects for its subject the human Ego.

There is undoubtedly, then, a very general interest in matters psychological, although few persons seem to possess a very precise or definite notion of what is comprehended in the term Psychology, applicable as it is to subjects as manifold and various as the points of view from which the idea which it embodies can be conceived. The art critic or the novelist looks at psychological principles from one point of view, the jurist or the physiologist from another. For the former Psychology is only a more or less felicitous intuition of different states of mind brought about by varied contingencies of individual and social life ; for the latter it is an exact, almost a mathematical formula of principles derived from experiments and long experience, so that one might almost say that the former regards it as a branch of art, and the latter as a branch of science.

Whilst the character and aims of Psychology are differently interpreted by the novelist, and by the jurist and physiologist, the disparity is even greater between their views and that of the general philosopher, by whom Psychology, like Ethics or

Æsthetics, is regarded not so much as a distinct science, governed by its own laws and exhibiting a special method of its own, but rather as a branch of knowledge governed by the supreme principles which are the basis of all general systems of philosophy, and vary according to the nature of each system. Thus, in the opinion of many philosophers, Psychology cannot be studied alone, but only as something derived from a general survey, wherein the principles of man's psychic nature and of his moral conduct are considered side by side with the principles of his physical nature.

The disparity between all these points of view is so great that any one unaccustomed to discern fundamental conceptions common to all might be tempted to believe that there is not one Psychology but many Psychologies, and that they are not even related to one another as different *species* of the same *genus*.

This diversity of view must not, however, make us judge contemporary thinkers too severely, for the fact that Psychology is frequently mentioned and discussed, though not always with scientific accuracy, at all events unmistakably shows the attraction of the subject and the importance that is attributed consciously or unconsciously to it.

Nor is this altogether a novel phenomenon. When public attention is called to a new study, people at once begin to train their thoughts and speech to accord with the newly developed idea, so that the new science, confined originally to a narrow circle, soon makes its influence felt among the general public, although its passage into current literature does not always proceed with that regularity and scientific accuracy which is desirable. Witness the misuse of the term Physiology some twenty or thirty years ago. Hardly had experimental research begun in this direction, than men of letters seized upon the new ideas and put them to the most arbitrary uses. Scarcely an essay was published which did not contain the inevitable word physiological, so that it might almost be said that everything that is now called psychological was then termed physiological. Nor has the term Physiology entirely disappeared in this connection, though for some time past the opinion has prevailed that Physiology cannot by itself explain the laws of the mind, and that Psychology is the more appropriate term.

The development of the moral sciences, such as History, Sociology, and Law, has led to the necessity of referring them to some common basis—viz. the study of the general phenomena of human consciousness. Thus, especially in works on law and sociology, we meet with preliminary considerations of a general nature, which seem to imply an exact acquaintance with the general principles and most recent results of the science of Psychology on the part of their authors, and yet one may be permitted to doubt whether these modern jurists and sciologists have more than a vague acquaintance with popular Psychology, or whether they have ever seriously studied the science itself.

The steady growth of the interest in psychological research renders it extremely desirable that the necessary scientific accuracy should be brought to bear on the subject, so as to secure the best possible result. As with the biological and physical sciences, which do not produce immediate practical results, so with Psychology—it should form the subject of a special study. As many readers are aware, psychological research has been prosecuted of late years with great enthusiasm and industry, especially in Germany and England, more recently in France and Italy. Although scientists may still differ as to the position which Psychology ought to occupy among the sciences, it is, nevertheless, an undoubted fact that, as regards experimental research, the study has already freed itself from dependence on other philosophic systems, and that among its numerous votaries there is growing up an ever increasing harmony of methods and aims which renders it practically autonomous. The majority of the better-known modern psychologists no longer occupy themselves with seeking a connection between the study of psychic phenomena and general systems of philosophy, but use the empirical method and keep as much as possible to objective facts. It is true that this procedure only goes back for about twenty years, and it is worth considering how the gradual disconnection of Psychology from the other philosophical sciences has come about, and why it was so much later in coming about than that of mathematics and the natural and moral sciences—a fact evidenced by the doubts still entertained by many whether it is indeed an independent science.

Like other branches of philosophy, Psychology in its original conception was far removed from what it has since become. It was evolved gradually, as the principles which unconsciously regulate the human mind came to be more generally understood and more clearly defined. Even now, especially among the uncultured classes, we observe that many persons unconsciously and by simple intuition govern their lives and their relations to others strictly according to psychological principles, though they do not possess any clear perception of the principles which they apply.[1] This was for a long time the case with all classes of the community; and when some ancient philosopher turned his attention to the consideration of psychic phenomena and laws, the majority of cultured persons did not believe that it was possible to organise those phenomena and laws scientifically, and form them into an exclusive object of study. Up to the middle of last century philosophy was the only science of the mind, and to occupy oneself with psychic phenomena was equivalent to studying the universal order of things under its ethical, logical, æsthetical, and metaphysical aspects. Psychology, as such, was either an introduction or a corollary: an introduction in the eyes of those who, like the English, took especial account of the practical importance of ethical and juridical problems; a corollary in the eyes of those who, like the authors of the great philosophic systems of the seventeenth century and of the Romantic period, had principally in view the establishment of certain transcendental ideas, from which they derived and dialectically elaborated all secondary conceptions. Amongst the philosophers of the empirical, or, to use a more modern phrase, the positivist school, which has always existed along with and opposed to the idealistic in the history of thought, it was natural that the necessity of gauging the motives which govern man's actions towards other men, or which compel him to create works of art, or to believe, for instance, in the supernatural, should make itself felt. Herein lay another and a patent incentive to psychological research.

In the history of thought in Greece a most important moment was undoubtedly reached when Philosophy, having abandoned the great cosmological theories of the earlier thinkers, turned with Socrates and the Sophists to the study of the psychological motives which determine men's actions in life, and attempted to found all moral laws on these alone. The metaphysical tendency continued even after Socrates; but it is a fact that the study of psychic phenomena, which Aristotle subsequently raised to great importance, has ever since been considered both by ancient and modern originators of philosophic systems as an indispensable foundation and starting-point of every hypothesis. Notwithstanding some

[1] See Spencer's interesting observation on the subject in *The Study of Sociology*, chap. xv.

partial attempt to emancipate itself, Psychology remained a branch of the philosophic trunk as late as the second half of the last century, and is not even yet considered by all to be entirely independent.[1] Many persons have sought an explanation of this, and some of the reasons adduced deserve attention.[2]

All the other sciences deal either with some aspect of the external and objective world or with some manifestation of man's intellectual or moral life, and contemplate such objects singly, separating them by means of a process of abstraction from the other component parts of the material or psychic world, as the case may be. Psychology, on the other hand, does not contemplate merely one side of man's thoughts or actions but the whole of his psychic being in its general modes of feeling, thought, and volition. If we admit this general difference, it is easy to comprehend the difficulty of separating the study of psychic phenomena from that of philosophy, which, for a long period at least, was governed solely by rational principles founded on the laws of the mind, which are the object matter of Psychology. It was difficult to separate the study of Psychology from that of ethics, inasmuch as ethical laws were mixed up with psychic laws, and it is notorious that ethical ideas were in the eyes of many philosophers—especially those who followed empirical methods—the principal object of philosophy, whilst even among students of metaphysics they constituted both the starting-point and the end of their speculations. On the other hand, ethical conceptions were influenced by metaphysical and theological ideas, which for a long time they were unable to shake off; and this also rendered any direct and independent study of psychic phenomena impossible.

A potent factor in the separation of the special sciences from an all-inclusive philosophy was the development of physical and biological research, which opened the door to philosophic speculation, and made it necessary to study natural and moral facts in their connection and evolution. The philosophy of the nineteenth century, romantic and positivist alike, is deeply imbued with the doctrine of evolution, the former confining itself almost exclusively to the laws governing the historical

---

[1] See, on the progressive evolution of the special sciences, Ribot in the Introduction to his work *La psychologie anglaise contemporaine*.

[2] See the reasons given by Wundt in his *Lectures on Human and Animal Psychology* (Eng. tr., Swan Sonnenschein & Co., 2nd edit.), p. 1.

evolution of thought, which it regarded as identical with Being, the latter looking especially to the evolution of natural phenomena. Of the two the positivist system is much more in accordance with the scientific spirit of our age, and it is therefore not surprising that it has more largely contributed to the formation of scientific Psychology.

The marvellous development in the last century of the moral —*i.e.* the historical, philological, social, and juridical—sciences, arising in great part from their adoption of rigorous scientific methods and the accumulation of a mass of material, is one of the striking features of nineteenth-century learning, and has been a potent factor in the formation of a distinct science of the mind. Each separate science, such as History, Philology in its numerous branches, Sociology, Political Economy, Statistics, and Law, has accumulated by degrees a vast mass of facts which possess the common characteristic of being pre-eminently *products* of the human mind. These sciences, though connected with the physical sciences and in a measure dependent on the data furnished by them, study particularly the psychic aspect of human nature in all its manifestations, so that one might say with truth that the moral sciences, though connected in a way with the natural sciences, form a whole and distinct system in themselves.[1] The moral sciences having detached themselves from philosophy in order to be placed on an empirical basis, have succeeded in obtaining, by means of the historical method, the results with which we are acquainted. And it was naturally to be expected that this should have gradually led to the adoption of the objective method, not only with regard to the concrete manifestations of the mind, which form the object of the so-called moral sciences, but also with regard to the psychic phenomena in their more general and abstract form. This general science of psychic phenomena aims at formulating the fundamental laws of all moral facts, and giving to the moral sciences a unity similar to that enjoyed by the physical. Those who first studied the problem of the *logical* methods of the moral sciences were in hopes of founding a general science of human nature (as Mill terms it), by which alone historical and social events could be scientifically explained. This is precisely what Psychology professes to do, seeing that the different moral sciences are no longer content with empirical research, but are anxious to examine mutual relations and to give a psychological explanation to

[1] See Dilthey's *Einleitung in die Geisteswissenschaften* (Leipsic, 1883), p. 5.

every historical and social fact—in other words, to make Psychology the foundation of their own superstructure.

In consequence of its general character, its connection with other branches of learning, and more especially of the importance of the questions connected with it and of the problems which it is called upon to solve, Psychology attracts students of different attainments in greater and greater numbers from other fields. The manifold sources from which psychological material is derived necessarily produces varieties of method and give rise to the most divergent views as to the nature and functions of the science. This is a natural result, not only of the very general character of psychic facts, but also of the different scientific training of those who dedicate themselves to their study.

I have no intention of tracing the history of Psychology from the earlier philosophers to the present time, for I should thereby exceed the limits which I have laid down for myself, and the subject has already been undertaken by others. In the brief survey I shall take of the most salient points in the evolution of Psychology and of the way in which it has gradually become severed from philosophy in its more general sense, it will be sufficient to refer to the works of my predecessors.[1]

[1] The principal works on the history of Psychology, which will be frequently quoted, are: for general Psychology, Siebeck's *Geschichte der Psychologie* (still in course of publication), of which the second of the two volumes published (Gotha, 1884) ends with St. Thomas Aquinas; for German and English Psychology, Dessoir's *Geschichte der neueren deutschen Psychologie* (2nd edit., Berlin, 1897). The evolution of Psychology is also touched upon by Külpe in his *Introduction to Philosophy* (Eng. tr., Sonnenschein, 2nd edit., 1901), and in his *Outlines of Psychology* (Eng. tr., Sonnenschein, 2nd edit., 1901); Natorp in his *Einleitung in die Psychologie nach Kritischer Methode* (Freiburg, 1888); Lange in his *History of Materialism* (1865). A brief but able summary of the history of Psychology is to be found in Mary Whiton Calkins's recent work, *An Introduction to Psychology* (Macmillan & Co., 1901).

CHAPTER I

HISTORICAL DEVELOPMENT OF PSYCHOLOGY

I. THE SEVENTEENTH AND EIGHTEENTH CENTURIES

A CONTEMPORARY writer divides the history of Psychology into three periods.[1] In the first period the Soul, which is the object of Psychology, is identified with the vital *principle*; the second limits that object to what can be learnt by means of *internal perception*; whilst during the third, or present stage we find that a phenomenon is considered a psychic phenomenon when it is subjective and forms an object of direct apprehension as opposed to what is *objective* or *physical* and can be thought of abstractly as existing *per se*, independently of the thinking subject.

Three periods of the history of Psychology.

Ancient philosophy after Socrates and mediæval philosophy are, as regards Psychology, dominated by the ideas of Plato and Aristotle. The soul is partly confused with the vital phenomena, and partly considered as a rational essence.[2] These ideas were maintained by the naturalistic philosophers of the sixteenth century, and even Descartes, who gave a totally new direction to philosophic speculations, does not differ much in his Psychology from the ancient and mediæval thinkers. Contrary to Aristotle, he considers the mind a purely thinking essence, entirely distinct from the body, the latter being that which has extension (*res extensa*), the former that which has no extension (*res cogitans*). Nevertheless, in regarding, as he did, *mens*, or consciousness, as the basis of all research concerning the moral world, he undoubtedly advanced the cause of Psychology, for the term *soul* used by

Descartes.

---

[1] See Külpe's admirable summary of the history of Psychology in his *Introduction to Philosophy* (Sonnenschein), p. 55.

[2] For ancient and mediæval Psychology see Hermann Siebeck's *Geschichte der Psychologie*, Th. i., n. 2, Gotha, 1880.

preceding philosophers was of a mystic character, and liable to very different interpretations.[1]

The two elements, mind and body, being connected in one point of the brain, the *glandula pinealis*, react on each other. From Descartes, therefore, is derived that dualistic conception of the spirit and the body which characterised for a long time the Cartesian school, though preparing the way later on for other psychological and philosophical conceptions. The spirit being limited, in his estimation, to the higher mental activities —*i.e.* the intellect—those psychic manifestations which could not be included therein came to be relegated to the level of matter; so that the lower animals became, for Descartes, mere automatons. This dualism gave rise to the spiritualistic and materialistic schools, the former of which considers the world as a creation of the mind, the latter as a product (ourselves included) of mechanical causation.

Man, according to Descartes, receives the spiritual essence from the Divinity, and that faculty, being inborn, does not require the help of experience to develop itself. On this principle of the dualism between soul and body, between the so-called *res cogitans* and *res extensa*, is founded the theory of the passions which Descartes expounded in his treatise *Des passions de l'âme* (1649), which, from a psychological point of view, is well worthy of note. In his opinion, feelings are also to be distinguished according as they refer to external objects and to our own body, or are derived directly from the soul. The latter, however, owing to the reciprocal influence of the corporeal and the spiritual essences, are fed and fortified by those which Descartes calls *esprits animaux*.

As against the dualistic theory two doctrines arose which were entirely opposed to each other, the one being metaphysical, the other empirical. The former finds its representative in Benedict Spinoza, whose fundamental principle was the absolute parallelism between thought and reality, applied also to the theory of feelings, and set forth by him in the third part of his *Ethics* (1677). In this he disputes the Cartesian hypothesis, and maintains that the decisions of the soul and the impulses or appetites of the body are not only simultaneous facts, but are one

Spinoza.

---

[1] Höffding (*History of Modern Philosophy*, i. 236) notes this as a merit of Descartes with respect to Psychology, and inclines to the belief that he owed it to the influence of Vives. With the use of the term *mens*, he tells us, Descartes has prepared the way for modern Empirical Psychology.

and the same thing, though they appear to us under different aspects, according as we consider them from the standpoint of the mind or that of extension.

Locke. The dualistic system found a much more formidable adversary in the theory of knowledge founded on experience, which practically owes its being to John Locke. Locke's *Essay concerning Human Understanding* (1690), besides marking an epoch by the novel method which it applies to philosophy and to the theory of knowledge, constitutes probably the first attempt at a scientific study of the mental processes. Acute observer as he was, Locke perceived and accepted as a premise that we cannot have knowledge without experience, and discarded the artificial dualism between the consciousness and the external world in favour of another dualistic conception, which, though far from satisfactory, was destined to help the solution of the problem. This consisted in distinguishing the *inner* from the *outer sense*; the former affording us cognition of our inner or psychic actions, the latter of external objects. The fundamental process of external perception is *sensation*, that of the spirit *reflection*, all perceptions and ideas of the external world being derived from sensation. The importance of such a doctrine was great, and was eventually to lead Psychology to a scientific explanation of the complicated processes of consciousness. Locke also attempted to explain the origin of ideas, which were considered by the earlier metaphysicians as pure and simple manifestations of the reasoning power. According to him, on the contrary, they are nothing but perceptions, which possess the peculiarity of combining the features of several individual perceptions so as to produce one common presentation. He attributes great importance to *reflection*, because it affords the direct proof of the spontaneity of our mind, which is invested with the power of producing, regulating, and preventing its own thoughts, as well as the motions of the body. This spontaneity, or volition of the mind, which distinguishes it absolutely from purely physical objects, Locke discusses at great length, noting, amongst other things, the difference between the will, which is the faculty of choosing from several thoughts or motions, and liberty, which is the possibility of putting into execution the thoughts or motions chosen by the will.[1]

It is clear that nothing but a dualistic system could be derived from such premises, the choice lying between the attribution of

[1] See *An Essay concerning Human Understanding*, Book II., chap. xxi.

an exclusive or preponderating value to *sensation* or to *reflection*. With Locke begins, one may say, that second period in the history of Psychology which for the ancient conception of the soul, more or less clearly understood as the vital principle, substitutes the notion of inner and outer sense, by which for a long period of time Psychology was kept distinct from the natural sciences. Amongst the English philosophers, who were always more or less favourable to Positivism, the tendency to attribute primary importance to experience and sensation as mediums of knowledge remained after Locke. Amongst the Germans, on the contrary, ever somewhat inclined, if not to spiritualism, at least to idealism, the notion prevailed of the greater importance of the inner sense, or reflection, considered as a spontaneous and original attitude of the soul. The psychological error into which both the Cartesians and the Empiricists had fallen was that of believing that the mental life manifests itself only during those clear and distinct states of consciousness in which we are quite certain of our sensations and ideas. The Empirical philosophers, starting with Locke from sensations from which they derived the whole of the mental life, differed greatly from the Cartesians, but failed to study sufficiently the nature of sensation.

Leibnitz endeavoured to conciliate the two doctrines, adding some original ideas of his own. In opposition to the Empiricists,

Leibnitz. who gave too much importance to the so-called external sensations, and as a complement to Locke's doctrine, he maintains that our consciousness is a spontaneous process, which manifests itself at all times independently of any external stimulus, and is therefore always active, even when, as during sleep, the soul (to use an expression of the period) "does not think."

Against the Cartesians and the spiritualists in general Leibnitz maintains that the states of consciousness, which at first sight seem to us simple, are in reality often exceedingly complex, and the result of many constituents; and that, therefore, between the dimmer sensations and the clearer states of consciousness, such as intellectual activity, the only difference is one of degree. Thus a *perception*, which is Leibnitz's name for a sensation, is a result of many sensations (*petites perceptions*), whilst the organic functions produce in us continual sensations, which have an influence on the whole of our mental state. According to Leibnitz, therefore, our psychic life consists in a complexity or a chain of facts, not all of which appear to us in a clear and distinct manner. Those of which we are clearly conscious Leibnitz calls *apperceptions*, whereas those of which we are only more or less dimly conscious he calls *perceptions*. He is also of opinion, in opposition to the Spiritualists and Cartesians, that we possess no inborn ideas, but only the predisposition or aptitude for forming them; and with this theory, subsequently completed and elaborated by Kant, he was able to bring into accord the theories of the Empiricists and of the Spiritualists. This fact explains his importance in the history of Psychology, as to him may be traced the origin of a school which entertained the possibility of making Psychology an independent science, although, owing to a very one-sided conception of knowledge, it attributed too exclusive an importance to the inner sense.

This school of Psychology (appropriately called *Psychology of the inner sense*, or of *internal experience*) was originated by Christian Augustus Wolff (1679—1784), amongst whose merits is that of having been the first to give the name of *empirica* or *experimentalis* to Psychology, and of recognising its importance as an autonomous science. His system is important enough in the history of our subject to warrant our discussing it at some length.

Wolff.

Psychology, according to Wolff, may be divided into two parts, empirical and rational or speculative, to both of which he gives an equal importance. Empirical Psychology comprises two principal parts, the one particularly connected with the cognitive capacity, the other with the desires and the reciprocal action of soul and body. All knowledge is the outcome of sensations, which are produced by variations of the sensorial organs, and are related to each other. The sensations can be reproduced by means of phantasmata. This form of cognition is, however, a simple form, a mere perception; and the mind can, by means of attention, distinguish the various parts of a compound perception, of which it can apprehend some parts more clearly than others. Thought and intelligence are the result of attention, the former consisting in a retrospective examination of what we have perceived, the latter being the faculty of representing things to ourselves distinctly. From cognition are derived pleasure and pain, and thence a judgment on the quality of the object, and lastly desire or repugnance.[1]

On the other hand, Rational Psychology treats of the soul in general, and of the cognitive faculty in particular. The soul is a simple substance—it is neither the body nor an attribute of

[1] See Dessoir, *Geschichte der neueren deutschen Psychologie*, 2nd edit. 1897.

the body, and the rapidity of its sensations is to be distinguished from the rapidity of the stimuli. Apperception is the outcome of the clearness of the several *perceptiones partiales*, and of the concurrent action of attention and memory.

Wolff treats also of the relations between the sensations and the cerebral activity which accompanies the process of attention : *Si eadem in cerebro excitatur idea materialis, eadem quoque in anima nascitur idea sensualis et contra.* The images produced by memory find in the brain corresponding *material ideas* ; but, except in the case of hallucinations, they are less vivid than those produced by perception. Some of Wolff's psychological ideas are well worthy of note. Thus the field of perception is constituted, in his opinion, by the number of perceptions of which we can be conscious at the same time, as in optics the space which the eye can comprise at a glance is called the field of view. From the sensations are derived the acts of the intelligence, judgments, and ideas. Wolff treats lastly of the question of the relations between the soul and the body. According to empirical Psychology, the soul depends on the body, inasmuch as we have sensations when we are struck by external impressions ; but the body, on the other hand, must be dependent on the soul, as otherwise we could not explain its voluntary and independent acts. He rejects both materialism and spiritualism or occasionalism, and follows Liebnitz's idea of pre-established harmony.

Wolff was the cause of awakening in Germany a decided interest in psychological studies, and we have in that country during the eighteenth century a great number of philosophers who gave those studies their special attention, whether as his disciples or his adversaries, or as striving to conciliate eclectically the different views. Thus we may note the school of the so-called popular psychologists (like Mendelssohn), of the materialists, and of other empirical non-materialist psychologists like Beausobre, Platner, and others. Most of these start from the *Empirical Psychology* of Wolff, a work of great merit, which is neither entirely speculative nor entirely experimental in its method. The importance of Psychology was at that time recognised by all ; Zimmermann, for instance, writing : "It is a fact that in our time all true philosophers declare that amongst the human sciences the most useful, although nowadays still the most imperfect, is the science of man."[1] But

---

[1] Quoted by Dessoir, *Geschichte*, etc., p. 133. The whole of this interesting period in the history of Psychology is illustrated by Dessoir with clearness and abundance of facts.

there is no denying the existence of a diversity of opinions as to the limits of Psychology, and especially as to the characteristics which distinguish it from Logic. Many important problems were discussed at that time regarding the nature and method of Psychology, and, amongst others, the question which was to be taken up again later, as to whether Psychology is to be counted a philosophic science—*i.e.* a branch of metaphysics—or a physical science. The old-fashioned dogmatists had a leaning towards the former opinion, whereas the younger and more empirical scientists followed the latter view.

During this period we find a first attempt at an experimental philosophy like what exists nowadays in the work of John Nicholas Tetens (1736—1807), a shrewd observer and a man of uncommon versatility, who kept clear of the metaphysical subtleties of the time.[1] Notwithstanding his partial adoption of the theories of Wolff, he differs from him on many points. He divided perceptions into the two categories of external and inner sense, subdividing the latter into perceptions of pain or pleasure on the one side, and thought and will on the other. His doctrine of sensations showed great originality, anticipating in many respects the results of the modern physiology of the senses. Thus the disciples of Wolff had never explained satisfactorily the so-called posthumous sensations. Tetens explains them by means of the continuance of the stimulus, and quotes the example of a live coal, which, being made to rotate rapidly, presents the appearance of a ribbon of fire. He also made experiments, and gave some chronometrical measurements with reference to the continuance of luminous and acoustic and even tactile sensations. He, therefore, may be said to follow a system of his own, founded on the observation of facts.[2] Thus he denies the materialistic hypothesis that the mental processes are equivalent to cerebral stimuli, inasmuch as it not only does not lend itself to observation, but is entirely unsatisfactory as an explanation. He does not, however, discard it as a naturalistic doctrine, but considers it an invaluable

[1] Tetens lived from 1736 to 1807, and, after being Professor of Physics and Metaphysics at the Academy of Rostock, and later of Philosophy and Mathematics at the University of Kiel, settled finally at Copenhagen, where he entered a State department.

[2] The importance of Tetens has been recognised by modern students of Psychology. Besides Dessoir (already quoted), pp. 120—129, account has been taken of his work by Wundt (*Mind*, ii. 515 and iii. 156), Strumpf (in his *Tonpsychologie*, i. 38), and others who have studied his philosophic theories and drawn comparisons between him and Leibnitz, Wolff, Kant, etc.

means of psychological research. As instances of the presentative faculty, Tetens indicates perception, fancy, and the poetic gift. *Perception* embraces all sense presentations ; *Fancy* reproduces them according to the law of co-existence and similarity ; and the independent *Poetic Gift* creates new images and presentations. Yet all these are connected, and may be considered as different degrees of one and the same fundamental activity. The *Representations*, or images of the memory, are defined by Tetens as " traces left on the soul by the modifications to which it has been subjected" ; *Feeling* as the subjective modification of the soul resulting from a given impression ; and *Will* as the determination of the soul to some manifestation of activity. From these fundamental notions Tetens rises to higher speculations ; but he always professed to abstain on principle from mixing up hypotheses with facts. Thus, with reference to the soul, so much discussed in his time, he was of opinion that psychological research ought to make it its aim, but not to take it as a starting-point.[1]

At this time especially, owing to the influence of English philosophy, there was, in fact, a strong tendency towards putting metaphysical questions on one side.

These attempts at forming an independent Psychology which should be solely based on observation and on experiments were not for the moment successful. In Germany, with the advent of other great philosophers, intellectual activity became absorbed by metaphysical questions, and Psychology became again one among the philosophical sciences with no special importance of its own ; and we must come down as far as Herbart in the nineteenth century to find a philosopher treating Psychology as a separate science. Its development continued, however, uninterruptedly in England, where, from Bacon downwards, philosophers never lost sight of the importance of experience. Of the two factors of Locke's Psychology, English philosophy dedicated itself specially to the external, seeking to explain the conditions according to which mental phenomena are combined and connected, and endeavouring to ascertain those conditions from the data afforded by external experience.

Amongst the first to evolve a strictly empirical psychological

---

[1] Tetens wrote (see Dessoir, *op. cit.*, p. 138) no less than sixty-five essays and books, not counting scientific articles published in two Kiel newspapers. Of all these writings, sixteen may be called philosophical, the others treating of various scientific and practical questions. His most important philosophic work is the *Philosophische Versuche über die menschliche Natur und ihre Entwickelung* (1777).

doctrine from Locke's philosophy, we find a philosopher who succeeded in combining the two contradictory doctrines of metaphysical idealism and empiricism. This philosopher is George Berkeley (1685—1753), who fills a conspicuous place in the history of Psychology with his *Theory of Vision* (1709) and his *Principles of Human Knowledge* (1710). The former contains an attempt at a scientific explanation of the origin of the idea of space, which, according to Berkeley, forms itself in our minds by the gradual blending, through habit and long usage, of visual and tactile sensations, actual and remembered. This theory, from which Berkeley deduced the metaphysical consequence of the phenomenalism of the external world, was both original and audacious, and can compare with the modern theories on the psychological origin of space. Berkeley, however, in his *Principles*, though starting from Locke's notion that all elementary and compound ideas come to us through sensation and reflection, arrives at the very remarkable conclusion, which is fully confirmed by modern Psychology, that there exist no general ideas, but only individual ones.

Berkeley.

A more thorough analysis of human knowledge, and of the psychological laws which govern it, was attempted after Berkeley by David Hume (1771). His psychological theories are set forth in his *Treatise on Human Nature* (1739—1740) and in his *Inquiry concerning Human Understanding* (1747). His fundamental principle was that our ideas are not *a priori*, but are a consequence of previous sensations, the origin of which he considers impossible to trace. Every well-defined disposition of the spirit has the tendency to endure and to colour subsequent impressions and ideas. Moreover, the ideas have a natural tendency to recall each other reciprocally; they have, that is to say, an associative tendency, one bringing another with it by means of a gentle force.[1] The conditions under which this association takes place are, according to Hume, similarity, co-existence in space and time, and causality. Hume shrewdly notes with regard to association, that in the inner world no less than in the external world there exists a potent and mysterious force of attraction. He also proposes the question whether it be possible to reconcile the principle of connection with the fact that all our sensations and perceptions are distinct and independent elements, and declares that it is too difficult for his intelligence.

Hume.

Hume's ideas, meanwhile, were becoming known outside

[1] See Höffding, *History of Modern Philosophy*, i. 430 foll.

England, and found a representative in an Italian scientist, Francesco Maria Zanotti (1697—1777), a Bolognese scientist and versatile writer, who published in 1747 a pamphlet, *Delle forze attrattive delle cose*, in which he developed ideas very similar to Hume's.

Zanotti.

David Hartley, a thinker whose importance as a psychologist is perhaps greater than Hume's (although in a sense he may be considered his follower), must be awarded a foremost place in the history of Psychology, owing to his attempt to explain psychic phenomena by scientific reasons and on simple principles.[1] Hartley's most important work, published twenty-eight years before the *Philosophic Essays* of Tetens, on whom it probably exercised influence, explains complex psychic phenomena and even the most elevated thoughts and feelings by means of the association of sensations and simple perceptions. He disputes Locke's theory of the existence of ideas derived from reflection, everything being derived, according to Hartley, from the association of sensations, which association consists in the conjunction of simultaneous or immediately successive perceptions. To this psychological association corresponds the physiological phenomenon of the conjunction of several vibrations in the brain, where they form one single vibration. This is the earliest beginning of a Psychology which, in place of seeking metaphysical laws and relations, relies entirely on experience and on the aid of the sister science of physiology. Hartley does not inquire into the relations existing between associations and vibrations; nor does he declare in favour of the materialistic or of the spiritualistic theory, both of which he considers one-sided. What he seeks to establish is the important fact that the mental life is developed little by little from elementary into more complex phenomena by means of continual associations and according to the three following secondary rules:—

Hartley.

1. Just as happens with the combinations of matter, complex perceptions constitute such a perfect unity that their component parts are not recognisable.

[1] David Hartley was born in Yorkshire in 1705. He studied theology and medicine, and, while actively attending to his profession as a doctor, occupied himself with philosophical studies. The work for which he is celebrated is entitled *Observations on Man, his Frame, his Duty, and his Expectations*, and was published in 1749. Its fundamental idea, which is to reduce all complex psychic phenomena to simple elements, was apparently suggested by a work of a little-known writer (Gay), who attempted to derive the more complex feelings by association from the more elemental. See Höffding's *History of Modern Philosophy*.

2. Those notions which at first were accompanied by full consciousness, become, through repetition, unconscious or automatic.

3. The force and vividness possessed by some perceptions are communicated to the other perceptions which become associated with them.

The importance of these theorems is obvious, constituting as they do the first attempt at a scientific explanation of complex psychic phenomena. Hartley's ideas, which at first passed unnoticed, became more generally known towards the end of the eighteenth century through Joseph Priestley, naturalist and theologian, who gave them a materialistic colour by affirming the identity of the mental and cerebral processes, and maintaining that the former can be understood solely through the study of the latter.[1]

Priestley.

Another naturalist of great merit, Erasmus Darwin (1731—1802), fought in the same cause, and, applying these ideas to the study of animals, endeavoured to explain the instincts by means of experience and association, regulated by the impulse of self-preservation, and by the necessity of individual adaptation to external conditions.[2]

E. Darwin.

The psychological doctrine of association was made in this way to pass the limits of pure Psychology and enter the field of biology. A totally different system was followed by the Scottish school of philosophers, for whom all speculation consisted almost entirely in the study of the mental processes, and whose principal representatives are Thomas Reid and Dugald Stewart.

These philosophers, as opposed to Hume, take as their starting-point the data afforded by the inner sense, or rather, as they called it, the common sense. Thomas Reid (1710—1796) set forth his theories in a work entitled *Inquiry into the Human Mind on the Principles of Common Sense* (1764). All psychic and intellectual processes, even the most difficult and complicated, such as those which lead to the consideration of the reality of the external world or of the causation of natural phenomena, can, in Reid's opinion, be explained in the simplest fashion by means of a sort of instinct which gives us a direct and unquestionable knowledge of the same. In his Psychology

Reid.

[1] Joseph Priestley, who lived from 1733 to 1804, is famous for his discovery of oxygen. His principal work is entitled *Disquisitions on Matter and Spirit* (London, 1777).

[2] Erasmus Darwin (1731—1802), grandfather of Charles Darwin, was doctor, naturalist, poet, and philosopher. His principal work is *Zoonomia, or the Laws of Organic Life* (London, 1794). See Höffding, *op. cit.*, p. 506.

he therefore gave up all attempt at explanation, reducing it to a pure empiricism and simple description of mental processes. Nevertheless, he and his school possess no little importance in the history of our subject, owing to their being amongst the first to give Psychology its proper value. He was also the author of *Physiological Research on the Muscular Sense* (1795), which is a notable attempt at psychological and physiological analysis.[1]

Reid's ideas were taken up by Dugald Stewart (1753—1828), who wrote various works, of which he gave a summary in his
Stewart. *Philosophy of the Active and Moral Powers* (1828).
He kept to Reid's descriptive method, and believed firmly in the possibility of reducing Psychology to the level of the natural sciences, which in his time followed solely the descriptive method. His Psychology possesses many merits, especially owing to his analysis of the associations, which he was the first to distinguish into two great classes—*i.e.* simple or spontaneous, and voluntary or regulated by attention—the former comprising associations of similarity, analogy, contrast, and contiguity—the latter comprising the relations intervening between the cause and the effect, the means and the end, the premises and the conclusion. This distinction, which was accepted and developed by modern Psychology, is important in that it recognises and gives relief to the active function of consciousness in the formation of logical processes.

A philosopher partly connected with the Scottish school and partly with the associationists is Thomas Brown (1778—1820), a
Brown. pupil of Erasmus Darwin, whose *Lectures on the Philosophy of the Human Mind* were published in 1820. They are important for the distinction they contain between touch and muscular sensation, and for a careful account of the laws of association.

The ideas of English philosophers were to find a favourable ground in France, where, however, they lost the experiential
Condillac. character noticeable in Locke and Hume, and assumed a more logical and metaphysical quality. The most notable philosopher of the time in France, Condillac, exaggerated

---

[1] Thomas Reid, who was at first a preacher, became later a Professor at the Universities of Aberdeen and Glasgow. Besides the works already quoted, he published the *Essays on the Intellectual Powers of the Mind* (1785) and the *Essays on the Active Powers of the Mind* (1788). See, with reference to Reid and the Scottish school, A. Seth's *Scottish Philosophy* (2nd edit., Edinburgh and London, 1890).

Locke's and Hume's ideas to the point of affirming that all the phenomena of our consciousness are derived from sensations which our consciousness passively receives—that is to say, we not only obtain from external impressions the contents and object-matter of our consciousness, as Locke held, but our inner activity itself comes to us from without.[1] Condillac therefore denied the existence of Locke's inner sense. The success obtained by this form of sensationalism in France and elsewhere was so great that in France it gradually assumed the place of Cartesianism. It is, nevertheless, a fact that these two philosophic systems, widely though they differ on some essential points, are not without some connecting links.

If Descartes denied consciousness to animals, which he held to be mere automatons, French materialism, working on the data of experience introduced by English philosophy, followed **French materialism.** the latter to its most extreme consequences by means of logical deductions as convincing as the reasonings of Descartes himself. If the acts of animals, which we believe to be indications of thinking, feeling, and willing, are nothing but the result of a cunningly devised mechanism, why should this not be so with the acts of man? This mechanism is naturally constituted by the brain and the nervous system, by means of which we receive impressions from the external world, and these, little by little, endow us with sensations, perceptions, and consciousness itself. Condillac, in this connection, gave his celebrated illustration of a statue which, on receiving, one after the other, the various sensations, becomes at last a living being.

These opinions were common to La Mettrie, Diderot, Helvetius, and Holbach,[2] the first of whom, in a work which has become celebrated, entitled *L'homme machine*, follows up Des-**La Mettrie.** cartes' idea, and extends the notion of psychological automatism from the lower animals to man. This intellectual movement was, without any doubt, inspired and helped on by the progress of the natural sciences; but it found, nevertheless, in

---

[1] Condillac lived from 1715 to 1780, his principal work on Psychology being his *Traité des sensations* (1754).

[2] Holbach (1723—1789) published in 1770 his celebrated work *Système de la nature*, the most remarkable and complete of the materialistic works of the time. Helvetius (1715—1771) published *De l'esprit* (1758), *De l'homme* (1773—1774). La Mettrie (1709—1751), the real founder of French materialism, wrote an *Histoire naturelle de l'âme* (1745), and *L'homme machine* (1748). Diderot (1713—1784) published his *Interpretation de la nature* in 1754. See on these philosophers Lange's *History of Materialism*, Vol. I., Part IV., chaps. i., ii., iii.

France itself at the time a lively opposition on the part of the more idealistic thinkers and of dispassionate observers.

Amongst the idealists Jean Jacques Rousseau ranks foremost. Though not himself a psychologist, Rousseau was a staunch believer in the essential difference between sensation and thought, and between spirit and matter, which, in his opinion, are two different substances.

J. J. Rousseau.

Rousseau's compatriot Charles Bonnet was distinguished as a psychologist and a severe critic in his psychological writings (of which the most important is his *Essai analytique sur les facultés de l'âme*, 1759) of the theories of Condillac, who derived all the phenomena of consciousness from a purely passive feeling.[1] In his opinion, man is not purely psychical nor purely physical, but is a psychophysical being. Thought, therefore, cannot be produced without the action of the nervous fibres; but the latter are by no means identical with thought itself, the origin of which is a mystery. Though Bonnet refused to admit the materialistic theory so generally accepted in his time, he nevertheless maintained that, to properly understand the formation and the connections of ideas, there is no other way but to examine the relations of the nervous fibres. On this assumption he made several important observations upon the physiological conditions of the mental processes, and brought into evidence the existence of an active psychical force which is put in motion either by pain or by pleasure.

Bonnet.

If we now cast a retrospective glance at this period, which is one of the richest in the history of thought, we have reason to be surprised at the great number of important psychological works produced during the space of a few years. The writings of Hartley, Tetens, Condillac, Bonnet, Reid, and La Mettrie belong more or less to the period between 1748 and 1765.[2] Psychological research at this time, in the absence of very great thinkers with profound and suggestive theories to offer to the consideration of the studious, occupied the attention of the latter, and attracted them by its analytical and minute methods

[1] Charles Bonnet, of Geneva (1720—1793), was the author of various works, of which the *Essai analytique* quoted above and the *Essai de psychologie* (1754) are the most notable. See, on Bonnet, Max Offner's interesting monograph *Die Psychologie Charles Bonnets* (in the *Schriften der Gesellschaft für psychologische Forschung*, Heft 5, Leipsic, 1893).

[2] Hartley's principal work came out in 1749, Condillac's *Treatise on Sensations* and Bonnet's *Essay* in 1754; Reid's first important work in 1764, and Tetens's writings are also of the same epoch. It must be remembered, however, that Reid published the other two works quoted in 1785 and 1788.

II. THE EARLY PART OF THE NINETEENTH CENTURY

Kant. Up to this time the notion of the unity of all the psychic functions had not yet been accepted, each function being attributed to some special faculty. Immanuel Kant, though denying to Psychology the character of a real science, placed it, nevertheless, on a secure philosophical basis by solving the problem formulated by Hume as to the relations between the multiplicity of our perceptions and the principle of their connection.[1]

Leibnitz had already shown that the soul is continually active; but he had not demonstrated the general forms of its activity, and his successors had not developed his idea. We have seen how the disciples of Wolff had with an *empirical* brought forward a *rational* Psychology, by means of which they sought to prove that the identity in all phenomena of the thinking Ego is a property of the thinking substance. Kant, on the contrary, considers this assertion a paralogism, the above-mentioned identity being nothing but an act of thought itself, and there being no reason for declaring it a property of any substance whatsoever. Kant is of opinion that, although we can have an idea of the phenomena of consciousness, we can know nothing of a mental substance; just as we can only have a science of physical phenomena, and not of the substance which is supposed to underlie them. We cannot, in fact, according to Kant, go beyond the thinking Ego to an absolute subject. Rational Psychology would consequently have no other object than to indicate the limits which reason may not overstep in the direction of materialism or of spiritualism, the notion of soul being made use of merely as a guiding principle of research. Psychology might, therefore, be a branch of study, but never a science. The same is true of empirical Psychology. It could never hope to become a science, because the phenomena of the internal world are so transient and uncertain as not to be susceptible of any exact determination. It is, therefore, impossible to apply mathematics or experiment to the mental processes, and empirical Psychology must consequently satisfy itself with being descriptive, without attempting to explain the mental phenomena

---

[1] See, on Kant's Psychology, Jürgen Bona Meyer in his work entitled *Kant's Psychologie* (1870); Alfred Hegler, *Die Psychologie in Kant's Ethik* (1891). See also K. Dietrich, *Die Kantische Philosophie* (Vol. II., 1885); A. Riehl, *Der Philosophische Criticismus und seine Bedeutung für die positive Wissenschaft* (Vol. I., Leipsic, 1876). As to the connection between Kant's Psychology and that of the followers of Wolff, see the last chapter of Dessoir's work already quoted.

which it observes. This dictum of the great philosopher of Königsberg was for a long time a decided stumbling-block in the way of the development of experimental Psychology. It is, nevertheless, a fact that, his scepticism notwithstanding, Kant formulated several epistemological ideas, which were subsequently of great use to Psychology. He denied the Wolffian notion of a substance (of this we can know nothing); but, on the other hand, he did not content himself with the purely empirical explanation given by the associationists. In his opinion, sensations constitute the *matter* of the consciousness, or the substratum indispensable to every form of thought. But this matter is not of itself sufficient to explain the development of the conscious processes, because the sensations must be arranged in order, and this arrangement is the work of an inner power, which Kant calls the *form* of thought. We have, however, two forms: one for the data of sense, the form of sensory intuition; the other for the intellect, which is the concept. The former is, moreover, subdivided according to space and time. All these forms express the inner synthesis to which the data of experience are subjected, a theory which was subsequently developed by modern Psychology.[1]

Kant has not given us a complete psychological analysis of his fundamental epistemological notions, although, as we have seen, he gave a new direction to the more general and fundamental questions of Psychology. For some time his work was left in abeyance. The idealist and romantic[2] philosophers, indeed, so far from following up Kant's psychological analysis, abandoned entirely the critical method in favour of metaphysical systems. These, however, were not really so detrimental to Psychology as would appear at first sight, and as is believed by many, contributing, as they did, not a few novel ideas to science in general and to Psychology in particular. Above all, they brought into notice the historical continuity and the incessant evolution of mental activity from the simpler to the more complex forms.

Hegel. Hegel's philosophy of the mind marked the culminating point of idealism, for in his system the idea is considered as what is most real in nature. The evolutionary idealism of Hegel and of the romantic philosophers is responsible for the

[1] Höffding, in his *History of Modern Philosophy*, Vol. II., says: "He [Kant] had here found a conception, which raised him as much above the atomistic Psychology, which lay at the bottom of empiricism, as above the spiritualistic Psychology, from which, until now, most idealistic systems had sprung."

[2] The word *romantic* is here used according to the distinction drawn by Höffding in his *History of Modern Philosophy*, which seems a felicitous one.

psychological notion of the *unity* of mind in human society, according to which history appears as the development of one single all-embracing spirit. In this manner Hegel was able to prove the close connection existing between the various products of the mind, and was one of the founders, if not the founder, of the historic method of research. This method, as is well known, having extended to every province of inquiry—artistic, social, historical, or judicial—has, through the *Psychology of Peoples*, been one of the principal agents in giving to Psychology a character of autonomy.

The evolution of Psychology owes much also to two philosophers of the metaphysical school, Herbart and Schopenhauer. The former endeavoured to formulate psychological laws in an original manner, and tried to apply to Psychology the rigorous method of the physical sciences and of mathematics. The latter, whose philosophic system embraced various manifestations of nature and of the spirit, penetrated with marvellous intuition into the world of consciousness, solving several mental problems to which little importance had been given before him.[1]

In Herbart's opinion the basis of Psychology is to be found in metaphysics. The soul, like the whole universe, is a compound of units; and the mental life consists in the conflict and also in the harmony of those units, some of which are blended together by means of *assimilations*, others unite in groups by means of *complications*, others, again, are at variance amongst themselves, the resulting whole constituting the human *Ego*. In this conception of the mental life, except for the substitution of the terms *assimilation* and *complication* for *association*, Herbart came very near to the psychological doctrines of Hume and Hartley (taken up at that time by James Mill[2]), in whose opinion consciousness primarily consisted in a multiplicity of sensations and perceptions. He is also particularly worthy of note

Herbart.

---

[1] Frederick Herbart lived from 1776 to 1841. His psychological theories appear already in his earlier more metaphysical works, written in 1808 and 1813; but were more fully treated in his *Lehrbuch zur Psychologie* (1816) and in his great work *Psychologie als Wissenschaft, neugegründet auf Erfahrung Metaphysik und Mathematik*, published in 1824—1825. Arthur Schopenhauer lived from 1788 to 1860. The first edition of his famous work *Die Welt als Wille und Vorstellung* is of 1819. In 1844 was issued an enlarged second edition, with a second part added.

[2] On James Mill see L. Ferri's *La Psicologia dell' associazione*, Part II., chap. i., p. 82 foll., and Ribot's study on that philosopher in *La psychologie anglaise contemporaine*, p. 55 foll.

for having been the first to dispute the theory which held the field of German Psychology after Wolff, and was even accepted by Kant, according to which consciousness is constituted by several distinct faculties.

Herbart reduces all mental forms to one single element, which he calls presentation (*Vorstellung*). From this proceed what we call feeling and volition. His theory, however, met with scant favour, its sole merit being that of containing the principle of mental unity. Nor was Herbart more successful in trying to reduce Psychology to the laws of mathematics, on the supposition that the presentations are permanent unities susceptible of quantitative measurement, which can be calculated with precision. One of his disciples, Drobisch, endeavoured to develop this part of his doctrine,[1] but with little success. Psychology was about to enter upon a new era with the physiological method; but the importance which such a purely metaphysical philosopher as Herbart attributed to that science was a very remarkable fact in his time, so that by some he is considered one of the pioneers of scientific Psychology.[2] This explains the authority and popularity which his work even now retains, especially in Germany.

The Psychology of Peoples, one of the most important branches of modern scientific Psychology, owes its origin in a great measure to Waitz and Lazarus, both followers of Herbart. The characteristic of Herbart's Psychology is that he considers the mental life as a compound of intellectual units, and that he attributes a preponderating value to its cognitive and perceptive aspect.

Whilst, with the English intellectualists, Herbart gives exclusive importance to presentation, his contemporary Schopenhauer is,

Schopenhauer. from a certain point of view, a decided anti-intellectualist. In Schopenhauer's opinion, what is most essential in man is not the intelligence, but the will, by which he means that mass of impulses which have their origin in our moral and physiological nature and over which reason possesses no power. The intelligence has no other function than that of illuminating the will, so that man may know his own self, though without any possibility of modifying his inner essence. The enduring quality which Herbart attributes to the presentation is by Schopenhauer attributed to the blind will. Hence a complete dualism between the two parts of the mind, which are united

---

[1] Drobisch (1802—1896) is the author, amongst other works, of an *Empirische Psychologie* (1842).

[2] For example, by Ribot, in his *Psychologie allemande contemporaine*.

only in appearance, and possess no equality in their mutual action, the will and not the intelligence being the governing force.[1] If we now wish to trace the genesis of this conception of the "will," which Schopenhauer was the first to elevate to the rank of a speculative system, we shall find that it has to be looked for rather in the history of ethics than in that of Psychology. The psychological motives of the acts of willing, when analysed carefully, cannot but appear different from the mental processes by means of which we arrive at the knowledge of the external world. Thus Aristotle distinguished moral will from cognition, and in modern philosophy Kant based his *Critique of Practical Reason* on the principle that we possess a spontaneous and free will, by which we can and must follow the precepts of morality. This moral principle was called by Kant the principle of willing what is good (*Wolhwollen*), and a disciple of his, Fichte, founded upon it his whole system of philosophy, whilst Herbart himself, determined intellectualist as he was, also retained that principle as the foundation of all moral systems.

Psychology owes much to Schopenhauer, because of the importance attributed by him to the subjective element in our consciousness. Schopenhauer, however, is not always very explicit in his doctrines, and, as Zeller rightly remarks,[2] notwithstanding his idealism, he presents many points of contact with the materialists and the physiologists, inasmuch as he ultimately places the seat of human will in physiological temperament and considers presentation a product of the brain. From him came the first impulse (subsequently so widely extended) to the study of all the so-called organic sensations and the feelings connected therewith, which have so much influence in the constitution of consciousness.

A psychologist whose works still enjoy a certain repute, Frederick Edward Beneke, attributes to Psychology an even

Beneke. more decided biological character.[3] As opposed to Herbart, he admits the existence in the consciousness of two kinds of spontaneous impulses or attitudes,

---

[1] Höffding rightly remarks on this point that "the unpsychological division between intelligence and will shows itself here in its crudest shape."

[2] Zeller, *Geschichte der neueren deutschen Philosophie*, p. 873. Schopenhauer's psychological theories appear in different passages of his principal work, but especially in Vol. I., Bk. II.

[3] Frederick Edward Beneke (1798—1854) wrote numerous works, and exercised a great influence, especially on the students of the University of Berlin, where he lectured, not wholly unmolested by the Hegelians, who predominated at the

sensation and motion, which develop themselves gradually from simple primitive forms by means of the continuous action of external stimuli. External impressions leave on the mind traces or dispositions which can, by means of renewed excitations, revert from the unconscious to the conscious state. What is, perhaps, most important in Beneke's work is the theory, which he illustrated by means of the analogy of the evolution of natural products, that from the lower and more elementary forms of mental life an uninterrupted evolution leads to the higher and more complex forms. This is what he calls the formation of new faculties, the latter at first sight appearing so different from their originals that one would hardly credit their possession of a similar nature.[1] Beneke's Psychology has an exclusively spiritualistic character, for he gives a maximum of importance to the inner sense, as distinguished by him (with all the psychologists from Locke down to the experimentalists) from the external sense. Introspection was, in the opinion of Beneke, the only possible method in Psychology, because of the inner sense being so much sharper and more exact than the external sense. A really scientific method in Psychology could not be hoped for while this dualism existed between the so-called internal and external sense, as introduced by Wolff, and the moment had not yet come to do away with it. Notwithstanding the progress which the natural sciences were making, no one as yet believed in a scientific unity which should abolish the artificial distinction between physical and mental phenomena.

Whereas in Germany there reigned after Kant a spiritualistic tendency, in France Condillac's ideas were still held in favour,
Cabanis. although a much greater importance was attributed to the historical evolution of thought than he had given to it. One of the most notable representatives of this school is George Cabanis (1757—1808), who published in 1802 his book on the *Rapports du physique et du moral de l'homme*, in which he insists particularly on the importance of the inner organic sensations, whilst Condillac had confined himself almost exclusively to outward impressions. Thus Cabanis was in a way a precursor of Schopenhauer, who, as we have seen, placed the essence of human nature in the aggregate of dim instincts residing in the organism.

time in that university. Amongst his writings are to be noted especially his *Psychologische Skizzen* (1825—1827), and his *Lehrbuch der Psychologie als Naturwissenschaft* (1833), a fourth edition of which appeared in 1877.
[1] See especially pages 210 foll. of the *Lehrbuch*.

A less original follower of Condillac was Destutt de Tracy (1754—1836); but the most celebrated psychologist of this school was Maine de Biran (1766—1824), who is thought by some the most notable psychologist of the nineteenth century in France. His decided natural bent towards the observation and analysis of his own mind led him into the field of psychological research,[1] where, like many others, he followed at first the theories of Condillac and Cabanis, and turned his attention principally to the conditions of the body which correspond to the states of consciousness.

De Biran.

Even at that early period de Biran has some felicitous inspirations, as when he discovers the principal obstacle to the introspective method to be the continual change of the states of consciousness, or, as he called it, "the ever revolving wheel of existence."

Later, de Biran attributes more and more importance to the spontaneous inner activity of consciousness, which manifests itself directly by means of an effort of will,[2] and does not require the agency of any external impression. De Biran, nevertheless, with an apparent inconsequence which reveals the former disciple of Condillac, refuses to attribute to this inner activity much power in the government of the will, which is influenced by unconscious phenomena, which we are unable to regulate, and which exist even during the moments that we are not aware of them. This theory of unconscious sensations, which was much discussed at the time, was an evident consequence of the theories of Cabanis and of Schopenhauer. De Biran attempted also to explain physiologically the relation between the active and the passive sides of consciousness by having recourse to the hypothesis of the co-operation of different nerve centres. He took as an instance sleep and somnambulism to demonstrate the double aspect of our nature, thus abandoning the old-fashioned method of pure introspection, and making use of other aids to the study of mental phenomena. But what de Biran principally insists upon is the direct consciousness which we possess of an inner activity. Although, in his reaction against Condillac's doctrines, he therein represents a marked progress in the history of Psychology, he was, nevertheless, very far from giving it an experimental character.

---

[1] He has left a *Journal intime*, wherein he had noted all his different states of mind. This was a natural consequence of the introspective method, which led to an almost purely literary or artistic conception of Psychology.

[2] See *Rapports du physique et du moral de l'homme*.

Maine de Biran's work was not continued in France for some time, Ampère (1775—1836), Royer-Collard (1763—1843), and Cousin (1792–1867) contributing nothing very original. Ampère followed mainly the English associationists ; Royer-Collard was principally noted for having introduced into France the theories of the Scottish school and particularly of Reid, and Cousin attempted to conciliate the Scottish theories with those of de Biran and others. Theodore Jouffroy,[1] on the contrary, followed exclusively the Scottish philosophers, and, as far as regards Psychology, kept entirely to the introspective method, not recognising any better means of studying mental phenomena, and even denying the existence of any connection between Psychology and Physiology. In conclusion, we find that Psychology in France had gradually passed from absolute materialism to pure spiritualism, the first represented by Condillac, the latter by Jouffroy.

Other French psychologists.

Jouffroy.

Sensationalism and materialism found very severe critics in the Italian philosophers Pasquale Galluppi and Antonio Rosmini. Galluppi (1770—1846), although a follower of Locke's empirical method, attributed very great importance to the original and spontaneous activities of the spirit, as may be observed especially in his work *Filosofia della volontà* (1832—1840).[2]

Galluppi.

An even more profound critic of sensationalism was Antonio Rosmini-Serbati (1797–1855). His *Psicologia* (1836 ; Eng. tr. 1884—1888) and his *Antropologia* (1838) are part of a complete system of philosophy wherein he treats with great acumen some psychological problems of a specially philosophical character. Rosmini exerts himself to prove the simplicity, the spirituality, and the immortality of the soul. In his opinion the spirit is not to be considered as distinguished from the body, as in the dualistic theory of the Cartesians. It is, on the contrary, united to the body, of which it is the form, the body being the matter of the soul. Body and soul are connected by a fundamental

Rosmini.

---

[1] Theodore Jouffroy (1796—1842) wrote various works, of which the most notable are the *Mélanges philosophiques*. Taine, in his book *Les philosophes classiques du XIX. siècle*, gives a good portrait of him and of other French philosophers of the first half of the nineteenth century, such as Cousin, Royer-Collard, etc.

[2] Pasquale Galluppi exercised much influence in Italy, his principal philosophic works, besides the one quoted, being : *Saggio filosofico sulla critica della conoscenza* (1819—1832), *Lettere filosofiche sulle vicende della filosofia* (1827), *Elementi di filosofia* (1820), *Lezioni di logica e metafisica* (1832—1836).

and continuous consciousness which we have of our own body (*sentimento fondamentale corporeo*), from which are evolved, by means of the intelligence, the two conceptions of body and soul (*res extensa* and *res inextensa*). Thus the sensitive faculty is not totally distinct from the rational, as was held by the Cartesian spiritualists, but the former is contained in the latter. The sensitive faculty perceives only relations, whereas the rational faculty perceives the absolute entity. It must be noted that Rosmini, notwithstanding the fact of his being one of the stoutest champions of the indivisibility and spirituality of the soul, in accordance with his principle of the inseparability of body and mind, develops a theory, according to which the mind extends beyond all known organic bodies to the very elements which compose them. He has, therefore, no difficulty in accepting the doctrine of universal animism.[1]

The future of Psychology was to be influenced not only by philosophic speculations, but partly also by the development of the moral sciences. One of the most illustrious French philosophers, Auguste Comte, was the first to turn his attention to the connections between the various positive, physical, and social sciences. In his opinion the latter are derived from the former by means of an increasing complexity and decreasing generality.[2]

Comte.

In Comte's classification the place of Psychology is filled by Sociology, which is the study of the more complex phenomena of social life; but his influence on Psychology was nevertheless indirectly beneficial, owing to the importance attached by him to the study of social phenomena, which the psychologists of the inner sense altogether neglected. He exaggerated, however, in the opposite direction by denying all value to introspection. Moral laws must be studied in connection with social phenomena, which on their part can only be understood with the aid of biology, the sole difference between biology and sociology consisting in the greater complexity of the latter. As for individual Psychology, Comte admitted it only in its then prevalent form of cerebral anatomy and physiology, or rather of phrenology. Although

[1] Besides those already mentioned, Rosmini's principal works are: *Nuovo saggio sull' origine delle idee* (1830; Eng. tr. 1883—1884), *Il rinnovamento di T. Mamiani*, etc. (1836), *Principii di scienza morale e storia comparata dei sistemi morali* (1831—1837), *Filosofia del diritto* (1841).

[2] Auguste Comte lived from 1798 to 1857, his ideas being expressed in the numerous volumes of his *Cours de philosophie positive*, translated into English and condensed by Harriet Martineau.

Historical Development of Psychology

sociology since Comte has deviated somewhat from the path he marked out, he possesses the undoubted merit of having been its founder.

Meanwhile, Kant's critical philosophy had extended its influence to England, where it was mainly represented by William Hamilton, **Hamilton.** who believed in the existence of a psychic substance, and, as a consequence, of unconscious states of mind.[1]

In a very different line John Stuart Mill, a philosopher of the positivist school, followed up the psychological side of positivism **Stuart Mill.** in his various works, and particularly in his *Examination of Sir William Hamilton's Philosophy.*[2] Mill cannot properly be considered a follower of the associationist doctrines. On the contrary, in his opinion the fundamental principle of Psychology is that consciousness constitutes a unity of connected parts, in relation to which the laws of association are but of secondary importance. As regards method, Mill cannot be said to have contributed anything new to Psychology, belonging to the inner sense school rather than to the experimental.[3] His important work is chiefly from the side of logic, where his analysis of the inductive method formed an epoch. He was, moreover, the first to examine the possibility of giving to the moral sciences a common basis in Ethology, or general science of human nature, as he called Psychology.

After Mill, who, in our estimation, closes the period of the inner sense and introspective school, begins what is called the New Psychology, which is what we are principally concerned with in the present work.

III. Modern Psychology

Modern Psychology being founded on the principle of the unity of **Modern** all branches of knowledge, the old-fashioned distinction **Psychology.** between inner and outer sense gradually disappears, and the physical and mental worlds are conceived of as different

---

[1] William Hamilton lived from 1788 to 1856, and was a professor in the University of Edinburgh. His principal works are the *Lectures on Metaphysics* (1858) and the *Lectures on Logic* (1860). The influence his doctrines exercised on Spencer is well known. See Höffding, *Einleitung in die englische Philosophie unserer Zeit.*

[2] Mill lived from 1806 to 1873. His *Examination of Sir W. Hamilton's Philosophy* appeared in 1865. See besides Ribot, *op. cit.*, p. 99, Ferri, *op. cit.*, p. 98, and Höffding, *op. cit.*, p. 24.

[3] See Ribot, *Psychologie anglaise contemporaine.*

aspects of the same thing. It is therefore important to trace the origin of this new system and to observe the points of contact as well as the differences which connect it with, or distinguish it from the preceding schools.

It is difficult to assign a date to the commencement of modern scientific Psychology. Three causes favoured its rise :—

(1) The observation of historical and social facts marking the progress of the moral sciences.

(2) The Psychology of the individual mind and the experimental method, connected with the advance of physiology.

(3) General biology, which had its development under the influence of the theory of evolution.

The first of these causes, consisting in pure observation, may perhaps be said to originate with Hegel, whose conception of historical evolution caused a vast amount of research in all branches of the moral sciences, giving rise eventually to the *Historical* school, and, later still, to what the Germans call the *Psychology of Peoples* (*Völkerpsychologie*). The second form of modern Psychology likewise has few precursors. We have already mentioned Berkeley, with his theory of vision, and Tetens, who was the first to measure the duration of images produced by different sensations, and whose ideas with regard to the experimental method in Psychology possess more than a merely historical interest.[1] Bonnet, psychologist and naturalist, attempted to employ in Psychology the method of the natural sciences ; Hartley and Priestley inquired into its connections with physiology. We must nevertheless distinguish amongst psychologists those who, recognising certain connections between mental and cerebral phenomena, admit the possibility of explaining the former by means of the latter, and those who in their experiments make use purely and simply of physiological methods. The former may be found even amongst metaphysicians ; the latter are mainly empiricists, although there have been some who have successfully combined the two methods. As to the third method of modern Psychology, it is entirely new, and may be said to possess no precedents to speak of. It was the cause of the development of genetic Psychology.

Before coming to the modern scientific psychologists, it may be well to glance at the materialistic school, which flourished in the middle of the last century. The philosophers of that school, like

---

[1] See Külpe, *Einleitung in die Philosphie*, p. 65 (Eng. tr. 1897 ; 2nd edit. 1901).

Büchner, Moleschott, Vogt, and Czolbe, not only were not psychologists, but in affirming as they did that thought is merely a product of the brain, practically denied the very existence of the science of Psychology. They exercised, however, an indirect influence through their demolition of old-fashioned spiritualistic ideas and their demonstration of a connection between cerebral and mental processes. Their materialistic exaggerations, on the other hand, were the ultimate cause of a reaction out of which the scientific Psychology of our own day was subsequently evolved.[1]

Materialists of the nineteenth century.

Amongst the physiological psychologists we must first of all mention Hermann Lotze, a man of varied and profound culture, naturalist, doctor, psychologist, logician, and historian of German æsthetics.[2] Besides publishing works on physiology and general pathology,[3] he wrote a *Medical Psychology, or Physiology of the Mind* (1882),[4] which is of great importance in the history of Psychology. His starting-point is the popular Cartesian theory of the reciprocal action between body and mind. Whilst he professes to see the same mechanical causation in physical and vital phenomena, he nevertheless stops short of the extreme consequences of such a principle. In his opinion, physical phenomena do not constitute a continuous series, but there exists a point where the physical phenomenon is, as he calls it, absorbed and changed into a state of consciousness. It must be noted, however, that at this time the principle of the conservation of energy had only been

Lotze.

---

[1] The celebrated work by Ludwig Büchner *Kraft und Stoff* went through sixteen German editions from 1855 (when it was first published) to 1889, not counting numerous foreign ones. Moleschott's principal work, *Der Kreislauf des Lebens*, appeared in 1852. The author lived from 1822 to 1893. Charles Vogt, who was for some years a lecturer at the University of Geneva, published several works of repute, such as *Köhlerglaube und Wissenschaft* (1855) and *Vorlesungen über den Menschen*. Heinrich Czolbe (1809—1873), who in his works shows himself superior to the other philosophers of his school, is noted for his *Neue Darstellung des Sensualismus* (1855), *Die Entstehung des Selbstbewusstseins* (1856), an essay called *Die Elemente der Psychologie vom Standpunkte des Materialismus*, etc.

[2] Hermann Lotze (1817—1881) was for several years a lecturer in the University of Göttingen, and afterwards in that of Berlin. He wrote much on different philosophical subjects, and consecrated his whole life to science and teaching.

[3] *Allgemeine Pathologie und Therapie als mechanische Naturwissenschaften* (1842) *Allgemeine Physiologie des körperlichen Lebens* (1851).

[4] *Medizinische Psychologie oder Physiologie der Seele*.

recently formulated,[1] and had not attained the importance which subsequently attached to it. Like the Cartesian, Lotze's Psychology is entirely spiritualistic. Physical phenomena are derived, in his opinion, from a psychical substance, or principle, and his researches are principally concerned with the connections between physical and mental phenomena. The material processes, according to Lotze, are only symbols which, being translated by the soul into a language proper to itself, produce sensations. The latter constitute the material upon which the higher mental faculties exert their activity, manifesting themselves even in the absence of any concomitant cerebral phenomenon. The material processes are not the cause, but the effect of mental processes.

Apart from these theories, which are not sufficiently well founded, Lotze had more success in results of a less general and more empirical character, and in his theory of local signs, which, in spite of subsequent modifications, offers the best explanation of the formation of the perception of space. He agreed with Schopenhauer in recognising feeling as a spontaneous force, in opposition to the Hegelian and Herbartian schools. Lotze, however, was principally occupied with philosophical problems, and did not contribute much to the advancement of Psychology, which was in his estimation a branch of applied metaphysics.

Results of a more positive nature are due to the researches of the physiologist Ernest Henry Weber, author of a celebrated work *On the Sense of Touch and Organic Feeling*,

Weber.

published in 1849. Taking up the attempts of Tetens and Bonnet at a time when the physical sciences were much more advanced, Weber collected some valuable data with regard to the connections between the external stimulus and the corresponding sensation, and succeeded in establishing the existence of a constant law which rules them.[2] He found a worthy successor in his pupil

---

[1] It was first stated in 1845 by Robert Mayer in his work *Die organische Bewegung in ihrem Zusammenhange mit dem Stoffwechsel*. Almost at the same time Helmholtz, a German, Joule, an Englishman, and Colding, a Dane, published works on the same subject. Helmholtz's essay *Ueber die Erhaltung der Kraft*, and Joule's *Matter, Living Force, and Heat*, were published in 1847.

[2] Weber lived from 1795 to 1878. He was a lecturer on anatomy and physiology in Leipsic University, and wrote various works on those subjects. The work above quoted (*Der Tastsinn und das Gemeingefühl*) was published in R. Wagner's *Handwörterbuch der Physiologie*, iii. 2, and republished by itself in 1851. See Ludwig's *Rede zum Gedächtniss an E. H. Weber* (Leipsic, 1878).

Gustav Theodor Fechner, a man of most varied attainments.[1]
Fechner. As regards his philosophic ideas, whereas Lotze was practically a follower of the Cartesian dualistic principle, Fechner, on the contrary, believed in a universal animism, by which matter and spirit are indissolubly connected not only in man and animals, but also in plants and the celestial bodies. The difference between the external and internal worlds depends rather on a different point of view than on substantial difference between the two, just as the convex and concave parts of an arc are one and the same thing considered under different aspects. More logical than Lotze, he understood the great importance of the principle of the conservation of energy, which he considers applicable to the physiological phenomena connected with mental activity. This parallelism once admitted, Fechner, like Weber, set himself to discover and formulate mathematically the ruling principle of both. At first he had imagined that the physical stimulus and the resulting sensation are directly proportionate; but subsequently, and, as he precisely notes, on the morning of October 22nd, 1850, he was struck by the notion that the mental process corresponds to a relative change in the physical state, so that the variation of intensity in the mental state is not directly correspondent to the intensity of the stimulus, but rather to the difference between the respective intensities of the said stimulus and of the pre-existing one.

Psychophysics is therefore the exact science of the connections between the functions of the body and of the soul, or, more generally, between the physical and mental worlds. Fechner preserves the old-fashioned distinction of inner and outer perception. The connection between body and mind may be direct or indirect. Sensations are in direct dependence on certain activities of the brain, of which they are the immediate consequences; but they depend also indirectly on the external stimuli whose action is conveyed through the nerves. The mental process

[1] G. T. Fechner may truly be called the founder of scientific Psychology. Born at Lansit in 1801, he studied physics and medicine, and became Professor of Physics at Leipsic in 1835. A disease of the eyes obliged him temporarily to give up lecturing, and he thereupon devoted himself to philosophic studies, obtaining later the chair of philosophy in the same university. He wrote various works and papers on psychology, physics, æsthetics, and philosophy. He died in 1887, Wundt pronouncing his funeral oration (see in Wundt's *Philosophische Studien*, vi. 477, *Zur Erinnerung an Gustav Theodor Fechner*). Fechner's principal and, we may say, epoch-making psychological work is his *Elemente der Psychophysik*, published in 1860.

being viewed as a direct emanation of the physical process, the latter may be considered the substratum or vehicle of the former; and those physical activities which are in more direct connection with the mental activities are called psychophysical. Psychophysics may therefore be divided into two branches, according as it studies the indirect or the direct relations intervening between consciousness and the external world. The former, the psychophysics of the external world, borrows its method from the science of physics, whilst the latter, or psychophysics of the inner world, presupposes a knowledge of physiology and anatomy, especially those of the nervous system,[1] and constitutes, in other words, so-called *Physiological Psychology*.

Fechner formulated the law which he named after Weber, as that by which the intensity of a sensation does not increase proportionately to the intensity of the external stimulus, but is commensurate to the difference between the sensation itself and the totality of the impressions already received. This law can be expressed with greater exactitude thus: sensation represents the logarithm of the stimulus. Fechner's work *Elemente der Psychophysik* (published in 1860) teems with data derived from his experiments in every province of sensation, and forms the starting-point of experimental Psychology.

Fechner's work was carried on by Wilhelm Wundt, lecturer at the University of Leipsic. He is a man of most varied attainments in all branches of science, and a philosopher and physiologist of remarkable merit. In 1874 he published the first edition of his *Grundzüge der physiologischen Psychologie*, which reached a fourth edition in 1893, and is still the most complete work on the subject. Wundt carried the application of the physiological method to Psychology to the utmost possible extent. He tests Weber's law, for instance, by means of a series of experiments in the same way that he experiments with regard to the duration of sensations, to mental and muscular reactions, to the span of consciousness, to the influence of attention on perception, to the nature of perceptions of time and space. In 1878 he founded in Leipsic the first laboratory of physiological Psychology, which soon obtained a world-wide renown. By means of the data obtained by his experiments, Wundt was able to formulate with precision general and fundamental principles in Psychology, and to arrive at a knowledge of mental phenomena hitherto unequalled. Wundt brought out in 1892 a new and entirely

[1] See Fechner, *Elemente der Psychophysik*, pp. 9-11.

rewritten edition of a psychological work which he had published for the first time in 1862. In it he expounds the principles of experimental Psychology in a simpler form and with fewer details than in his *Grundzüge*; but the work in which his ideas are given with greatest clearness and precision, together with the latest results of the study of Psychology, is his *Grundriss der Psychologie* (1896).[1] Wundt is also the author of a large number of papers published in his *Philosophische Studien*. Not satisfied with the definition of Psychology and of psychological phenomena as compared with physical given by his predecessors, Wundt re-examines the whole question from the beginning, and arrives at the conclusion that there is no substantial difference between Psychology and the natural sciences, the external world existing only in so much as it is perceived by our consciousness, and consciousness existing only insomuch as there is an object to be perceived—*i.e.* the external world. The only difference between the physical and psychical sciences lies in the point of view from which they consider their object. Psychology studies it in connection with the direct impression it creates on our consciousness, whereas the physical sciences make abstraction of the effects produced on our consciousness and are concerned with general laws. That which appears directly to our consciousness is constituted by qualities, or values, which manifest themselves either as sensations or as feeling and will. The two latter are what lend an eminently qualitative character to the mental processes, the will being that which represents the spontaneous character of the mental life, and distinguishes it from a merely physical mechanism. These ideas are dealt with at great length in Wundt's *System der Philosophie*. As a consequence of his principle that the phenomena of consciousness and those of nature are the same thing differently considered, follows the adoption, in the case of Psychology, of the methods of the natural sciences, and especially of Physiology. Thus we have Physiological Psychology, which is not, as has been erroneously believed, a branch of Physiology, but simply an application of physiological methods to Psychology. The experimental method completes what introspection can only partly achieve, and gives a more exact basis to psychological research; but it is by no means sufficient in itself, and can only be applied to the simpler mental processes. As regards the more complex ones, Social Psychology, or, as it is also called, the

---

[1] The *Grundriss der Psychologie* has already reached a third edition, and has been translated into English and Italian.

Psychology of Peoples, studies the great mental phenomena which are the outcome of man's life as a member of society. In addition to historical documents, Psychology appeals to the data supplied by mental evolution in children and animals as well as by mental diseases. By means of the experimental method the mental life can be reduced to its constituent elements—*i.e.* sensations and simple feelings. Proceeding from these elementary forms in a contrary and synthetic sense, we are thus enabled to understand the more complex mental formations (*Gebilde*), such as perceptions, emotions, and volitional processes, and also the connections between them. Wundt goes on to consider how these mental processes have formed themselves in the individual and in the species, and, lastly, endeavours to establish the laws of Psychology by means of some few general principles which govern the development of all mental processes.

To this period belongs the psychologist Adolph Horwicz, who also attempted a complete treatment of psychic phenomena based on the results of physiology. His *Psychological Analyses founded on Physiology* were published in three volumes between 1872 and 1878.[1] The work, though possessing undoubted merit, is obscure and unmethodical, the author, while professing to be guided by pure experience, launching forth into general theories, and pushing his anti-intellectualism to the point of considering feeling as the primitive faculty of mind and the "direct expression of the soul's impulse towards self-preservation."

Horwicz.

Psychology was meanwhile making great progress in England as well as in Germany. Foremost in the rank of psychologists in England are Spencer and Bain. Herbert Spencer was the first to develop the theory of a progressive evolution of consciousness parallel to that of living organisms. Spencer's *Principles of Psychology* is the application of the philosopher's general ideas to a special branch of experience rather than a study of mental phenomena empirically considered. His dominating notion is the principle of evolution as set forth in his *First Principles*. In his *Principles of Psychology*[2] are comprised

Spencer.

---

[1] *Psychologische Analysen auf physiologischen Grundlage, ein Versuch zur Neubegründung der Seelenlehre* (Part I., Halle, 1872 ; Part II., 2 vols., Magdeburg and Halle, 1875 and 1878).

[2] *The Principles of Psychology* (London, 1855). On Spencer's *Psychology*, see Ribot, *op. cit.*, p. 161 foll. ; Ferri, *op. cit.*, p. 163 foll.[; Höffding, *Einleitung* p. 203.

a synthetical and an analytical part, preceded by a study of the data and inductions of Psychology. Spencer examines first of all the nervous system, which is the *sine quâ non* of consciousness, and is of opinion that the object of Psychology consists in determining the connection between the series of physical phenomena and the corresponding series of mental phenomena. The individual cannot be considered as an abstract psychic entity, but as what he really is—viz. a psychophysical being, who has to adapt himself to his surroundings. Therefore there can be no sharp distinction between Biology and Psychology, for there can be no interruption in evolution, which is a universal and continuous process observable in every form of existence. Life consists in a perfect harmony between the outer and the inner worlds. Thus consciousness, like the bodily organism from which it is inseparable, is subject to a progressive evolution from simpler to more complicated forms, or, as we may say, from a homogeneous to a heterogeneous form. Spencer in his *general synthesis* studies the evolution of consciousness with regard to its several aspects of space, time, speciality, complexity, and so forth ; in his *special synthesis* he examines the various forms of consciousness, such as reflex action, instinct, memory, intelligence, feeling, and will. Both these, being detailed studies of the logical forms of thought, belong rather to Epistemology and Logic than to Psychology proper.

Spencer's work possesses immense importance in the history of Psychology, and testifies to the greatly beneficial influence exercised during the last century on Psychology and the moral sciences by biological studies. Just as Biology was beginning to consider all organic beings, including man, as connected with one another by a continuous chain of evolution, so Psychology ceased to consider man as an isolated being in order to explain the origin of conscious phenomena by means of the evolution of the species. Thus Spencer maintained the necessity of supplementing the individual method in Psychology with the social and physiological methods, and divides the first into two special sciences, *subjective* and *objective*, the latter being properly a biological science.

Bain. The next most notable modern English psychologist is Alexander Bain, a pupil of Mill, who infused a modern spirit into the analytical method of the Scottish school. His two principal works, on *The Senses and the Intellect* and on *The Emotions and the Will*, are amongst the best of modern

Psychology. The first was published in 1855, and in it Bain follows mainly the English doctrine of association. His other work, on *The Emotions and the Will*, is more original,[1] and aims at a complete study of the will and of the feelings, which had up to then been sacrificed to the study of the intelligence.[2] Bain was the first to classify the feelings according as they are the outcome of anger, of sympathy, of fear, or may be defined as æsthetic, ethical, intellectual, ideal, etc. His book is for this reason, as well as for the minuteness of its method of observation, one of the most complete on the subject. What especially distinguishes him from his English predecessors is that he abandons the purely descriptive method and explains the formation of more complex phenomena by reducing them to their constituent elements. Let us take, for example, the first chapters of Part II., which refer to the will. Bain examines the primitive elements of volition, the gradual development of the volitional power, as manifested in the motions of the body, the action of thought and feeling on the will. Step by step he succeeds in establishing the intimate connection existing between the various functions of consciousness, and ends by demonstrating the voluntary character pertaining to thought-concatenations and the continual and reciprocal action of feelings and ideas. His work was the first to be written independently of all philosophical presuppositions and on data furnished by introspection tested by biology, and it has the merit of being free from the schematic design so apparent in Spencer's *Principles of Psychology*, which give one the impression of a continual searching for the same rules in Psychology as govern organic evolution. Bain's book, together with Fechner's *Elements of Psychophysics* (published in 1860), marks the beginning of purely empirical Psychology. Though he did not himself make use of experiment, Bain knew how to adapt the data afforded by the biological sciences as well as the general principles of philosophy, so that many of his theories have since found full confirmation in experimental Psychology. If a criticism is to be passed upon him, it is that his method is not always as rigorous as it should be, and that

---

[1] This work was published in 1859, and went through a third and revised edition in 1875. Bain published also a work on *Moral and Mental Science* in 1868, and one entitled *Mind and Body* in 1873. His theories had been studied by Ribot, *op. cit.*, p. 249 foll., Höffding, *Einleitung*, etc., p. 85 foll., and Ferri, *op. cit.*, p. 133 foll.

[2] The earlier philosophers (Descartes, Spinoza, etc.) had always placed the manifestations of the feelings and of the will in a subordinate position to the intellectual processes.

he seems often to lose sight of essential points in the multitude of secondary details. He is also often too exclusively descriptive, to the detriment of the scientific explanation of psychic phenomena, and his classification of the emotions is too artificial, based as it is on the erroneous application of the same criterion to physical and mental phenomena.

An English philosopher of the period who had some points of contact with Bain was Samuel Bailey. He also insisted on the application to Psychology of the method of the natural sciences ; but he was rather a logician than a psychologist, and resembled in many ways the eighteenth-century writers.[1]

Bailey.

Meanwhile, the doctrine of evolution had in England more than in other countries extended from the natural sciences to almost every other branch of learning, and especially to Anthropology and Psychology, and naturalists and physiologists had begun to couple the study of mental processes with that of the evolution of organic forms. The ancient barrier between man and the dumb animals once overthrown, the mental processes which distinguish the former were looked for in their elementary form in the latter, and it gradually came to pass that Psychology, upon the data afforded by Anthropology, Sociology, Comparative Anatomy, and Physiology, was able to delineate an evolution of psychic phenomena similar to that of physical forms.

The theory of evolution had an ardent follower in George Lewes, who has many claims to be reckoned one of the founders of the new Psychology.[2] He was the first in England to give special importance to the physiological problems connected with Psychology. In all his studies his main endeavour was to trace back mental phenomena to organic causes. Lewes is more speculative than Bain, and concerns himself only with the more general problems of Psychology. In his estimation, consciousness is nothing but the result of organic harmony, and he seeks for no other unity ; so that his point of view is one-sided. Nevertheless, it helped towards the subsequent establishment of the two parallel unities, which are nowadays recognised by experimental Psychology, the mental and the physical.

Lewes.

---

[1] Samuel Bailey (1791—1870) published various works, amongst others *Letters on the Philosophy of the Human Mind* (3 vols., 1855—1863) and *The Theory of Reasoning* (1851).

[2] G. H. Lewes (1817—1878) wrote a *History of Philosophy* (1845); *Life and Works of Goethe* (1855); *Physiology of Common Life* (1860); *Problems of Life and Mind* (3 vols., 1874—1879); *The Physical Basis of Mind* (1877).

Another consequence of the doctrine of evolution was the recognition of the importance of pathological mental phenomena in explaining normal states of mind. Just as the human mind in the present is the result of a lengthy evolution of the species, which, in an infinitely abbreviated form, repeats itself in the individual, so do mental maladies follow a process of retrogression from which may be inferred what happens in normal cases. In this way the study of pathological states is of great help to psychological science.

One of the first to apply these theories was Maudsley, whose influence has been most marked in French Psychology, which concerns itself especially with the connection between normal and abnormal mental cases.[1] Maudsley inclined even more than Lewes towards materialism, so that for him Psychology is entirely absorbed by Physiology, and the study of conscious phenomena by that of the nervous system. In his opinion, consciousness is not the most important factor in man, but is, on the contrary, an epiphenomenon—that is to say, an addition to what constitutes the essence of an organised being—viz. its impulses and instincts.

Maudsley.

The connection existing between the biological and the new psychological schools induced many professional naturalists to turn their inquiries towards mental phenomena. The founder of this new Biology was an English naturalist, who, though treating a special part of Psychology, exercised an influence upon the whole of this branch of study—viz. Charles Darwin. With his famous work on the *Expression of the Emotions in Men and Animals*, published in 1872, he opened the way to the observation of physiological phenomena which accompany the various states of the mind, a study subsequently continued with great success by others. To Darwin we owe one of the first and ablest essays on the Psychology of infants.[2]

Charles Darwin.

Amongst other Englishmen who studied the mental processes we have Laicock, author of a celebrated theory (1838) of *unconscious cerebration*, more fully developed in subsequent works.[3]

---

[1] Henry Maudsley wrote: *Physiology of Mind*; *Pathology of Mind* (1867, republished in 2 vols. in 1876, one volume treating of the physiology, and the other of the pathology, of the mind); *Body and Mind* (1870); *Body and Will* (1883); *Responsibility in Mental Diseases* (1874), which last has been translated into French and Italian.

[2] *Biographical Sketch of an Infant*, published in *Mind* in 1877.

[3] Laicock dealt with many psychological and physiological questions in his book *Mind and Brain* (1860).

With Maudsley, he was one of the first to consider pathological mental phenomena in their connection with normal states of mind. Another physiologist incidentally connected with Psychology was Carpenter,[1] whilst Huxley also makes various noteworthy psychological observations in his numerous zoological works. Lastly, we must not omit Morell and Murphy—of whom the first was influenced by the German theories of Herbart's school, and the second endeavoured to reconcile the new ideas on evolution with the old-fashioned theory of association.[2]

Laicock and other English psychologists.

The Psychology of Peoples, which constitutes a very important part of general Psychology, has a twofold origin: idealistic and positive. The former is connected with the philosophy of Hegel and with the development of juridical and historical studies in Germany; the latter derives its source, on the contrary, from Comte, and is a result of biological ideas applied to social questions.

Psychology of Peoples.

The last-named form of the Psychology of Peoples finds its principal representative in Herbert Spencer, who in his *Social Statics* (1850) had compared social evolution to organic evolution, and in his *Principles of Psychology*, published some years later, had maintained the impossibility of explaining the phenomena of consciousness by means of individual analysis alone.[3]

This branch of science received important contributions from the anthropological studies of Lubbock and Tylor on the origin of civilisation and primeval man,[4] through which much light is thrown on the psychological conditions of primitive humanity. The researches on primitive civilisation found

Lubbock.

---

[1] Amongst the numerous works on Physiology, Zoology, Botany, etc., of which Carpenter is the author, the best are: *Zoology and Instinct in Animals*; *Principles of Human Physiology* and *Principles of Comparative Physiology* (published from 1816—1851); *Mental Physiology* (published 1874).

[2] Morell wrote an *Introduction to Mental Philosophy on the Inductive Method* (1861), and Murphy a book entitled *Habit and Intelligence in their Connection with the Laws of Matter and Force* (2 vols., 1869).

[3] Spencer's *Principles of Sociology* (1876) is the principal work by him which treats of ethnographic Psychology, and studies various mental forms to be found in the individual considered as living in society.

[4] Edward Burnett Tylor's principal works are: *Researches into the History of Mankind* (1865); *Primitive Culture: Researches into the Development of Mythology, Philosophy, Religion, Art, and Custom* (1871); *Anthropology: an Introduction to the Study of Man and Civilisation* (1881). Sir John Lubbock (now Lord Avebury) is the author of: *Prehistoric Times, as illustrated by Ancient Remains and the Manners and Customs of Modern Savages* (1865: in 1880 this

their complement in a comparison with the intellectual and moral condition of savages in the present time. Something in this line was done by Lubbock, in his work on Prehistoric Times; but the first to attempt a complete study of the life of savage peoples, based on copious ethnographical data, was Theodor Waitz. This German scientist, following the lead of Herbart, aimed at giving a scientific basis to Psychology, which he considered a fundamental part of philosophy, in opposition to Fichte, Hegel, and Schelling, who had assigned to it a purely secondary importance. Apart from various other works on general Psychology, his most important work deals with the *Anthropology of Peoples in a State of Nature*, which he did not live to finish.[1] Another well-known writer on ethnographical and sociological subjects is Adolph Bastian;[2] and, of course, Herbert Spencer's sociological studies afford a notable contribution to ethnographical Psychology.[3] Comparative mythology and the study of languages have also had their part in the general result, especially through the works of Max Müller, whose vast range of culture embraces both English and German science.[4]

These scientists, mainly of the positivist school, were not noted for the precision of their methods, and followed (Spencer not excepted) a purely empirical and descriptive system. Amongst

work had reached its fifteenth edition); *The Origin of Civilisation and Primitive Condition of Man* (1870).

[1] Theodor Waitz (1821—1864), some time professor at Marburg, wrote various works on Herbartian principles, amongst which was a *Lehrbuch der Psychologie als Naturwissenschaft* (1849). Of his principal work, *Anthropologie der Naturvölker*, the first four volumes came out from 1859 to 1865, the fifth and sixth in 1867 and 1872. Waitz is also the author of a work entitled *Die Indianer Nordamerikas* (1865), which is a kind of supplement to the preceding.

[2] Adolph Bastian, professor at the University of Berlin, is the author of *Der Mensch in der Geschichte* (1860); *Beiträge zur vergleichenden Psychologie, Ethnologische Forschungen* (1871); *Das Beständige in den Menschenrassen* (1868).

[3] Besides the *Principles of Sociology* (1876), Spencer published eight volumes (1873—1882) of a work entitled *Descriptive Sociology*, on the customs of the savage and half-civilised peoples of the present day.

[4] Max Müller's famous work on the *Science of Language*, which has been translated into nearly every language, came out in two series from 1861 to 1864. Müller is also the author of *Essays on Comparative Mythology* (1858); *Lectures on Origin and Growth of Religion as illustrated by the Religions of India* (1878); *Natural Religion, Physical Religion, Anthropological Religion, Theosophy of Psychological Religion* (lectures, 1891—1892); *Science of Thought* (1887), translated into German under the title *Das Denken im Lichte der Sprache* (1888).

Historical Development of Psychology 45

Lazarus and Steinthal. the Germans, on the contrary, we find a greater scientific rigour of method and exposition, Lazarus and Steinthal, both followers of Herbart, being, one may say, the creators of the "Psychology of Peoples." The former published in 1855 his celebrated work on *The Life of the Soul*,[1] which sets forth the results of researches on the psychical evolution of peoples and the principles of the new science. Lazarus does not keep to the purely descriptive and empirical method hitherto applied to the moral sciences. He endeavours to fix the laws of the evolution of ideas and of feelings, and to make of Psychology a science occupying the same position in respect to the historical and social sciences as Physiology and Physics do in respect to the natural sciences.[2] Steinthal concerns himself especially with the relations between Psychology and the science of language.[3] Steinthal and Lazarus edited together from 1860 to 1870 a *Review of the Psychology of Peoples and of the Science of Language*.[4] Its object was to collect data and observations on the intellectual and moral life of peoples, and it numbered some of the most able men amongst its contributors. In a great work, of which the first two volumes have already appeared, Wundt is now giving a scientific shape to the Psychology of Peoples based on the data furnished by individual Psychology and by the moral sciences.

Thus, with Spencer and Bain in England and with Fechner, Lazarus, and Steinthal in Germany, Psychology was becoming an important and autonomous science. Nevertheless, especially in Germany, some authors persisted in the old-fashioned methods of pure introspection, as, for instance, Franz Brentano **Brentano, etc.** in his *Psychologie vom empirischen Standpunkte*, of which only the first volume has appeared[5]; Th. Lipps in his

[1] *Das Leben der Seele* (2 vols., 1856—1857; 2nd edit., enlarged in 3 vols., 1876—1882).

[2] See Bouglé's observations in his little work entitled *Les sciences sociales en Allemagne* (Paris, 1896, p. 18 foll.).

[3] *Einleitung in die Psychologie und Sprachwissenschaft* (Berlin, 1871), which is practically a revised and enlarged edition of a work published by Steinthal in 1855 entitled *Grammatik, Logik, Psychologie, ihre Principien und ihr Verhältniss zu einander*.

[4] *Zeitschrift für Völkerpsychologie und Sprachwissenschaft*. It was subsequently continued as the *Zeitschrift des Vereins der Volkskunde*. See, on Lazarus and Steinthal, Ribot in his *Psychologie allemande contemporaine*, and on Steinthal, Bouglé, *op. cit.*

[5] On the evolution of modern Psychology, see Lange's *History of Materialism*, Bk. II., Sect. III., chap. iii. In this chapter, written with Lange's usual clearness,

Grundsachen des Seelenlebens (1883)[1]; Wilhelm Volkmann in his *Lehrbuch der Psychologie*; Ulrici[2]; Fortlage, and others.

On the other hand, the number of works of the experimental school was daily increasing in number. One of the most important from every point of view is Harald Höffding's *Psychologie in Umrissen*.[3] Höffding is a professor in the University of Copenhagen, and is considered a follower of the German school, although he has several points of contact with the English psychologists.

Höffding.

His work is remarkable for clearness of style and for its unerring grasp of the object and character of Psychology. Höffding deals principally with psychological questions of a general and philosophical nature, as the relation between body and soul, conscious and unconscious states, the different elements of mind, and on each of them he brings to bear a remarkable originality, coupled with clearness and abundance of data. He rather neglects the study of the sensations, but analyzes in a masterly manner the phenomena that have to do with feeling, with the will, and with the reciprocal action of the three fundamental psychic elements, so that consciousness appears as a single unity based on the will.

The study of Psychophysics was followed in Germany by some very able men, such as Donders, Müller, Helmholtz, Hering, Goldscheider, Exner, Mach, Stumpf, Zeichen, Ebbinghaus, Münsterberg, Külpe, Lipps, Merkel, Mennmann, and many others who have contributed to the great progress it has made.[4]

German psychophysics.

are shown the various origins of *Scientific Psychology*—viz. the beginning of physiological German Psychology, of the Psychology of Peoples, and of English Empirical Psychology. Franz Brentano's work came out in 1874. Brentano has many points of contact with modern scientific Psychology, and his observations are always worthy of attention.

[1] Th. Lipps was the author of *Psychologie der Kosmik* (*Philos. Monatshefte*, 1888—1889); *Psychologische Studien* (1895).

[2] H. Ulrici, *Gott und der Mensch* (1866; 2nd edit. 1874).

[3] First German edit. 1887; 2nd, 1893, translated into English.

[4] Elias Müller, *Zur Grundlegung der Psychophysik, kritische Beiträge* (1878); H. Helmholtz, *Handbuch der physiologischen Optik* (1867; 2nd edit. 1886), *Die Lehre von den Tonempfindungen*, etc. (1863; 4th edit. 1877), *Die Thatsachen der Warnehmung*; Ewald Hering, *Ueber das Gedächtniss* (1870); *Der Raumsinn, der Temperatursinn*, etc. (Hermann's *Handbuch der Physiologie*, Vol. II.); A. Goldscheider, *Neue Thatsachen über die Hautsinnennerven* (1885); *Untersuchungen über den Muskelsinn* (1889); S. Exner, *Die Grosshirnrinde* (Hermann's *Handbuch*, Vol. II.), Ad. Elsas, *Ueber die Psychophysik* (1886); E. Mach, *Untersuchungen über den Zeitsinn des Ohrs* (1865); *Grundlinien der*

Ebbinghaus, who is a lecturer in the University of Breslau, is the author of several important works, among others of one *Ueber das Gedächtniss* (1885). He has deserved much credit as Editor of the *Zeitschrift für Psychologie und Physiologie der Sinnesorgane*, which publishes psychological works and reviews of any work on Psychology or on subjects related to Psychology. He is now publishing a new work entitled *Grundzüge der Psychologie*, and is justly considered one of the ablest German psychologists. Stumpf, who is a lecturer at the University of Berlin, is the author of an important book entitled *Tonpsychologie* (1883); to the eminent physicist Mach and to Ziehen we are indebted respectively for *Beiträge zur Analyse d. Empfindungen* and *Leitfaden der Physiol. Psychol.* (1893; Eng. tr. 1895; 3rd edit. 1899), besides other works. Both these authors follow the method of so-called psychophysical materialism, endeavouring to reduce all the processes of the mind to sensation, and to explain their connection by the help of cerebral physiology. To the same school, though differing from it in many points, belongs Külpe's *Grundriss der Psychologie* (1893; Eng. tr. 1895; 2nd edit. 1901), which is based entirely on the experimental method, and is one of the most notable works on modern Psychology. Külpe has published various other special works on Psychology, all notable for breadth of view and clearness of style. A more decided champion of the psychophysical method is Hugo Münsterberg, professor at Harvard University, U.S.A. Besides publishing various much-discussed papers, such as *Die Willenshandlung* (1888), *Beiträge zur Experimentellen Psychologie* (1889, 1892), *Ueber die Aufgaben und Methoden der Psychologie* (1891), he has recently given a complete exposition of his system (which, as we shall see, is opposed to the doctrines of most modern psychologists) in his *Psychology and Life* (1899) and in his *Grundzüge der Psychologie*, which is still in course of publication. Besides Külpe, we have several psychologists of Wundt's school who have kept themselves clear of all materialistic theories, such as Merkel, Kirschmann, Mennmann, Meinong, Kieson, Pflaum, G. F. Lipps, Alfred Lehmann (a Dane, and the author of some important studies on sense, hypnotism, and on the corporeal manifestations of the mental processes),[1] and others.

Lehre von den Bewegungempfindungen (1875). The most important works of Merkel, Mennmann, and other disciples of Wundt will be quoted in the course of the work.

[1] Alfred Lehmann, *Die Hauptgesetze des menschlichen Gefühlslebens* (1892); *Die Hypnose und die damit verwandten normalen Zustände* (1890); *Die körperlichen Aeusserungen psychischer Zustände*, and other works.

There exists in Germany a most extensive literature on Hypnotism; suffice it to quote Moll, Forel, Preyer, Heidenhaim, **Pathological Psychology.** Dessoir, Wetterstrand, Wundt.[1] Pathological Psychology is also represented by some very able men in Germany, such as Kussmaul, author of *Die Störungen der Sprache* (1877), and one of the first to introduce a science of the mechanism of language. Amongst alienists Kraft Ebbing, and especially Emil Kräpelin have furnished important contributions to the study of Psychology, the former being the author of various works on mental pathology, and of important papers on experimental Psychology published, in collaboration with other writers, in the *Psychologische Arbeiten*, edited by him.

Nor is the Psychology of Infancy neglected in Germany. As far back as the end of the eighteenth century we have **Psychology of childhood.** Dietrich Tiedermann's famous *Beobachtungen über die Entwicklung der Seelenfähigkeiten bei Kindern* (1787); later, the works of Semig and others. In 1881 Preyer, the physiologist, published his celebrated work *Die Seele des Kindes* (Eng. tr. 1889), which is still the most complete work on the subject from a biographical point of view. We must not omit to note Strümpell, Groos, author of *Die Spiele der Menschen* (1889; Eng. tr. 1902), and W. Ament, with his recent work *Die Entwicklung von Sprachen und Denken beim Kinde* (1899).

Animal Psychology has been much studied in Germany, although there is not yet an extensive literature on the subject. **Animal Psychology.** Strümpell's work on the mental life of animals compared to that of man (1878) is worthy of note, as is Hugel's *Das Seelenleben der Thiere* (1884), Schneider's *Der thierische Wille* (1880),[2] and especially Karl Groos's *Die Spiele der Thiere* (1896), in which may be traced the influence of the modern theories of experimental Psychology. Lastly, we have Wundt's work *Vorlesungen über die Menschen und Thierseele* (Eng. tr. 1894; 3rd edit. 1901).

Psychology has acquired a great importance in Germany within these last years, so that its usefulness is recognised even

[1] Besides Lehmann's works, the most important in Germany are the following: A. Forel, *Der Hypnotismus*; R. Heidenhain, *Der sogenannte thierische Magnetismus* (4th edit. 1889); Moll, *Der Hypnotismus* (1889; Eng. tr. from 2nd edit., 1890); Preyer, *Vorlesungen über Hypnotismus* (1890); Wetterstrand, *Der Hypnotismus und seine Anwendung in der praktischen Medicin*; M. Dessoir, *Das Doppel-Ich* (1889); Wundt's work *Hypnotismus und Suggestion* is contained in Vol. VIII., Part I., of the *Philosophische Studien*.

[2] Schneider is also the author of a book called *Der menschliche Wille* (1880).

by those who, as anatomists, physiologists, sociologists, historians, and political economists, do not make it their special object of study. This is especially the case as regards Experimental Psychology and the Psychology of Peoples, which some psychologists are now endeavouring to bring into harmony with each other. In this connection we must note Alfred Biese's *Entwickelung des Naturgefühls* (1888), whilst works on the subject have likewise been published by Stein, Wenzel, Pflaum, and others. On empirical questions and on questions of method we have works by the pen of such eminent philosophers as Zeller, Avenarius, Dilthey, Paulsen, Windelband, Ziegler, Sigwart, Natorp, Jodl, Volkelt. To Jodl and Cornelius we are indebted for two complete psychological treatises. The former's *Lehrbuch der Psychologie* (1896) treats mostly of fundamental questions, whilst the *Psychologie als Erfahrungswissenschaft* by Cornelius enters into more detailed particulars.[1]

In England Spencer and Bain had soon numerous followers. James Sully began with a work called *Sensation and Intuition: Studies in Psychology and Æsthetics* (1874), and in 1892 published an important treatise in two volumes entitled *The Human Mind*, which is an enlarged edition of his shorter *Outlines of Psychology* (1884; 2nd edit. 1895). In it, with excellent method and profound erudition, he endeavours to conciliate the different tendencies of the principal modern psychologists. Sully's method of observation and power of analysis are quite out of the common, and, like Höffding and Wundt, he possesses a clear conception of the unity of the mental processes and of the importance of the will. He is the author of *Studies of Childhood* (1895), which may be considered the best descriptive work on the Psychology of Infancy.[2]

Sully and other English psychologists.

A very original writer who holds a foremost place amongst contemporary psychologists is James Ward, whose article published in Vol. XX. of the *Encyclopædia Britannica* is one of the most important modern treatises on Psychology. Whereas the greater part of English psychologists attribute most importance to external factors in the formation of con-

---

[1] Stein, Windelband, Zeller, Volkelt are the authors of various short papers which we shall have occasion to quote later on. Sigwart has published several psychological writings in *Kleineschriften* (1881); Ziegler wrote *Das Gefühl* (1893); H. Spitta is the author of *Einleitung in die Psychologie als Wissenschaft* (1886); and P. Natorp of *Einleitung in die Psychologie nach kritischer Methode* (1888).

[2] See also Sully's *Illusions* (1881), *Pessimism* (1877), and other works.

sciousness, Ward gives particular prominence to the subjective factor; hence the importance attributed by him to attention and to feeling. Another distinguished writer is G. Croom-Robertson, who, like Ward, forsakes the descriptive in favour of the explanatory and genetic method. Modern Psychology is indebted to him for some very remarkable observations on the muscular sense and on visual perception. G. F. Stout, Reader in Philosophy in Oxford University, and editor of *Mind*, is to be noted for his *Analytic Psychology* (1896), and especially for his *Manual of Psychology* (1899; 2nd edit. 1901), a work full of information and remarkable for the excellence of its method. Like Sully, Stout endeavours to conciliate the various schools of modern Psychology, and has no preference for the purely experimental method.

A somewhat different line is followed by Francis Galton and Grant Allen, who may be considered the most important representatives of the naturalistic school in England. Francis Galton is well known for his theories on hereditary genius, and more particularly for his doctrine of general images. Grant Allen follows the experimental method in Psychology, and is the author of important works on physiological æsthetics, on colour-sense, etc. Pathological Psychology has in England two notable representatives in Hollander and Mercier; and there are besides many English philosophers like Sidgwick, Seth and others, who interest themselves in psychological questions.

The Psychology of infancy has had various representatives in England besides Sully. Thus Charles Darwin published in 1877 his *Biographical Sketch of an Infant*, and after him come Pollock, Warner, and Romanes. The last named published in 1889 his well-known *Mental Evolution in Man*, and is the author of several works on the intelligence of animals, in which he follows, with good result, a prevailing descriptive method. Sir John Lubbock (Lord Avebury) is also well known in this connection for his work *Ants, Bees, and Wasps* (1882), which has gone through a great number of editions, and has been translated into various languages. A more serious attempt at explaining the psychical laws in animals is due to C. Lloyd Morgan, Professor of Biology at Bristol, and author of *Animal Life and Intelligence* (1890) and of *Habit and Instinct* (1896).[1]

[1] F. Pollock is the author of a paper entitled *Record of an Infant's Progress in Language* (1878); Francis Warner of *The Children: How to Study Them* (1887); Romanes of *Animal Intelligence* (1882), and *Mental Evolution in*

Historical Development of Psychology

Psychological studies have found some of their most enthusiastic followers in America, where the experimental method **American psychologists.** has met with such great favour that the country now possesses some of the best psychological laboratories. One of the leading promoters of the movement is George Trumbull Ladd, professor at Yale University, who published in 1890 his *Elements of Physiological Psychology*, which in 1894 was followed by his *Psychology, Descriptive and Explanatory*, both of which works are conspicuous for clearness, precision, and breadth of ideas. Ladd's system closely resembles the dominant method in modern Psychology which we have seen adopted by Stout and Sully.[1] A somewhat different method is followed by Dewey, author of a *Psychology* on speculative lines. A man of strikingly original ideas, and as profound as he is brilliant, is William James, professor at Harvard University, whose *Principles of Psychology* (1891) is one of the most important works on modern Psychology, in which the experimental and speculative points of view are most admirably connected and harmonised. His dominant principle is that of the spontaneity of consciousness which is apparent in the connections between the mental processes. James, therefore, rejects the theory of the English Associationists, who tend to reduce the mental life to a mechanism of associated perceptions. James excels in the analysis of the phenomena of consciousness, of which he succeeds with great ability in tracing the connections and reciprocal relations. More successful than others in combining the descriptive and experimental methods, it is a pity that, in his desire to present the mental processes as a whole, he omits to examine separately their component parts.[2]

An author of note in recent times is J. Mark Baldwin, professor at Princeton University, and author of an excellent *Handbook on Psychology* published in 1891, in which he ably avails himself of the various methods of psychological research. He is principally known for his doctrine of the parallelism between the evolution of mental processes in the

Animals (1883); C. Lloyd Morgan of an *Introduction to Comparative Pyschology* (1887).

[1] Ladd is also the author of a *Primer of Psychology* (1895) and of several philosophical works which treat of psychological questions.

[2] W. James is the author also of *Psychology* (1892, an epitome of the *Principles*), *The Will to Believe, and Other Essays in Popular Philosophy* (1899), *Talks to Teachers* (1899), *Psychological Varieties of Religious Experience* (1902), besides shorter papers

individual and in the species, which has inspired him to write an original work entitled *Mental Development in the Child and in the Race* (1895), which has been translated into French and German. In this work Baldwin shows himself a past-master in the use of the explanatory method with reference to the Psychology of infancy and to the Psychology of peoples, in the felicitous combination of experiment and observation, and in the use which he makes of biological and psychological data, and of subjective and objective observation. He subsequently developed his ideas more fully in a volume entitled *Social and Ethical Interpretations in Mental Development*, which deals with Social Psychology. Apart from Tarde's book on the same subject, it is a work which presents the greatest originality, and constitutes one of the most determined attempts at solving the problem of the psychological relations between the individual and society. Other works by the same author on educational and biological interpretations are expected with much interest.[1]

A recent psychologist of merit is Edward Bradford Titchener, Professor of Psychology in Cornell University, and author, besides numerous articles, of *An Outline of Psychology*, entirely on experimental lines (published in 1896, and now in its third edition), and of two volumes on *Experimental Psychology* (1901) as a guide to laboratory practice. Amongst other American psychologists we must not omit to note Sanford (author of a *Course in Experimental Psychology*), Cattell, Münsterberg (who, though a German, may be counted amongst American psychologists, being now professor at Harvard University and writing in English[2]), Warren, Angell, Patrick, Bryan, Calkins, Delabarre, Tawney, Jastrow, Franklin, and Urban (author of notable works on *Affective Memory*, on the *Logic of the Emotions*, etc.). The American psychologists have a greater affinity with the Germans than the English in their application of the experimental method in conjunction with the descriptive. Psychological studies have met with great favour in America, especially in their application to Sociology (witness the writings of Giddings, Lester Ward,[3] and

[1] Baldwin's *Social and Ethical Interpretations* has also been translated into German and French. He has recently published a short, popular treatise *The Story of the Mind* (1899; translated into Italian 1901), and is the author of shorter articles, as well as the editor of an exhaustive *Dictionary of Philosophy and Psychology*, and of *Development and Evolution* (New York, 1902).

[2] Münsterberg has published in English *Psychology and Life* (1899).

[3] Giddings, *The Principles of Sociology* (1896); Lester Ward is the author of *Outlines of Sociology*, besides numerous articles in the *Monist* and elsewhere.

others. The Psychology of childhood has been studied in America by Granville Stanley Hall (professor at Clark University), Baldwin (already quoted), Shima, Tracy, Chamberlain, A. R. Tylor, and others.[1]

Just as the new Psychology could not entirely throw off the influence of the earlier philosophers in England and Germany, **French psychologists of the nineteenth century.** so that the German psychologists are characterised by a strong tinge of idealism and the English of empiricism, so in France the sensationalism of the eighteenth century has a marked effect on the Psychology of the nineteenth. The earliest important works of the kind are those of Hyppolite Adolphe Taine (1828—1893), **Taine.** in *Les philosophes classiques du XIXme siècle* (1856). Taine shows himself a follower of Cabanis and of the sensationalists, and gives a very able criticism of the spiritualistic theories which predominated in France up to the middle of the century with Cousin, Jouffroy, Laromiguière, Royer Collard. In *L'Intelligence* (published in 1870) Taine gives us a complete exposition of his doctrines. Although this work, treating of intellectual phenomena, has a pre-eminently logical and ideological value, it does not neglect the study of the sensations, based upon the data furnished by the physiology of the senses.

With Taine there begins in France a new era in Psychology. The importance of this science, its comprehensive character, and its points of contact with other branches of study were understood by him to their full extent, and he was not slow to avail himself of the help of other sciences, such as Physiology, Sociology, History, and Art. Where he was not so successful was in his attempt to reduce complex phenomena to their elemental parts, his analysis appearing to lack a guiding principle capable of demonstrating the evolution of the mental processes. The markedly intellectual character of his work was an obstacle to a complete comprehension of consciousness. There is not a word in it about the subjective aspect of consciousness, nor about the feelings and the will, nor, consequently, about their influence on intellectual phenomena.

[1] The best-known work by Granville Stanley Hall is *Children's Lives* (1896); A. F. Chamberlain is the author of *The Child and Childhood in Folk Thought*; A. R. Tylor wrote *The Study of the Child*; Frederick Tracy (professor in Toronto University) *Psychology of Childhood* (1893), etc. See, on the Psychology of childhood in North America and elsewhere, J. Schimpfl, *Stand der Kinderpsychologie in Europa und Amerika (Zeitschrift für pädagogische Psychologie*, 1899, Heft. 6).

Psychology in France owes much to Ribot. He has the merit of having made himself well acquainted with the modern Psychology **Ribot and others.** of England and Germany, and of having introduced into France and Italy the works of Bain, Spencer, Lewes, Maudsley, Lotze, Fechner, and Wundt. Ribot did not content himself with popularising the works of others, but struck out a line of his own, and soon became famous with his three works on the Maladies of the Will, of Memory, and of Personality. As we shall have several occasions of examining Ribot's theories, it must suffice meanwhile to note the manifest influence exercised upon them by the English school of Psychology, and especially by Lewes and Maudsley. In his later works his theories have been somewhat modified to suit the temperate idealism of contemporary English and German Psychology. He is principally noteworthy for his analysis of mental phenomena, and for his ability in applying data furnished by pathological phenomena to the explanation of normal phenomena.[1] With his *Revue philosophique* and other publications, and through the medium of his lectures, Ribot was the cause of attracting many to the study of Psychology, and of calling attention to abnormal and pathological states of consciousness in the insane and in persons under the influence of hypnotism. The most notable of his successors are Alfred Binet, author of *Psychologie du raisonnement* (1886), *Les altérations de la personnalité* (1891), *La fatigue intellectuelle* (1898); Pierre Janet, author, amongst other works, of *L'Automatism psychologique* (1889; 2nd edit. 1894); Fr. Paulton, who wrote an exhaustive work on *L'activité mentale et les éléments de l'esprit* (1889), and another on the *Phénomènes affectifs et les lois de leur apparition* (1887); Léon Dumont, author of a fine work on the *Théorie scientifique de la sensibilité* (1875); Feré, who in 1887 published some interesting experimental data on *Sensation et mouvement*, and (1892) an important work on the *Pathologie des émotions*. Some of the French psychologists are alienists as well, *e.g.* Despine, author of *Psychologie naturelle* (1868); Ballet, author of *Le langage intérieur*

---

[1] Ribot's works are the following: *La psychologie anglaise contemporaine* (1870; 3rd edit. 1891; Eng. tr. 1873), *L'hérédité* (1873; 5th edit. 1894); *La philosophie de Schopenhauer* (1874); *La psychologie allemande contemporaine* (1879; 2nd edit. 1892; Eng. tr. 1886); *Les maladies de la mémoire* (1881; 9th edit. 1894; Eng. tr. 1882); *Les maladies de la volonté* (1883; 10th edit. 1895; Eng. tr. 1897); *Les maladies de la personalité* (1885; 3rd edit. 1894; Eng. tr. 1891); *La psychologie de l'attention* (1889; 2nd edit. 1894; Eng. tr. 1890); *La psychologie des sentiments* (1896; Eng. tr. 1899); *L'évolution des idées générales* (1897; Eng. tr. 1899); *Essai sur l'imagination créative* (1900).

et l'aphasie (1866); Sollier, whose *Psychologie de l'idiot et de l'imbécile* has been translated into German; Bourdet, and others. On psychophysical lines we have the works of the Belgian Delboeuf, who is also author of a work called *La matière brute et la matière vivante* (1890). The physiologist Richet is author of an *Essai de psychologie générale*, nor must we omit to mention Bourdon, Henri, Flournoy, Beaunis, Philippe, all of whom follow the experimental method, which the numerous psychological laboratories have recently rendered more and more popular. The results of psychological investigations are published in the *Année psychologique*, edited by Binet, Beaunis, and Henri, and appearing yearly since 1895. This publication, besides containing papers by eminent psychologists of all countries, gives a complete review of all psychological books and articles as they are published. Hypnotism has also been much studied in France (witness the important works of Bernheim, Richet, Janet, and others). The study of nervous maladies has received a powerful impulse from Charcot (1825—1893), famed for his anatomical researches on the structure of the nervous centres.[1]

The Psychology of Childhood has been ably dealt with by Bernard Perez, Queyrat, Compayré, Binet; that of animals, studied by Flourens in the first half of the eighteenth century, was made the subject in recent times of an important work by Espinas, *Les sociétés animales* (1877), whilst later still we have Alfred Binet's *La vie psychique des micro-organismes* (1891).[2]

The Psychology of Peoples has an eminent exponent in Gabriel Tarde, author of several important works, amongst which are *Les*

[1] Binet et Henri, *La fatigue intellectuelle* (1898); Ch. Féré et Binet, *Le magnétisme animal*; Despine, *De la folie* (1875); Paul Sollier, *Le problème de la mémoire, essai de psycho-méchanique* (1900); Delboeuf, *Examen critique de la loi psychophysique* (1883), *Le sommeil et les rêves* (1885), etc.; Bourdon and Henri have both published various papers on psychophysiology in the *Année psychologique* and in the *Révue philosophique*; Beaunis, *Les sensations intérieures* (1889), etc.; Flournoy, *Des phénomènes de synopsie* (1893); Bernheim, *De la suggestion* (1884), *Hypnotisme, suggestion, psychothérapie* (1891); Richet treats of hypnotism in *L'Homme et l'intelligence* (1884); Charcot published in 1874 his *Leçons sur les maladies du système nerveux faites à la Salpêtrière* (4th edit. 1880), and is the author of *Les localisations dans les maladies du cerveau et de la moëlle épinière* (1876—1881).

[2] Bernard Perez is the author of *L'enfant de trois à sept ans* (1886), *Psychologie de l'enfant* (1878; Eng. tr. 1885), *L'art et la poésie chez l'enfant* (1888), *Le caractère de l'enfant et de l'homme* (1892), etc.; F. Queyrat wrote *L'imagination et ses variétés chez l'enfant* (1893); G. Compayré published *L'évolution intellectuelle et morale chez l'enfant* (1893); Binet is the author of various papers on the Psychology of childhood published in the *Revue philosophique* and in the *Année psychologique*. Flourens wrote *De l'instinct et de l'intelligence des animaux* (1841).

lois de l'imitation (1890), *L'opposition universelle* (1891), *La logique sociale* (1895), besides others connected with law and criminal sociology. Tarde endeavours to explain historical and social evolution by means of a few general psychological laws, and to point out the spontaneous character (much neglected by naturalistic psychologists) of the manifestations of the human intelligence. His works are deservedly extremely popular both in France and elsewhere. An author equally at home in experimental Psychology and in the Psychology of peoples is Bourdon, professor at Rennes University, and author of an interesting work entitled *L'exposition des émotions et des tendances dans le langage* (1892).

Whereas all the above-mentioned authors (Tarde perhaps excepted) follow a strictly empirical method, a more philosophical character is to be observed in the writings of Alfred Fouillée, whose various works on Ethics, Law, Sociology, General Philosophy, and Psychology are all equally deserving of praise. His principal psychological work is entitled *Psychologie des idées forces* (1893) ; in this he partly follows Schopenhauer by ranking as a primary psychological principle the volitional impulse (which he calls *l'appetit*). At the same time he differs from him in recognising the close connection between the said impulse and the cognitive elements of consciousness, owing to which an idea becomes a force. Fouillée, profound philosopher as he was, has a very clear conception of the character and of the laws of consciousness, and he ably confutes the theory of those psychologists who (especially in France) assign to it the secondary function of illuminating intermittently the vital mechanism.

To this purely philosophical school are also to be assigned the writings of Guyau, of which the most important, psychologically speaking, is his *Genèse de l'idée de temps* (1889), and those of Henri Bergson, author of *Essai sur les données immédiates de la conscience* (1889) and *Matière et Mémoire* (1896), both notable works. These writers, and others such as Ralier, Rauh, Duprat, etc., follow a system which differs from that of the naturalistic alienists who introduced experimental Psychology into France. A more speculative and metaphysical character is to be noticed in the writings of Ch. Renouvier and D. Mercier, and other contemporary French philosophers, who make use of Psychology as a starting-point for their philosophical doctrines.[1]

[1] Ralier, *Cours de philosophie* : Vol. I. *Psychologie* (1898) ; Rauh, *De la méthode dans la psychologie des sentiments* (1899) ; G. L. Duprat, *L'instabilité mentale* (1899) ; *Les causes sociales de la folie* (1900) ; Ch. Renouvier, *La psychologie*

Although Italy is not so advanced as other nations in psychological studies, it is but just to say that these have always been **Psychology** more or less cultivated in this country, and within the **in Italy.** last few years have received an impulse which promises well for the future. Rosmini and Galluppi were followed by a series of spiritualistic philosophers like Mamiani and Conti, for whom Psychology was an accessory of metaphysics. A much greater importance was attributed to it by the disciples of the positivist school, who, from the eighteenth century downwards, did nothing but preach in a more or less modified form the theories of Locke, of the English associationists, and of the French sensationalist. To this school belong Genovesi, Gioia, Romagnosi, and Carlo Cattaneo (1801—1869). Cattaneo was the first in Italy to give importance to the study of social and of historical consciousness, to which study he applied the name of Psychology of Associated Minds (lectures given from 1859 to 1863). Italian positivist Psychology has an able exponent in Pietro Siciliani (born 1835). Keeping pace with the progress made by Positivism abroad, and especially in England with the biologists and evolutionists, he was the means of widening the scope of Psychology in Italy. One of his principal works is *I prolegomeni alla moderna psicogenia* (1878), which has been translated into French. Another positivist philosopher, Andrea Angiulli (1837—1890), whose merits lie principally in the pedagogical line,[1] has dealt incidentally with psychological questions, and founded in 1881 a review entitled *Rassegna critica di opere filosofiche, scientifiche e letterarie*, wherein they are frequently discussed. Meanwhile, the positivist movement in Italy had very much increased and given rise to heated controversy with the followers of spiritualism. One of the most famous Italian positivist psychologists **Ardigò.** and philosophers is Roberto Ardigò (born 1828), professor in Padua University, who has embraced in his numerous works every branch of philosophical thought. In 1870 he published *La psicologia come scienza positiva* (3rd edit. 1882), in which, as opposed to the spiritualists, he maintained the complex character of consciousness and its intimate connection with physiological phenomena. His ideas are expounded with great clearness in his last work, entitled *Unità della coscienza*

---

rationelle; D. Mercier, *Psychologie* (1897), *Les origines de la psychologie contemporaine* (1898).

[1] Andrea Angiulli, *La filosofia e la ricerca positiva* (1868), *Questioni di filosofia positiva* (1873).

(1898). In some respects he follows the theories of Spencer, Bain, and Herbart ; but he differs from them in attributing a preponderating importance to cerebral physiology in the explanation of complex mental phenomena.[1]

Sergi. Experimental Psychology in Italy owes much to Giuseppe Sergi,[2] professor at the University of Rome, author of *Principii di Psicologia* (1874) and of several other works, such as *Elementi di Psicologia* (1879), which has been translated into French (*Psychologie physiologique*, 1887), and *Principii di psicologia*, of which the first volume, which appeared in 1894, is entitled *Dolore e piacere, storia naturale dei sentimenti*. Sergi's ideas are more advanced than those of other Italian psychologists, as he is a staunch believer in the theory of the dependence of mental on corporeal phenomena, so that he may be said to follow Maudsley, Richet, and other physiological psychologists. Another psychologist worthy of note is Tito Vignoli, author of various psychological papers, and of an important work entitled *Della legge fondamentale dell' intelligenza nel regno animale* (1877), which has been translated into English and German.

Many alienists in Italy have taken up the study of Psychology. Thus Enrico Morselli, professor at the University of Genoa, is an alienist and anthropologist, as well as a psychologist of great merit. His *Introduzione alle lezioni di psicologia patologica e di psichiatria* (1881) has been translated into German. He founded the *Rivista di filosofia scientifica* (1882—1892), which became the organ of the Italian positivist school, and dealt especially with psychological questions. Another alienist and psychologist of mark was Buccola, who in 1883 published a celebrated work entitled *La legge del tempo nei fenomeni del pensiero*. The author unfortunately died prematurely, and before he could follow it up with other works. The Psychology of mental diseases has also been dealt with by S. de Sanctis (whose work on dreams—*I Sogni*, 1899—is perhaps the best we have on the subject), Tanzi (professor at the Istituto di studi superiori of Florence), Tamburini, Guicciardi, Ferrari, and others. The physiologist Angelo Mosso, professor at Turin University, has contributed largely to the study of Psychology with his works on Fear, on Fatigue, and on the Temperature of the

Mosso.

[1] R. Ardigò is the author of *Il fatto psicologico della percezione*; *Il vero* (1894); *La scienza sperimentale del pensiero*; *La ragione*.
[2] Giuseppe Sergi is the author of *Teoria fisiologica della percezione* (1881); *L' origine dei fenomeni psichici e la loro significazione biologica* (1885); *Le degenerazioni umane* (1888); *Psicologia per le scuole* (1890).

Brain, which have been translated into several languages, and deservedly enjoy a world-wide reputation. Professor Patrizi, of Modena University, is also the author of some notable works. Amongst those who combine the study of Psychology with that of general philosophy we may quote Francesco de Sarlo (professor at the Istituto di studi superiori of Florence), Fornelli (professor at Naples University), Cesca, Faggi (professor at Palermo University), Dandolo (professor at Messina University), Mantovani, Marchesini, and especially Filippo Masci (professor at Naples University). The last named has published some excellent works on the Origin of Instinct, on the Comic Sense, or Sense of Humour, on Psychophysical Materialism, etc., and it is to be hoped that he will soon collect them into one general treatise.[1]

Positivism in Italy, with the aid of biology, gave rise to a new and original branch of study which can be considered essentially Italian, namely, Criminal Anthropology and Sociology, whose most eminent exponents are Lombroso, Ferri Sighele, Garofolo. The Psychology of Childhood has been studied by Colozza, Vitali, Paolo Lombroso, De Sanctis, and others.

Criminal anthropology in Italy.

Notwithstanding the favour shown to Positive Psychology in Italy, there are several psychologists with different views, like Boratelli, professor at Padua University (who, in his celebrated work on Kant, follows the Kantian theories tempered with ideas borrowed from Lotze), and other eminent philosophers such as

---

[1] Tito Vignoli is the author of *Peregrinazioni psicologiche* (1895), etc.; Enrico Morselli of *Semejotica delle malattie mentali* (1885 *sqq.*). The English translation of A. Mosso's *La Paura* came out in 1896; of his *La fatica* in 1903; and of his *Temperatura del cervello* in 1901. F. de Sarlo is the author of *Saggi filosofici* (2 vols., 1895—1897); N. Fornelli of *Gli studi di psicopatia in Francia* (1878); A. Faggi of *Principi di psicologia moderna* (1897); G. Dandolo of *La coscienza nell' uomo*; *Le integrazioni psichiche* (1898); G. Mantovani of *Psicologia fisiologica* (1896). The first edition of Cesare Lombroso's *L'uomo delinquente* came out in 1876; Enrico Ferri's *Sociologia criminale* came out in 1891, but is in reality the third edition of a shorter work entitled *I nuovi orizzonti del diritto e della procedura penale*, which appeared in 1880. F. Masci is the author of *Coscienza, volontà, libertà* (1884); *Genio naturale dell' Istinto* (1887); *Il Materialismo psicofisico e la dottrina del parallelismo in psicologia* (1901). F. Benatelli published several psychological essays, some as early as 1852. His *La coscienza e il meccanismo interiore* appeared in 1872, his *Elementi di psicologia e logica* in 1892. Carlo Cantoni wrote a *Corso di filosofia* (Vol. I.: *Psicologia*, 1866); A. Chiappelli published in the *Giornale Napoletano di scienze e lettere* in 1880, and in the *Filosofia delle scuole italiane* in 1885 several excellent papers on the nature and value of modern psychological research.

Tocco, professor at the Istituto di studi superiori, Florence and Chiappelli, professor at Naples University.

As in other countries, so in Russia, Psychology has had many difficulties to contend with. Metaphysical philosophy, in its opposite forms of Mysticism and Materialism, has hitherto shackled psychological research in that country. It was not until 1885 that a Psychological Society was founded in the University of Moscow. This society inaugurated in 1889 a philosophical and psychological review, which published all the more important contemporary articles written on the subject in Russia.

Russian psychologists.

Specially distinguished in the psychological line are Lopatine, Troitsky, and above all Grote (1852—1899), who founded and directed the psychological laboratory in the University of Moscow and has published several works of merit.[1]

We have more recently a number of younger men who have applied themselves almost exclusively to experimental Psychology, such as Tokarsky (the successor of Grote in the direction of the Moscow laboratory), Marine, Worobiow, Bernstein, Bělkin, Ejner, and others. These researches found much favour amongst physiologists, one of whom, Setchenow, brought out a volume of psychological studies on materialistic lines in 1863, when the field was still held by idealistic and spiritualistic metaphysics. His work made a great sensation at the time, and is still held in much esteem for the clearness of its method and ideas.

Amongst other notable physiologists and alienists we must note Betchtesen (who since 1896 has edited an important review of Alienism, Neurology, and Experimental Psychology), Orchansky (professor at the University of Charcow, who has written several notable works on Weber's Law, on Nervous and Mental Phenomena, and on Heredity), Sikorsky (who has occupied himself with great success with the Psychology of the Russian people), Tschige, and others. The moral and philosophical sciences which have a connection with Psychology, such as Æsthetics, Philology, etc., have been studied from the psychological point of view in the writings of Gitetsky, Obolensky, and others.

The studies which deal with so-called spiritualistic and telepathic phenomena have a celebrated representative in Russia

---

[1] *The Psychology of Sensations; The Reformation of Logic; The Conception of the Soul and of Mental Energy in Psychology; Nietzche and Tolstoi; The Critique of Progress; Lectures on the History of Philosophy in the Seventeenth and Eighteenth Centuries.*

in the person of Akiakow, a man of uncommon talent, whose works have been translated into many languages. These studies not having yet entered into a really scientific phase, and being, therefore, most uncertain in their methods and results, it is impossible to gauge their real value with regard to the understanding of mental processes.[1]

We have thus ascertained that Psychology is studied in all civilised countries, a fact which is in a great measure due **Psychological** to the numerous psychological laboratories which have **laboratories.** been recently founded. In Germany, besides the Leipsic laboratory (founded in 1878), we have those of Göttingen, Bonn, Berlin (managed by Professor Stumpf), Freiburg; in France those of Paris and Rennes; in America those of New York, Philadelphia, Worcester, Yale, Providence, Cornell University, Wisconsin, Illinois, Harvard, Chicago, Toronto. There are others at Copenhagen, Gröningen, Geneva, Liège, Brussels, Rome, Turin, Stockholm, Cambridge and London.

These studies brought in their train the publication of various psychological periodicals, of which the most notable is **Periodicals.** Wundt's *Philosophische Studien*, founded in 1883. Besides this we have in Germany the *Zeitschrift für Psychologie und Physiologie der Sinnesorgane*, in France the *Année psychologique*. *Mind* was founded in England in 1866. In America we have the *Psychological Review* (1894) and the *American Journal of Psychology* (1887). Other philosophical periodicals have begun to give importance to psychology: as, for instance, the *Revue Philosophique* (founded in 1878 by Ribot), the *Vierteljahrschrift für wissenschaftliche Philosophie*, the *Rivista filosofica*, the *Rivista di filosofia, pedagogia e scienze affini*, etc. Even the numerous periodicals dealing with the science of mental diseases reserve a place for psychological research. The same is the case in regard to recent periodicals dealing with the Psychology of Childhood and in general with all those connected in any way with Psychology.

This science has now attained such a degree of maturity as to warrant an examination into the results obtained, with the view of ascertaining what new ideas have been introduced and in

---

[1] Not knowing the Russian language, I have only been able to acquaint myself with works translated into French or German (*e.g.* some of those of Setchenow, of Grote, and one or two others). For the above information on Russian Psychology, I am indebted to Ossip-Lourié's recent work, *La philosophie russe contemporaine* (Paris: Alcam, 1902).

what main points it differs from the more old-fashioned Psychology. In a critical survey of this kind it is necessary, where such a proceeding is possible, to pass from elementary to more complex questions. This method cannot, however, be always followed, owing to the general character of Psychology, which makes it impossible not to mix up philosophical problems with the more simple questions under discussion. After having discussed the object of Psychology, I shall deal with the relations between mind and body, and pass thence to the methods of Psychology, to the composition and development of mental life, and to consciousness. Lastly, I shall examine the laws of Psychology. Throughout this survey I shall attempt to make clear the points on which the best contemporary psychologists agree, as well as those on which opinions differ; and in the latter case endeavour to find the causes of disagreement, and to show which appears to be the more probable and acceptable solution.

CHAPTER II

OBJECT AND SCOPE OF PSYCHOLOGY

IF we open any psychological treatise of the old school, we find Psychology defined as the science of the inner phenomena in man.

Object of Psychology. "The object of Psychology," says Beneke, one of the most eminent representatives of the aforesaid school, "comprises every thing we can apprehend by means of internal perception and sensation."[1] This definition is based on a philosophical conception originating with Descartes and subsequently accepted as a psychological principle by Locke, according to which there is an absolute division between the physical, or external world and the inner world of consciousness. We have an external experience, according to Locke, when an external stimulus, touching a part of our body, awakens a sensation in the mind; whereas internal experience consists in the elaboration of the perceptions derived from external experience, and is distinguished by a peculiar mental activity. It is owing to this activity of consciousness that from the elementary we pass to more complex perceptions, such as the apprehension of relations and of abstract notions.[2] Although, on the one hand, Locke's philosophical theory gets rid of the absolute separation between Psychology and the Natural sciences, which had prevailed from Descartes downwards, on the other hand the distinction he drew between "sensation" and "reflection" was destined to bring about a return to the aforesaid separation.

We have seen that after Wolff there arose in Germany a school of psychologists who, in attempting to reconcile the idealism of Leibnitz with the empirical theories of Locke, created the so-called "Psychology of the inner sense." This school, it must be

[1] Beneke, *Lehrbuch der Psychologie als Naturwissenschaft* (4th edit. 1877), p. 1.
[2] Locke, *Essay on Human Understanding*, Book II., chap. i.

remembered, did not limit itself to the consideration of these inner phenomena, but, in studying the essence of the soul, frequently indulged in purely metaphysical speculations. One of the most noteworthy attempts at building up a scientific system of Psychology upon this principle is due to Herbart, who imagined a mechanism of presentations governed by the impulse of self-preservation.

This theory lasted until quite recently, one of its most eminent representatives being Franz Brentano, who, however, did not accept the ultimate consequences of the system, which would have led back to the Cartesian dualism between spirit and matter. He rightly observed how, on the one hand, there are facts which do not form the special object either of Psychology or of the natural sciences, but of a science to which we give the name of Metaphysics, and, on the other hand, there cannot be said to exist a sharply defined distinction between the natural sciences and Psychology, for there are many physiological processes intimately connected with mental phenomena. These last have recently [1] become the object of an intermediate science, called Psychophysics, or, more recently, Physiological Psychology. Brentano argued from this the artificiality of all classifications of the sciences, and concluded that Psychology should be simply defined as the *science of the soul*. He also rejects the definition of Psychology as the "science of psychic phenomena," because it implies that inner, like outer phenomena are manifestations of something which has a real existence; whereas he is of opinion that any clear knowledge and certainty we possess regarding them can only be the result of direct perception.[2] Brentano, however, in conformity with the old psychological school, concludes that the only means of arriving at an exact knowledge of these phenomena consists in introspection, coupled with the observation of other individuals.[3] The definition of Psychology as a *science of the soul* has been adhered to even in modern psychological works of a scientific and empirical character; but it has lost its original metaphysical sense, and may be interpreted as meaning that "Psychology is the science of everything connected with feeling, thinking, and willing." This empirical

[1] Brentano wrote in 1874, so that the term "recently" must be referred to that date.
[2] Brentano, *Psychologie vom empirischen Standpunkte* (Leipsic, 1874), pp. 6, 7, 24, 25.
[3] Amongst modern psychologists of note who follow the theory of the inner sense we can note Lipps (*Die Grundthatsachen des Seelenlebens*, 1883) and Volkmann (*Lehrbuch der Psychologie*, 2nd edit. 1875—1879).

school has been called by Lange, in his History of Materialism,[1] a Psychology "without soul." The notion that underlies it was especially upheld by Mill, who, with Hume, maintained that Psychology should confine itself to the general and particular laws of consciousness, whereby one mental state is produced by another. Although Mill cannot be numbered among the psychologists of the modern school, he was the first to eschew in his Psychology all inquiry as to the substance of the soul. Among German psychologists, on the contrary, who are in many respects the pioneers of the experimental movement, the contrary took place. Thus the physiologist Lotze, who advocated the application of biological methods to Psychology, retained the Leibnitzian notion of a substantial substratum underlying mental phenomena, although his contemporary Fechner, the founder of Psychophysics, rejected all idea of such a substratum, both as regards mental and physical phenomena. Bain is the first psychologist who confined himself exclusively to the empirical method, his object being to study the phenomena and laws of consciousness irrespective of any philosophical presupposition. With his works on *The Senses and Intellect* (1855) and on *The Emotions and the Will* (1859) it may be said that modern empirical Psychology begins. He is neither a spiritualist nor a materialist, but a pure Psychologist who aims at conferring on Psychology the same degree of objective exactitude which has been attained by the natural sciences.

Entirely opposed to the above is the materialistic school. In the eyes of materialistic authors a psychological science, in the proper sense, has no *raison d'être*, for the comprehension of mental phenomena comes as a natural result of the study of the cerebral processes. The only reality is matter; what we take to be phenomena of consciousness are only apparently such. This physiological materialism has left its traces in several modern psychologists, with whom we shall have to deal later on.

A modern philosopher who has had a marked influence in the history of Psychology is Herbert Spencer, who could neither accept the negative conclusions of the materialists nor content himself with the psychological ideas professed by the spiritualistic school. Dominated by the idea of biological evolution, the laws of which he endeavoured to fit to the mental processes, he could not help recognising the great difference which exists between biology and psychology.

Scientific character of Psychology.

[1] Lange, *History of Materialism*, Vol. II., Part. III., chap. iii.

"Psychology," he says, "is a totally unique science independent of, and antithetically opposed to, all other sciences whatever. The thoughts and feelings which constitute a consciousness and are absolutely inaccessible to any but the possessor of that consciousness form an existence that has no place among the existences with which the rest of the sciences deal. Though accumulated observations and experiments have led us by a very indirect series of inferences to the belief that mind and nervous action are the subjective and objective faces of the same thing, we remain utterly incapable of seeing, and even of imagining, how the two are related. Mind still continues to us a something without any kinship to other things; and from the sciences which discover by introspection the laws of this something, there is no passage by transitional steps to the sciences which discover the laws of these other things."[1] Spencer is therefore of opinion, as opposed to Comte and his followers, that it is impossible to create a psychological science based solely upon introspection, which, however, he considers the starting-point of all psychological research. To this, which he calls "subjective Psychology," Spencer adds, as a complement, what he defines as "objective Psychology." Consciousness not being able to exist without a brain and a nervous system (or, in other words, without a biological organisation), there must necessarily exist a series of connections and relations between the two which cannot be gauged by mere introspection, but require to be examined by means of some other psychological method resembling the methods of biology.[2] The two "Psychologies" are not of equal value, the "objective" Psychology being non-existent without the "subjective," but together they constitute "a double science, which, as a whole, is quite *sui generis*." Spencer, however, treats the question rather as a philosopher than as a psychologist.

The same may be said of Adolph Horwicz, in his work *Psychologische Analysen auf physiologischen Grundlagen* (published in 1874). Horwicz (like others of his time, not excepting Wundt, in his first work published in 1863) deals only with theoretical questions. His style, moreover, is obscure and abstruse, and his fundamental idea, that all psychical phenomena are derived from feeling, is wholly metaphysical.

The empirical method, as inaugurated by Bain, had numerous ollowers in Europe and America, and Binet dates from 1874 the

[1] *The Principles of Psychology*, Vol. I., Part I., chap. vii., p. 140.
[2] *Op. cit.*, i. 141.

beginning of this new phase in psychological studies.[1] Wundt instituted in that year the first laboratory of physiological Psychology at Leipsic, Ribot (who had already published some notable psychological works) founded the *Revue Philosophique*, and Charcot began his researches on hypnotism in hysterical subjects. The Psychology of Peoples was also well advanced, and the distinction between Philosophy and Psychology was beginning to be admitted by all.[2] All the principal works on Psychology which have appeared since that date and constitute "contemporary Psychology," or what is also called "the new Psychology," are written in accordance with the above views. Such are the works of Sully, Ribot, Ladd, Ward, Höffding, Baldwin, James, Jodl, and some of those of Wundt, in all of which we find that theoretical questions dealing with the proper definition of Psychology and of its relation to natural or moral science are altogether avoided, or only incidentally discussed.

Various definitions of Psychology.

To quote one who is essentially a representative of this empirical school, we find that Höffding defines Psychology as the "science of the soul," but adds that this is quite a provisional and inadequate definition, which merely serves to place Psychology, as the science of that which thinks, feels, and wills, in contradistinction to Physical Science, which deals with that which moves in and fills space. "Psychology," he continues, "is as little bound to begin with an explanation of what Mind is, as Physics is obliged to begin with an explanation of what Matter is. . . . It will be our endeavour to preserve Psychology as a pure science of experience, and to distinguish sharply between the given facts and the hypotheses employed to classify and explain them."[3]

Similar definitions are given by Sully, Jodl, and others.[4] We must not think, however, that contemporary Psychology entirely eschews questions of a general character; and Höffding, who, besides being a psychologist, is also a philosopher of no mean merit, discusses with masterly ability the problem of the body and the soul, and the general character both of mental and of biological phenomena. That the necessity of a deeper insight into the

---

[1] See A. Binet, *Introduction à la psychologie expérimentale* (Paris, 1894), p. 1.

[2] Ribot explicitly makes the distinction in the Introduction to his *Contemporary English Psychology*.

[3] *Outlines of Psychology*, p. 1.

[4] Sully, *The Human Mind* (London, 1892), Vol. I., p. 1, and also his smaller manual *Outlines of Psychology* (2nd edit., London, 1895), p. 1; Jodl, *Lehrbuch der Psychologie* (Stuttgart, 1896), c. i., *Aufgabe und Methode der Psychologie*. The other contemporary authors above quoted give similar definitions.

question was making itself always more felt can be perceived in other psychological works of the empirical school, as, for instance, in William James's *Principles of Psychology* (1891). In his opinion Psychology is the "science of mental life" with regard to its phenomena and its "conditions." He rejects the English theory of "associationism," and maintains that in Psychology a large place must be given to cerebral physiology. Mental phenomena, however, extend far beyond the limits of nervous physiology, and James succinctly defines their distinctive character as consisting in the fact of striving after future aims and choosing the means to reach them, this being, as he rightly observes, what distinguishes an intelligent from a mechanical act. James, however, does not proceed to inquire what should be the real object and which the best method of Psychology. Jodl, in his recent work *Lehrbuch der Psychologie* (1896), does not go much beyond Höffding and James. Psychology is defined by him as "the science of the forms and natural laws of phenomena of consciousness in their normal course, as these are related to the processes of physical life and to the adaptation of the organism to outward conditions, and form altogether what we call the mental functions or processes." Like Sully and Höffding, Jodl carefully distinguishes Psychology from the natural sciences, such as Psychiatry and Physiology, with which it has affinities, and also from some of the philosophical sciences, such as Logic, Ethics, and Æsthetics, with which he considers that Psychology is much more closely connected than with the natural sciences. His failure to give us a more profound definition of Psychology is all the more remarkable, as he places it amongst the philosophical sciences.

Inquiries into the aim and real nature of Psychology must necessarily enter the field of Epistemology, and the attraction which philosophical questions exercise on German psychologists has made the latter dwell particularly upon this aspect of the subject.[1]

Fundamental characteristic of Psychology.

The mistake of the older psychologists, Locke and Kant not excepted, consisted in considering the mental life almost exclusively from the standpoint of knowledge, or rather of perception. What else, indeed, was Kant's "synthesis" and Locke's "reflection" but an intellectual process? Consciousness was divided into the three faculties of knowing, feeling, and willing; but as these were

[1] A notable example of this is afforded by H. Münsterberg's recent book *Grundzüge der Psychologie* (1900), of which the first volume is entirely devoted to philosophical questions connected with Psychology.

thought to be separate and disconnected, it was impossible to arrive at an adequate solution of the problem of the inner constitution of consciousness. The intellectualist theory reached its extreme point in Herbart, for whom consciousness was constituted of a mechanism of presentations which in his view were primitive mental elements, and not subject to any transformation in their goings and comings. These theories evidently could not be expected to throw any light on the subject. Schopenhauer was the first to draw attention to the important part played by the subjective elements of consciousness—*i.e.* will and feeling. These subjective elements are, in his opinion, the expression of the inner nature of the soul, and cannot be considered equivalent to presentation, seeing that the latter refers directly to the external world. This notion, on the other hand, was exaggerated by Schopenhauer when he sought to make it into a universal principle, thus creating a hylozoistic system which recalls the primitive systems of natural philosophy. Moreover, in accordance with his metaphysical ideas, he committed the grave psychological error of establishing a dualism between knowledge and will, not admitting any connection or even any reciprocal action between the two. There is, however, no doubt that Schopenhauer's fundamental principle was destined to bear fruit in modern Psychology by undermining the ancient division between consciousness and matter, between what is subjective and what is objective, or, in other words, the ego and the non-ego. The new school did but continue and develop the ideas of Kant, who was the first to point out the indivisibility of the terms subject and object as recognised by Schopenhauer. The world, says Schopenhauer, is will and idea; but the former, in his opinion, is of paramount importance, the latter being of secondary moment. It was consequently necessary to give to this metaphysical principle a solid basis in psychological observation, as well as to find a connecting link between the two elements indicated by Kant in his *Practical Reason*—viz. knowledge and will. This connection is still to seek in the positivist philosophy of the nineteenth century, the very definition of Psychology given by Spencer marking the culminating point of the intellectualist conception of the nature of consciousness.

Spencer holds that the object of Psychology is to find the connection between physical and mental phenomena, which present, in his opinion, an undoubted parallelism. The question is what place is here assigned to the feelings and to the will? They do not correspond to any external phenomena, because we do not find in the natural world anything which can be called a process of the will or a feeling. For this reason Spencer pays less attention to these two aspects of the mental life than to perceptions and ideas, and thus leaves his definition far from satisfactory from an epistemological point of view. The Cartesian dualism had almost disappeared from these new intellectualist conceptions, because, although we find it in a somewhat metaphysical form in Spencer, his contemporaries, such as Bain and Fechner, adopt the above-mentioned psychophysical parallelism merely as a means of research. From the admission that Psychology can and must have recourse to physiology, physics, and the natural sciences in general, followed, as a consequence, the removal of the barrier between physical and mental phenomena, and the recognition of an intermediate zone in which the "external world" mingles with the "internal world," and calls into existence that new branch of science which goes under the name of psychophysics. At the same time we find an ever-increasing tendency in psychologists to attach importance to the subjective mental processes—*i.e.* to the feelings and to the acts of the will—in which the mental life finds its principal expression. This can be observed in Bain's book on *The Emotions and the Will* (1859), in Wundt's first work on Psychology (1863), in Horwicz, and in others. What is, therefore, the main difference between Psychology and the natural sciences? What difference exists between the world of perceptions and the dominion of the will? The answer appears to be the following: The world may be considered as a presentation only if we abstract from the subject, that is from ourselves; on the other hand, it is both presentation and will when we consider it as it presents itself directly to our consciousness. Whatever we observe in our consciousness, whether in one separate state or in successive and connected states, we perceive directly, without requiring any special logical process, for the phenomena of consciousness present themselves to us immediately without the intervention of any other process. What, then, do we find in our consciousness by means of this direct perception? The very two elements which the old-fashioned Psychology had kept separated—*i.e.* feelings and perceptions. We find present, on the one hand, perceptions and representations of the memory, ideas, conceptions—in a word, different forms of knowledge; on the other hand, feelings of pleasure, of pain, impulses, desires, resolutions—that is to say, different manifestations of the subjective part of consciousness, which may all be comprised under the denomination of "processes of the will." From this it might be supposed that presentations tally perfectly with the objects of the so-called external world, and, therefore, that the natural sciences, which deal with the external world, may be said to form a part of Psychology. A contemporary school of philosophers, indeed, upholds the coincidence of presentations with external objects [1]; but this system (which has been justly defined as "a primitive and ingenuous realism") does not pay enough attention to the marked difference existing between objects as they appear to our consciousness and as they are in reality. Colours, sounds, forms, the whole material which goes to make up our sensations, are not properties of things, but phenomena produced by a substratum which we can only conceive if, by means of a process of abstraction, we divest the object of those very properties under which it appears to our consciousness.

The external world is confined in this way to purely mechanical forms of motion—*i.e.* to "matter." This fact, which had been dimly recognised by the ancients, and was first formulated by Galilei, gave a new direction to the natural sciences, which it freed from the naïve phenomenalism of primitive systems. Although, moreover, the natural sciences start from presentations, they do not stop there, but proceed to inquire into the causes which bring them into being, so as to arrive at a scientific conception of an "object" by itself, external to our own consciousness.[2] Consequently presentations are subjective phenomena of consciousness, and are only to be considered objective when they refer to external objects, and constitute the material of the so-called "external world." Feelings and impulses, on the contrary, are essentially subjective, and it is through these that mental phenomena acquire their peculiar character of spontaneous inner phenomena.

Whilst, therefore, we maintain the distinction between *external* and *internal*, we hold that the natural sciences consider the world under the *external* aspect, after abstracting the subjective

---

[1] This so-called "Philosophy of Immanence" which has arisen lately in Germany numbers amongst its representatives Schuppe, Schubert, Soldern, Kaufmann, and others. Wundt recently expounded and confuted their theories in three long articles in the *Philosophische Studien*, Vols. XII. and XIII. (1896 and 1897).

[2] On this subject see Külpe in his *Einleitung in die Philosophie* (p. 63): "Jeder der sich mit naturwissenschaftlichen Beobachtungen beschäftigt hat, weiss dass er vor allem auf die Erkenntniss der gegenstandlichen, des von subjektiven Zuthaten befreiten Objectiven bedacht sein muss." See also Wundt, *Grundriss der Psychologie*, p. 2; and Hans Cornelius, *Psychologie als Erfahrungswissenschaft* (Leipsic, 1897), p. 2.

elements of consciousness, whereas Psychology considers it from the *internal* point of view, and with reference to those very elements. The terms *inner perception* and *inner sense* can be used only if applied to those mental processes which have their origin in our consciousness, or, so to speak, in our personal character, as is the case with the feelings and the will. Thus, an impulse or an emotion is perceived by us directly within ourselves, and we can only indirectly refer it to anything external. As, on the other hand, these subjective processes are always connected with presentations and objective phenomena, it follows that the whole contents of our consciousness forms a unity; and consequently that the object of Psychology and of the natural sciences is one and the same, although considered from different points of view. According to those who consider presentations as identical with the objects of the natural world, Psychology should confine itself purely to the subjective forms of consciousness, such as recollections, feelings, etc., leaving on one side even actual presentations. But this, in our opinion, is an arbitrary and quite unjustifiable exclusion.[1] Psychology may therefore be defined as the *science of direct subjective experience*, and the natural sciences as the *science of indirect objective experience*. This conception of knowledge, while completing that given by Locke, is based, as regards direct experience, on a new principle discovered by modern Psychology—viz. the principle of the variability of presentations considered directly or from a psychological point of view. It is a fact that presentations considered in themselves alone, irrespective not only of feelings and impulses, but also of representations of the memory, are comparatively unchangeable and permanently at the disposal of the observer. If we further consider that the variability of presentations is only apparent when they are considered directly, or psychologically, we must of necessity come to the conclusion that their variability is caused by the subjective

Fundamental characteristics of psychical phenomena.

---

[1] Some examples will illustrate the different points of view of Psychology and of the natural sciences. Let us suppose a botanist and a psychologist both intent on examining a certain plant. The botanist, as an observer of nature, will endeavour to study it objectively and completely in abstraction from the feelings which it may engender, or the recollections which it may evoke; he will examine its different parts, he will compare it with other plants, and he will finally classify it accordingly. The psychologist, on the contrary, will allow himself to follow the series of perceptions which the plant calls forth through association and the various feelings which are engendered within him, and by following the course of these complicated mental processes he will endeavour to ascertain their origin and the several psychological principles by which they are governed.

elements of consciousness—viz. feelings, impulses, recollections—all of which find their typical expression in the processes of the Will. The Will, therefore, is the typical and characteristic mental function which distinguishes the phenomena of consciousness psychologically considered, and we thus arrive at an exact distinction between physical and mental phenomena, according to which the former are *objects* and the latter *processes*.[1]

We must consequently reject the old definition of Psychology as the science of internal phenomena, as opposed to physics, which deals with external phenomena. There is also no reason for the distinction, founded on the fact that the phenomena of the external world occur in space, those of consciousness in time. As conscious phenomena include presentations, some of which occur in space, there is no reason to exclude space from the mental processes. As regards time, even the followers of the old school of Psychology are obliged to admit that it comprises not only mental but natural phenomena. Neither must we forget that the distinction in question was based on the antiquated belief that time and space are innate notions in the human mind. Like the simpler sensations, they are the result of certain relations between the elements of consciousness, and are, consequently, complex mental processes, produced by a combination of mental activity and experience ; and not, as in Kant's opinion, innate forms within which the material, afforded by external sensations, arranges itself.

There are also other objections to the notion that Psychology and the natural sciences have a common object. Thus, although we may abstract the physical phenomena, which are part of our consciousness, we cannot separate an individual, who is a psychological being, into two distinct entities, seeing that the mental and the biological parts are inextricably connected. Many mental phenomena being intimately connected with, and dependent on, physiological facts, it was natural that some authors should uphold with Spencer the existence of a subjective and an objective Psychology, the latter having the same point of view as the natural sciences. It is, however, easy to reply that the above-mentioned Psychologies are merely two aspects of the same science, which begins by studying the simpler mental phenomena which are directly dependent on physiological processes, and passes gradually to the consideration of more complicated phenomena which have their origin in the combination of the former. Both

[1] See E. B. Titchener, *An Outline of Psychology* (3rd edit., New York, 1899), p. 7, etc.

these orders of phenomena are of the same psychic nature and governed by the same laws, and thus differ from physical phenomena. It must, however, be borne in mind that whereas it is generally admitted that internal and external facts form an inseparable whole, which it requires a process of abstraction to consider from a subjective and from an objective standpoint, there is, on the contrary, great difference of opinion on the question of the relation of these facts to one another and to the perceiving subject, one school of psychologists, followers of the experimental method, professing opinions on this point which have given rise to no little discussion.[1]

Every one agrees that mental phenomena should be considered as "what has been lived through" (in German, *Erlebnisse*); but this expression, which ought to be taken as meaning an "event," a "fact which has taken place" (in German, *Ereigniss*), is interpreted by psychophysical materialists as meaning the product of a living and physical individual.[2] The facts which form the object of the different sciences, except philosophy, says Külpe,[3] are facts of experience. Psychology, like all the special sciences, deals with events, its characteristic feature being that any existing event may form an object of psychological investigation.[4] As the relation of Psychology to the natural sciences cannot be expressed in terms of a specific subject-matter, it follows that the distinguishing characteristic of mental phenomena consists not in their belonging to a particular class of events, but in the fact that these events are "dependent on the individuals by whom they are experienced" (*von erlebenden Individuen*). This important point once admitted, the doctrine of mental processes (taking the word "doctrine" in the sense given to it by the natural sciences) must aim at demonstrating their dependence on certain corporeal processes which take place in the brain.[5]

Relations between physical and mental phenomena.

---

[1] See the interesting controversy between Wundt (*Philosophische Studien*, 1895; *Über die Definition der Psychologie*) and Willy (*Vierteljahrschrift für wissenschaftl. Philos.*, 1897; *Die Krisis in der modernen Psychologie*), Ebbinghaus (*Grundzüge der Psychologie*, p. 8) and Külpe (*Einleit. in die Philosophie*, 2nd edit.; Eng. tr. 1897, 2nd edit. 1901).

[2] See the work already quoted, pp. 14 and 15, in which Wundt shows up the mistake of giving to *Erlebniss* a different sense from *Ereigniss, Geschehen, Vorgang*, etc.

[3] See O. Külpe, *Outlines of Psychology*, p. 1; and also Wundt's already quoted work, *Ueber die defin. der Psychologie*, pp. 14 and 15.

[4] *Outlines of Psychology*, p. 2.

[5] *Op. cit.*, p. 6, *Über Aufgaben und Methoden der Psychologie*. This

Münsterberg is even more explicit. Granted, he says, that a first mental process is in all cases accompanied by a certain physical process, and that the latter necessarily produces a second physical process which we empirically connect with a second mental process, it is an inevitable consequence that the second mental process, must follow the first. "The empirical fact of the connection between the several elements of consciousness and the elementary cerebral processes does not, therefore, in the least explain psychical phenomena. If, on the contrary, these connections are established empirically, the indication of the causal connection between the several cerebral processes offers a real explanation of the coexistence and succession of the elementary units of consciousness, an explanation which the mental phenomena alone do not afford."[1]

Much the same opinion is held by Ebbinghaus, another eminent German psychologist. "It is not," he says, "that Psychology is distinguishable from other branches of science, such as Physics or Biology, because its subject-matter is different, as is the case, for instance, with Zoology as distinguished from Mineralogy or Astronomy. It deals with the same objects considered from a different point of view. It is not the science of a part of the world, but of the whole world from one particular aspect. It deals with forms, processes, and relations, the properties of which are essentially determined by the properties and functions of some organised individual. It is, moreover, the science of all those individual peculiarities which have a decisive influence on the behaviour of individuals in respect to external circumstances [die für seine Art, die Welt zu erleben, wesentlich massgebend sind]. Psychology," he continues, "studies how the world presents itself to the eye of man, or to the eye of a butterfly, or even to an individual without eyes; how the consciousness of a so-called objective world is formed, and how this objective world comes, little by little, to be thought of as peopled with

theory has been even more completely developed by Münsterberg in his *Grundzüge der Psychologie*, Vol. I.

[1] *Ueber Aufgabe und Methode der Psychologie*, p. 27 : " Die empirische Feststellung der Beziehungen Zwischen den einzelnen Elementen des Bewusstseinsinhaltes und den elementaren Gehirnprocessen bietet somit nicht die geringste Erklärung der psychischen Elemente ; sind diese Beziehungen aber erst einmal empirisch festgestellt, so bietet die Aufzeigung des Causalzusammenhangs Zwischen den einzelnen Gehirnprocessen in der That eine wirkliche Erklärung für die Coëxistenz und Succession der elementaren psychischen Inhalte." See also *Psychology and Life*, p. 60 ; *Grundzüge der Psychologie*, p. 457.

things and energies, or even with gods and magical forces. In fact, Psychology," Eblingham concludes, " considers the world from an individual and subjective point of view; whilst Physics considers it as if it were independent of us [von den Erlebnissen der Individuen]." [1]

This mode of conceiving the object of Psychology, however, does not overcome the difficulty of the relation of physiological cerebral phenomena to the perceiving subject. Granted that the individual is of a two-fold nature, physical and mental, it is, nevertheless, a fact that the study of the physical processes must be kept quite distinct from that of the mental processes. Of the latter we have a direct perception; whilst the former, which belong to the general order of physical phenomena, can only be studied by means of the indirect method which makes complete abstraction of all subjective impressions.

There are, however, weightier objections, founded on logical and epistemological reasons, to the theory which distinguishes Psychology from the Natural sciences, according to the different standpoint which they severally assume. There are some who maintain that the Natural sciences also must make use of direct intuition; whilst in the opinion of others Psychology, so far from being a science based solely on direct experience, requires, like the physical sciences, to transform and elaborate the data it has collected.

Recent discussions on the subjective character of mental phenomena.

The former objection can best be met by the reply that, granted that the natural sciences presuppose an intuition of natural objects and phenomena, this constitutes merely subjective common-sense impression, and not scientific knowledge. The progress of the natural sciences has always consisted in modifying and correcting the data of the senses; nor could they be called sciences, in the proper acceptance of the word, before the principle was established that, in order to understand natural phenomena scientifically, it is necessary to put aside all subjective impressions, and to substitute an abstract idea in the place of an image of the senses.[2]

---

[1] Hermann Ebbinghaus, professor in the University of Breslau, *Grundzüge der Psychologie* (Erster Halbband, Leipsic, 1897), pp. 7-8. This work is still in course of publication. To the foregoing authors must be added Ziehen, *Leitfaden der physiologischen Psychologie* (2nd edit., Jena, 1893; Eng. tr. 1895, 3rd edit. 1899); Mach, *Beiträge zur Analyse der Empfindungen* (Jena, 1886); Avenarius, some time professor at Zürich University, and author of a *Kritik der reinen Erfahrung* (Leipsic, 1888); and, amongst the French and Italians, Despine, Sergi, and others. Cf. Külpe, *Einleitung in die Philosophie*, p. 63.

[2] Amongst other supporters of this theory is Carlo Cantoni, professor in the

The second objection, which has found an able supporter in Rickert, not to mention Münsterberg, already quoted, deserves to be specially examined. According to this opinion, the mental world, being as complex as the physical world, requires, like it, to be reduced to its elemental units, by means of a process of simplification. Were not this the case, the psychologist's task would merely consist in giving an empirical description of facts observed, a description which would vary according to the individual. It is not only psychological, but also material data which are revealed to us directly; and in each case they must be submitted to a process of transformation, during which abstraction must be made of the perceiving subject. In this manner the science of nature arrives at the purely abstract conception of the atom, and Psychology at the no less abstract conception of the sensation, which is, in the words of a contemporary German philosopher, "das letzte Ding" of consciousness.

To this theory there are several objections. To begin with, when it is said that Psychology reproduces the phenomena of consciousness in the manner in which they present themselves, it is not meant that these phenomena must be represented in the form in which they appear to each individual at a given moment of his mental life. On the contrary, although it is understood that the ultimate object of Psychology consists in studying mental phenomena as they appear subjectively to consciousness, this does not exclude the process of elaborating such phenomena and so arranging them as to render possible a scientific treatment and explanation. Again, when it is affirmed that Psychology reduces all mental phenomena to sensations (though, as we shall see, this is inaccurate), what else is meant by the term sensation than an eminently subjective phenomenon consisting in a given *quality* accompanied by a certain degree of intensity? And what is a quality, if not a purely subjective fact? However much we may elaborate and divide into its component parts the sum total of mental phenomena, when we arrive at the sensation, we find that it cannot be reduced to an objective form, that it is a primary element, the result, may be, of a process of abstraction, but possessing all the characteristics of a subjective, mental, and immediate phenomenon. Besides sensations, moreover, we have simple feelings which are also the result of abstraction, and are the most charac-

University of Pavia, who confuted certain other modern psychological theories in the *Rivista Psicologica* (Anno I., Vol. II., 1900), in an article on the "Concetto e carattere della Psicologia."

teristic and typical elements of the inner, mental, and subjective life. The processes of abstraction and of scientific elaboration in Psychology merely constitute, therefore, its *method*, and do not influence the essential nature of the science. In being obliged to have recourse to such methods, Psychology resembles all the other sciences, for even History, which, according to Rickert and Münsterberg, differs from Psychology and from the Natural sciences, in being the science of pure facts, whereas they deal with abstract ideas—even History is constrained to have recourse to those processes. The case of the Natural sciences, on the contrary, is quite different. For these it is absolutely necessary to abstract from perception and to keep to purely abstract ideas. An *atom*, for instance, is an abstract idea because we can represent it to ourselves only in thought and not in any sensible form. A sensation appeals, on the contrary, in all cases to the senses, although it is always accompanied by various other mental phenomena, and the process of scientific elaboration consists in isolating it from these concomitants. The process of abstraction in this case is consequently limited, and does not arrive at a pure idea, as in the case of the atom.[1]

Psychology, therefore, however much it may elaborate and transform the data upon which it works, cannot do away with the direct and subjective character which distinguishes them absolutely from the elements of physical phenomena. Nor can we accept the argument which is made use of to deny the subjective character of Psychology—namely, that it has to deal not only with the processes which we perceive, but also with those which are not perceived, and which are unconscious. Strictly speaking, it is true that nothing which is outside the domain of consciousness should form part of the study of Psychology. Yet we may hold that Psychology has the right to extend its researches to facts outside consciousness, thus leading to a representation of phenomena constructed on the analogy of those which we directly perceive and can, therefore, reproduce within our consciousness.

---

[1] The principal representatives of the theory which is here discussed are, as we have said, Münsterberg, who gives a very clear exposition of it in his *Psychology and Life* (1899), especially in chap. i., pp. 1-35, and in his *Grundzüge der Psychologie*, still in course of publication; and H. Rickert in his book *Die Grenze der naturwissenschaftlichen Begriffsbildung* (1896), of which only the first part has appeared as yet. This theory is also followed by Külpe in his *Einleitung in die Philosophie* (Eng. tr. 1897, 2nd edit. 1901).

Granted the general subjective character of Psychology, it follows that mental processes possess certain peculiarities which distinguish them absolutely from physical processes. These special characters are two : first, will or impulse, without which no mental phenomenon can be conceived of as taking place. The second characteristic consists in the end which the will has in view, and for which it selects the most suitable means. The object, therefore, represents the intellectual aspect of the mental life, whilst the will represents the impulsive, spontaneous, or subjective aspect.[1] Physical phenomena do not possess a will nor an object, nor have they feeling of æsthetic or moral value. The differences which distinguish them are differences of quantity, and these quantitative differences would be totally inadequate to enable us to understand the intrinsic qualities—that is to say, the "value" of the mental processes—if we had never had an immediate and direct knowledge of the same. Could we observe a brain in the act of thinking and follow the most imperceptible motions of its cells and fibres, we should still be unable to understand what that brain thought or felt if we had never perceived in ourselves some kind of mental process. The brain and its movements form a part of the domain of presentation or of the physical world, and the fact that it serves as a direct and material substratum to thought leaves its character quite unchanged.[2]

Psychology must therefore follow another path, for it could never throw the slightest light on the laws of consciousness by deducing them from the laws governing cerebral phenomena, even could these be exactly known. The latter is an indirect method, to which recourse can be had only when direct psychical experience fails, and has only a passing and supplementary value. " Psychology must therefore study the mental processes in their formation and evolution, following them up from their simple to their more complex forms, and seeking the laws of their progressive development."

Aim and position of Psychology as a science.

[1] See James, *Principles of Psychology*, i. 1, etc.
[2] Even if we attained a perfect knowledge of cerebral phenomena, the inner nature of the mental processes would still be distinct from them. "If we could see every wheel in the physical mechanism," says Wundt, "whose working the mental processes are accompanying, we should still find no more than a chain of movements showing no trace whatsoever of their significance for mind" (*Human and Animal Psychology*, p. 446). Wundt says the same in several of his works, notably in his *System der Philosophie*, p. 583. The same ideas are more or less clearly expressed in the *History of Materialism*, Vol. I., Part III., chap. ii.

Psychology is the science of direct experience, and deals with facts as they present themselves to consciousness, without making abstraction from our feelings or impulses, as must be done in the case of the Natural Sciences. We may illustrate from the history of knowledge. At first humanity ingenuously believes that the physical world is just what it seems, and therefore conceives that world in accordance with its own modes of feeling, attributing to it feelings and impulses like those of a conscious being. Little by little it learns to abstract from such feelings and impulses, and to consider the external world as a system of objects ruled by mechanical laws. Here we have the great scientific reform of the sixteenth century, separating the physical and mental worlds, which had been hopelessly confused, and with Descartes' philosophy we come upon that dualism which has lasted until quite recently. At the present time we have reverted to the primitive unity, but in a different way, and maintaining the distinction between presentations, as such, and the contents of consciousness.[1]

In another chapter we shall discuss the methods which are available to Psychology in this investigation. For the present we shall content ourselves with having determined its object and nature.

The character and object of Psychology once determined, there remains the question of its place amongst the sciences—whether, that is to say, it should be considered a special or a philosophical science. In the opinion of the old-fashioned psychologists Psychology was a part of philosophy, some considering it in a special sense preparatory to philosophy, seeing that it deals with general mental phenomena and constitutes the necessary foundation of logic, ethics, æsthetics, and metaphysics. Even at the present time, in schools and universities, Psychology is studied as a part of philosophy, and it is only in a few universities (especially in America) that there are special psychological chairs. In theory, however, these ideas have been somewhat modified, and the great development of psychological science has given it the place and importance of an independent branch of study.

---

[1] Avenarius, in his *Kritik der reinen Erfahrung*, and in *Der menschliche Weltbegriff*, gives a very able survey of the development of thought and scientific knowledge. In a more empirical and positive manner Baldwin has endeavoured to do the same for the child in his *Mental Development in the Child and in the Race* (Part III., chap. xi.).

Whilst there are still some who believe that Psychology may be numbered amongst the natural sciences, it is more generally considered a moral science of a very general character, for whereas the various moral sciences deal with the concrete manifestations of consciousness, whether literary, artistic, social, or religious, Psychology studies consciousness itself, and only in its general forms. The necessity of a fundamental science is all the more felt owing to the development attained by the moral sciences, as it is the only means by which a scientific unity of treatment and a satisfactory explanation of moral phenomena can be obtained. Thus the position of the special sciences is as follows: on the one hand, the physical, chemical, and biological sciences, and above them all the science of Dynamics; on the other hand, the moral, historical, philological, and social sciences, with Psychology at their head. On the former is based the philosophy of nature, on the latter the philosophy of the spirit. Thus Psychology amongst the moral sciences would be analogous to Dynamics amongst the physical, being a special science like the latter, although of a very general character.

Psychology and the moral sciences.

But besides being the basis of the moral sciences, Psychology has many points of contact with the natural, physical, and biological sciences, owing to the connection existing between all the various facts and phenomena which form the object of the several branches of learning. Human life is evolved amongst physical surroundings, to which man has to adapt himself, while at the same time he is himself a psychophysical being, composed of physical and of psychical elements. The historian requires the help of the natural sciences to explain the influence of the climate, the soil, and the general physical conditions of a country on a given civilisation.[1] In the same way the philologist requires their help to explain the physiological causes of certain changes and evolutions in a language when spoken by a different race, or by the same race after a long lapse of time. Similarly, the political economist is dependent on the natural sciences for finding the reasons of certain connections between the means of production and consumption, or the causes of changes in methods of production. Finally, and above all, experimental Pyschology requires the help of the biological sciences,

Psychology and the natural sciences.

[1] See Bernheim's very interesting observations on the various historical methods in his *Lehrbuch der historischen Methode* (2nd edit., Leipsic, 1894), especially chap. v., §§ 3 and 4.

the application of whose methods to psychological research marks, as we have seen, the most important moment in its history.

Nor is this all, for Psychology is also closely connected with the philosophical sciences—such as Logic, Ethics, Æsthetics, and Metaphysics. It is now generally admitted that the science of Logic cannot exist without a foundation of exact psychological data, seeing that a logic based only on metaphysical principles is out of the question. It is not possible to give a scientifically correct definition of logical processes in general, of concepts, of modes of reasoning, and of judging, except by placing them in connection with other mental processes of which they represent a more developed and conscious form. The science of Logic is consequently now generally regarded as a continuation of scientific Psychology, and cannot be reduced to a merely formal art of drawing conclusions, as it used to be in the past. The associations of ideas, which are the starting-point of logic, are themselves mental processes, and, as such, fall within the province of Psychology, without the help of which they cannot be properly understood.

Psychology and the philosophical sciences.

Psychology and logic.

The relations between Psychology and Epistemology are even closer, for whereas logic can, up to a certain point, avail itself of the traditional forms of thought, epistemology cannot. The latter science, having for its object the investigation of the origin and development of the fundamental and general principles of human knowledge, clearly cannot dispense with the data of Psychology, which investigates the laws of thought, without which no form of knowledge could exist. This connection between Psychology and Epistemology was well understood by philosophers such as Locke and Hume, to whom the knowledge of psychological phenomena owes much of the progress it has made since their time.

Psychology and epistemology.

Ethics and Æsthetics are in a similar position. Ethics, which follows the evolution of moral ideas, especially in social institutions where they manifest themselves most clearly, has its basis not less in individual Psychology than in the Psychology of peoples and in sociology. Any attempt to make it independent of the one or the other would be little else than a return to the methods of old-fashioned speculative ethics, which are now happily obsolete. Æsthetics also has assumed an increasingly scientific character since the appearance, about twenty years ago, of the works of Fechner, Taine, and others. Fechner was the first to study the psycho-

Psychology and ethics and æsthetics.

logical laws, in relation especially to the evolution of æsthetic feeling in the individual, while Taine studied them with especial regard to history.[1] No purely metaphysical science of Æsthetics, treating of beauty in the abstract, would satisfy modern scientific requirements. What we need is to be shown the actual manner and conditions of the development of the feeling for beauty, just as we look to Ethics to show us the moral principles to be deduced from history and from the actual conditions of society. Both Ethics and Æsthetics are philosophical doctrines belonging to the Philosophy of the Mind, which embraces, besides them, the philosophy of religion, of history, of law, and of society, all of which, on their part, require the help of the corresponding moral sciences, such as the history of religions, civil history, science of law, sociology, and, above all, of Psychology. The Philosophy of Mind, in conjunction with the Philosophy of Nature, constitutes the science of Metaphysics, which is the science of the supreme principles of knowledge and action in man.

The philosophical sciences, whether of Nature or of Mind, must necessarily have recourse to hypotheses, and cannot have, therefore, the same positive character as the special sciences. Let us take as instances Sociology and Ethics, the former being a special, the latter a philosophical science, although some Positivist philosophers would make no distinction between the two. The main difference between them consists in the fact that Sociology deals only with the origin and development of the various forms of social life, without considering their evolution in the future, nor putting forward rules as to man's conduct in respect to the State, the family, and the different contingencies of life. Ethics, on the contrary, endeavours to determine the ideal goal, towards which humanity *should* tend in accordance with a moral law, which, unlike the laws governing the evolution of society in the past, is not susceptible of demonstration. Modern Ethics borrows an ever-increasing quantity of data from Sociology; but the latter can never be substituted for the former, for it lacks two of its distinctive features—the *appreciation* of social phenomena and the *consideration of the future*. Sociology does not express any opinion whether a given religion, or a given form of government or of society, be good or bad, nor does it attempt to trace for humanity its future line of conduct, but rests satisfied with explaining social phenomena in

Philosophy and positive science.

[1] See Fechner's notable work *Vorschule der Æsthetik* (two vols., Leipsic, 1876), and Taine's well-known *Philosophie de l'art* (1865).

the past and in the present.[1] The same difference is to be noticed between that part of Psychology which treats of feeling and Æsthetics, between the juridical sciences and the Philosophy of Law, between History and the Philosophy of History, between Biology and Chemistry on the one side and the Philosophy of Nature on the other.[2]

This, however, does not mean that the special sciences and the philosophical sciences are entirely distinct, and that no connection exists between them. The latter have more frequent recourse to hypothetical theories than the former, but there is no doubt that in general biology, in comparative anatomy, in the science of language, or in comparative mythology, hypothetical theories are so frequent that there are not wanting those who deny them the character of positive sciences. Nor is it easy for the special sciences to refrain from making occasional use of the notions proper to their corresponding philosophical sciences, and it is a commonly accepted fact that when the study of a special science becomes most profound, it finds itself in the proximity of philosophical questions, and that scientists often indulge in philosophic speculations after years spent in minute research.

All this, however, does not sufficiently explain the fact that Psychology is considered to possess a greater philosophical importance than the other special sciences. The real cause of this is to be found in our definition, which is more than a mere empirical enumeration of the contents of Psychology, and is epistemologically important. Not to speak of sciences of a less general character, even Dynamics, which is the basis of all physical and natural sciences, cannot be taken as a logical starting-point, for it is but the result of a process of abstraction, by means of which presentations, or objects, are separated from the subjective part of consciousness, in order that they may be better studied and that we may find out the special laws that govern them—in this case the laws of motion. However much we may endeavour to imagine to ourselves an objective world, existing independently of our mind, we cannot dispense with the latter as a necessary starting-point of any investigation or

Psychology and dynamics.

[1] See H. Höffding, in his *Ethik* (Leipsic, 1888), p. 182. On the relations between Psychology and the moral and philosophical sciences, see H. Münsterberg, *Grundzüge der Psychologie*, Vol. I.

[2] Ethics, Æsthetics, Logic, and other branches of philosophical science are sometimes mistakenly called sciences of the mind. Even Fouillée falls into this mistake, in his book on the *Mouvement idéaliste et la réaction contre la science positive* (Introduction).

hypothesis. It may, indeed, be argued that the objective world is just as necessary a correlative to consciousness. But we must recollect that the objective world does not appear to our consciousness in the shape in which the physical sciences present it; but rather in the primitive form in which Psychology studies it—*i.e.* as presentation and will. These two parts of consciousness are subsequently separated by means of a process of abstraction, out of which is evolved a system of pure presentations governed by special laws and necessarily hypothetical.

The importance which Logic has for the theoretical sciences is possessed by Ethics with regard to the practical sciences. Any moral judgment which we pass on individuals, on society, or on history pertains to ethical science, which has for its object the general principles of moral judgment, and is of the greatest importance in examining the inmost meaning of human actions and establishing an ideal goal towards which they should tend. The discussions as to the possibility of a science of ethics free from religious dogma and independent of metaphysical systems are notorious, and any definite answer as to the value of this science must depend upon the answer to the question whether it is capable of formulating ethical rules of conduct inspired by high ideals. This question—complex as it is in itself—has been rendered even more difficult, owing to the confusion which is frequently made between the natural and the moral sciences. If we limit the notion of science to the physical and biological branches, we must be content with a purely naturalistic morality, which some will not be slow to connect with a utilitarian standard and other dubious consequences.[1] This problem cannot be solved unless we complete the meaning of the term "science" by extending it to those branches which have assumed of late so great an importance, and which form the natural basis of Ethics.

This is especially the case with those dealing with the evolution of society and religion, where the moral nature of man is particularly manifest. Sociology alone cannot explain all ethical motives and views, but requires the help of Psychology, and especially of

---

[1] The answer to the question respecting the value of science for ethics, so much discussed some years ago with so little precision and clearness of view, and even entirely denied by some, depends upon the definition we give of science. If, as by many, science is confusedly believed to correspond to the science of nature, we can understand how absurd it must appear to found scientific ethics on physiology or general biology. Ethics, like Æsthetics, must rest upon Psychology and the moral sciences.

the Psychology of peoples, which, through the study of the action and evolution of the will in the individual, arrives at a conception of the general laws of man's conduct in society.

Both the science of ethics and scientific logic therefore have their starting-point in the psychological fact of the existence of certain moral impulses, which are generally developed from simple to more complex forms. Other philosophical sciences, moreover, have their origin in Ethics, among which may be mentioned Pedagogy, which has no little practical importance.

These are the reasons which, in our opinion, raise Psychology above the level of other special sciences. It would be impossible for ethics and logic to find a satisfactory basis in the natural sciences, as has been proved by the unsuccessful attempts made in that direction. The original germ of theoretical knowledge and practical action in man resides in his consciousness, and not only in one part of his consciousness, but in the whole, comprising alike the subjective and objective aspects. As we have seen, Psychology is the science which studies the evolution of mental processes just as they present themselves, and it is therefore natural that it should possess a greater philosophical importance than any other of the special sciences—a fact which further explains why it should have developed into an autonomous department of knowledge. The object of Psychology being man, it must be borne in mind that man has always been inclined to consider his power of creating everything which passes under the name of science, art, religion, social and civil institutions, etc., as a supernatural gift. This circumstance was long an obstacle in the way of putting that power to the same objective scrutiny which is applied to natural phenomena and even to the products of the mind. The results of an objective study of the products of the human mind, however, having been found satisfactory, it was natural that the same methods should come to be applied to the mind itself, in conjunction with other methods proper to the natural sciences. This was the origin of modern scientific Psychology, which no longer considers mind, or consciousness, as a supernatural gift, but eschews metaphysical speculations as to its origin and destiny and the search after a hypothetical and unchangeable substance underlying the mental processes, and treats psychological phenomena as real and of importance in themselves. Whereas Metaphysics seeks for the absolute and real in a hypothetical world, Psychology places it instead in the mind of man, from which spring all knowledge,

Psychology and the special sciences.

action, and belief. Accordingly, while divesting the soul of all supernatural attributes, it gives it a very real importance, considering it the origin of all our beliefs, knowledge, and acts, following, we may say, a middle course between the two extreme theories of the spiritualists and the materialists.

On one side we have seen that Psychology is the basis of the special moral sciences; on the other that it has points of contact with the biological science of Physiology; and, lastly, that it is connected with Ethics and Logic. We must now turn to its limitations, which it is of particular importance to consider on the side of philosophy, as there exists a widespread opinion that Psychology is a part of the latter science. Wolff's school, we have already noted, distinguished Psychology into two parts, empirical and rational, the former having for its object the description and explanation of the phenomena of consciousness, and the latter the discussion of questions concerning the essence of the soul, its destiny, its immortality, etc. Modern Psychology, being above all things empirical, leaves metaphysical questions to philosophy. This principle we find accepted by all modern psychologists, who, if they touch upon metaphysical questions at all, do so only when they are connected with the subject they happen to be treating, and generally by way of illustration. Thus Höffding, James, Wundt, Sully, and others, when they deal with such questions as that of the connection between body and spirit, consciousness and unconsciousness, attribute much more importance to facts than to theories, and found their hypotheses always on the former. Even psychologists, who still believe in the existence of a mental substance underlying the mental processes, recognise nevertheless that this is a purely philosophical question, which must be excluded from all psychological discussions.[1]

In the opinion of these psychologists, Psychology should only deal with mental problems just as physics should only consider physical phenomena, leaving the arduous questions concerning the essence of energy and matter, the atomic theories, and all

Limitations of scientific Psychology.

---

[1] The most notable of these psychologists is Külpe, who, in his *Einleitung in die Philosophie*, discards the notion of "actuality" in favour of "substantiality"; but is of opinion that the question is one belonging to philosophy (see § 23, p. 188, etc., *Die Psychologischen Richtungen in der Metaphysik*). There are not wanting, however, those who still think that Psychology is only an introduction to philosophy, amongst them Spitta, who entitles his book *Introduction to Psychology as a Science* (*Einleitung in die Psychologie als Wissenschaft*). Psychology, in Spitta's estimation, reduces itself to a *Selbsterkenntnisslehre* (p. 36).

cosmological ideas in general to natural philosophy.[1] It is certain, nevertheless, that we can trace no clear line of demarcation between Psychology and the philosophy of the mind, when we bear in mind the very general character of psychological questions as soon as they become at all complex. The confusion between Psychology and philosophy is especially to be guarded against when we enter the field of the Psychology of peoples, which is often mistaken for the philosophy of history, of society, and of religion, although the latter are really part of the philosophy of mind.

We shall have to deal with this question farther on,[2] so that it may here suffice to say that the Psychology of Peoples concerns itself only with the more simple and general facts, which are the outcome of social life, whilst the Philosophy of Mind studies the whole evolution of historical, religious, social, and intellectual phenomena in man, with a view to understanding the psychological laws which have governed it in the past and are likely to shape its course in the future. It is therefore natural that with the continual and increasing development of the moral sciences and of Psychology, the Philosophy of Mind should have greatly gained in importance in the eyes of modern philosophers.[3]

The same difficulties occur when we inquire into the limitations of Psychology with regard to certain special sciences, such as sociology, physiology, psychiatry, and general biology. A distinction must here be made between the moral and the natural sciences, Psychology having a greater affinity with the former, which deal with the mental aspect of life. But whereas the various moral sciences are concerned with different groups of concrete facts, Psychology studies the primary conditions indispensable to the production of such concrete manifestations—that is to say, the general processes of consciousness, or, in other words, the different forms of intuition and thought, feeling and willing. Psychology

---

[1] See, on the connections between Psychology and philosophy, the Introduction to Ribot's work *La psychologie anglaise contemporaine*, and Flournoy's *Metaphysique et Psychologie* (Genève, 1890). See also Höffding in *Outlines of Psychology* (p. 11 foll.) and the chapter entitled "Psychology and Philosophy" of W. James's *Text-book of Psychology* (p. 461).

[2] See chap. iv. (a).

[3] See, for example, Wundt's *System der Philosophie* and Paulsen's *Einleitung in die Philosophie*. A comparison of these works with Spencer's *First Principles* is useful, this work dealing especially with physical and cosmological problems, in accordance with the character of the time in which it was written.

finds itself, therefore, with respect to the moral sciences, in the same position as general physics or dynamics with regard to the natural sciences. Just as the phenomena of the external world are all phenomena of motion, so the intellectual and moral actions of man are all processes of consciousness. Psychology is to be considered, therefore, the basis of the moral sciences.[1]

In this manner we have determined, with sufficient exactness, the line of separation between the moral sciences and Psychology. The old-fashioned theories failed in doing this, owing to the restricted limits within which they confined the science of Psychology. Psychology, according to those systems, being only an introduction to gnosiology and metaphysics, was deprived of its most important characteristic—viz. that of being the most general, fundamental, and explanatory of the moral sciences. Nor must we be led into error by the definition given above, according to which Psychology studies the results of experience from the subjective and individual point of view. It must be understood that the term *individual* does not signify that the study of the mental processes is to be left to the subjective judgment of each individual, for no science could exist under such conditions. Science presupposes generalisation, is a product of processes of abstraction, and based entirely upon concepts. For this reason the term *individual* must be understood in a general sense. This being a contradiction in terms, it is best to use the term *subjective* in place of *individual*. Considered in this way, Psychology is the science which studies the general forms of mental processes, considered as a whole, under their objective and subjective aspects, and as manifested not in this or that particular individual, but in an abstract individual, taken as a general type.[2]

The connections existing between Psychology and the natural sciences are not so apparent as between Psychology and the moral sciences, and can be reduced chiefly to questions of method. The subject-matter of science, whether physical or mental, being the same, it is possible to apply to the mental sciences the methods of the physical sciences; but their aims being quite different, the laws of Psychology must necessarily be different from those of the natural sciences. Thus cerebral processes are quite different from mental processes, notwithstanding the fact that the latter cannot be produced without the former. Even that part of

[1] On this question see Wundt, Vol. II., Part II., of his *Die Logik der Geisteswissenschaften*, especially chap. i. and ii. See also Sigwart's *Logic*, Masci, etc.

[2] See Spitta, chap. i. of his *Einleitung in die Psychologie als Wissenschaft*.

Psychology which studies the elementary mental functions, such as sensations and the simpler perceptions, where the aid of physiology and of physics is continually required, preserves a sharply defined distinction between physiological and psychical phenomena, a *sensation* being essentially different from the physical and physiological stimuli which produce it. Psychology cannot concern itself with the relations between the physiological and the mental phenomena, but must stop at the mental manifestations, considering physical phenomena only in so far as they complete the former. Consequently, general, or, as some call it, higher Psychology and physiological Psychology are not two distinct sciences, but two branches of the same science.

We have already alluded to the question whether Psychology can arrive at an *explanation* of mental phenomena, or must content itself, as was Kant's opinion,[1] with describing them. In the latter case, Psychology could not be called a real science, as the object of all scientific research consists in finding the reasons of facts.[2] We have already rejected the opinion held by many psychologists that the only explanation of the mental processes is to be found in physiological causes. The aim of Psychology, therefore, if it is to be a real science, consists in finding an explanation of mental facts in the mental world itself, considering their evolution, their concatenation, and their connection. The study of psychological methods and of the development of the mental life will enable us to judge whether it is possible to attain that result.

[1] See chap. i., pp. 40, 41.
[2] See on Kant's opinion on this matter, Natorp's observations in his *Einleitung in die Psychologie nach Kritischer Methode*, p. 101 foll. Natorp concludes that the only real explanation of mental phenomena is to be found in their physiological causes. See also an article by Ebbinghaus, "Ueber erklärende und beschreibende Psychologie " (*Zeitschrift für Psychologie*, Vol. IX.).

CHAPTER III

MIND AND BODY

WE have already alluded to the principal differences which exist between physiological phenomena and mental processes. Both are, however, very closely connected, and together make up the individual, who is a psychophysical being. The connection between these two orders of phenomena has been the starting-point of various theories and metaphysical systems. It will be well, therefore, to begin with an examination of the results reached by modern Psychology, with the help of the biological sciences, and especially of anatomy and physiology.

The terms "mind" and "body" suggest ideas of a metaphysical nature, according to which the mind and the body are conceived as entities possessing a real and concrete being entirely distinct from the phenomena pertaining to each. With these empirical Psychology has nothing to do. To the psychologist, the terms "mind" and "body" merely indicate two abstract ideas, representing the mental processes as a whole on the one hand, and biological phenomena as a whole on the other. A distinction is, nevertheless, necessary. Not all corporeal phenomena, but only the phenomena pertaining to the nervous system, are in direct relation to mental processes; wherefore it might be more appropriate to entitle the present chapter: "The Mind and the Nervous System." On the other hand, the more general term "body" is justifiable if, besides considering that the nervous system is closely connected with all the other parts of the organism, one bears in mind that it is also designed to unite all its several parts into a whole endowed with a certain amount of independence of external surroundings. Thus the nervous system expresses perhaps better than any other term the conception of the bodily organism, considered in the co-ordination and connection of its several parts.

Various conceptions of the relation between mind and body.

The fact that the organism is a *conditio sine quâ non* of our thinking faculty afforded food for reflection to the earliest philosophers of antiquity, some of whom invented psycho-physiological theories to explain the fact that external impressions call forth sensations. It is notorious that the ancients placed the seat of some of the mental processes, such as the feelings and the emotions, in the heart, or in the diaphragm. Empedocles, Heraclitus, and some of the Sophists endeavoured to explain the relations between the action of the external world and our body. The first philosopher who attempted to give a scientific explanation of biological phenomena, in accordance with his general philosophical views, was Democritus, whose explanation was entirely materialistic, as was the case with most of the pre-Socratic philosophies. Neither ancient nor mediæval philosophy admitted any specific difference between physical and psychical phenomena, both being contained in the notion of the "vital principle." In the pre-Socratic period, however, the tendency was towards a naïve form of materialism, very different from the more modern. On the one hand, the phenomena of the external world were conceived very much as we conceive the feelings and the subjective impulses, the universe being considered to be endowed with a will similar to the will of man; on the other hand, the thinking faculty was credited with the same qualities of fixity, immutability, etc., as natural objects. Even Plato gives no well-defined distinction between mental and the physiological processes, both being comprised in the general conception of soul, as distinguished into the rational and sensible, according as the higher faculties of the mind or the senses were considered. Aristotle, carrying on Plato's idea, admitted three grades of life, arranged in a progressive series of increasing perfection: the vegetative or nutritive, the sensitive or animal, and the rational or human soul. In Aristotle's opinion the two lower grades, as well as the rational soul, are to be found in man, the human intellect being divided into two parts: the one passive or sensible, the other active or speculative.

These Aristotelian ideas continued throughout the Middle Ages, the neo-Platonic philosophers and the Scholastic after them attributing a divine and supernatural character to the rational soul, whilst the sensible soul was merged in the physical world. A distinction between body and soul founded on general principles came much later with Descartes as the result of the scientific activity of the sixteenth and seventeenth centuries, which led to the mechanical conception of the universe.

Descartes, on the principle that the physical world is governed by mechanical laws, was induced to distinguish it as a *res extensa* from the world of consciousness, the *res inextensa*, or *res cogitans*. The two series of phenomena, however, are both to be found in man, who, as an organic being, is subject to physical laws, but is not subject to them as regards his reasoning powers. We have seen that Descartes considered the precise point of conjunction between the body and the soul to be the *glandula pinealis*. In Descartes' opinion the nerves of the sensorial organs and of the organs of locomotion meet in the brain, the former carrying external impressions to the brain cavities by means of a subtle substance which also fills the brain; the latter running in an opposite direction from the brain to the muscles.[1]

Descartes and the Cartesians.

These ideas show the influence of the old theories of the vital principle, so that we may say that, from a psychological point of view, Descartes marks no progress whatever. In his estimation consciousness was limited to man, and the materialists of the eighteenth century had only to develop this conception to arrive at the conclusion that man also is a machine which receives impressions and reacts by means of movements.[2] As the materialists had endeavoured to substitute for the Cartesian dualism the monistic conception that the only form of substance or reality is matter; so for the spiritualists or pure idealists (such as the post-Kantian metaphysicians), the only real principle was the thinking faculty. Between these two extremes of monism—materialistic and spiritualistic—the Cartesian dual hypothesis has found most favour among philosophers, even to the present day. We consequently come across two principal psychological tendencies in the history of philosophy—a monistic tendency in its materialistic and spiritualistic form, and a dualistic.

The great problem which presented itself to the Cartesian philosophy was that of giving a satisfactory explanation of the manner in which the mind and the body, the phenomena of consciousness and of the physical world, become connected in an apparent unity. The earlier followers of Descartes, such as Malebranche and Geulinx, evolved the so-called theory of "occasionalism," which closes the way to any empirical explanation by considering the connection between physical and mental phenomena to be directly occasioned by the divine will. From a more exalted point of view Spinoza substituted for the dualism between matter and spirit the conception of a divinity pervading the universe, and from which all things are

Spinoza and Leibnitz.

[1] See Wundt's "Gehirn und Seele" in the *Essays* (Leipsic, 1885), p. 91, etc.
[2] See Bain, *Mind and Body*.

derived. Leibnitz developed the notion of a pre-established harmony between the monads, each of which is part matter and part spirit. These theories were, however, of too metaphysical a character to furnish in themselves a sufficient explanation of the relations between body and soul; and those philosophers who preferred the more limited field of psychological research reverted to the dualistic Cartesian theory. This system, owing to its simplicity and clearness, appealed to the eighteenth-century mind, with its leaning towards formal precision and subtle classifications and distinctions. The greatest representative of this neo-Cartesian philosophy was a disciple of Leibnitz, whom we have already had occasion to mention—Christian Augustus Wolff, whose theories had great vogue in Germany during a large part of the eighteenth century. We have seen how he conceived the distinction between inner sense and external sense, so closely connected with the dualistic conception of consciousness and the body. In Wolff's opinion, as opposed to Leibnitz, the world is not a harmonious conglomeration of simple monads, independent of each other and endowed with a soul; but the soul itself is the only simple monad, and therefore essentially different from matter, which is indefinitely divisible. These purely philosophical questions were connected with others of a physiological nature, which had already been touched upon by Descartes, and were a subject of discussion among his followers, whom the metaphysical theories of Spinoza and Leibnitz did not satisfy. The study of the anatomy and physiology of the brain was in its initial stages at this period, and it was natural that when nearly all the special sciences were dominated by metaphysical ideas, and philosophical problems were frequently mixed up with empirical research, physiology and anatomy should lend themselves to support the psychological theories then in vogue. The "seat of the soul" was the favourite thesis of anatomico-metaphysical discussions of this kind, to which Wolff contributed his theory of the faculties, subsequently to make its influence felt upon physiology as well. This idea was a consequence of the eighteenth-century habit of mind, which, seeking after formal distinctions and classifications, omitted to study the genetic relations between the different branches into which it divided all human learning.[1]

[1] Wundt remarks (*op. cit.*, p. 93) that "Wolff, so zealous in his classifications in every province of learning, too often imagined that science has done everything when it has arranged its ideas in a well-ordered system, and treated inner experience like a country of which the first thing to know is its territorial division into provinces and districts."

Physiology and anatomy were not long in adopting this new path, and endeavoured to find in the human brain the various seats of what in Psychology were called the faculties. The first to clearly formulate these anatomical notions was a German, Francis Joseph Gall,[1] the founder of phrenology. Gall denied the possibility of finding the "seat of the soul," and was of opinion that we must be satisfied with localising its various faculties in the brain. Although his researches were of a somewhat fantastic nature, and his science has since fallen into discredit, it is nevertheless a fact that Gall possesses considerable historical importance for having initiated researches on morphology and on the functions of the brain which have since made continual and considerable progress. Gall's theory is well known. From the external shape, and more especially from certain protuberances of the cranium, he argued the shape of the brain, and thence the mental characteristics of the individual. In this manner he discovered twenty-seven dispositions, or aptitudes, of the soul, which he localised externally on the surface of the skull. At the time Gall's theory met with great success. We have seen how Comte himself considered Gall's phrenology as the only possible form of individual Psychology.[2] But with the improvement of means of research and of the methods of vivisection, cerebral anatomy was enabled to take up a more scientific position, and a reaction set in against Gall's theory.[3]

Gall and phrenology.

The French scientist Flourens was the first to begin those experimental researches, which for a long time held undisputed sway, to the exclusion of Gall's doctrines.[4] In Flouren's opinion the brain alone was the organ of the intelligence and of the will, and all other nerve centres served only to regulate the vital functions and the movements of the body. As opposed to Gall, he does not admit of a localisation

Anatomical and physiological theory of Flourens.

---

[1] F. J. Gall (1758—1828) lived after 1807 in Paris, and was the author of several works, amongst others the *Anatomie et la physiologie du système nerveux en général et du cerveau en particulier, avec des observations sur la possibilité de reconnaître plusieurs dispositions intellectuelles et morales de l'homme et des animaux par la configuration de leur tête* (4 vols., Paris, 1810—1818).

[2] See Wundt, *op. cit.*, p. 95.

[3] The history of these theories is given in the second chapter of Höffding's admirable *Outlines of Psychology*, besides Wundt's often quoted work. Höffding's treatment of the subject is masterly.

[4] Jean Pierre Flourens (1794—1867) wrote various works on anatomy and physiology, some of which are celebrated: *Recherches expérimentales sur les propriétés et les fonctions du système nerveux dans les animaux vertébrés* (1824);

of the mental faculties in the brain; and is of opinion that, if we remove one part, the remaining parts become, after a certain time, quite equal to accomplishing the functions pertaining to it. In this manner, instead of the destruction of one particular mental process, we have a weakening of the entire intelligence proportionately to the quantity of cerebral substance removed from the brain. Flourens arrived at these conclusions after a long series of experiments conducted upon various animals, and his ideas predominated down to the second half of the nineteenth century, when new doubts arose, and the question of localisation or absolute homogeneity was again hotly debated amongst men of science.

The faith in the theories of Flourens was first shaken by Broca, who proved, by means of experiments, that the seat of the important centres of speech is in the third frontal convolution of the left hemisphere.[1] This important discovery was brought about partly by the observation of pathological cases, in which it was noted that, as a result of apoplectic strokes, articulate speech was lost, while the speech muscles were not in any way affected; a fact which proved (anatomical examination confirming it) that in these cases there was an injury only to a part of the brain, the natural inference being that it was the injured part which had the sole function of connecting the various sounds, so that their combination should form a proper language, and not a series of disconnected sounds. This discovery justified the hope that the centres of each single mental process would also be discovered, and that Gall's theories might be completely confirmed. New light was shed on these researches by the microscopical observation of cells and fibres, ushering in the studies on the nervous system, which have since

Expériences sur le système nerveux; *De l'instinct et de l'intelligence des animaux* (1841); *Examen de la phrénologie, réfutation des doctrines matérialistes de Gall, Spurzheim et Broussais* (1842—1845); *Psychologie comparée* (1864).

[1] The Frenchman Paul Broca (1824—1880) was the author of several medical and anthropological works. His discovery dates from 1861. He founded in 1876 the Anthropological Institute, and is the author of various craniometrical studies. His numerous works on the subject appeared in the *Journal de Physiologie* and in the records of the Anthropological Society. Having turned his attention to the brain, he published various works on the anatomy of the cerebral convolutions and on cerebral localisation, especially that of the centre of speech. See *Bollettino della Societa Anatomica Fisiologica* (1861—1863), and a paper on aphasia, which he called "Aphemia" (1863). For more minute particulars on the question of the anatomy and physiology of the brain, see J. Soury, *Les fonctions du cerveau* (Paris, 1890).

acquired so much importance. These observations clearly proved the impossibility of accepting the notion put forth by Flourens, that the nervous system forms a homogeneous mass, whereof each part possesses the aptitude for every single function. It was ascertained that the sensory nerve-fibres, on reaching the brain, spread out into different directions, terminating in distinct ganglia or groups of cells, and that, conversely, the motor nerves start from different localities of the brain in bundles of fibres, which radiate to the various parts of the body. Thus, by means of experiment and of pathological observation, a certain localisation of the mental functions came to be established, but in a very different sense from that of Gall's theory. The Viennese anatomist Ludwig Türck had already noted that the motor nerve-fibres terminate in that part of the brain which is called the region of the central convolutions.[1] Subsequently an English physiologist, Ferrier, and two Germans, Fritsch and Hitzig,[2] ascertained, by means of experiments made upon animals, that a stimulus acting on certain limited areas of the brain causes corresponding muscular action on the opposite side of the body; and that, by depriving the brain of those parts, that action is notably affected.[3] The fact, however that a certain region of the brain regulates muscular action does not signify that in it lies the seat of the will. The willing faculty presupposes other faculties, such as feeling and perceiving, and is therefore accompanied by a complex series of physiological processes, which require the co-operation of all the nervous centres. The same may be said, and perhaps with greater reason, of the intelligence, which, in the words of the anatomist Munk, " has its seat in all the cerebral convolutions, and not in any special one, because it is the result of all the presentations derived from sensible perceptions."[4] Munk himself attempted to localise in the brain the seats of the processes of apprehension and recognition of

Ferrier, Munk, Goltz, etc. Discussions on the functions of the brain.

---

[1] L. Türck (1810—1868) is the author of several papers on the anatomy and physiology of the nerve centres.

[2] Gustav Theodor Fritsch (b. 1838), sometime professor at Berlin University, is the author of works on ethnography, anatomy, and physiology, of which several were written conjointly with Hitzig. Eduard Hitzig (b. 1838), alienist and professor at Zürich and Helle, is the author of *Untersuchungen über das Gehirn* (1874—1876); *Ueber die Funktionen der Grosshirnrinde*; *Ueber den heutigen Stand der Frage von der Localisation im Grosshirn* (1877).

[3] See Wundt, *Essays*, p. 101; Höffding, *op. cit.*, p. 53.

[4] Hermann Munk (professor at Berlin University), *Ueber die Funktionen der Grosshirnrinde* (Berlin, 1881); quoted by Höffding, *op. cit.*, p. 41, note.

elementary sensory impressions, such as those of sight and hearing. Notwithstanding the fact that this theory was limited to the localisation of certain elementary mental processes, and did not pretend to assign any special seat to the more complicated and general processes of the will and the intelligence, it was nevertheless hotly disputed by Goltz, an eminent anatomist, head of the so-called Strasburg school.[1] Goltz does not revert to the theories of Flourens, some of which, on the contrary, he rejects entirely, such as the doctrine that each part of the brain can do the work of the other parts. He proves that by removing a considerable part of the two cerebral hemispheres the intelligence is irremediably weakened; but he also considers it as proved that, when the injury to the brain is not of too great an extent, the animal recovers perfectly without such formation of new centres as is supposed by the supporters of the theories of localisation.[2] It is interesting to read of the results obtained by Goltz and his interpretation of them, which is entirely opposed to that of Munk and others. The discussion between him and those whom he calls the "new phrenologists" is not yet closed, and in the present state of the question it would be very difficult to say which side is in the right. Very probably the solution will be found to lie in a middle course between the two theories.

Appeal has been made in the course of the discussion to arguments of a more speculative character, such as the general laws of organic evolution, which is synonymous with everincreasing differentiation and complexity.[3] When, however, we consider the very general character of these laws, we see how either theory, by appealing to one particular point of view, can be easily adapted to them. Thus the theory of localisation is especially concerned with the differentiation of the various organs, which are appropriated to different functions; whilst the other theory gives, on the contrary, a preponderating importance to the connection existing between those organs themselves.

Questions just as complicated arise with regard to the nervous system so much studied of late years. Notwithstanding the greater perfection attained by modern methods of research and the powerful aids afforded by microscopical investigation, it is a

---

[1] See Soury, *op. cit.*, pp. 5—147, the chapter on Goltz and the Strasburg school. Goltz, who is the author of numerous works on anatomy—*e.g. Ueber die Verrichtungen des Grosshirns* (1881)—is a lecturer at Strasburg University.
[2] See Höffding, *op. cit.*, p. 42.
[3] For instance, Soury, *op. cit.*, pp. 35, 36.

fact that the student of histology is confronted with problems of capital importance with regard to the relation between the mental action on the one hand, and the cells and nervous fibres on the other, for which he is still unable to find a satisfactory and decisive solution. This being a point on which there is not even that comparative degree of agreement which exists with regard to cerebral localisation, it would be vain to enter into a minute analysis of the various opinions upon it here. Nor would it be opportune to hazard an opinion on questions as to which ideas differ so much amongst those who alone, both from technical training and continuous methodical study, are competent judges. It may, nevertheless, not be without interest to note some of the most contested points, especially as they are connected with experimental Psychology.

Modern histological research.

In order to obtain a clear idea of the state of the question, we must go back, and examine the theories which were for a long time universally accepted with regard to the nervous system. We have seen that a great step was made in the discovery that the nerve-substance is constituted of cells and fibres, and that the former perform a more important function than the latter in that they elaborate the impressions received, whereas the fibres are merely filaments, which transmit the impressions from the periphery to the centres and from one cell to another. Another fact known for some time to anatomy is that the grey substance is principally formed of cellular matter, whilst the white substance is essentially constituted by fibres. In what anatomical relation do these two elements of the nervous system stand to each other? This is the question which occupies contemporary anatomists and physiologists. According to the classical theory, as formulated five-and-twenty years ago by Gerlach,[1] the cells and fibres constitute a continuous tissue, in which each part is uninterruptedly connected with every other. This theory recommended itself by its simplicity, and it was only about fifteen years ago that it began to be questioned, in consequence of the painstaking researches of such men as Golgi (who is also worthy of note for his improvements in technical methods of research), Waldeyer, Kölliker, Ramon y Cajal, and others.

Golgi, Waldeyer, Kölliker, etc.

In attempting to give a summary of the state of knowledge with

[1] Joseph Gerlach, professor at Erlangen, expounded his theories in the *Handbuch der allgemeinen und speciellen Gewebelehre des menschlichen Körpers"* (1848).

regard to cells and nervous fibres, we may begin by observing that anatomists and physiologists are divided into two opposite camps. The nerve-cell is formed of a nucleus and prolongations, or projections, one of which is always distinguishable and is called the "axon," or "axis cylinder-process," whilst the others are termed "protoplasmic processes," or "dendrons." According to Golgi, to whom we owe the minute description of these different kinds of projections, the protoplasmic processes have a chiefly nutritive function, and the nerve-processes a nervous function. The different nerve-processes of the various classes of cells present different characteristics. Some, although emanating from collateral ramifications, preserve their individuality and are directly continued into a nerve-fibre. Others, also emanating from collateral ramifications, lose their individuality, so that it is not possible to follow them up. The nerve-fibres present the same peculiarities, if we start from the point of arrival at the centre; for whereas some, though sending out ramifications, can be followed throughout up to a nerve-process starting from a ganglion, others, on the contrary, are lost in their ramifications. The ramifications of both categories of fibres and nervous processes constitute an extremely fine nervous network, spreading throughout all the organs of the central nervous system. Several anatomical facts go far to prove this theory. The nerve-cells which do not possess protoplasmic processes have special and more direct connections with the blood-vessels, so that the latter may even be observed to penetrate into the former (unipolar cells of the sympathetic nerve; nerve-cells of the *Lophius piscatorius*, etc.).

Many histologists, on the other hand, deny the nutritive function of the protoplasmic processes, to which they attribute, on the contrary, the function of conductors of the nerve-current; while some are of opinion that the direction of the nerve-current in the protoplasmic processes is different from that in the axons: centripetal in the former and centrifugal in the latter; or, taking the nerve-cell as centre, cellipetal and cellifugal. According to His, Farel, Lenhossek, Van Gehuchten, and Ramon y Cajal, the termination of the axon and of its ramifications is as independent as that of the protoplasmic processes, and the reciprocal relations between them are simply relations of contact or articulation. The cell with its projections would thus form a comparatively independent unit, called "neurone" (a term first used by Waldeyer). This doctrine gives weight to some very plausible theories; for instance, the waking and sleeping states would find their explanation in the lengthening and shortening of the projections.[1]

Recent studies have brought to light several peculiarities of the nerve-cell, Apathy especially having made the discovery that the nerve is an aggregate of primitive fibrillæ, which penetrate into the cell like a network, and differ according to the different zones of the cell itself. These facts, however, are for the present limited to the lower animals, and it is not possible to draw conclusions with regard to the higher animals. On the other hand, Golgi has observed a network existing inside the nerve-cells which does not appear to be in connection with the axon, and a peripheral network which is apparently in connection with the axon. But how these connections are to be explained, and what possible connection there may be between the discoveries of Nissl, Apathy, Bethe, and Golgi, are questions which still await an answer, especially as we may say with Golgi that "the present state of knowledge on the structure and the relations of the nerve-cells does not permit the construction of theories regarding the organisation and mechanism of the functions of the nervous system in general" (*Comptes rendus de l'association des anatomistes.* Lyon, 1901).[2]

These difficult questions notwithstanding, it is certain that there exist some well-established anatomical and physiological facts which Psychology must take into account. The most important

---

[1] The researches of Camillo Golgi (professor at Pavia) are developed in his work *Sulla fine anatomia degli organi centrali del sistema nervoso* (Reggio: Emilia, 1885). Of this work there is an amplified German edition: *Untersuchungen über den feineren Bau des centralen und peripherischen Nervensystems* (Jena: Fischer, 1894). Waldeyer (professor at Berlin University) published in the *Deutsche medicinische Wochenschrift* (No. 44, 1891) a paper, "Ueber einige neuere Forschungen im Gebiete der Anatomie des Centralsystems." Ramon y Cajal (professor at Madrid) wrote an important work, translated into French by Azoulay under the title *Les nouvelles idées sur la structure du système nerveux chez l'homme et chez les vertébrés* (Paris, 1895). On the latest histological theories, with reference to Psychology, see Azoulay's article in the *Année psychologique*, Vols. I., II., III., and also H. Donaldson, *The Growth of the Brain*.

[2] See Golgi, "Di nuovo sulla struttura delle cellule nervose dei gangli spinali" (*Bollettino della società medico-chirurgica di Pavia*, 1899, No. 1); Apathy, "Nach welcher Richtung hin soll die Nervenlehre reformiert werden (*Biologischer Centralblatt*, No. 9); Ramon y Cajal, *Nuevas aplicaciones del metodo de coloracion de Golgi* (Barcelona, 1889); F. Nissl, "Mittheilungen zur Anatomie der Nervenzelle" (*Allgemeine Zeitschrift für Psychologie*, 1st edit. 1894).

circumstance, recognised by all students of anatomy, histology, and cerebral physiology, is the extremely complex character of all the physical processes which occur in the brain. The cerebro-spinal nervous system is formed of a series of co-ordinated parts, so disposed that from the lower to the higher centres a gradually increasing complexity of functions is observable.[1] Amongst the simpler centres the spinal cord and sympathetic system are connected with all those so-called reflex or automatic movements which accompany particularly certain vital functions. These movements (and especially those of the intestines) are comparatively independent of the higher centres. This independence is much greater in the inferior animals than in man, the connection between the various centres being much more apparent in the latter. The *medulla oblongata* is the seat of nerve-centres connected with other extremely important vital processes, such as respiration and the regulation of the movement of the heart and of the vascular muscles.

Experiments carried out on animals have demonstrated that these centres—namely, the spinal cord and the *medulla oblongata*—are capable of producing, if stimulated, certain comparatively purposeful movements, but that they are incapable of producing a spontaneous movement independent of external stimuli, and especially of co-ordinating the different movements even in the simplest way. The co-ordination of movements belongs, according to some, to the cerebellum; but opinions differ very greatly on this subject, so that it is not possible to pronounce a final judgment.[2] Lastly, we have the cerebral hemispheres with the *cortex*, chiefly composed of grey matter, which contain the centres of the more complicated mental processes, the *cortex* being the recipient of stimuli originating in the so-called external senses, as well as of internal stimuli, produced by the functions of the viscera and of the muscles. External and internal stimuli meet in the brain, and constitute, so to speak, the material which the *cortex* has to

---

[1] Goethe says: " Je unvollkommener das Geschöpf ist, desto mehr sind diese Theile einander gleich oder ähnlich, und desto mehr gleichen sie dem Ganzen. Je vollkommener das Geschöpf ist, desto unähnlicher werden die Theile einander. Je ähnlicher di Theile einander sind, desto weniger sind sie einander subordinirt. Die Subordination der Theile deutet auf ein vollkommeneres Geschöpf."

[2] Of recent works on the cerebellum, *Il Cervelletto*, by Prof. L. Luciani, of the University of Rome (Florence, 1891), deserves especial notice.

elaborate and transform. All the nervous centres are therefore necessary to the regular accomplishment of the mental functions. Without the lower centres we could not have impressions and sensations ; without the higher centres, and especially without the *cortex cerebri*, these impressions could not be combined together, and the movements which they determine could not be co-ordinated with other movements.[1] The higher centres are not only entrusted with the positive function of elaborating the impressions received from lower centres and of originating what are called the central impulses, but they have also a negative function, which consists in regulating the impulses which come from the lower centres. This latter function, however, as we shall see, is comprised in the former, because the suppression of an impulse comes as an immediate consequence of an act of choice, which is itself a process of the will, and has therefore a positive character. Some psychologists, English and French especially, such as Lewes, Maudsley, and Ribot, consider the principal function of the higher centres to be that of regulating and checking the impulses originating in the lower centres. This theory is closely connected with their conception of consciousness and of the genetic evolution of the will as nothing but a progressive transformation of a simple reflex action.[2] We shall, however, have occasion to point out that this is not sufficient to explain the origin of the processes of the will, and gives no proper idea of the importance of the *cortex cerebri* in the elaboration of mental actions, for it must be remembered that the *cortex* is the starting-point of those central impulses which are one of the most important elements in conscious life.

The theory of the co-ordination of the nervous centres, disposed, so to speak, in a hierarchical order, is, however, admitted by all psychologists, Physiology having placed this notion in the rank of accepted facts, and Psychology recognising it as of great importance

Co-ordination of the nervous centres.

[1] See, with regard to the co-ordination of the parts of the nervous system, the second chapter of Maudsley's *Physiology of Mind* ("The Mind and the Nervous System"), p. 109 foll. See also James's *The Principles of Psychology*, I. ii. ; Ladd's *Elements of Physiological Psychology*, Part I., p. 17 foll.; but the best exposition of the functions of the nervous system and of histological questions is to be found in *Grundzüge der Psychologie*, by H. Ebbinghaus, Vol. I., Bk. II. p. 89 foll. ("Vom Bau und den Functionen des Nervensystems"). See also Jodl's *Lehrbuch der Psychologie*, p. 43, and Baldwin, *Mental Development in th Child and the Race*, chap. xiv.

[2] See Maudsley, *Physiology of Mind*, iii. 184, and Ribot, *Les maladies de la volonté* (Conclusion).

in the explanation of the relations between body and mind from an epistemological point of view.

As the most typical instance of this hierarchical co-ordination (to make use of an expression introduced by Ribot), some modern psychologists (such as Wundt, Höffding, and Baldwin) adduce the relations existing between the various nervous centres with regard to articulate speech.[1] The observation of abnormal cases has thrown much light on the subject. Various elements are essential to articulate speech, the first of which is the voice, which forms, so to speak, the material of language. The voice must, however, be modulated, and its various sounds must be differently modulated and connected according to a certain rule, so as to form an articulate language, in contradistinction to the primitive speech, which consists in cries such as we find in animals and in the first stages of infancy. In this modulation of sounds two different operations are distinguishable—a simple and mechanical operation, consisting in producing and variously combining the vocal sounds, and a more complex one in the formation of syllables and words, these functions being accomplished in different centres. The simple emitting of a cry has the character of a reflex movement, which is probably originated in the *medulla oblongata*; the formation and combination of sounds is accomplished in the brain itself; and finally the more complex combination of sounds forming syllables and words depends upon still other centres in the *cortex cerebri*. It is clear that in the absence of the more elementary mechanisms which furnish the material to the higher centres the latter could not form by themselves an articulate language; and that, conversely, in the absence of the higher centres the vocal sounds could only form a series of cries and not a logically connected speech. In certain mental diseases, which have been recently attentively studied, the gradual retrogression from the perfect mechanism of developed speech to the primitive forms of inarticulate cries can be closely followed.[2]

We must now return to the question of the functions of the nerve-centres in relation to the phenomena of consciousness. The problem was first raised in this form by philosophers who, like the Cartesians, attempted to fix the seat of the soul, and,

---

[1] See Wundt, *Essays*, p. 11, and Höffding, *op. cit.*, p. 42; and on the mechanism of language and its disorders in pathological cases, see Kussmaul, *Die Störungen der Sprache* (1877), and Ballet, *Le langage intérieur et les diverses formes de l'aphasie* (Paris, 1886; 2nd edit. 1888), especially pp. 1—17.

[2] See Ballet, *op. cit.*, p. 6, 7, and Baldwin, *op. cit.*, chap. xiv.

later on, by Wolff and his disciples, who divided consciousness into a number of faculties, each corresponding to a special portion of the brain. Subsequently, when these studies threw off the shackles of philosophical theories, a number of data were brought to light of which Psychology and Philosophy itself were not slow to avail themselves.

The question of the relation between mind and body has in all times presented a markedly philosophical character. During the eighteenth century and the early part of the nineteenth it was discussed in a purely speculative manner, and with more or less abundance of words and vacuity of ideas. Lately, however, the discoveries of physiology and of histology have had a beneficial effect on the manner of dealing with the subject, concerning which a much greater clearness of view is now observable. Let us first examine the opinions of the seventeenth- and eighteenth-century philosophers.

We have already witnessed with what facility one may pass from the spiritualistic ideas of Descartes to the ideas of the materialists. Descartes was principally concerned to find the seat of the soul, or rather the point in which body and soul are united, and his conclusions in this direction had the effect of stimulating physiological research. Man alone, moreover, he held, was endowed with consciousness, while the lower animals were practically machines or automata. It was a short step from this to consider man himself as an automaton, deprived of all spontaneous mental energy; a theory of which La Mettrie's *L'homme machine* (1748) gives the clearest expression. The theory of psychological automatism had many followers after La Mettrie, such as Condillac and Holbach, and has reappeared in our own days in a more modern form, especially in France and in England,[1] where philosophical materialism has never ceased to hold the field alternately with spiritualism. Automatism involves the complete passivity of the mind, which itself is taken as the collective term for certain properties of the organism, so that this school may be said to follow a monistic theory, and to reduce all phenomena of nature, physical and mental, to the one single principle of matter.

The spiritualistic aspect (which was the principal one) of Descartes' doctrine continued meanwhile to develop itself, especially in Germany, where it inspired the systems of Spinoza, Leibnitz, and Wolff.

[1] See, with reference to La Mettrie, Lange's *History of Materialism*, II. ii. 49 foll.

Kant's theory that there can only exist a science of phenomena, and that thought and reality are indissoluble terms, each implying the other, effected a truce between the materialists and spiritualists of his time. After Kant, Idealism reigned supreme in Germany, and reached its climax in Hegel, who proclaimed the act of thinking to be the only real entity, its laws being the laws of the universe. It must be borne in mind that the idealists and metaphysical spiritualists, both before and after Kant, with the exception of Wolff, were not so much concerned with psychological problems (as had been the case with the French materialists) as with such philosophical questions as the relation between thought and reality, the determination of the notion of substance, and the like. After Wolff we find no psychologists amongst the idealists, the first noteworthy psychologists after Kant being Herbart, Beneke, and Lotze. The first two did not go into the question of the connection between the mind and the organism, but kept to Descartes' dualistic principle, affirming the doctrine of reciprocal action. Lotze was the first, after the materialists, to go deeply into the question. It is now necessary to retrace our steps, and to single out from the complicated course of philosophic thought the facts which have principally contributed towards attracting the attention of students to a question which had been much discussed during the eighteenth century by French materialists.

The relations between mind and body in modern philosophy.

When Lotze published his principal psychological work, *Medizinische Psychologie oder Physiologie der Seele* (1852), a great change had taken place in scientific ideas, owing to the progress of the physical, chemical, and biological sciences, culminating in the discovery of the conservation of matter and energy, made by Mayer, and confirmed by Joule, Colding, and Helmholtz.[1] Physiology especially was placed on a new basis by this discovery. The metaphysical explanation, according to which

[1] Robert Mayer lived from 1814 to 1878; his principal work, *Die organische Bewegung in ihrem Zusammenhange mit dem Stoffwechsel*, in which he expounded his famous theory of the conservation of matter and energy, was published in 1845. A year later Colding, a Dane, published his *Researches on the General Forces of Nature and their Reciprocal Dependence*. Joule's work on *Matter, Living Force, and Heat* appeared in 1847, in which year William Helmholtz (who died only a few years ago) published his essay *Ueber die Erhaltung der Kraft*. Helmholtz is well known as an indefatigable worker in the fields of physics, physiology, philosophy, and Psychology. Regarding these important scientific discoveries, see Höffding's *History of Modern Philosophy*, Vol. II.; and see also Max Planck's *Das Prinzip der Erhaltung der Energie* (Leipsic, 1887).

organic phenomena were supposed to be derived from an imaginary vital principle, was now discarded in favour of the explanation common to all physical phenomena—viz. that organic and vital phenomena, like all other phenomena of the external world, are the result of physical causes.[1] This principle was, nevertheless, much disputed, and is even now rejected by several authors of repute.

Before arriving at a scientific demonstration of the mechanical concept of vital phenomena, biology passed through various stages, which it is not uninteresting to note.

The most ancient theory regarding the phenomena of life is the theory of "animism." The primitive conception of the phenomena of nature consisted, as we have seen, in a general animation of matter, the physical world being imagined as similar to the human body in possessing a spontaneous will. This conception of universal animation is called in the history of philosophy "hylozoism." We need not come down to modern times to find a contrary doctrine in the "mechanical" theory originally formulated by Democritus, which, with the modifications brought about by the progress of science, has remained the basis of the scientific conception of life. This theory, while conceiving of the "soul" as a living substance, imagined the world as the result of the concurrence of an infinite number of material atoms. The theory of universal animism underwent sensible modifications at the hands of the Platonic and Aristotelian philosophers, who, in rejecting the materialistic ideas that followed from the doctrine of Democritus, established a dualism between external physical phenomena and organic phenomena. The Platonic and Aristotelian theory considered the soul only in connection with the latter. It was conceived of in various degrees—vegetative, animal, and rational; the lower degrees being considered almost identical with matter, the higher degrees being entirely independent of it. Hence vital phenomena came to be considered as entirely different from material phenomena, and a theory which went by the name of "vitalism," and afterwards met with a considerable amount of success, was formulated by the celebrated Doctor Galenus,[2] and

Theories regarding vital phenomena.

Animism and vitalism.

---

[1] See Mosso, "Materialismo e Misticismo" (*Nuova Antologia*, December 1st, 1895); J. Bernstein, *Die mechanistische Theorie des Lebens* (Braunschweig, 1890); Wundt, *Logik*, II. 533, etc.; Lange, *History of Materialism*, Bk. II.

[2] See Wundt, *Logik*, II. i. 533, etc. ("Die biologischen Richtungen"). On Galenus see *History of Materialism*, I. iv. 119 foll.

lasted, with modifications, down to the middle of the nineteenth century, by which time physiology had entered upon a new phase. Albert von Haller and John Müller, the founder of the physico-chemical school in physiology, are the two most celebrated representatives of the vitalistic theory.[1] Müller's theories found redoubtable opponents among his own pupils, some of whom are the founders of modern biology in its various branches, such as Helmholtz, Brücke, Du Bois-Reymond, Virchow, and Schwann.[2] The opposite extreme was represented by a theory which assimilated vital phenomena to external mechanical phenomena, considering the body a "natural machine," and appearing to find confirmation in the discoveries of physiology.

The gradual spread of discovery in the fields of anatomy and physiology is well known. The discoveries of Cesalpino and Harvey on the circulation of the blood, of Haller and Fontana on the irritability of the animal parts, of Spallanzani on the conditions of fecundation, demonstrated that the general conditions of the vital processes are subject to the same laws which govern physical phenomena. These discoveries having occurred simultaneously with others in physical science, it is not uncommon to find scientists, especially in recent times, who are physicists and physiologists at the same time.[3] Thus electric science has its origin in the naturalistic observations of Galvani.[4] Similarly the biological sciences were much influenced by the progress of chemistry, branching out into organic and physiological, which from Berzelius and Liebig down to our own days has made considerable progress. We have already noted the discoveries regarding the nervous system; but we must here note the fact that the investigations into the nature and velocity of the nervous current made by Helmholtz, Du Bois-Reymond, and others, were founded exclusively on the results of experimental physics.[5]

The mechanical conception of vital phenomena.

[1] Albert Haller (1708—1777) is celebrated for his work *Elementa physiologiæ corporis humani* (1757—1766). Johannes Müller (1801—1858) published in 1834 a manual on the Physiology of Man. J. Liebig also followed the vitalistic theory.

[2] See A. Mosso, "Materialismo e misticismo" (*Nuova Antologia*, 1° Decembre, 1895, p. 444).

[3] *E.g.*, the brothers Henry, Ernest, and Edward Weber and Helmholtz.

[4] On all these discoveries see J. Bernstein's *Die mechanistische Theorie des Lebens* (Braunschweig, 1890), p. 3 foll. See also Golgi, *Lo sperimentalismo nella Medicina* (Pavia, 1884). See Bernstein, *ut supra*, pp. 8, 9.

[5] See Bernstein, *ut supra*, pp. 8, 9.

In this manner the mechanism of organic phenomena was proved to possess the general character of physical phenomena, with the result that the vitalistic theory was superseded. It was, nevertheless, impossible to accept so simple a theory as that of the "natural machine," for whilst science demonstrated the fact of biological phenomena being regulated by general physical laws, it pointed out at the same time the enormous complexity of such phenomena. Supposing the individual organism to be a mechanism, it is such a delicate and complicated species that it cannot in any way be compared to what may be made by man. The fact, however, was established that there is no theoretical difficulty in admitting that all the vital processes, even those hitherto unexplained, may be subject to the same laws as other phenomena. On this question the student finds himself in the position of one confronted with a complicated piece of machinery which he cannot understand, although he never doubts that it works in obedience to the laws of mechanics.[1] The years 1845 to 1860[2] were a period of phenomenal progress in natural science. In 1845, as we have seen, Mayer published his work on the conservation of energy, which was immediately followed by the works of Joule, of Colding, and of Helmholtz, on the same subject. To this period belong the physiological discoveries of Claude Bernard; and in 1852 the celebrated German physiologist Karl Ludwig (1815—1895) published his *Manual of Physiology*, "the first treatise written with the express intention of introducing the mechanical conception of life."[3] But the work which more than any other caused a revolution in biological ideas was Darwin's *Origin of Species*, which was published in 1859.

Darwin's importance with regard to biology cannot be overrated. Even making allowance for the necessary changes brought about by the continual progress in comparative anatomy, his ideas remain the starting-point of an entirely novel conception of organic nature. The greatest obstacle in the way of assimilating biological and physical phenomena was, and still is, the fact that vital phenomena, though resulting from a combination of chemical elements and physical forces, possess some other element which is not to be found in purely physical phenomena. In other words, they bring us into the presence of a spontaneous energy, which

---

[1] See Bernstein, *op. cit.*, p. 18.

[2] See Mosso's paper quoted above, p. 444.

[3] See Mosso, *ut supra*, and his article published in the *Nuova Antologia* of June 15th, 1895.

gives them a character of purposefulness. This fact for a long time was attributed to a supernatural power; but no explanation was given in that way of the origin of species, and Darwin's principle that the characters of the different species are the result of a great number of small individual variations, fixed and transmitted by means of heredity, was thus the beginning of an entirely novel interpretation of organic evolution. These variations, he pointed out, take place through the action of the surroundings, to which the individual must adapt himself in order to live, and of the struggle for existence. The former principle of the adaptation to environment accorded perfectly with the mechanical interpretation of life,[1] mechanical and chemical adaptation, which has been proved to occur in the case of many vital phenomena, seeming to afford an explanation of the production of several organic forms. Darwin, however, did not assign enough importance to "functional," or internal, adaptation,[2] which is of the utmost importance for the interpretation of biological phenomena, seeing that, amongst the causes of organic modification, none is more characteristic of the organism itself than the inner spontaneous volition which manifests itself in the "function" of a given organ. This inner volition explains organic "teleology," and affords, together with the mechanical causes of organic variations, a relatively complete explanation of vital phenomena. The interpretation of biological facts has consequently both a physical and a psychological side.[3] Nor can it be otherwise, the individual not being purely physical or purely psychical, but psychophysical. It is therefore just as hopeless to attempt, as some writers do, to explain vital phenomena from the point of view of purely physical determinism, as it is to consider the psychical aspect alone in the explanation of the individual.[4]

A theory entirely opposed to the above is the ancient theory of the "vital principle," which has lately been brought forward again. One of the most authoritative exponents of this form of neo-vitalism is Professor Bunge,[5] of Basle,

Neo-vitalism.

---

[1] See Bernstein, *Die mechanistische Theorie des Lebens*, p. 18.

[2] See, on the biological theories of adaptation, Wundt in his *Logik*, II. i. 545, etc.

[3] Wundt, *Logik*, II. i. 551: "Das Problem der Entwicklung ist überhaupt kein rein physiologisches, sondern zu einem wesentlichen Theile zugleich ein psychologisches Problem."

[4] Amongst modern determinists are to be mentioned Delage and Dantec, whose works have recently aroused some attention.

[5] Bunge is the author of a *Lehrbuch der physiologischen Chemie* (2nd edit. 1889). This school numbers also amongst its followers Rindfleisch (see *Aertzliche*

a pupil of Ludwig. The chief argument of the neo-vitalists is the one alluded to by Virchow as far back as 1856. On the principle of *omnis cellula a cellulâ* Virchow affirmed that we cannot go beyond the cell in the explanation of biological phenomena, and that although the cell is composed of chemical elements, the fashion in which the latter are combined is entirely *sui generis*. Virchow considered the cell the substratum of vital energy, and on this basis he constructed his cellular theory of life and disease.[1] The Neo-vitalists, having noticed the great complexity of some of the vital phenomena, which were formerly supposed to be simple, hint, though they do not affirm explicitly the possible existence of a vital force of a different nature from general physical forces.

All these attempts are wanting in a scientific basis. However difficult the explanation of certain organic phenomena may be, science has ascertained that their components are similar to chemical elements. The "vital principle" in itself explains nothing. It is a provisional formula which indicates our state of ignorance on the subject, but serves no other useful purpose. The progress of physical science and of chemistry will eventually clear up several obscure points ; and we cannot afford meantime to give up the mechanical theory of life, which has been up to now the only theory which gives even a partially satisfactory explanation of biological phenomena.

We must now return to the question of the relations between mind and body. The mechanical explanation of biological phenomena exercising as it did so marked an influence on the biological sciences and physiology, it was natural that it should produce an effect on Psychology, which has so many points of contact with the latter, and indirectly also on general philosophy. Lotze, in his capacity of psychologist, philosopher, and physiologist, first reopened the question of the relations of mind and body, placing himself on the modern standpoint in accordance with recent scientific discoveries. His philosophical principles were, however, entirely spiritualistic. In his opinion, we can only obtain an exact knowledge of internal phenomena because we have a direct perception of them ; whereas of external phenomena, which are apprehended indirectly, we

Philosophie, 1888), Haacke, and others. Against these tendencies see Bernstein and Mosso, *loc. cit.*, and a paper published by Mosso in the *Nuova Antologia* of December 1st, 1890, p. 446 foll.

[1] See Bernstein, *op. cit.*, p. 22.

can but have an imperfect notion, a *cognitio circa rem*. He thus rejects Descartes' dualism, which gives to spirit and matter an equal value. Lotze's idealism herein reminds one very much of Berkeley's. On the other hand, he stoutly maintains the principle of the mechanical causality of biological phenomena, although he refuses to admit that the physical energy which is spent in physiological processes is preserved as such. In his opinion, this energy, although remaining intact as to quantity, can be transformed into a force of a different kind—namely, psychical energy.[1] The point at which this transformation takes place Lotze held to be the seat of the soul, herein approaching very near to the Cartesian theories of the reciprocal influence of mind and body. Similar ideas we find in Beneke.

Meanwhile, and immediately following Lotze's earlier writings, there had arisen in Germany a new school of materialistic philosophers. In common with preceding materialists, they considered the mental phenomena as one of the aspects, or functions, of matter, which alone is real. To this they added the notion of the continuity and continual transformation of matter and energy, with which they thought to explain the production of mental phenomena. The polemical discussions to which materialistic theories gave rise about the middle of the nineteenth century are so well known that it is hardly necessary to enlarge upon them, or to quote passages from the works of such men as Charles Vogt, Lewis Büchner,[2] James Moleschott, Henry Czolbe, Ernest Haeckel, and others.

The materialistic theory which, through the works of the French writers, with their flavour of amiable scepticism, had so successfully appealed to the taste of the eighteenth century, obtained no less a vogue during the years between 1860 and 1880, owing to the enthusiasm which recent scientific discoveries had awakened. The natural sciences were looked to for the solution of every problem, physical or moral; and for some time moral and philosophical science did little more than strive to appropriate and adapt to their own uses the laws of the natural sciences. Few books have had in our day the success of Büchner's

---

[1] See Lotze, *Allgemeine Psychologie*, p. 461.

[2] Büchner's famous work *Kraft und Stoff* appeared in 1855, was translated into thirteen languages, and reached its sixteenth edition in 1888. Moleschott's work *Der Kreislauf des Lebens* came out in 1852, as did Vogt's *Physiologische Briefe*. Both have been translated into French and other languages.

Mind and Body

Force and Matter,[1] passages of which have been quoted by some as irrefutable scientific truths.

The progress of experimental science had very much popularised the materialistic theories which came as a reaction against the excessive idealism that, in Germany principally, had resulted in a surfeit of abstract concepts to the detriment of all positive truths. Another reason in its favour has always been its great simplicity, which appeals to every one. The idea that material facts, which can be apprehended by the senses without the necessity of any process of abstraction, and can be submitted to precise measurement and determination, are the only form of reality has appeared in the eyes of the majority so simple a proposition as not to require demonstration. It is also a necessary consequence of the modern specialisation of pursuits that those who are particularly concerned with natural phenomena, and biologists especially, should involuntarily lean towards one-sided views, which impel them to accept with facility materialistic doctrines. We have, therefore, three theories concerning the relations between spirit and body: the more ancient dualistic, or Cartesian, theory, and two monistic systems, one of which reduces everything to the spirit, and the other to matter.

We must now examine these theories critically, in order to ascertain if there exists no other doctrine more satisfactory from an epistemological point of view. The first, or Cartesian, theory was founded on the principle that the material and spiritual elements exercised upon each other a continual influence, the mental life consisting in the harmony of spirit and body (which, in the opinion of the earlier Cartesians, depended directly on divine will). It is not surprising that this theory should have lasted throughout the seventeenth and even the eighteenth centuries, considering the backward condition

Modern theories on the relations between mind and body.

---

[1] A second edition of the English translation was completed from the tenth German edition, 1870. Paulsen, in his *Einleitung in die Philosophie* (p. 69 foll., note), writes with regard to this work: " Man mag das Buch in philosophischer Hinsicht geringwertig, man mag seine Behandlungsweise und seinen Stil unerfreulich, sein Ungeschick im begrifflichen Denken unerträglich finden, so bleibt doch die Thatsache, dass es seit 1855 in 16 Auflagen von dem deutschen Publikum gekauft und gelesen, auch in 13 fremde Sprachen übersetzt und hier wiederum in zahlreichen Auflagen gekauft und gelesen werden ist. . . . Fragt man sich welchen Vorzügen das Buch seine grosse Verbreitung und Wirksamkeit verdankt, so wird man auf zwei Stricke kommen: es bietet erstens eine Menge in populärer Form mitgetheilter naturwissenschaftlicher Kenntnisse, zweitens Verachtung der Kirche, der Theologie und des Bekentnisses."

of biological science, which was held in thrall by the metaphysical notion of the vital principle; but it is surprising that such a doctrine should count adherents in modern times, when the principles of mechanical causality and of the conservation of energy are generally accepted by science, some psychologists [1] even believing that, in accepting it, they are following an empirical method, entirely free from all metaphysical taint.

Theory of dualism.

In the preceding chapter we have seen that the object of Psychology is the study of all psychical facts as they present themselves directly to our consciousness by means of presentations, together with the mental phenomena which accompany them, such as feelings and impulses. The sciences of physical nature, on the contrary, have for their object the study of presentations, considered as existent by themselves and independently of all impulses or feelings. Now, all these presentations, which we call external objects, form to our mind a whole whose several parts are connected by a causal relation. The causal principle, which is one of the most important axioms in logic, as applied to the relations between external objects, assumes a particular form which is termed physical, or mechanical causality. This principle is not solely founded on the general notion that every fact must be both the cause and effect of other facts; but it also shows that the quantity of matter and energy which forms the substratum of physical phenomena remains unaltered, though its form varies. Between the cause and the effect there exists, therefore, an equivalence of value. Quantitative equivalence is the distinctive characteristic of mechanical causality, whilst it is entirely absent in the case of psychical causality, which has to take into account such subjective and variable elements as feelings and impulses. Consequently, although external facts have their part in mental phenomena, the latter cannot possess that character of comparative fixity which alone renders a quantitative measurement possible. In its absence there can be no exact correspondence of cause and effect. Moreover, the mental processes, considered by themselves, entirely lose the character of quantity, retaining only that of quality. For example, a sensation, taken by itself, is purely a qualitative fact (endowed with a certain amount of intensity), and nothing more; and if the notion of quantity cannot be applied to sensations, it is even less applicable to the feelings, which are

Physical and psychical causality.

---

[1] For instance Ladd, who enters upon a lengthy defence of the theory of reciprocal influence in his *Elements of Physiological Psychology*, p. 657 foll.

eminently qualitative facts. We have, therefore, two causal series—a mechanical series, which is quantitative, and a psychical series, which is qualitative. We cannot, however, insist too much on the fact that there are not in reality two distinct series, that the distinction is merely an abstraction of our own thought. The presentations which we think of as connected according to mechanical causality are part of the general contents of consciousness, which consists, in its turn, of a series of processes connected in accordance with psychical causality. Moreover, the term mental energy is not to be understood in the same sense as physical energy, but rather as indicating the whole mental activity in its progressive development. But if it be thus established that psychical and physical causality form only one causality, the Cartesian dualism between the spiritual and material principles falls of itself. Nevertheless it must be remembered that this monistic point of view is not the starting-point of psychological and physical research, but only its ultimate conclusion. Such research must start from scientific data, and these show on the one hand a series of physical facts extending from inorganic phenomena up to the most complicated biological phenomena, such as the cerebral processes, which mingle with the phenomena of consciousness; and on the other hand a series of mental facts extending from the elementary forms of sensation, which are closely connected with physiological phenomena, up to the highest and most complex processes of logical thought and to the creations of the imagination.

The psychologists of Wolff's school, as well as the more recent psychologists who distinguished between inner and outer facts, gave great weight to this fact. To many the assimilation of phenomena pertaining to the organism, and especially of cerebral phenomena, to the physical phenomena which take place without us is difficult to understand; and the fact that certain sensations which are determined by stimuli produced within the organism are called "inner sensations" increases the confusion. It is indeed a fact that these sensations, which have been carefully studied of late years, seem to afford a proof of the impossibility of severing the organic and the mental orders of phenomena.[1] How is it possible, for instance, to distinguish the psychical and the physical in the sensations, which, indicating as they do, though it may be in a vague way, the state of our organs, are connected with some of our most intense feelings and most deeply rooted instincts? Moreover, as empirical observation,

[1] See Beaunis's *Les sensations internes* (Paris, 1889).

which does not go much beyond the surface of facts, shows us a connection of reciprocal action and reaction between mental processes (especially the emotions) on the one hand, and physiological phenomena on the other, the theory of their reciprocal influence upon each other appears at first sight the most obvious and natural, which no doubt is the reason why many popular treatises of descriptive Psychology take it as their starting-point.[1] Science, however, should not rest content with vague impressions, and should be particularly cautious in those cases in which the differences between various orders of phenomena are not well marked, and where it is therefore harder to discover the fundamental principle which characterises one phenomenon amongst various others. Now, however closely a sensation be connected with the stimulus which determines it, and however indistinguishable the latter may sometimes be from the sensations produced (as in the case of organic or diffused, or, as some call them, inner sensations), it remains an incontrovertible fact that a sensation, as an elementary psychical phenomenon, is essentially different from the physical stimulus. This is accordingly where the Cartesian and Wolffian theory of reciprocal influence meets with serious difficulties. Given the double series of phenomena, physical and psychical, how is it possible to admit that the one mingles with the other in such a manner as causally to modify it? It is a fact that beings who are endowed with consciousness, and human beings especially, are in constant relation with their physical surroundings, without which it would even be impossible to imagine them, and that they continually modify and are modified by them. But in the changes which they can bring about they have so little power of separating the physical phenomena from physical causes that it remains, on the contrary, the continual aim of man to penetrate always farther to the root of physical causality, so as to better enable him to divert natural phenomena to his own ends.

It will never be possible to alter the specific character of mechanical causality, from which it follows that the dualistic conception, which at first sight appears to tally with the results of experience, is in reality completely at variance with them, and cannot be accepted on any consideration.[2]

[1] One of the best known among these is Hack Tuke's *Illustrations of the Influence of the Mind upon the Body in Health and Disease* (1872). See also Ladd, *op. cit.*
[2] This theory is ably confuted by Ebbinghaus, *Grundzüge der Psychologie*, i. 27 foll. See also Höffding's *Outlines of Psychology*, p. 55, and Masci's

The spiritualistic and materialistic monistic theories are even more unsatisfactory. The former has, as we have seen, several points of contact with the dualistic conception, admitting as it does the reciprocal passage from the psychical to the physical series of phenomena. Lotze, who is the foremost modern representative of this school, was of opinion that we can never have a perfect knowledge of our inner states, and that, as to external phenomena, we can only have a confused notion *circa rem*.[1] Such a view is, however, inadmissible, for it must be borne in mind that the external objects are presentations, the inner and the outer being inseparable except by means of an artificial process, which is only possible when the presentation does not refer to a present object, but to an image of the memory. In this manner external objects are reduced to psychical facts, and it is therefore clear (as corroborated by popular experience) that we can have a much more exact knowledge of physical phenomena than of psychical processes, for external objects are susceptible of quantitative measurement, which is impossible in the case of the phenomena of consciousness.

Monistic theories.

The spiritualistic theory.

The assertion that physical states can at a given point be transformed, or, in Lotze's own words, be absorbed into intensive states, is subject to even graver objections than the dualistic theory. If it is not possible to admit the commingling of the two series, it is even less possible to believe that the one should "absorb" the other and transform its character entirely. Such an idea cannot be entertained by any one who is even slightly acquainted with the main principles of modern physics. Physical causality cannot be changed into a different causal series founded on different principles, nor can it derive its origin from it, for no physical phenomenon can be explained otherwise than by means of another physical phenomenon, nor can it be transformed into anything but a physical phenomenon.[2]

Although the materialistic hypothesis cannot boast of more valid reasons on its side, it has the merit of being more in harmony with the data and the principles of the physical sciences, and of dealing with mechanical causality, irrespective of psychical

excellent work *Il materialismo psicofisico e la dottrina del parallelismo in psicologia* (Naples, 1902), p. 75 foll.

[1] See Lotze, *Medizinische Psychologie*, p. 261 foll.

[2] These theories are ably confuted in F. Masci's *L'idealismo indeterminato* (Napoli, 1898), ii. 9 foll.

causes.[1] Materialists, on the other hand, pay too exclusive regard to the principles of physical nature, to which they endeavour to subject every form of knowledge. Where there cannot exist quantitative and objective measurement, the materialists see no possibility of science. Materialism, in all times, has sought to do away with psychical facts in favour of natural facts, and to reduce the moral to the mechanical laws of the physical world. Further, whereas scientific progress has gradually eliminated all subjective elements from our conception of the external world, so that we think of it as independent of the conscious subject, and as solely governed by fixed mechanical laws, no similar process of elimination is possible with regard to the psychical world. Thus, although it may be evident to some that a mental process is no less real than a physical phenomenon, there exists, on the other hand, a widespread opinion that only what can be subjected to quantitative objective measurement is really existent. The continued favour in which materialistic ideas have been held can be explained partly by the character of comparative fixity proper to physical phenomena, which renders possible an objective measurement and an exact determination of their component elements, and partly by the fact that the progress of the physical and natural sciences is largely owing to this very character of stability. The mental processes, on the contrary, have no stability of form, are continually changing, and, being merely processes, are not susceptible of precise measurement. Hence they are not only deprived of the estimation in which the exact sciences are held, but are even considered by some as endowed with a purely fictitious existence, and of being nothing but illusions.

The materialistic theory.

We must hope that psychological, like physical, theories will gradually rid themselves of all subjective elements. That thought, or better still, the mental processes, have a real existence is a fact which does not call for subtle demonstrations. We feel that we possess ideas, feelings, desires, and volitions, there being nothing more directly and immediately apprehended than what happens in consciousness, and, in order to prove it on logical principles, we need only have recourse to the axiom

Reality of psychical facts.

---

[1] Lange, in his *History of Materialism*, Vol. III., chap. ii., § iii., p. 158, very aptly says: "We may shortsightedly abuse the mechanical theory of things as we will; it has, nevertheless, the grand merit that it lets us look into an infinity of problems, while at the same moment it affords us a first small victory as a pledge that we are on the right path."

of identity, which is the simplest of all. Even admitting, with some of the less advanced materialists, that these processes have their origin in physical phenomena, and represent a form of the transformation of energy,[1] it is impossible to deny that they possess an "actual" existence of their own, and that they may be studied by themselves. Nor is it satisfactory to say that they are the product of an illusion, for that implies the admission that there exists a conscious subject to whom cerebral phenomena appear, through the effect of an illusion, in the shape of mental processes, such as perceptions, ideas, feelings, and so forth. The term conscious subject is nothing less than a collective way of describing all those mental processes which we are asked to believe are but the product of illusion.[2] However much we seek to sever ourselves from our consciousness, we must always return to it, as the origin of all ideas which we have of the external world and of consciousness itself. Recalling Schopenhauer's witticism, we may compare the materialists to Baron Münchausen, who tried to raise himself out of the water by his own hair.[3]

If the reality of mental phenomena is directly patent to us, the question of whether it is derived from some form of physical energy is of an essentially metaphysical character, and belongs to the highest order of philosophical problems. We are here confronted with the same difficulties which beset the dualistic and spiritualistic theories. How can the passage from one causal form to another take place? However closely we follow the chain of physical causes and effects, we shall always find that a physical fact can but determine another physical fact and never a process of consciousness.[4] Even pure materialists have recognised this to

[1] In the first edition of the *First Principles* Spencer inclined towards this opinion. In the second he was more cautious, recognising that psychical energy is different from physical energy, and that the two cannot be said to be connected by any causal dependence. See, on these questions, Paulsen in his *Einleitung in die Philosophie* (Bk. I., chap. i., p. 4).

[2] Some fine criticism of these materialistic theories, as also of the other two mentioned above—viz. dualism and spiritualism—is to be found in G. F. Stout's *Manual of Psychology* (1879), p. 43 foll.; also in Cantoni's "Studi sull' intelligenza umana," published in the *Atti dell' istituto lombardo di scienze e lettere* (Milan, 1870—1871).

[3] See *The World as Will and Idea*, Bk. I., § vii. Various modern psychologists, who cannot be called materialists, adhere to the notion that consciousness is a product of illusion, amongst them Taine.

[4] This impossibility of reducing mental processes to physical causes has been recognised by many physicists and physiologists, and even by positivist philosophers. Thus Tyndall (in *Fragments of Science*, 5th edit., p. 420) says

the extent that, not being able to explain mental phenomena, they have had to have recourse to the *extrema ratio* of denying their existence and of attributing the feeling we have of their existence to an illusion. The eighteenth-century materialists, on the other hand, were of opinion that consciousness is a "function" of the brain, and this idea has been entertained by some modern materialists such as Vogt, who is the author of the celebrated saying that "the brain produces thoughts as the kidneys secrete urine." The products of the brain, such as cholesterin, creatin, xanthin, etc., are known to physiological science, but they are purely material, and not susceptible of comparison with what we call the mind itself.

Confutation of materialism.

Recent psychophysical materialism is less consistent, for, although admitting that even the most elementary mental process has an entirely special character of its own, it treats it merely as an epiphenomenon, or as something superadded to a physiological fact. The real explanation of mental phenomena, according to this view, is to be found in the cerebral mechanism. Here, however, in addition to the fact that consciousness plays much more than a passive part in the evolution of the species, we find ourselves met by the usual difficulty—How can a series of material phenomena explain a totally different order of facts?[1]

It is impossible to bridge the gulf which separates the series of physical facts from the series of mental facts, nor is it possible to deny the existence of one or the other of those series, without going counter to the most incontrovertible data furnished by experience and to the fundamental principles of physical science. How are we, then, to solve the problem of the relations between

that "the passage from the physics of the brain to the corresponding facts of consciousness is unthinkable"; and Spencer (*Principles of Psychology*, i. 862) confesses that "no effort enables us to assimilate them." These declarations do not, however, prevent both writers from falling into certain grave contradictions, of which hereafter (see chap. vi.). Cf. James, *The Principles of Psychology*, i. 147, 148. Bernstein's opinion is also worthy of note, because not often met with amongst psychologists. In his *Die mechanistische Theorie des Lebens*, pp. 12, 13, he says: "Scheint unserem Verstande, welcher gezwungen ist nach dem Gesetz der Causalität zu denken, nicht möglich die Grundeigenschaften der Psyche, die Empfindung, Wahrnehmung, und Vorstellung aus rein materiellen Processen abzuleiten."

[1] See Masci's ably expressed objections to the materialistic theories in his *Il materialismo psicofisico e la dottrina del parallelismo in psicologia* (Napoli, 1901), pp. 65—68, 94, 95, 109—128. On the functional notion see Höffding, *op. cit.*, p. 60; Stout, *Manual of Psychology*, p. 49 foll.; and Ladd, *Elements of Physiological Psychology*, p. 654.

the body and the soul, if we are unwilling to restrict ourselves to a purely descriptive system?

Taking common and primitive experiential knowledge, we find it entirely ignorant of the physical phenomena which accompany consciousness, of which alone it has an immediate feeling. When, however, we consider consciousness from a critical and scientific point of view, we make use of a process of abstraction to isolate it from its accompanying organic and physical phenomena. As a matter of fact, we are unable to imagine a mind, a series of conscious processes, or one single conscious process, as existing alone and independent of the organic phenomena which constitute its physical substratum. Similarly, an organism existing apart from certain physical surroundings is unthinkable. Whatever idea we may entertain as to the origin of mental energy—whether we believe it to be a transformation of physical energies, or to be spontaneous, or to be due to supernatural causes—whatever theory we may hold regarding the ultimate destiny of the soul, we cannot avoid recognition of the fact that we possess no record of mental facts unaccompanied by cerebral or nervous phenomena. Amongst organic beings we find a series of forms ranging from the more simple and homogeneous to the most complex, we observe that mental phenomena in all organic beings follow the same process of increasing complication; but we find also that every mental process has its foundation, so to speak, in an organic substratum which closely resembles it in its general characters. Taking man, who is naturally the most direct object of our consideration, we find that each individual has a consciousness of his own, just as he possesses an organism of his own. The organism and the consciousness are consequently closely connected elements, only separable by means of a process of abstraction. The individual, therefore, presents a double aspect—physical, anatomical, and physiological on the one hand; mental and conscious on the other. In other words, there cannot exist a purely mental or a purely physical individual, but we have in all cases a psychophysical being. From this it follows that the doctrines which consider the evolution of the species from a psychical or a physical standpoint alone must necessarily be one-sided and unsatisfactory. The purely psychical doctrine has been upheld by the spiritualists of all ages; the purely physical, which believes that organisms are developed through biological causes alone,[1] is quite recent. Further, the mental and physical

Theory of psycho-physical parallelism.

---

[1] For example, that of Dantec. See his recent book *Le déterminisme biologique*

aspects of the individual present a singular correspondence, which enables us to establish a kind of parallelism between them. It is, for instance, an accepted fact in anthropology that just as the human intelligence is of a higher order than that of animals, so the brain, as compared to the other centres, is proportionately larger in man than in animals.[1] Recent anatomical and physiological investigations have rendered more and more evident the correspondence existing between the functions of consciousness and of the nervous centres. That species of hierarchy, for example, which we have noticed in the nervous system, in which the lower centres are in a manner subordinate to the higher, finds its counterpart in the co-ordination of the various mental processes, of which the more complex are the result of simple elements variously combined. The whole of the processes of consciousness thus form a vast network, which may be compared to the complexity of the organs of the neural system. A yet more precise correspondence has been recently discovered by experimental Psychology in the relation (which can be mathematically determined) between the stimulus and the sensation. The terms of this proportion are the nervous energy and the mental phenomenon ; but nervous energy has as yet only been measured in the peripheral elements, the relation between the perception and the central cerebral energy being still unknown.

Modern Psychology has further succeeded in ascertaining with increasing precision certain correspondences which, though less susceptible of mathematical measurement, present a certain constancy of character, and are noticeable in all cases of mental phenomena which are accompanied by very accentuated states of feeling. In all cases of emotion, for instance, the physical and the mental aspects are easily discernible. In willing an outward action, the external manifestation is an essential part of the action itself, without which it could not exist. Even in those states of consciousness in which the cognitive element prevails there is a physical counterpart manifesting itself in definite feelings, such as fatigue, drowsiness, tension, exhilaration, etc., which are inseparable from all actions of the mind. There are to be noted, besides, other facts which belong to the field of pathological Psychology. It is well known that mental maladies, especially those which

(1896), and of Delage, *La structure du protoplasma et les théories sur l'hérédité et les grands problèmes de la biologie générale* (1895). This theory is followed by those psychologists who accept the doctrine of psychophysical materialism.

[1] See Höffding, *op. cit.*, p. 53.

follow a distinctly progressive course, are not only characterised by abnormal mental conditions, but also by affections of the nervous centres ; and that certain injuries to the centres are almost always followed by definite mental disturbances.[1] Likewise certain chemical agents, acting directly on the brain, produce mental effects of a given nature.

All this goes to prove the parallelism between the two series of mental and physiological phenomena, though we must be careful to note that this "parallelism" is not to be understood in a mathematical sense.

It was natural that theories on this subject should at first be purely metaphysical. The Cartesian dualism, which admitted a reciprocal influence between the mind and the body, was followed by Spinoza's theory, in which the two parallel series of phenomena were represented as an emanation from the Divinity, a conception of the world, according to which there exists a perfect order and correspondence between things as between ideas : *ordo ac connexio rerum idem est ac ordo et connexio idearum.*[2] Leibnitz formulated a similar, though even more idealistic, conception. In our own day experimental Psychology has placed the conception on a more scientific basis.

The correspondence between the physical and mental series of phenomena has its starting-point in the mathematical relation between the stimulus and the sensation, which Gustav Theodor Fechner was the first to formulate in the law which he named after Weber. He greatly extended the principle, and, going far beyond a mere parallelism between physiological and mental facts, conceived of all physical and all mental manifestations as two different forms of the same activity, whence his theory has been called one of identity.[3] This notion has more recently been developed by Harald Höffding, who goes even farther than Fechner in affirming that mind and body are two aspects of something which we cannot think of as resembling

Theory of identity.

---

[1] This subject has been ably dealt with by Ribot in his various works of pathological Psychology. We must not forget that pathological anatomy, as regards mental diseases, is still in a very primitive condition.

[2] Spinoza, *Ethics*, ii. 1—13, iii. 2.

[3] R. Falkenberg (*Geschichte der neueren Philosophie*, Leipsic, 1886) calls Fechner's system an "idealistisch gewendeter Spinozismus." Concerning Fechner's philosophical ideas see his *Elemente der Psychophysik*, p. 3 foll. "Die ganze Welt," says Fechner, "besteht aus solchen Beispielen die uns beweisen, dass das, was in der Sache Eins ist, von zweierlei erscheint, und man nicht von einem Standpunkte dasselbe als vom anderen haben kann."

either. Thus, in his view, the sensation we may have at a given moment corresponds to the state of our brain at that moment, seeing that one and the same essence operates in consciousness and in the brain.[1] A similar theory has been more recently developed by a Russian psychologist, Van Grot, who has endeavoured to demonstrate the identity of the two series of physical and mental facts by analogy with the recent theories on energy in the fields of physical and chemical science.[2]

A still less admissible theory is that of the modern neo-Thomistic school, in which modern scientific Psychology, after the overthrow of Descartes' dualistic conception, is returning to the animistic idea of S. Thomas, who merged the notions of body and mind in the indefinite conception of Soul.[3]

But to assert the identity of these two principles is equivalent to leaving entirely on one side the results at once of modern biology and of Psychology. It is now generally admitted that biological phenomena are neither more nor less than chemical processes, which, in their turn, are manifestations of general physical phenomena. On the other hand, the science of Psychology has proved that all mental processes, from the sensations up to the most complicated mental phenomena, have a qualitative character which distinguishes them absolutely from physiological processes. The problem is: how is it possible to bridge the gulf between the two series of facts, which modern science has only served to widen?

Finally, an empirical theory has been put forward by Bain in a short work entitled *Mind and Body : Theories of their Relations* (1873).[4] In Bain's opinion mind and body, physiological phenomena, and facts of consciousness are simply different aspects of the same thing, a view followed to a large extent by Spencer,

[1] See *op. cit.*, p. 64 foll. Höffding quotes among his precursors in this theory of identity, besides Spinoza, Leibnitz and Fechner, also Kant, who first alluded to it in the first edition of his *Critique of Pure Reason*. Höffding quotes also his compatriots Creschow and F. C. Sibbern. He expounded and defended his ideas at length in a paper published in the *Vierteljahrschrift für wissenschaftliche Philosophie*, Vol. XV., entitled " Psychische und physische Activität."

[2] See Nicolas van Grot, " Die Begriffe der Seele und der psychischen Energie in der Psychologie" (*Archiv für systematische Philosophie*, Vol. IV., June 30th, 1898).

[3] See D. Mercier (professor at the Catholic University of Louvain), *Les origines de la psychologie contemporaine* (1898), especially chaps. iv. and v., and his *Psychologie*; also the numerous articles published on the subject in the *Revue néo-scholastique*.

[4] See also the article by the same author in *Mind*, Vol. VIII., p. 402 foll.

who also sees a species of parallelism or correspondence between physical facts and the mental series which it is the object of Psychology to explain.[1]

All these theories on psychophysical parallelism have in different degrees an eminently metaphysical character. Bain and Spencer are more empirical than Höffding and Fechner; for the former limit themselves to the notion of a unity which presents itself under a double aspect, whereas the two latter imagine an original activity which manifests itself in two different forms.

<small>Interpretation of the concept of parallelism.</small>

The whole conception, however, is necessarily vague and hypothetical, and consequently, though adapting itself to a philosophical discussion, falls outside the scope of psychological research, which should confine itself to experience, and should reject all hypotheses, except those which are purely provisional. The theories of Fechner, Höffding, and Van Grot, and especially of Spencer and Bain, have moreover the serious defect of being too "intellectualist" in regarding consciousness too exclusively from the intellectual and cognitive point of view. This is a consequence of a tendency which has hitherto been too prevalent in Psychology. According to these theories, it would appear that consciousness consists only of sensations and perceptions—in other words, of cognitive elements. Psychology adopted a properly scientific method when, about the middle of the nineteenth century, owing principally to Bain, Spencer, and Fechner, it abolished the old-fashioned distinction between the external and internal worlds, and began to adopt for its own use the methods of physical and physiological science. On the other hand, modern Psychology has had to recognise that there are other elements in consciousness, besides sensations and perceptions, which have no direct connection with the external world, but are entirely subjective. These mental factors, to which Schopenhauer was the first to call attention, are the feelings and the processes of volition. In the external world we do not find anything resembling a feeling or an act of willing, nor anything resembling a qualitative (æsthetic or moral) value. In a presentation, considered by itself, there is neither aim nor will, so that the only identity which can be found between the external and the internal world is that which may exist between the two series of external objects and of presentations. But where can we find in the external world anything corresponding to, or identical with, the feeling or the will? This theory of identity leads

[1] *Op. cit.*, Part VIII. (see above, chap. ii.).

inevitably to the result that one or other of the two series, physical or mental, loses its specific character, transforming itself into an indefinable *tertium quid.*

Wundt's theory is much more tenable. Accepting, as he does, psychophysical parallelism as an empirical fact, with regard to elementary cognitive phenomena, he greatly widens the scope of the experimental psychological method instituted by Fechner, and gives the doctrine an interpretation which makes it impossible to regard it as a revival of the old Cartesian dualistic theory of the *influxus physicus.* Wundt does not admit that either of the two causal series can enter into and modify the other, still less absorb it,[1] and thus keeps clear of the dualistic and, at the same time, of the spiritualistic and materialistic theories.

Psychophysical parallelism must therefore be considered as merely an empirical statement that certain physical and physiological conditions correspond to mental processes; that the content of a sensation, and ultimately of an act of thinking, has always a physical side; and that feelings and acts of willing, while referring indirectly to perceptive processes, are accompanied by more or less accentuated physiological phenomena.

Nor must we be led into error by the fact, constantly adduced by physiologists and psychologists, that cerebral phenomena are the direct cause of conscious processes. They are the proximate cause, but by no means the only one, for the whole of the external physical world is more or less directly the cause of mental processes. Moreover, neither feeling nor willing find anything corresponding to them in external phenomena, for the external manifestations of the emotions and of the processes of the will are in all cases physical facts and nothing more, and have in themselves no attribute of value or "finality." Even considered from the point of view of cognition, consciousness does not follow a parallel course with the physical processes, thought being much less shackled by mechanical connection than is the case with what is called "the real." Thought takes the most varied shapes, and can even detach itself completely by means of its abstract conceptions from reality, and create an intellectual world of art and science, endowed, so to speak, with a life exclusively its own.[2] Another

[1] See the papers already quoted from the *Philosophische Studien*, "Ueber die Definition der Psychologie" (Vol. XII., Part I., 1895) and "Ueber psychische Causalität und das Princip des psychophysischen Parallelismus" (Vol. X., Part I., 1894).

[2] See Jodl, *Lehrbuch der Psychologie*, p. 77 foll., where all the objections to the theory of absolute parallelism are very ably set forth.

proof of the non-existence of an absolute parallelism between the mental and the physical can be found in the fact that not all cerebral processes are accompanied by corresponding phenomena of consciousness. It is very probable that, in order to produce a mental phenomenon, the cerebral, like the physical and peripheral, stimulus has first to reach a certain degree of intensity. We can only, therefore, say that the theory of parallelism is applicable as regards the cognitive elements, and even then only up to a certain point. It is quite insufficient to explain the relation between mind and body, or to be taken as the foundation of psychological science.[1]

Having thus given a sketch of the principal theories on the question of the body and the mind, we shall now examine the methods adopted by modern Psychology.[2]

[1] Amongst modern philosophers R. Ardigò inclines towards the theory of absolute parallelism; see his book *L'Unita della coscienza* (1898), Part I. Fouillée, on the contrary, points out the differences between the two series of facts; see *L'Evolutionisme des idées-forces* (1900).

[2] The question of the relations between mind and body, and the results obtained by physiology and histology is exhaustively treated in all the principal modern works on Psychology, and has produced an extensive literature in the shape of pamphlets and papers published in the philosophical reviews. The best survey of the question is perhaps the one given by Ebbinghaus in the recently published first part of his *Grundzüge der Psychologie* (Leipsic, 1897, Bk. I., §§ 3 and 4). See also, besides Wundt and Höffding, already quoted, Sully, *The Human Mind*, Part. I., chap. iii.; James, *The Principles of Psychology*, I., ii., iii.; Baldwin, *Handbook of Psychology*, Vol. II., Part III., chaps. i., ii. See also a notable, though rather one-sided, book by Lewes, *The Physical Basis of the Mind* (London, 1877; 2nd edit. 1893). A learned criticism of psychophysical parallelism is to be found in Masci's recent work *Il materialismo psicofisico e la dottrina del parallelismo in psicologia* (Naples, 1901).

CHAPTER IV

THE METHODS OF PSYCHOLOGY

THE discussion raised in the preceding chapters in regard to the object of Psychology, the relations between mind and body, and **Uncertainty** the reality of mental phenomena, finds a practical **of psycho-** application when we come to consider the methods to **logical** **methods.** be followed in psychological research. In no other science is the question of method so much debated as in Psychology.

The question necessarily arises how Psychology can possess so extensive a literature and have collected such a quantity of scientific data, if psychologists are still at variance as to what method they ought to follow. Conversely, if method has a decisive importance with regard to psychological research, doubts may arise as to the value of the above-mentioned works and of the data they contain. It must be borne in mind, however, that questions of method always come after the method itself has been, more or less consciously, adopted, just as questions of metre arose long after poets had been in the habit of composing verses. In every manifestation of the mind the unconscious always precedes the conscious. It is nevertheless a fact that no other science has witnessed such violent discussion over questions of method as Psychology has. Chemistry, Physics, Geology, and History, for instance, are satisfied with a few fundamental principles, which serve as a starting-point for research ; and the fact that Psychology requires to examine more critically the various methods which present themselves seems to point to some peculiar characteristic which distinguishes it from all other special sciences.

Psychology possesses, as we have seen, a character of generality which distinguishes it from the special sciences, allying it to **Psychological** Philosophy, and more particularly to Logic and Ethics. **research has** And it is this philosophical character which renders it **an inherent** **character of** necessary for Psychology to select carefully the prin- **generality.** ciples upon which to found its deductions, and to be very particular in regard to its methods of research. The philosophical sciences have the peculiarity of offering a much wider scope to discussion than the special sciences, owing to the fact that they are in themselves practically a criticism of scientific principles.

Psychology, moreover, on its own account presents difficulties unknown to other special sciences, owing to the fact that the object of its study is the processes of consciousness considered in their more general form as types. It has, therefore, many points of contact with other sciences, and occupies an intermediate position between the two great fields of Natural and Moral science. It might reasonably be objected that the necessity for having recourse to the help of other sciences is common to all branches of learning. For it is with the development of knowledge as with the evolution of organic or social forms: the increasing differentiation of knowledge into numerous branches has increased the mutual dependence of all these branches upon one another, though, naturally, in different degrees. Geography and anthropology, for instance, make such frequent inroads into the domains of natural, historical, and social science that it is difficult to draw a line of demarcation between them. Those sciences, however, have for some time possessed the advantage, only lately acquired by Psychology, of being entirely untrammelled by any dependence on philosophy and metaphysics, and being free to follow a strictly empirical method. Psychology, on the contrary, connected as it is with logic, epistemology, ethics, and æsthetics, has been, until quite recently, prevented from placing itself on an independent scientific footing by being obliged to deal with questions of a purely speculative order.

England was the first country in which Psychology acquired an empirical character, although even there it lacked a scientific method. On the Continent, from Descartes to Leibnitz and even later, Metaphysics reigned supreme, and the solution of psychological problems was always made to depend on general philosophical premises, and was not considered of much importance. In order to find a real psychological method, we must come down as late as Christian Augustus Wolff, who is the pioneer of that steady and methodical study which was taken up by the German universities and had so great an influence on the evolution of philosophical thought.

Historical survey of psychological methods.

In our brief survey of the historical development of Psychology, we have already noted that Wolff and his school considered "introspection" as the only means of obtaining a knowledge of the mental processes. This was a result of the distinction between inner and outer sense, the former being regarded as the means of obtaining cognition of the phenomena of the mind, the latter of those of the external world. Wolff's school dominated in Germany during the whole of the eighteenth century, and, with few exceptions, due to the influence of French sensationalism, the German psychologists of that period did not swerve from the method of pure introspection. Amongst the exceptions we have already mentioned Tetens, who was the first to make some attempts at experimental Psychology in the direction of the measurement of the duration of sensations. The principles of introspection and of the "inner sense" were an inheritance from the preceding metaphysical schools, which, from Descartes downwards, considered the soul, consciousness, or *res cogitans* as a supernatural essence, which could be understood only by means of a special, almost mystical, intuition. The mystical origin and tendency of the inner sense and introspective school were proved later on, especially in France, where, at the beginning of the nineteenth century, a reaction took place against the ideas of the sensationalists and materialists of the eighteenth century, and a new school of spiritualistic and mystic philosophers, led by Royer Collard, Cousin, and Jouffroy, made those principles the foundation of their psychological doctrines.[1]

The introspective method.
Recent criticisms.

Jouffroy may be called the last, and perhaps the most ardent, follower of the doctrine of the inner sense and of the introspective method, a doctrine and a method which were natural to a mind, like Jouffroy's, entirely closed to external objects, and absorbed in its own "Ego."[2] We cannot say that Psychology owes much of its progress to introspection; for, if we examine the results achieved in recent times through the exclusive application of that method, we find that scarcely anything has been added to the Psychology of the time of Wolff.

It has been often remarked that mental phenomena, owing to their instability and fluctuation, are not as susceptible of direct observation as the phenomena of the external world. We have seen that Kant considered this a permanent obstacle to Psychology ever becoming a real science.[3]

The introspective method started from the mistaken assumption

---

[1] See A. Seth, *Scottish Philosophy* (2nd edit., Edinburgh and London, 1890).

[2] Taine, in one of his best works, *Les Philosophes classiques du XIXième siècle* (1856), gives an excellent description of the psychologists of this school.

[3] The defects of the purely introspective method have been enumerated and ably described by Höffding, *Outlines of Psychology*, chap. i., p. 16.

that mental phenomena resemble what are called "objects," that they possess the stability of physical phenomena, and that they can be studied by the same methods. Just as a naturalist arrives at the knowledge of the composition of a mineral or the structure of a plant by examining it minutely and by making abstraction from any other impression which may warp the serenity of his judgment, so the psychologist, by concentrating all his attention on the examination of his mental acts, is enabled to perceive their whole mechanism, their origin and development, and to classify them accordingly. In these days we can hardly understand the implicit confidence which was reposed in the introspective method even as recently as the middle of the nineteenth century. It was not then understood that mental phenomena are in a state of continual change, that they are not "objects," but "processes," and therefore cannot, like physical phenomena, be reduced to a fixed and permanent substratum. Presentations were supposed to be unities, which cannot be separated into other elements, and the same notion obtained as regards feeling and acts of willing.

The old-fashioned metaphysicians, moreover, tended to neglect certain mental phenomena as less important and therefore less worthy of their attention. The sensations, for example, were left to the physiologists; nor was it imagined that their study would one day become the basis of psychological research.

The confidence in the introspective method had its origin in the belief that Psychology was a branch of Metaphysics, and the corresponding spiritualistic idea that we can have an exact cognizance only of the facts of consciousness. This principle once accepted, it naturally followed that an accurate study of the mental processes should have been considered unnecessary and that the scientific exigencies of the old psychologists should have been satisfied with incomplete classifications, made according to entirely subjective principles. As a consequence, it was not only impossible properly to observe certain mental processes, but it was natural that many of them should entirely elude observation. To be dominated, for example, by a strong emotion and to follow simultaneously the phases through which it passes is a contradiction in terms. As the word implies, to be dominated by a passion excludes our having the mastery over our actions, and consequently the possibility of stopping to observe and examine them. The contradiction is even greater if we consider the degree of calmness necessary for an objective and dispassionate study such as Psychology demands. When, under the influence of a powerful emotion, we stop to reflect, the emotion tends to be weakened, and may even disappear altogether. Indeed, the possibility of feeling impressions, which temper the strength of a passion, is in itself a sign that the emotion was not very strong from the beginning.[1] The same is the case with the current of our thoughts. If we follow a series of presentations, whether connected by a simple association or by a logical concatenation, the intellectual or imaginative process (owing to the necessity of directing the attention to the development of the process itself) is immediately affected, and becomes, with the added element contributed by the attention, a new state of consciousness, distinct from the first.

If these states are not susceptible of exact observation, others elude observation entirely. The introspective method naturally requires a mind matured and accustomed to follow the inner processes. How can a child, for instance, make observations of this sort? Or can one imagine a savage making psychological observations on himself? The study of pathological cases of mental disorders becomes impossible with this method; for we cannot imagine a lunatic having a full consciousness of his condition, and possessing sufficient serenity of mind to make observations on himself. The introspective method, therefore, limits psychological observations to a certain period of life in a mentally normal man, and, even within these limits, can give but very uncertain results, whilst it renders any analysis of the mental states in animals quite out of the question. The Psychology of inner perception is consequently condemned to an inevitable poverty of results and want of precision. The psychologists of this school, thinking to follow the empirical method, were often led on to conceptions, which overstepped the bounds of experience and assumed, in many cases, the nature of mystical visions.[2] The Psychology of the inner sense consisted

---

[1] See Brentano, *Psychologie vom empirischen Standpunkte*, p. 36.

[2] To give an idea of the vagueness of the majority of spiritualistic psychologists and of the almost mystic character they attributed to psychological observation, it will suffice to quote the following passages from T. Jouffroy's essay " Objet, certitude, point de départ et circonscription de la psychologie," written in 1823, and published in his *Mélanges philosophiques* (Paris, 3rd edit. 1860): "Au dedans de nous et dans les profondeurs de notre être, un principe se développe continuellement, qui va saisir hors de nous les réalités que le monde contient, et en conçoit des notions plus ou moins complètes, plus ou moins distinctes

mainly in a species of literary dilettanteism, which took the form of a "journal intime," wherein were noted the thoughts that passed through the observer's mind. A good idea of these pseudo-scientific writings can be obtained from the so-called psychological fiction of the present time, which has much analogy with them.[1]

This had been already noted by Immanuel Kant, who was of opinion that it was useless to occupy ourselves with the intimate account of the involuntary course of our thoughts and feelings, seeing that it only leads to mental confusion, and may even, under the influence of so-called superior inspirations or of forces extraneous to the will, plunge us into superstition and endless terrors, making " supposed discoveries out of those things we have ourselves introduced into our minds, like Bourignon, or Pascal, and even an otherwise admirable intellect, Albrecht Haller, who through the long-continued though often interrupted diary of his spiritual condition at last reached the point of asking a famous theologian, his former academic colleague, Dr. Less, whether in his extensive treasures of divine learning he could not find consolation for his troubled soul."[2] He goes on to point out the difficulty of an exact study of the phenomena of our own consciousness, arising from the fact that " in place of observing ourselves, we are apt to introduce extraneous elements into our consciousness." Kant accordingly proposed to found his empirical Psychology on the observation not of self, but of others.

Kant's criticism upon the introspective method.

Introspection, however, held the field for many years, and

. . . il embrasse ainsi le visible et l'invisible, l'apparent et le caché et élève dans son sein une image du monde, qui est la connaissance humaine . . ."
"Le nous qui est une réalité, sent en lui-même persister avec lui des attributs invariables comme lui ; ce sont ces attributs qui le constituent, lui et non toute autre réalité. Mais par delà ces attributs dans lesquels il se sent immédiatement et par lesquels il se manifeste à lui même, il conçoit quelque chose de plus fixe encore, de plus immuable . . . ce n'est plus ni le moi, ni une action du moi : ce n'est ni un phénomène ni une réalité individuelle ; c'est quelque chose d'une troisième nature, qu'il ne comprend que négativement . . . c'est l'objet de l'ontologie" (p. 199). The same idea was held by the Scottish philosophers, of which Jouffroy was a follower.

[1] See Lange's able criticism of the introspective method in his *History of Materialism*, Vol. III., p. 168 foll. ; also Sully's *Illusions* (1881).

[2] Quoted by Lange, *History of Materialism*, Vol. III., p. 169. See Höffding, *History of Modern Philosophy*, Vol. II., p. 301 foll. The same happened to Maine de Biran, though by nature of a positive turn of mind, and not given to mystic speculations.

even during the second half of the nineteenth century books were published in defence of the introspective method.[1]

Herbart's criticism. A new method was attempted by Herbart, who marks an important epoch in the history of Psychology for two principal reasons : first, because he wished to reduce all the phenomena of consciousness to simple elements or units ; secondly, because he endeavoured to combine systematically the results of English associationist Psychology with those of German metaphysics, and to found an empirical Psychology, logically based on rational principles. But notwithstanding this tendency towards a species of mechanical science of the mind, the starting-point of Herbart's system of Psychology is entirely natural, and, in spite of his efforts to give it a precise and mathematical shape, his method consists solely in inner intuition and in the subjective analysis of the mental elements. Some of the most notable points in his works are his analyses of certain psychological questions which have nothing to do with mathematics. Herbart's attempt, we repeat, is of importance as an indication of a desire for a more scientific method than existed before him, and although, owing to the adoption of the experimental method, Psychology took afterwards a different course, this should not blind us to his merits, or lead us to deny all scientific value to his attempts, even though they proved unsuccessful. Herbart is not to be judged according to the standards of to-day. If we consider that at the time his works appeared (from 1816 to 1824) psychological studies were under the dominion of the "faculty" theory, which was responsible for the aberrations of Gall, we may have an idea of the importance of his doctrines and of his beneficial influence on Psychology. Even to-day the principle of the inner sense and of introspection has some eminent upholders, who have, however, been obliged to make concessions to the new methods of research. One of the ablest contemporary psychologists of this school is Brentano, who, nevertheless, adopts the scientific method to the extent of

[1] Such as Fortlage's *System of Psychology as an Empirical Science according to the Observation of the Inner Sense* (1855). In his *History of Materialism* (1866), Vol. III., p. 143, Lange gives a most able criticism of this school of psychologists, and especially of Fortlage. He insists that there exists no difference between inner and external sense, and notes that even if Kant's fears of hallucinations and madness consequent on the abuse of introspection were exaggerated, this method is nevertheless the means of giving to the most fantastic conceptions of metaphysics the appearance of empirical deductions.

denying the possibility of inner "observation" in the proper sense.[1]

An important event in the history of thought, which had, after a certain time, if not immediately, a great influence over the moral sciences, was the advent of Positivism. We have seen how Auguste Comte comprised under that name certain doctrines which had made their appearance here and there, and were especially due to English philosophers, and how he proclaimed science, and consequently, observation and experiment, to be the basis of all knowledge. A deathblow was dealt in this way to the metaphysical conceptions of the idealistic school which were flourishing in Germany, where Hegel's philosophy held the field. Wishing to reduce all science to objective knowledge founded on facts, Comte naturally repudiated the introspective method in favour of external observation. In what was the latter to consist? The ideas, feelings, and activity of man manifest themselves in social institutions and in the products of nature and of art. These are preserved for us by history, so that from them we are enabled to reconstruct the evolution of the human mind, in the same manner as the fossils discovered under the earth's surface enable us to reconstruct the forms of extinct animals and plants.

Influence of Positivism and of the Natural Sciences. The ideas of Comte.

Comte considered Psychology and sociology as subordinate to biology, because the latter studies phenomena of a less complex nature than the former. Comte was therefore the first to conceive a social Psychology based upon biology.[2] On an entirely different principle Hegel founded at the same time, in Germany, a social Psychology based upon the philosophical principle of the evolution and concatenation of the manifestations of the human mind. As regards individual Psychology, Comte, whose ideas coincided with those of the French materialists, was of opinion that the mental processes could only be explained by means of the biological phenomena which attend them, and that the best way to the solution of the problem lay in the phrenology of Gall.[3]

Neither Comte nor Hegel, however, can be called psychologists

---

[1] He distinguishes between " innere Wahrnehmung " and " innere Beobachtung " (*Psychologie vom empirischen Standpunkt*), and criticises those who, like Fortlage, place exclusive reliance on inner observation.

[2] See Comte's *Cours de philosophie positive* (2nd edit. 1864), Vol. I., p. 30, etc., and Vol. III., p. 761, etc.

[3] See a criticism on Comte and his followers in Brentano's *Pyschologie*, p. 39 foll.

in the strict sense, for neither treats Psychology as a separate science. The first German psychologist of note, after Herbart, is Edward Beneke, who, however, did not contribute anything new to psychological science. Although a follower of the introspective principle, Beneke was, much more than his predecessors, under the influence of physiology, conceiving consciousness as a gradual development from the more primitive faculties (in his estimation, sensation and motion) to the higher faculties. The necessity of a method more consonant with the exigencies of science was making itself felt also amongst the followers of the classic introspective school.[1]

Whilst philosophers were thus casting about for a method in Psychology which, while adapting itself to their speculative tendencies, should yet afford a certain amount of precision in its results, attempts were being made in the domain of biological science, and especially of physiology, to arrive by a different way at more exact and positive results in the study of mental facts. The beginnings of Psychology must be looked for not only in general philosophy, but in various special sciences, such as physiology, zoology, sociology, each of which has contributed to the building up of the new science.

Physiological Psychology is sometimes erroneously confused with experimental Psychology. Although possessing some points of contact with it, it really forms a distinct branch by itself, dealing principally with the cerebral, nervous, and physiological phenomena which accompany the mental processes. Its origin is ancient, dating, one may say, from the time when the existence of relations between body and spirit was first realised, and it has always been distinguished by a materialistic tendency. It was first scientifically formulated by the psychologists of the eighteenth century, such as Priestley, the French materialists, and some of the followers of Wolff. Gall's and Spurzheim's phrenology is a complete system for explaining the processes of consciousness by means of cerebral phenomena. Physiology, however, was still hedged in by superannuated prejudices, and had not yet detached itself from the other natural sciences.[2] Gradually,

[1] Beneke entitles his principal work a *Manual of Psychology, considered as a Natural Science.*

[2] Biology itself was not separated entirely from natural history before the beginning of the nineteenth century, with Bichat, Lamarck, and Treviranus. Lamarck was the first to use the term "biology" in 1801; that same year Bichat pointed out the necessity of distinguishing a special group of physiological sciences from the other natural sciences.

nevertheless, the close relations between the nervous system and the mind forced themselves even upon those who, like Lotze, were most averse to materialism. Lotze was the first to adapt spiritualistic philosophy to the data of biological science ; but the real solution of the question of method lay in a combination of the experimental with the introspective, and for that it was necessary that the former should attain such a degree of perfection as to be applicable to mental phenomena.

We have seen that this combination had been attempted by Tetens in the eighteenth century ; but for a long time he had no imitators, and it is only recently that he has acquired the reputation he deserves.[1] After Tetens we find the experimental method of physiological Psychology applied by Weber, who, however, was considered to be solely a physiologist,[2] none of his contemporaries believing that his researches could have so marked an influence on Psychology.

Rise of Experimental Psychology. Weber.

Weber was the first to notice the existence of a certain proportional relation between the stimulus and the sensation ; but he did not extend his experiments to other besides tactile sensations, nor did he formulate any law on the subject.

The merit of extending these experiments beyond the limits of physiology and physics, and of applying them to psychological phenomena, is due to Gustav Theodor Fechner (1801 —1887) and Wilhelm Wundt. The fundamental principle of Fechner's psychological doctrine is the result of a happy combination of observation and philosophical speculation of the highest order, and its genesis cannot be understood without a knowledge of Fechner's theories on the relations between body and soul, with which we have dealt in the preceding chapter. It is a noteworthy fact that, whilst on the one hand his theories soared to the boldest heights of mystic speculation, on the other hand he descended to the mathematical determination of the minutest particulars of the most elementary psychophysical relations. Fechner admitted no difference between body and soul, but considered them as the same thing looked at from two different points of view.

Fechner.

The material world is the external form of divinity, the spiritual world the internal, the difference between them being only

---

[1] We have already mentioned Wundt's studies on Tetens in *Mind*, Vols. II. and III. ; also Stumpf, Dessoir, etc., on the same subject.

[2] We have already quoted Weber's paper on the sense of touch and on organic feeling (1846).

phenomenal, such as that which exists between the concave and convex sides of an arc.

Fechner, unlike his contemporary Lotze, does not admit of any break in the continuity of the physical causal series, and although it has not been demonstrated that the law of the conservation of energy applies to the material processes which accompany the mental activity, he is of opinion, nevertheless, that we have every reason for believing that that law does actually apply to them, as to all other physical phenomena.[1]

Fechner received from his master, E. H. Weber, the idea of a constant relation existing between the external stimulus and the sensation. This led to his formulating the psychophysical law, which he called by Weber's name, but which is also often called Fechner's law. Fechner had originally imagined a directly proportional relation between the stimulus and the sensation; but he subsequently arrived at the conclusion that the variation of the one is not directly proportional to the variation of the other. The variation in the intensity of the mental state is not proportionate to the actual force of the stimulus, but to the difference between the amount of energy manifested by the corresponding material state and that existing previous to the action of the new stimulus. Therefore, if we represent with da the intensity of the mental state, with $d\beta$ the variation of energy, and with β the pre-existing energy, we have the following formula:—

$$da = k \frac{d\beta}{\beta};$$

or, in other words, the sensation increases as the logarithm of the stimulus—that is to say, that in order that the former may increase in an arithmetical ratio, the latter must increase in a geometrical ratio.

The results of Fechner's experiments were set forth by him in his *Elemente der Psychophysik* (1860), wherein are to be found mathematically formulated the relations existing between stimulus and sensation in the case of the tactile organs and of sight and hearing. He also published several shorter papers in elucidation of various points of his theory and in reply to objections. One of the most notable appeared in *Philosophische Studien* in 1888,[2] and

---

[1] See Wundt's address, "Zur Erinnerung an Gustav Theodor Fechner" (*Philos. Stud.*, Vol. IV., p. 471).

[2] The year after his death, which occurred in 1887. The article is in Vol. IV., p. 161 foll., of *Philosophische Studien*.

is, according to Wundt, the clearest and most complete exposition of his doctrine.

Fechner with his psychophysical law opened the way to scientific Psychology. Henceforth Psychology definitely discarded all metaphysical influences in favour of experimental methods, which seemed to render possible the measurement of the phenomena of consciousness.

Meanwhile, three important works had appeared in England —*i.e.* Alexander Bain's *Senses and the Intelligence* (1855), *The Emotions and the Will* (1859), and Herbert Spencer's *Principles of Psychology* (1885). We have already alluded to their contents in chap. i. Somewhat in the style of Fechner, Bain, in the above-mentioned works, of which the latter is the more important, applies the method and data of physiology and of other biological sciences to physical research. He has some points of contact with the Scottish philosophers, though differing from them considerably, for whereas they admitted no other method but pure introspection, Bain assigns great importance to objective experience, and does away with the barrier between the "external" and "internal" worlds. Like the German psychologists of the beginning of the nineteenth century, he tried to treat Psychology as a natural science, but evinced in so doing a much more scientific spirit, and confined himself much more strictly to empirical methods. Bain may, indeed, be considered the real founder of that modern empirical Psychology, which differs considerably from experimental Psychology in that it does not rely only upon experiment, but assigns great importance to pure objective observation. Bain may with reason be placed alongside of Fechner owing to the abundance of data he has furnished, and to the novelty of the method he introduced; for if Fechner was perhaps more systematic and profound, Bain, on the other hand, was superior as an observer. We must now follow the course of experimental research in Germany.

The new English Psychology.

Bain's analytical Psychology.

Fechner had rightly entitled his work *Elemente der Psychophysik*, as it created, so to speak, a new science occupying an intermediate place between physical science and Psychology, and claiming as its object the study of the relations existing between the physical and mental aspects of life. After Fechner and Weber, various psychologists and physicists turned their attention to experimental researches of a psychophysical nature. Such were Fick, Helmholtz, Hering, Donders, and

Experimental research in Germany.

others.[1] But the chief merit of carrying out this transformation belongs incontestably to Wilhelm Wundt.

Experimental Psychology enters with Wundt upon a new phase. With Fechner it was "psychophysical" in the sense that it aimed principally at being "an exact science of the relations between the body and the soul, or, in general, between the bodily and spiritual, the physical and psychical world."[2] Wundt, on the contrary, in his "physiological Psychology" makes use of all physiological data which may contribute to a knowledge of the physical processes attendant upon mental phenomena, while at the same time he applies to the study of the elementary phenomena of consciousness certain methods proper to physiology. His physiological Psychology is, therefore, quite different from that of the materialists of the eighteenth century, as also from that of the English psychologists and physiologists of the nineteenth (such as Carpenter, Lewes, Maudsley, etc.), who pretended to explain the phenomena of consciousness by means of physiological and cerebral phenomena. Physiological Psychology, with Wundt, is combined with experimental Psychology, whereas other modern authors have kept more strictly to the former. The most complete work of the kind in English is Ladd's *Elements of Physiological Psychology* (1887—1890),[3] which, though very similar to Wundt's system, maintains a theory of dualism and of reciprocal pyschophysical influence.

Wundt began his scientific career as a Professor of Physiology in Heidelberg University, and distinguished himself especially by his studies on the nervous system and on the mechanism of the nerves.[4] From these his attention was turned to the mental phenomena which are connected with them; and as early as 1858 he published his *Beiträge zur Theorie der Sinneswahrnehmung*, in which he confuted the nativistic doctrines dominant amongst physiologists, regarding the origin of perceptions of time and space, and maintained the necessity of giving to psychological theories a

---

[1] Amongst Helmholtz's works (1821—1894), those that have a special importance with regard to Psychology are *Die Lehre von den Tonempfindungen* (1863) and *Die Thatsachen der Wahrnehmung* (1878). Hering has some important papers on "Space," "The Sense of Temperature," etc.

[2] Fechner, *Elemente der Psychophysik*, Vol. I., p. 8.

[3] The author epitomised this work in his *Outlines of Physiological Psychology* (1891). Another work of the kind, although with a materialistic bent, is Sergi's *Psychologie physiologique* (1888).

[4] Wundt's *Lehrbuch der Physiologie* came out in 1865; his *Untersuchungen zur Mechanik der Nerven und Nerven-centren* in 1871—1876.

physiological foundation. He also published other works of a psychological character, such as his *Lectures on the Soul in Man and the Lower Animals* (1863, and republished entirely revised in 1892)[1]; but his real work as a psychologist began when, in 1871, he took the chair of Philosophy in the University of Leipsic. In 1874 he published the *Grundzüge der physiologischen Psychologie*, in 1878 he founded the first laboratory of experimental Psychology, and in 1883 the periodical entitled *Philosophische Studien*, which published the experiments made in that laboratory. Wundt, like Fechner, is a philosopher, and although his *System der Philosophie* appeared in 1889 after his principal psychological work, some of the more fundamental philosophical ideas which it contains and which are connected with psychological questions had been already set forth by him in the latter.

We have already investigated the epistemological ideas on which Wundt founded his psychological method. The object of Psychology is to study the processes of consciousness in their general form; but, on the other hand, it is a principle founded on experience that nothing happens in consciousness which has not its counterpart in certain physical processes.[2]

Philosophical vindication of the experimental method in Psychology.

A simple sensation, the combining of sensations into presentations, the associations of the latter, and, lastly, the processes of apperception and of the will, are all accompanied by physiological phenomena; whilst other somatic processes, such as simple or complex reflex processes, though not comprised within the bounds of consciousness, are nevertheless important subsidiary adjuncts of its phenomena. In the study of mental phenomena some of the experimental methods which physiology applies to the study of nervous phenomena may consequently be made use of. Physiology and Psychology meet here on a common ground, the neural phenomena being the object of the former, and at the same time the indispensable and direct cause of the mental processes. All phenomena of consciousness, however, are not in an equally favourable condition for measurement. The parallelism of the mental and physiological series of phenomena extends indeed from the simple process of sensation to the more complicated processes of association of impressions and ideas; but each series preserves its own peculiar characteristics, and the laws governing one cannot

[1] Translated into English under the title *Human and Animal Psychology* Sonnenschien, London).

[2] See *Grundzüge der physiologischen Psychologie*, Vol. II., p. 644.

by any means always be taken as the substitute or completion of the laws governing the other. The mental series, moreover, comprises other processes closely connected with the presentative, which constitute the most characteristic part of consciousness —viz. the processes of feeling and willing. To these psychophysical parallelism does not extend. We have already seen (chap. ii.) that the fundamental characteristics of mental phenomena consist in their possessing a given qualitative value, in being always directed towards a given end, and in appearing as acts of volition. As these characteristics cannot, like physical phenomena, be determined in a purely quantitative fashion, the methods of physiology are not applicable to them. Although, moreover, the two series of qualitative and quantitative values are not separated by any sharply defined line of demarcation, and although the qualitative phenomena present a number of gradations from simpler forms of a less qualitative character to complex forms which possess that character in a more marked degree, Wundt is of opinion that the experimental methods can be applied only to the simpler forms. As to the more complex forms, Wundt thinks that we ought to rest satisfied with the investigation of external phenomena, such as customs, myths, and languages, which constitute the special object of what is called social or ethnographical Psychology (*Völkerpsychologie*),[1] and of which we shall have to treat later on. We must now see what development was given by Wundt and by his school to the experimental method introduced by Fechner.

The experiments made in psychological laboratories may be divided into two classes—those which refer to the measurement of the sensations and to the study of perceptions, and those which aim at determining the duration of certain mental processes. The former, which are called "psychophysical," have their centre in Weber's law; the latter, which are called "psychometrical," have been much extended of late years, and promise to contribute very important results to general Psychology. There are also some noteworthy experiments partly connected with the above, such as those dealing with the measurement of the extension of consciousness and of the attention, or with the retention of psychical impressions, or their reproduction and association. We may first examine the class of so-called psychophysical experiments.

Various experimental methods.

---

[1] See Wundt's *Outlines of Psychology* (Introduction, § 3).

Fechner, in his *Elemente der Psychophysik*, had already indicated the principal methods for the measurement of sensations ; Wundt and his disciples improved on those methods considerably.[1] Every sensation presents two elements— quality and intensity. Psychological experiments aim at measuring the intensity of sensations. As regards the intensity, the limits are determined by the *threshold* of consciousness, and the *height* or *upper limit* of sensibility. The psychophysical method must, consequently, have two principal objects in view— namely, the determination of the so-called " limit values," between which variations of the stimuli are followed by variations of sensation, and the determination of the regular relations existing between these variations. The threshold and the upper limit are naturally variable, rising and falling through the action of various causes, and sensibility with them. The feebler the stimulus required to cause a sensation, the greater the sensibility ; and conversely, the higher the upper limit of the stimulus, the greater the sensitivity to stimuli (*Reizempfänglichkeit*). There are two methods for determining the threshold of consciousness—the so-called "ascending," and the "descending" method.[2]

These methods may be used in combination, so that an average can be taken of the results obtained, the threshold being ascertained as exactly halfway between a just perceptible and a just imperceptible stimulus. The upper limit of sensibility

Psychophysical method.

[1] The most complete work on the subject is still Wundt's *Grundzüge der physiologischen Psychologie*, of which an amplified fourth edition appeared in 1893. Vol. I. of the fifth edition has already appeared, and the two other volumes will appear shortly. A period of nineteen years elapsed between the first and the fourth editions, and Wundt, in the Preface to the latter, has reason to say: " When this book came out for the first time nineteen years ago, experimental Psychology was still obliged to have recourse to the natural sciences. Little by little things have changed, and it has slowly formed for itself a special method." Other important works on experimental Psychology are Külpe's *Grundriss der Psychologie* (Eng. Tr.) ; Ladd's *Elements of Physiological Psychology* (1887); Ebbinghaus, *Grundzüge der Psychologie* (Part I., 1897 ; in course of publication); Sergi, *La psychologie physiologique* (1888) ; E. C. Sanford, *Course in Experimental Psychology* (1894; 2nd edit. 1898); Titchener's recently published *Experimental Psychology*. All the principal text-books of modern Psychology treat more or less at length of the experimental methods ; see those of James, Baldwin, Sully, Höffding, etc. See also Binet's *Introduction à la psychologie expérimentale* (1894), and Mantovani, *Psicologia fisiologica* (Hoepli, Milan, 1896).

[2] See *Grundzüge der physiologischen Psychologie*, Vol. I., p. 334 foll.

can be determined by means of a simple process, which consists in gradually increasing a given stimulus until it reaches the point where no new sensation can be perceived.

In order to determine the relation existing between the variation of the stimuli and that of the sensations, various methods have been adopted, their object always being to determine, at different parts of the scale comprised between the threshold and the upper limit, the variation in intensity of sensations which accompany variations in the intensity of the stimulus.[1] We have thus two kinds of sensibility—a so-called absolute sensibility, which corresponds to the threshold of consciousness, and consists in perceiving even the most infinitesimal sensation, and a "sensibility of difference," corresponding to a "threshold of difference," and consisting in the power of perceiving degrees of difference in the scale of sensations.[2] We have said that both the threshold and upper limit, as also the sensibility to difference, are variable quantities. This variability is the consequence of the different conditions in which the experimenting subject may find himself. Experimentalists classify these conditions under three different heads—viz. attention, expectation and habit, practice and fatigue.[3] The greater the attention brought to bear upon the stimulus, the greater also is the absolute sensibility and the sensibility of difference. This is a very important factor, and requires to be properly regulated, so that the attention be kept constantly in one direction and maintained at the highest possible pitch. There are various states of consciousness which can have an influence on the attention and, indirectly, on the sensibility. Thus depression or agitation or physical discomfort are apt to diminish the intensity of the attention; whilst, on the contrary, a strong interest in the work on hand and a great faith in its result render the attention keener. Expectation and habit may also modify the subjective conditions of the individual under observation. Expectation renders the sensibility more acute, for it resolves itself into a preparatory attention, which serves to strengthen the attention itself.[4] Habit also may be a cause of error, in that the individual, after a certain number of experiments, is apt to acquire

---

[1] *Grundzüge*, Vol. I., p. 336.

[2] These terms were first used by Fechner. See *Elemente der Psychophysik*, Vol. I., p. 242.

[3] O. Külpe, *Outlines of Psychology*, p. 37 foll.

[4] Külpe, *loc. cit.*, p. 42.

a disposition of the mind or nerves towards the reception of a determinate stimulus. In a series of sensations this disposition may easily lead to an erroneous appreciation, as some sensations may appear more and others less intense than they are in reality. Naturally this factor should be taken into account by observer and experimenter alike, and it should be reduced as much as possible to a constant value. Further disturbing causes are practice and fatigue.[1] Practice tends to sharpen and facilitate perception; fatigue, on the contrary, renders it slow and obtuse.

There are various methods for establishing the relations which exist in a scale of sensations between each of the latter and the corresponding stimuli. The most generally adopted method, which resembles the system employed in determining the threshold and upper limit of sensation, is the so-called method of "minimal variations,"[2] which has various forms, collectively described sometimes as "gradation methods" (*Abstufungsmethoden*).[3] A process they all have in common is to vary by imperceptible degrees the central stimulus up to a point at which a corresponding change takes place in the judgment of the observer. This general method comprises two principal forms—of "just noticeable differences" and of "mean gradations" (*der mittleren Abstufungen*), also called the "method of more than noticeable differences" (*Methode der uebermerklichen Unterschiede*).[4] The former consists in establishing what variation of intensity of the stimulus is required to produce a change in the sensation. The difference in the stimulus which corresponds to that difference in the sensation was called by Fechner "threshold of difference." The latter, which is somewhat more complicated, consists in the

---

[1] Külpe, *op. cit.*
[2] The term "Methode der Minimaländerungen" is Wundt's. See *Grundzüge*, Vol. I., p. 336.
[3] Külpe, *op. cit.*, p. 53.
[4] These two principal forms comprise various applications to different experimental cases. Thus Külpe (*loc. cit.*) divides the methods of decreasing gradations into four classes: (1) The method of minimal variations applied to the determination of the stimulus (also called "method of just noticeable stimuli"); (2) the method of minimal changes applied to the comparison of stimuli, or method of equivalents (method of equivalents); (3) the method of minimal variations applied to the determination of differences (method of minimal or just noticeable differences, or simply method of minimal changes); (4) the method of minimal changes applied to the comparison of differences (method of supraliminal noticeable differences, or mean gradations). The classification we have given is Wundt's (*Grundzüge der physiologischen Psychologie*, Vol. I., p. 336 foll.). See also Ebbinghaus, *Grundzüge der Psychologie*, p. 66 foll.

appreciation we give of a sensation as compared with other sensations.[1]

The other method[2] embraces two forms—that of "average error" and that of "correct and incorrect instances." The first is founded, says Wundt, on the principle that the smaller the difference of the stimulus perceptible in a sensation, the smaller will also that difference of the stimulus be which is no longer perceptible. One may consequently suppose that the exactness with which, given a first stimulus, a second is graded (*abgestuft*) in order to appear equal to the former, is inversely proportional to the magnitude of the threshold of difference. Therefore, given a certain intensity of stimulus, the method consists in diminishing the intensity in such a manner as to produce a sensation indistinguishable from the first. The precision with which this happens is inversely proportionate to the errors committed on the average.[3] The average of the errors committed in a great number of observations is the mean error, which may be of two kinds—"constant" and "variable." The method of "correct and incorrect instances" is founded on the fact that when two not very different stimuli, A and B, are made to act upon a sense-organ, owing to the oscillation of the sensibility of difference and other causes, sometimes A appears stronger than B and sometimes B stronger than A. The proportion between the number of correct instances and the total number of cases may serve as a measure of the sensibility of difference. By extending the observations to a large number of cases, the variable conditions, which exercise a disturbing influence on the results, are eliminated.[4]

These methods have for their object the insurance of the maximum precision attainable in psychological analysis. Till now it has not been possible to obtain measurements equally exact for every kind of sensation, but the results already obtained warrant the hope of better things in a not distant future.[5]

After sensations we must consider presentations of time and

[1] See Külpe's description of this method, *op. cit.*, p. 57.

[2] Külpe has a special section on the subject ("The Error Methods"), *op. cit.*, p. 64. Wundt puts them together with the other methods mentioned. This purely formal difference is the only one between the two authors.

[3] Wundt, *op. cit.*, i. 338. See also *Logik*, II. ii. 175; and Ebbinghaus, *Grundzüge der Psychologie*, p. 68 foll.

[4] Wundt, *Grundzüge*, Vol. I., p. 340; Külpe, *op. cit.*, p. 64 foll.; Ebbinghaus, *Grundzüge*, p. 70 foll.

[5] A notable attempt at eliminating as much as possible all individual errors which may concern not only Psychology but several other sciences, natural

of space. Space-presentations are mainly tactile and visual; time-perceptions acoustic. As regards the former, it is first of all necessary to determine the smallest distance between two tactile or visual stimuli that is requisite, in order that they may be separately perceived, and thereby afford a "perception of space." This minimum distance is called "threshold of space." The tactile threshold of space varies according to the different sensibility of the skin in the various parts of the body, and experimental Psychology has collected numerous data on the subject.[1] The muscular threshold, or threshold of "movement," varies also according to the different articular surfaces. Visual presentations are more complicated, as different elements come into play according as they refer to one eye or to both eyes. The question here is to find not only the threshold of visual extension, but also the threshold of the distinction between linear visual extensions, the threshold of the distinction of depth, and the threshold of the perception of movement in objects.[2] The perceptions belonging to the sense of hearing, or time-perceptions, are simpler.[3] Besides these there are also experiments regarding the "localisation" of sensations and presentations. These may be of tactile, visual, and muscular, as well as of acoustic presentations. The localisation of the latter, it ought moreover to be noted, is always the result of an indirect process, inasmuch as acoustic presentations give us no direct perception of locality.[4]

We have already alluded to "psychometry," or the measurement of the duration of mental processes. Psychometrical experiments are also called "experiments of reaction," the duration of the mental processes being the time between the action of the stimulus and the reaction which follows on its perception, and which consists in a movement. These reactions and the experiments concerning them are of various

Psychometrical methods.

---

and moral, is contained in a work by Fechner, edited by Professor G. F. Lipps. The work is entitled *Collectivmasslehre* (Leipsic, Engelmann, 1897), and is written with the object of establishing a standard of measurement applicable to several objects. This may be compared to Quetelet's attempt at formulating the so-called principle of large numbers. With regard to the value of these methods as applied to the moral sciences, see chap. vii. Regarding Fechner's work, see a paper by Lipps, published in the *Philosophische Studien*, Vol. XIII., Part IV. (1898), p. 579 foll.

[1] Wundt, *op. cit.*, Vol. II., p. 20, etc.   [2] *Ibid.*, p. 96, etc.
[3] *Ibid.*, p, 47, etc.   [4] *Ibid.*, pp. 32 and 93 foll.

kinds.[1] The simplest form is that of a "simple reaction following upon sensational impressions." The time which elapses between the impression and the reaction is called "time of reaction." The methods of these experiments are taken from physiology, and consist in the use of various instruments of precision, such as Hipp's chronoscope, the pendulum chronoscope, and control hammer. Experiments of reaction are simple and composite. The conditions of observation may change in both, owing to various causes, external (*i.e.* inherent in the quality or intensity of the impression) or, more frequently, internal (depending on the state of consciousness of the observer). The stimulus may, for instance, be preceded by some sign, which causes it to be expected, or it may arrive unexpectedly. On these conditions depend the different directions taken by the attention, upon which a disturbing influence may also be exercised by simultaneous stimuli, whether of a similar nature or the reverse. Disturbances may also be caused by poisonous substances, such as alcohol, chloroform, morphia, tea, etc., or they may be the result of permanent mental derangement.[2] As for composite processes of reaction, they come into existence when to a simple process other mental acts are added which cause changes in the subjective conditions and also in the duration of the reaction. There are four kinds of mental processes which have formed the object of experiments in respect to duration: (1) the act of recognition; (2) the act of distinction between two or several presentations; (3) the act of choice between two or several movements; (4) the act of association of one presentation with another; with which are connected simple acts of logic.[3]

We have said that the span of consciousness and of attention may be studied experimentally. There are two methods for doing **Measurement of the span of consciousness and of attention.** this: the first consists in ascertaining how many impressions produced and received simultaneously, and, if possible, instantaneously, we are capable of embracing; the second consists in putting into action a series of similar sense-stimuli, and in ascertaining how many new impressions may be added to one already received, before the latter is effaced from the consciousness.[4] The former method shows

---

[1] Wundt, *op. cit.*, Vol. II., p. 305; Külpe, *op. cit.*, p. 421; Binet, *Introduction à la psychologie expérimentale*, p. 103 foll.

[2] See Buccola, *La legge del tempo nei fenomeni del pensiero* (Milan, 1883).

[3] Wundt, *op. cit.*, Vol. II., p. 363 foll.

[4] *Ibid.*, p. 287 foll.

how many impressions may approximately be apperceived in a given moment, affording thereby a knowledge of the span of apperception, but not of consciousness. The span of consciousness is obtained by means of the second method of successive stimuli. Both processes are to be found graphically described in treatises of experimental Psychology.[1] The apparatus used to ascertain the number of impressions simultaneously apperceived is the so-called "tachistoscope"; for testing the extent of consciousness, there exists a complicated apparatus described by Wundt.[2] The oscillations of attention are also subject to measurement. One of the most important causes of disturbance of attention is the action of several sensorial stimuli. If all external impressions capable of disturbing the attention are eliminated, the stronger becomes the action of subjective impressions, caused, for instance, by breathing and by the action of the muscles,[3] especially those belonging to the organs which are being subjected to the stimulus—*e.g.* the tension of the tympanum, and so forth. For these experiments the graphic method, which marks the course of the oscillations by means of curves, is preferable. The graphic method is also used with success in experimenting upon those emotional states which accompany very strong physical commotions.

The last and most complicated class of experiments is that regarding mnemonic and associative processes, which are connected **Mnemonic and associative experiments.** with the span of consciousness. We have, first of all experiments concerning the apperception of simultaneous or rapidly succeeding impressions, amongst which are to be noted so-called "experiments of complication," the object of which is the association of different presentations. For these Wundt invented a special pendulum.[4] There are also experiments on time-presentations, on the influence of time upon the mnemonic processes,[5] and, lastly, on simultaneous and successive associations. As regards the feelings, experiments have had to be limited to the more elementary forms.[6]

[1] Wundt, *op. cit.*, Vol. II., p. 290.   [2] Wundt, *op. cit.*, Vol. II., p. 292.
[3] *Ibid.*, p. 297.   [4] *Ibid.*, p. 405.
[5] For an excellent epitome of recent experimental results in this department see Ward's supplement to Art. *Psychology* in Enagel Brit. Vol. XXXII.
[6] See, on this subject, A. Lehmann's *Die Hauptgesetze des menschlichen Gefühlslebens* (translated from the Danish into German: Leipsic, 1892). See also, as regards psychological experiments in general, Baldwin's *Dictionary of Philosophy and Psychology*; Sanford's *Course in Experimental Psychology* 1894); Titchener's *Experimental Psychology*; see also Binet, *op. cit.*

Psychological experiment has consequently reached such a development as to constitute an important branch of Psychology.

Criticisms on the experimental methods. But this result has not been obtained without opposition; for no sooner had Fechner published his *Elements of Psychophysics* than there began a heated controversy regarding his methods.

The point most open to discussion was, of course, the principle embodied in what he calls Weber's law. Psychometrical experi-

The value of Weber's law discussed. ments, on the other hand, owing to their character of greater simplicity, and to the fact that they were already used by physiologists, were attacked less on the ground of their direct results as in regard to their importance in general Psychology. The discussions on Weber's law, which are to be found in various treatises, deal with two principal points—

Various interpretations of Weber's law. its interpretation and its intrinsic value.[1] As regards its interpretation, one of the following three meanings is generally attributed to Weber's law—a physiological, a psychophysical, or a psychological.[2]

According to the first of these interpretations, which is of course followed by physiologists, the logarithmic proportion is not to be looked for as existing between the external stimuli and the sensations, but between the stimuli and the nervous excitation, the latter increasing in an arithmetical ratio, whilst the stimuli increase in a geometrical ratio. The sensations, on the contrary, are directly proportional to the nervous excitation.[3] This assertion is, however, purely hypothetical, owing to the insufficient number of experiments bearing on the subject. Nor does this theory take sufficient account of the complicated nature of the process of judging sensational intensity, such a process implicating not only the sensory but also the apperceptive centres.

The psychophysical interpretation, of which Fechner is the principal exponent, considers Weber's law as the expression of

---

[1] See Wundt, *op. cit. passim*; Fechner "Ueber die psychischen Massprincipien und das Weber'sche Gesetz" (*Phil. Stud.*, Vol. IV., p. 2, 1887); Ribot, *La psychologie allemagne contempaine*; Jodl, *Lehrbuch der Psychologie.*, Part II., chap. iv., pp. 210—235; Külpe, *op. cit.*; Grotenfeld, *Das Weber'sche Gesetz und die psychische Relativität*; Delbœuf, *Examen critique de la loi psycho-physique* (1883); Hering, *Die Grundlagen der Psycho-physik* (1876); G. E. Müller, *Zur Grundlegung der Pyscho-physik* (1878); Elsas, *Ueber die Psycho-physik* (1886); J. Merkel, "Die Abhängigkeit Zwischen Reiz und Empfindung" (*Philos. Stud.*, Vols. IV., V., and X.).

[2] Wundt, *op. cit.*, Vol. I., p. 390 foll.

[3] This theory is held by G. E. Müller, Dewar, M. Kendrik, Mach, Ebbinghaus, etc. James also follows it in his *Principles of Psychology*, Vol. I., p. 548.

a reciprocal relation between the corporeal and psychical activities. This view, however, makes the unjustifiable assumption of the equality of equally noticeable sensational differences. Moreover, it offers no explanation of the logarithmic relation which is held to govern physiological process and psychical experience, merely asserting that it is a fundamental fact.

There remains, therefore, the third, or psychological interpretation, of which the principal exponent is Wundt.[1] According to him, Weber's law is to be explained by means of the psychological processes, which occur in comparing the sensations to be measured. It refers, therefore, rather to a process of the attention, by which we compare two mental states, than to the sensations alone. We measure thus two different mental states, but without referring them to any fixed quantity. This measurement seems to indicate the possibility of a physiological explanation, which as yet is but dimly seen, owing to the limited knowledge we have of the central nervous processes. In our opinion, Wundt's psychological explanation, besides being consonant with the general character of the mental processes, explains also the intrinsic meaning of Weber's law.

There have not, on the other hand, been wanting those, such as Hering and others, who have endeavoured to deny all value to Weber's law on the ground that it does not give a quantitative measurement of the mental processes, being founded upon the minimum differences that we perceive between several sensations, differences which cannot be compared with any minimum sensation, which should serve as a standard of measurement. We cannot say, for example, that a given sensation of colour is two or three times greater than another.[2] Consequently Weber's law lacks the quantitative precision which is the principal characteristic of a natural law, and is therefore nothing more than a statement of the commonly observed fact that there exists a certain relation between stimulus and sensation.[3]

It is certain that an attempt to compare the intensity of sensation with the intensity of stimulus, susceptible of quantitative measurement, would lead to no useful result. Sensations and

---

[1] Wundt, *op. cit.*, Vol. I., p. 393, and *Logik*, II. ii. 183 foll.

[2] See Münsterberg, *Grundzüge der Psychologie*, Vol. I., p. 263, etc. ("Die Unmessbarkeit des Psychischen").

[3] E. Hering, " Ueber Fechner's Psycho-physichen Gesetz " (*Sitz. Ber. der Wiener Akad. Mathem. Naturwiss.*, Class III., Vol LXXII.). See Jodl's criticism on Hering in his *Lehrbuch der Psychologie*, p. 224 foll.

stimuli are of an entirely different nature and not susceptible of comparison. For this reason it is necessary to make use of different systems of measurement for the physical and the psychical series of phenomena. The stimuli naturally can be reduced to quantitative units, whereas sensations can only be compared with other sensations—that is to say, with purely intensive states.[1] It is a fact that the differences between the various sensations have all the same value when taken by themselves, and that they only acquire a special meaning when placed in a certain relation with others, so that one may say that this is purely a "difference" and not a constant "value." Fechner, however, maintained the "difference" hypothesis—*i.e.* that to a constant relation between the stimuli there corresponds a constant "difference" of sensations—although he ultimately admitted that Weber's law can also be interpreted in the sense that a constant "relation" between the sensations corresponds to a constant relation between the stimuli. This latter theory, maintained also by Wundt,[2] makes Weber's law a special case of the general psychological law of relativity, according to which every mental state has a value only insomuch as it finds itself in a relation with other simultaneous or successive states.[3]

It is necessary to emphasise the essentially "psychological" character of experimental Psychology, which, instead of basing itself purely on external observation and on physiological data, has sought to render introspection more perfect and exact in its results. "The increase of scientific exactitude must come," says H. Münsterberg, in *Psychology and Life*, p. 38, "from the use of more refined methods in self-observation, and all the work done in our modern laboratories of experimental Psychology is in the service of this endeavour, while the methods of histology and comparative anatomy, of pathology and vivisectional physiology, all in-

Psychological character of the experimental method.

---

[1] Fechner, in his last paper on this subject ("Ueber die psychischen Massprincipien und das Weber'sche Gesetz," in *Philos. Studien*, Vol. IV., Heft. II., 1887), recognised that Weber's law is susceptible of a twofold interpretation—psychological (*Unterschiedshypothese*) and physiological (*Verhältnishypothese*). The former is based only on the difference between the sensations, and is purely subjective; the latter corresponds to the constant relation of the stimulus, and is therefore a constant relation of sensations. See Wundt., *op. cit.*, Vol. I., p. 397; Külpe, *op. cit.*; Jodl, *Lehrbuch der Psychologie*, p. 223.

[2] Who formerly maintained the other theory. See *op. cit.*, Vol. I., p. 397.

[3] The purely psychological hypothesis is also sustained by Zeller, Delbœuf, Schneider, and Ueberhorst.

dispensable for the psychophysiological problems, are unknown, and ought to remain unknown, in our psychological laboratories. The hope that physiological Psychology will give us a fuller acquaintance with the psychological facts as such is therefore an illusion."

This opinion was not shared by those physiological psychologists for whom there can be no other scientific method than the physiological, and the idea of solving psychological problems by means of physiology has reappeared recently in that section of the experimental school which has espoused a species of psychophysical materialism, and which, though essentially German, has many adherents in all countries. One of the most eminent representatives of this doctrine, none other than Münsterberg himself, although recognising that the cognition of mental phenomena can only be obtained through introspection, maintains that, owing to the psycophysical nature of the individual, the laws which govern the formation, association, and development of such phenomena have to be studied by means of the cerebral phenomena, which go together with them. Even the psychological value of Weber's law is considered by these psychologists as purely provisional, on the assumption that so soon as we become exactly acquainted with the physical and chemical composition of the nervous processes we shall be enabled to find an absolute standard of measurement for all sensations.[1] Psychophysical materialism, however, as has been noted before, is guilty of inconsistency in declaring direct observation to be the only source of psychological knowledge, and in believing it necessary at the same time to have recourse to a totally different order of facts to serve as an explanation.

Psychophysical materialism discussed.

Experimental Psychology is an essentially "individual" method, which studies the mental processes as they take place in the individual considered in the fulness of his development and mental faculties; in other words, it supposes an adult and normal individual. Modern scientific Psychology has, however, devised other complementary methods, which are necessarily limited to elementary mental processes, and can all

The genetic methods.

[1] H. Münsterberg, *Ueber Aufgabe und Begriff der Psychologie*, 1891, p. 29 foll. In his last works Münsterberg's ideas on this subject appear somewhat modified. A fine criticism of these theories is to be found in F. Masci's already quoted work *Il materialismo psicofisico e la dottrina del parallelismo in psicologia*, p. 61 foll.

be comprised under the appellation of "genetic" methods, in that they study the formation of the mental processes in the individual, or in humanity, or in all living creatures.[1] Thus we have the "Psychology of infancy," "of peoples," and "of animals."[2] As a kind of check to these methods, which deal with progressive evolution, "pathological Psychology" studies mental retrogression and abnormal states of the mind.

The "ontogenetic" method, or "Psychology of infancy," has been for long in the hands of somewhat empirical observers, who have not been guided in their researches by very clear and precise principles. The works of Darwin, of Romanes, and of Preyer (whose book on the subject is classical), were followed by others which were all more or less of a biographical and descriptive character. The first to bring this branch of study into connection with general Psychology was J. M. Baldwin, in whose *Mental Development in the Child and the Race* the results of observations on the infant, the adult, and the race are continually connected and compared. Baldwin, in making use of the experimental method in his studies on infancy, does not omit to take into account the circumstance that an infant is incapable of that degree of concentration of attention necessary for experimental introspection. As he rightly remarks,[3] the Psychology of infancy is superior to that of animals and to pathological Psychology, because the child becomes eventually a man (which does not happen with animals), whilst when consciousness is in a pathological state, all its functions are more or less out of gear. The Psychology of infancy, moreover, allows of experimentation up to a certain point, and further affords an opportunity of following up the parallel course of mental and physiological evolution.

<small>The Psychology of infancy.</small>

A wider field is open to the Psychology of peoples, which is so closely connected with the evolution of the social and historical sciences. The scientific character of the latter only dates from the beginning of the nineteenth century, when they received a great impetus, especially in Germany, thanks to the progress of positive philosophy. The main

<small>Psychology of Peoples.</small>

---

[1] Cornelius, *Psychologie als Erfahrungswissenschaft*, p. 10.

[2] The first of these methods has been named ontogenetic, the other two phylogenetic. Experimental individual Psychology has also been called "functional" by some psychologists (cf. Titchener, *Outline of Psychology*, p. 21 foll.).

[3] See *Mental Development*, etc., chap. i.

principle of this school was to consider the facts connected with history and law in their natural evolution, explaining each event as the result of a series of other preceding or concomitant facts. The historical evolution of social structures, however, was not dealt with in Germany for its own sake, but rather as a consequence of philosophical speculations, which have more connection with it than with history, literature, or language, so that these studies may be said to have consisted more of reflections upon the "philosophy of history" than of "sociological" research.

On the other hand, several important ethnographical and historical works based directly upon facts made their appearance in Germany, notably the work of Bastian.[1] In England, where the doctrine of biological evolution was daily gaining ground, we find the important works of Tylor and Lubbock on the physical and mental conditions of primitive man.[2] Anthropology and sociology were in this way preparing the foundation of a new branch of scientific research. The curiosity of scientists had been further awakened by the accounts of travellers and explorers concerning the habits and customs of savage peoples, and the idea naturally suggested itself of comparing them with the customs of the present day and of primitive man. With these ideas Waitz wrote his voluminous *Anthropology of Peoples in a State of Nature*.[3] Sociological studies were daily becoming more popular, greatly favoured by Spencer's philosophy of evolution, which had introduced a new system of interpretation of historical and social facts.[4] The science of language, which had made such remarkable progress, afforded important materials to the study of comparative mythology: suffice it to quote the classical works of Max Müller.[5] Language, religion, and customs, therefore, were being studied in their origin, evolution, and reciprocal bearings, and the necessity

Anthropological and linguistic research.

[1] Bastian's work, *Der Mensch in der Geschichte*, appeared in 1860. He also edits a *Zeitschrift für Ethnographie*.

[2] The first works of Tylor and Lubbock on primitive civilisation compared with the present customs of savage peoples appeared in 1865.

[3] Waitz's great work, in six vols., *Anthropologie der Naturvölker*, was published between 1858 and 1872, and his book about the *Indianer Nordamerikas* in 1865.

[4] H. Spencer, *The Principles of Sociology* (1877). Spencer published also a work, in eight vols., entitled *Descriptive Sociology* (1873—1882), which is a collection of data regarding the customs of savage and semi-civilised peoples.

[5] M. Müller, *Essays on Comparative Mythology* (1858).

of finding an explanation of social and historical facts which should resemble the chain of cause and effect in natural phenomena, and which should be similar to the explanation of individual psychological facts, was daily and increasingly apparent.

The theories of Lazarus and Steinthal. The first attempt of this kind had been made by M. Lazarus, a pupil of Herbart, who published in 1855 a series of monographs, under the comprehensive title of *The Life of the Soul*, which dealt with the psychological aspect of various questions concerning art, language, customs, and certain forms of social life.[1] Lazarus took as his starting-point the individual Psychology of Herbart, who, in his estimation, " had given it a solid basis by seeking for the laws of mental life, . . . and, with the help of observation, speculation, and mathematical calculation, had created a science of statics and mechanics of the soul."[2] Psychology having therefore arrived with Herbart at its highest development, it was only necessary to apply it to the general mental phenomena, which individual Psychology had up to then neglected, explaining them " in accordance with psychological laws."

Steinthal published in 1871 a work of the same kind, entitled *Introduction to the Psychology and to the Science of Language*.[3] Taking his start, like Lazarus, from Herbart's mathematical Psychology, Steinthal attempted to explain the mental evolution of man up to the appearance of language, and to follow the development of the latter from simple and concrete onomatopœtic forms to the abstract expressions of logical thought. A powerful help and encouragement to these studies was afforded by the *Journal of Ethnographical Psychology and of the Science of Language*, founded in 1860 by Lazarus and Steinthal with the object of collecting essays on the psychological aspects of religion, art, language, social life, etc., which had appeared in different places and at different times.[4] The nineteen volumes of this periodical contained a very important series of monographs

[1] *Das Leben der Seele, in Monographien ueber seine Erscheinungen und Gesetze* (3 vols., Berlin, 1855; 2nd edit. 1875; 3rd edit. 1883).

[2] Lazarus, *op. cit.*, Preface, pp. iv. and v.

[3] *Einleitung in die Psychologie und Sprachwissenschaft*, which is a modification of another published by the same author in 1855, and entitled *Grammatik, Logik, Psychologie, ihre Principien und ihr Verhältniss zu einander.*

[4] *Zeitschrift fur Völkerpsychologie und Sprachwissenschaft*, herausgegeben von Professor M. D. Lazarus and Professor D. H. Steinthal. It lasted until 1889.

by some of the most eminent specialists, such as Delbrück on the science of language and comparative mythology, Lübke on the history of art, etc. Its object is explained in the Introduction by Lazarus and Steinthal.[1] This periodical was principally devoted to the science of language, which, amongst the moral sciences, was at that time the richest in data. This was the origin of a new science, which has been called "Psychology of Peoples" or "Ethnographical Psychology" (*Völkerpsychologie*). Lazarus and Steinthal have the merit of having been the first to understand the importance of these researches; although, in their estimation, the Psychology of peoples was not an independent but an applied science, whose object consisted in explaining social, linguistic, and religious phenomena according to the principles of individual Psychology.

Numerous objections have been raised against it, both by students of the various moral and philological sciences and by psychologists, which are sufficiently important to call for notice. The various moral sciences, though not easily distinguishable, owing to their mutual connections and interdependence, have each of them a special aspect of human phenomena to deal with. Thus the historian first ascertains the truth of certain events, and then seeks for the motives which have inspired those who have taken part in them. The sociologist, after having surveyed the actual conditions of society, looks for the origin of present institutions, and follows up their formation and evolution. Instances might be multiplied. Now, these sciences all consider different manifestations of the mind and the will, of which the causes must of necessity be mental, and their ultimate explanation a psychological one. Consequently the moral sciences make use of Psychology as a fundamental explanatory science, just as the physical and natural sciences find the ultimate explanation of natural phenomena in dynamics. On the other hand, the Psychology of peoples having for its object (in the opinion of Lazarus and Steinthal) the explanation of historical and social facts by means of individual Psychology, it follows that that science intervenes quite superfluously between general Psychology and the moral sciences, that explanation falling wholly within the province of the latter. An eminent linguist, Hermann Paul, in his *Principien der Sprachgeschichte*,[2]

Objections to ethnographical Psychology.

---

[1] "Einleitende Gedanken über Völkerpsychologie und Sprachwissenschaft."

[2] H. Paul, *Principien der Sprachgeschichte* (2nd edit., Halle, 1886). See in the Introduction, p. 8 foll., the "Critik der Lazarus-Steinthalschen Völker-

denies that the object of the "Psychology of peoples" is to give the psychological reasons of facts, of which the moral sciences, according to Lazarus and Steinthal, should merely give a description. Taking as an instance the science of language, Paul proves that its office does not stop short at studying the phonetic variations, but that it looks for the laws which govern them, both with regard to the physical organisation of the vocal organs, as also with regard to association of ideas and other psychological causes. If we, on the other hand, take some modern historical work, such as Mommsen's *Roman History*, we find besides a complete and exhaustive exposition of facts, a minute psychological examination of the actions of all the personages concerned. The psychological explanation of historical and social facts is a growing necessity, which is taken into consideration nowadays by all works dealing with those subjects, even political economy feeling the necessity of a psychological basis.[1] It might, therefore, be argued with an appearance of reason that the so-called "Psychology of peoples" has no defensible *raison d'être*, seeing that it resolves itself partly into individual Psychology and partly into the different moral sciences. It is, however, necessary to note several circumstances which attended the birth of that science, as well as the changes that have subsequently taken place.

At the time when Lazarus and Steinthal wrote their principal works, the introspective Psychology, to which Herbart had attempted to give a mathematical form, with his statics and mechanics of presentations, still prevailed in Germany. Experimental Psychology had hardly yet appeared, for it was in 1860 that Fechner brought out his *Elements of Psychophysics*, which, at the time, passed almost unobserved. Gradually, however, experimental Psychology came into prominence with the works of Horwicz, Wundt, and others, and, as we have seen, it is pre-eminently an individual method. Now, the individual, considered alone and severed from intercourse with his kind, is an abstraction of the mind which we do not meet with in reality, and of whose existence we have no proof. Modern sociology has proved the absurdity of the individualistic

psychologie." This work is also founded on Herbart's Psychology. See the criticism on the third edition by O. Dietrich in the *Zeitschrift für romanische Philologie*, Vol. XXIII.

[1] On the psychological interpretation of historical facts, see Bernheim, *Lehrbuch der historischen Methode*, chap. v.

theories, so much in vogue during the eighteenth century. The individual is born and passes through the various stages of his development in a community of other individuals like himself, owing many of the physical and moral qualities which he possesses to his surroundings. Psychology, like the physical sciences, makes use of abstraction only as a necessary means, not as a general scientific principle. But when we reject the possibility of constructing an individual Psychology not founded on experiment, we must remember that not all the psychical manifestations of the individual are of that simple nature which, in the present state of knowledge, is the *sine quâ non* of experimentation. There exist much more complicated mental processes, which are the product of social life and which would be unthinkable apart from it, such as language or (which is equivalent) logical and abstract thought, religious and social feelings. Individual Psychology being thus limited to certain simple forms of social life, the "Psychology of peoples" can be no longer considered, as Lazarus and Steinthal considered it, simply an application of the principles of individual or general Psychology, but acquires a more important aspect as an integral part of the latter. Ethnographical Psychology comes in where the experimental method cannot be applied.

Specific character of social psychological processes.

Let us now examine its various modes of proceeding.[1] The principle on which it is founded is that certain forms of mental life are the result of man's living in a society, and are unthinkable if we consider the isolated individual. The most important "social" manifestation of man, without which he cannot have relations with other men, is language, which is the result of a combination of physiological and mental factors, which follow the same course in the species and in the individual. Language is essentially the vehicle of human thought, and supposes an intellectual development capable of forming abstract notions; it therefore embraces some of the most complex processes of mental activity.[2] Another important product of social life is found in religious and mythological ideas which have existed in all times. These ideas constitute the original germ of those mental activities whose object is the knowledge of the universe and man—in other words, of

---

[1] Concerning the new interpretation to be given to the Psychology of peoples, see Wundt's fine article "Ueber Ziele und Wege der Völkerpsychologie" (*Philosophische Studien*, 1887, Bd. IV., Heft I.).

[2] On the general development of language, see H. Paul, *Principien der Sprachgeschichte*. See also Wundt, *Ethik*, Part I., chap. i., pp. 2, 3.

science and philosophy. A third and no less important manifestation of social life consists in all that concerns the relations between civilised men, and which goes under the generic appellation of manners and customs. Still other important products of social life are to be found in the fields of art and literature.

We have often said that the object of Psychology is to discover the general and typical forms of the mental processes, and that it should consequently eschew all that presents a singular and individual character.[1] The various moral sciences, on the contrary, are not confined to the formulation of general principles on the evolution of language, of religion, or of manners and customs, but concern themselves also with the development of one particular form of language, religion, or society, so that they are all of too limited and particular a character to serve as a complement of individual Psychology. They may be of use in checking its results, but they cannot compensate for its shortcomings. The Pyschology of peoples, as we have said, has for its object social mental products; but it studies them only in the earlier and more general forms, which are in a measure similar to individual mental processes, and can be better understood by means of direct observation. For this reason many modern works on anthropology and criminal sociology, such as those by Ferri, Lombroso, Sighele, and others, cannot properly be included under the name of social Psychology. We have, on the other hand, good examples of ethnographical Psychology in the splendid work by J. M. Baldwin, entitled *Social and Ethical Interpretations in Mental Development*, in Biese's *Entwicklungsgeschichte des Naturgefühls*; in Bourdon's *L'expression des émotions et des tendances dans le langage*; and also in several most original works by G. Tarde (chiefly *Les lois de l'imitation*), which occasionally overstep the limits of Psychology and enter the field of the philosophy of history.

Difference between Psychology and the moral sciences.

Difference between the Psychology of peoples and the history of philosophy.

Notwithstanding these theoretical distinctions, it is inevitable that some of the moral sciences should be occasionally confused, especially in their general principles, with the Psychology of peoples. This is the case, for instance, with Sociology which, in studying the general features of social life in all its manifestations, necessarily invades the field of ethnographical Psychology, especially when it deals with the primitive states of civilisation. Similarly, both Sociology and

[1] Paul says as much in his *Principien der Sprachgeschichte* (Introduction, p. 10) : " Die Psychologie hat es niemals mit der concreten Gestaltung einer einzelnen

Ethnographical Psychology may be confused with the Philosophy of History. This science, which has for its object the laws governing historical events, acquired a scientific character with Giovan Battista Vico, and owes much of its progress at the beginning of the nineteenth century to Hegel's idealistic philosophy. Hegel's Philosophy of History embraces the Psychology of peoples, sociology, and the history of religion and art ; but after Hegel these various branches were separated. The philosophy of history, although it has its foundation in history as well as in individual and ethnographical Psychology and sociology, keeps nevertheless a special end in view, for, whereas these sciences aim at collecting and explaining certain facts, the philosophy of history endeavours to distinguish the laws which govern them, comparing historical laws with the other laws of the universe in order ultimately to form a synthetic judgment on the general value of the historical facts themselves.[1] Consequently, though it may be possible to mistake part of the philosophy of history for sociology, and even for history itself, it is absolutely impossible to mistake it for ethnographical Psychology. The latter deals only with certain psychological phenomena of the social consciousness, whereas the philosophy of history extends to all history, and does not confine itself to principles, but deals also with facts.

The Psychology of animals has received a good deal of attention in recent years, though as yet it lacks scientific exactness. Romanes, Flourens, and others are rather collectors of anecdotes than methodical observers. On the other hand, Charles Darwin, and various zoologists, such as Brehm, have collected some reliable information ; whilst Vignoli and Lloyd Morgan have recently succeeded in giving to animal

The Psychology of animals.

Menschenseele, sondern nur mit dem Allgemeinen Wesen der seelischen Vorgänge zu thun. Was berechtigt uns daher den Namen dieser Wissenschaft für die Beschreibung einer concreten Gestaltung der geistigen Eigenthümlichkeit eines Volkes zu gebrauchen ?"

[1] See Bernheim, chap. i. of his *Lehrbuch der historischen Methode*, where he deals with the connections between " history on the one hand, and philology, political science, sociology, philosophy, anthropology, and the natural sciences on the other." See also Barth, *Die Geschichtsphilosophie Hegels und der Hegelianer bis auf Marx und Hartmann* (1890); F. Jodl, *Die Kulturgeschichtsschreibung, ihre Entwicklung und ihr Problem* (1878) ; E. Gothein, *Die Aufgaben der Kulturgeschichte* (1889); G. Simmel, *Die Probleme der Geschichtsphilosophie* (1892). The latter work, which had a certain vogue in Germany, is rather unsatisfactory, and cannot be commended for its clearness.

Psychology a more scientific character.[1] The difficulties of this branch of Psychology are considerable, owing to the necessity of reconstructing the mental life of animals by means of a process of induction, based on certain similarities which it probably has with our own. It is not surprising, therefore, that hasty and even fantastic conclusions are sometimes arrived at. Up to a certain point animals are susceptible of being experimented upon, but in a far less degree than man, and in a different way, both as regards the experiment itself and the aptitudes of the animal.

As regards pathological Psychology, several questions are hotly debated. It is natural that alienists, whose special occupation is the study of mental diseases, should often attribute to the latter a greater importance as means of arriving at a knowledge of normal mental states than really belongs to them. It is an undoubted fact that mental disturbances are accompanied by certain abnormally developed mental conditions, which help to explain the origin and development of the corresponding normal conditions. Moreover, the dissolution of states of consciousness can very well be appealed to in explanation of the inverse and normal process of evolution. Aphasia, for example, has been of great use in the explanation of the functions of speech, amnesia for that of association of ideas, and so forth. We must be careful, however, not to exaggerate the importance of this method of study. French contemporary Psychology, for instance, has been based almost solely upon the observation of morbid cases, with the result that the student is often in doubt whether he is reading a work on normal or abnormal Psychology. In the use of this method, it must always be borne in mind that the data of normal individual Psychology are the starting-point; and that a clear knowledge of normal cases must precede that of abnormal ones. Within certain limits, experiment may be applied to the study of pathological Psychology, provided the very different conditions as compared to normal cases[2] are taken into account.

Pathological Psychology: its recent progress.

Little need be said concerning the help afforded to Psychology by the study of criminals, which, as a subdivision of the science of

---

[1] See Vignoli, *Della legge fondamentale dell' intelligenza nel regno animale* (Milan, 1877), Introduction; C. Lloyd Morgan, *Introduction to Comparative Psychology*, iii. 50 foll.

[2] Ribot combines with great ability the psychiatric and the psychological methods. The experimental studies of E. Kraepelin, the alienist, who edits a publication entitled *Psychologische Arbeiten*, are also worthy of notice.

mental anomalies, affords some very useful data concerning the impulses, social instincts, etc.

Fierce controversy has raged of late years as to the value of so-called hypnotic experiments conducted on subjects in a state of artificially produced sleep. In these cases also it must be remembered that an experiment made upon a person in a hypnotic state, and under the influence of another person's suggestion, can have little value from the psychological point of view, owing to the fact that the subject is deprived of just that condition which is essential in ordinary experiments—viz. the consciousness of his own self, of his own actions, and of what is taking place within himself. These hypnotic states, if compared with certain normal mental conditions (such as semi-consciousness) which they resemble, may help to throw light upon the latter, but cannot of themselves explain the course of the fundamental processes. On the contrary, it is through the knowledge of the latter, acquired by means of experiments conducted upon adult and normal subjects, that we are enabled to understand the hypnotic states themselves. What data can a person under hypnotic influence furnish regarding the relations between the stimulus and the sensation, the extent of consciousness, the retention of images and ideas, and so forth, when that person sees and feels solely through another's will, which he is obliged blindly to obey?[1]

In all indirect psychological methods it is, therefore, necessary to draw a sharp distinction between psychological research and the researches proper to the sciences which are auxiliary to Psychology. It is sometimes undoubtedly hard to say where Psychology ends and some special science begins. Psychological considerations of a general nature are to be found in any work dealing with the moral sciences; but what distinguishes Psychology from the latter is its character of high generality, in virtue of which it deals not with some particular mental manifestation, but with all mental manifestations treated as types. Many works are published nowadays under the title of psychological studies, or essays, which, as a matter of fact, are special treatises on some particular subject of a historical, philological, or social nature, and therefore deficient in the principal characteristic of Psychology— namely, generality.

Having thus enumerated all the methods which may serve the purposes of Psychology, we shall proceed to examine their

[1] See Wundt's important work *Hypnotismus und Suggestion*, published in *Philosophische Studien* (1892, Vol. VIII.).

comparative merits. We have had occasion to see that introspection is the basis of the experimental method, for without it no perception of the mental processes would be possible, and consequently there would not exist a psychological science. The experimental method, it is well to repeat, does not simply consist, as is sometimes thought, in a deduction of the mental processes from a knowledge of the physical processes which accompany them, but in the application of physiological methods to psychological analysis. If introspection is necessary to the experimental method, it is as necessary to the objective method—*i.e.* to comparative Psychology in general, to the Psychology of peoples, of infancy, of animals. It is a commonly known fact that we can only have an indirect knowledge of the feelings and thoughts of others, being obliged, so to speak, to reconstruct them in accordance with their external manifestations and by analogy with our own modes of thinking and feeling. Needless to say, this process of induction is accomplished naturally, and with intuitive rapidity. Another aid to the interpretation of the mental states of others, and of the processes of consciousness in general, is the recollection we have of our own past mental acts. This, though an indirect method, is closely allied to direct inner perception, of which we may say it is an attenuated form.[1] This being the case with respect to adult and normal individuals, it is all the more so with infants and animals, whose mental processes we can only approximately comprehend through the resemblance which their actions bear to our own. The same may be said of the Psychology of peoples. Here it is not possible to penetrate into the state of mind of other persons; but it is a case of reconstructing states of consciousness from documents which have no meaning by themselves, but only in proportion to the psychical contents that we attribute to them. The difficulty of this operation is manifest. We are able to translate more or less exactly the written symbols of an ancient tongue, because the outer forms of a language change very slowly, even though the meaning may have

[1] Külpe, in his *Outlines of Psychology*, divides the methods of Psychology into two principal categories—direct and indirect methods. The former embrace introspection and the experimental method, with which are connected the physical and mental relations of dependence and the dispositions of the psychophysical individual. The latter comprise the mnemonic and the linguistic methods, and the auxiliary methods which are concerned with pathological and hypnotic mental states, as well as with mental evolution and the mental productions of history, art, and literature.

undergone a complete transformation. It is consequently necessary not only to reconstruct the words, but also the primitive meaning of a document, and in this the assistance of introspection is invaluable as a starting-point for inductive research. In this way all the methods of indirect Psychology are reduced to interpreting the mental states through the direct knowledge we have of our own states of consciousness. Introspection is, therefore, the centre of all research and the immediate source of any knowledge we may possess of our mental processes. Other methods can only serve to direct and to complete it,[1] so that Comte's notion of substituting external observation for introspection must absolutely be rejected. Social and historical facts, moreover, are neither more nor less than manifestations of individual consciousness; and we have no other way of arriving at a knowledge of the latter than by means of the observation of our own mental states.[2] If this holds good with regard to the observation of the mental acts of other individuals similar to ourselves, and of historical documents, of children, of animals, or of the insane, it does so to a still greater extent in the case of the physiological phenomena which accompany mental processes. In themselves these are merely quantitative physical facts, whose qualitative value depends upon the interpretation we put upon them : without this they are for us as meaningless as the words of an unknown tongue.[3] On the other hand, no interpretation can be arrived at without the direct cognition of the facts of consciousness, obtained by means of introspection aided by experiment.

What, then, is the relation of the experimental method to

[1] Höffding (*Outlines of Psychology*, p. 24) distinguishes the methods of Psychology into two classes, subjective and objective, in which he agrees with Spencer (*Principles of Psychology*, Vol. I., Part I., chap. vii.). Subjective Psychology is founded on direct introspection; objective Psychology is to be distinguished, according to Höffding, into physiological and sociological. The latter embraces the Psychology of infancy, of animals, of peoples, of language, of literature, etc. James, in his *Principles of Psychology*, distinguishes psychological methods as falling within three divisions—introspective, experimental, and comparative (pp. 185—194). The same distinction is made by Sully, Baldwin, Jodl, Stout, and others.

[2] See a criticism of Comte's theory in Brentano, *Psychologie vom empirischen Standpunkte*, p. 39 foll.

[3] Lange, in his *History of Materialism*, notes as much. Cf. Wundt's *Human and Animal Psychology*, p. 453; as also his writings concerning the "Definition of Psychology," and on the "Psychophysical Problem" (*Philosophische Studien*, Vols. X. and XII.), in which he discusses at great length the theories of the neo-materialists.

other psychological methods? Some modern psychologists consider these different methods as distinct branches of Psychology, which may be separately treated.[1] Others, on the contrary, while disposed to adopt the experimental method, do not consider it necessary for psychological analysis, but are of opinion that it should be restricted to the elementary processes more closely connected with nervous phenomena, and, moreover, that it should be completely separated from the rest of Psychology, and made into an intermediate science of physiological Psychology. In all other things (seeing that the followers of these theories adhere, as a rule, to the old-fashioned method of pure inner perception) psychological analysis should proceed on its own way untrammelled by any connection with other sciences, and relying solely upon the direct intuition of mental facts.

Value and limitations of the experimental methods.

There are also those who, mixing up experimental with physiological Psychology, believe that it is nothing but a branch of physiology. This theory, which had a certain vogue about twenty years ago, at the time of the first psychological experiments, counts but few supporters at the present time, even among physiologists.[2] We have already discussed and rejected it, together with the theory of the psychophysical materialists, which is based upon a false interpretation of the principle of psychophysical parallelism and of Fechner's law. On the other hand, the first of these theories, which concerns itself directly with the position and value of experimental Psychology, as compared with other psychological methods, offers greater scope for discussion.

The criticisms brought to bear upon the experimental method in Psychology at the present time, when it has produced such excellent results, consist mainly in pointing out that the field of psychological experiment is very limited, and that it can never be applied to the more complex mental processes. This point requires elucidation. During recent years experiments have been made in various psychological laboratories and especially in Leipsic with regard to the measurement of various sensations. Psychometrical experiment, moreover, has been applied to some exceedingly complicated processes. There is consequently every reason to hope that they will achieve in the future yet more important results, and that they may even have a practical appli-

[1] For instance, Spencer, *Principles of Pyschology*, Vol. I., Parts I. and VII.
[2] Amongst the most noteworthy supporters of this theory are Lewes and Maudsley.

cation, as in the case of mnemonic experiments, to present methods of education.[1] It is nevertheless certain that experiment cannot overstep the limits, beyond which mental phenomena assume a primarily qualitative aspect and elude all exact measurement. The intrinsic value, for example, of a religious, æsthetic, or moral sentiment cannot be determined quantitatively ; and even could their course be ascertained with exactitude, it would possess but a limited importance, owing to the fact that their mode of acting depends far more on their intrinsic and qualitative value than on the time they require to develop, or on their relation with external causes.[2] In the case of sensations, presentations, and simple associations, where the qualitative aspect is secondary, the experimental method finds no obstacle. Measurement, moreover, of sensations is possible only in so far as there exists a constant relation between them and external stimuli. Thus, when a given stimulus acts upon us, we respond to it with a certain sensation, which must inevitably take place. It is quite different in the case of mental processes, which are not directly caused by external impressions, but have a purely internal, or, as it is called, "central," origin. Just as it is exceedingly difficult to localise complex cerebral functions, owing to the extreme complexity of the neural processes which take part in them, so it is not always possible to say what consequences may follow upon a central stimulus, owing to the number of associative processes to which it may give rise. In this case we must rest satisfied with very general data, which cannot be obtained through experiment, but only through observation. The greater number, moreover, of these complicated processes are the result of a gradual evolution of the species, and of the association of many individuals, so that their genesis must be sought for in the history of the social community.

We do not, however, intend to detract from the value of experiment in psychological research. It is certain that, if we wish to judge Psychology by the standard of the physical sciences, the latter are far superior to it in exactness. Pyschology, however, should be judged by a very different criterion, and in accordance

[1] A book has been published recently by Binet and Henry entitled *Fatigue intellectuelle*, which is founded on laboratory experiments, and may be of great utility with respect to pedagogical methods and their applications.

[2] On the limits of the experimental method in Pyschology see J. M. Baldwin's *Handbook of Psychology*, Vol. I., p. 29 ("Limitation of the Experimental Method"); Stout's *Manual of Psychology*, p. 26 foll. ; Titchener's *Outline of Psychology*, p. 42 foll. ; Ladd's *Psychology Descriptive and Explanatory*, p. 22.

with very special principles. Nor must it be forgotten that it deals with " quantities of value," and not with " values of quantities." There are, moreover, physical sciences which are not always able to avail themselves of the experimental method. Meteorology, Geology, Astronomy, and Geography have to be satisfied with observation without experimentation, achieving, notwithstanding, very important results. Even the sciences which make large use of the experimental method have sometimes to limit its application and to complete it by means of observation. This is the case with the Biological sciences. The same occurs with Psychology, which in its methods is somewhat similar to biology. The latter has, in general, to limit its experiments to simpler cases, seeing that the more complicated organisms lend themselves far less to experiment, in the first place because they are less likely to survive the removal of some organ, and, in the second place, because their more complex biological conditions are an obstacle to exact induction. By means of experiments on animals of simple organisation and by comparing the results obtained with what has been observed in the more complicated processes, it has been possible to explain the causes of many biological phenomena, and to ascertain their course with a certain amount of precision. The moral sciences, during the nineteenth century, have adopted a similar method, trying to find an explanation of salient historical and economical events through the study of simple facts of lesser importance. In the case of biological science, experiment and observation complete and check one another reciprocally. The former points out the conditions required for the occurrence of a given phenomenon ; the latter finds confirmation of the results thus obtained in those cases where the conditions are more complicated. Nor can it be otherwise in the case of Pyschology. Although the experimental method may only be applied to the more elementary processes, these are capable of throwing much light upon the mode of evolution of the more complicated ones, seeing that the fundamental laws of psychological activity are the same in both. If it is possible, therefore, to apply the experimental method to the simpler mental processes, the results obtained should not be left in isolation, but should serve, on the contrary, as a foundation for psychological research, and afford a standard of reference for the data of observation. The measurement of the intensity and duration of sensation, of the extent of consciousness, and so forth, would be nothing but a useless

Relation between the experimental and other psychological methods.

pastime if it did not find some practical application.[1] For
the same reason Histology would be without value if it did not
afford an exact notion of the anatomical structure of organisms.
Similarly, the experimental results obtained by Physics and
Chemistry serve to complete the data obtained by various sciences
of pure observation which deal with extremely complex facts. This
is the case of Physics with regard to Meteorology, of Chemistry
with regard to Mineralogy, Geology, etc. In Psychology, as in
Chemistry, Physics, Philology, or History, a fact or a document,
which by itself has no particular meaning, acquires significance
when it is taken in connection with other data referring to
the same subject. From a quantity of individual observations
a general law is evolved, which may link together an entire class
of phenomena. Biology, in its various forms of histology, pathology, and anatomy, affords us continual examples of this.[2] In
Psychology, for instance, it often happens that a fact which has
been ascertained in the laboratory contains, so to speak, the
germ of a similar process which takes place in a much more
complex form in the intellectual and social evolution of the
species. For example, the fact, so often confirmed by laboratory experiments, that a presentation is not an indivisible unit,
but that it consists of various elements, differently arranged
in every case (so that it can never be completely reproduced),
finds its confirmation in the observations of the Psychology
of peoples, where it has been proved that in the evolution of
ideas and feelings a given line of thought or disposition in the
social mind (what is known as the "spirit of the time") never
reproduces itself a second time in the exact form of the first.
Experimental Psychology, therefore, with respect to the Psycho-

[1] It would be better in that case, says Wundt (*Hypnotismus und Suggestion*),
to apply oneself to the improvement of sewing machines.

[2] In an admirable essay on experiment in medical science, *Lo sperimentalismo
nella medicina* (Pavia, 1884), Camillo Golgi quotes, as an example of the connection between single and complex facts, the observations on the nuclei of certain
cells in tadpoles, salamanders, and other animals. These observations showed
that such nuclei have sometimes a granular and sometimes a filamentary structure,
and that the filaments in the latter case exhibit various forms—skein-like, ring-shaped, and so forth—these peculiarities of structure being related to the proliferation of the cells, and characterising the different phases of the process of
separation. Other observations showed that similar facts are to be observed
in the case of vegetable tissues; that kindred structural changes take place in the
development of the fecundated egg, etc. From these and such-like insignificant
facts there issues a biological law which embraces both the animal and vegetable
kingdoms, both normal and pathological life (pp. 40, 42).

logy of peoples, performs the same office that histology performs with respect to anatomy, justifying Professor James in calling it "microscopical Psychology."[1]

There is no separation, therefore, between the experimental method and other psychological methods, nor are there, as some think, several Psychologies. Experiment and observation are nothing but different methods of the same science, and we cannot therefore detach experimental Psychology from the rest of Psychology, and make of it a separate and intermediate science between Psychology and Physiology. An intermediate science is meaningless. Every science has a special object and special principles, which it can borrow from no other science. It has been held by some that the object of physiological Psychology should be the study of the relations between the body and the soul, and hence that it should be a psychophysical science. This is the earlier theory of Fechner, subsequently abandoned by him. It is difficult, however, to understand the meaning of a "psychophysical" science, seeing that we have no facts, outside the range of Weber's law, to confirm it, and it has besides an entirely metaphysical character. In reality we have only qualitative and psychological values on the one hand, and dimensions or quantitative and physical values on the other. If physiological Psychology has been enabled momentarily to assume the appearance of an independent science, it is owing to the fact that, when it first came into existence, the attention of psychologists was concentrated upon it. Now, however, that it has reached a certain degree of development, it has become incorporated with the rest of Psychology, and must rank as one of the methods of the latter.

Unity of the various psycyological methods.

It is also a mistake to emphasise the antithesis between experimental and introspective Psychology to the extent of making them distinct sciences. The instance has been adduced of theoretical physics, which is distinguished from experimental physics. But whence does the former take its data, if not from the latter? A theoretical physical science not founded on experimental observation would have no scientific value whatever. Seeing, moreover, that pure observation, in the case of individual

---

[1] *The Principles of Psychology*, Vol. I., p. 192. Wundt, in a paper published in *Philosophische Studien*, Vol. X., p. 123, etc., says that he has arrived at a knowledge of the laws governing the higher processes of consciousness, by starting from experimental observations on the more simple presentations. See also Münsterberg, *Psychology and Life*, p. 112.

mental processes, has a very limited value, what would a theoretical Psychology be reduced to? It must be borne in mind that theoretical physics makes use of mathematics, to which Psychology can only exceptionally have recourse.

General Psychology should consequently be based upon experimental Psychology; but it is essential that the results obtained by other means be harmonised and compared, so as to give a complete and precise notion of the origin and development and of the laws of the processes of consciousness. The task of the psychologist does not, therefore, consist in reducing all psychological research to the experimental method, but in connecting the data afforded by experiment with those obtained by means of the genetic methods and of pathological Psychology. In this line we have some recent works, such as Baldwin's *Mental Development in the Child and the Race*, and *Social and Ethical Interpretations in Mental Development*, which are especially important, and have opened up new fields of psychological inquiry and speculation. Amongst the few recent treatises of general Psychology wherein the results of the various methods are blended together we must mention Höffding's. Most authors treat of experimental Psychology by itself, and when, like Külpe, they wish to confine themselves to it entirely, they are obliged to sacrifice a considerable portion of their subject.

Recent attempts at blending the psychological methods.

We must now pass to another no less important question. Given that pure observation in individual Psychology is a fallacious method, is it to be entirely eliminated? Although Wundt answers categorically in the affirmative,[1] his assertion cannot, we think, be unreservedly accepted. It is obvious that the pure introspective method, as practised by the old-fashioned Psychology, has done its work, but it has, nevertheless, a place in modern investigation. If the most important task with which Psychology has to deal is that of bringing together the data afforded by the various methods of research, it follows that, although the experimental method must necessarily be its basis, because of the precision of its results, it is bound to include in its view the different character and connections of mental processes. And this cannot be done except through the aid of pure introspection and "memory" of its

Preponderating value of the introspective method.

[1] See *Outlines of Psychology*, p. 22: "Pure observation such as is possible in many departments of natural science is, from the very character of psychical phenomena, impossible in individual Psychology."

data.[1] Various modern psychologists, such as Bain, James, Höffding, and Stout, have already adopted these lines with marked success; whilst others have committed the mistake of treating their subject in too schematic and arid a fashion, quite contrary to its nature and to the immense variety of its methods and data.[2] Psychology should, above all, deal with human facts which have actually taken place, and consequently should have its foundation in the experience of life.[3]

[1] See Ladd, *Psychology Descriptive and Explanatory*, pp. 24, 25, where he denies that psychological induction should be limited, like physical induction.

[2] See Villa, "La question des méthodes en psychologie" in the *Revue scientifique*, September 22nd, 1900.

[3] Ladd is therefore right, in a sense, when he says in the Preface, *op. cit.*: "'The cry which must be ever ringing in the ears of the genuine psychologist is this—"Back from book and laboratories to actual and concrete human life."'"

CHAPTER V

PSYCHICAL FUNCTIONS

THE application of scientific methods, and especially of the experimental method, to Psychology, has brought about a general conception of the psychical life substantially different from that of the old-fashioned psychologists. The composition and development of the life of consciousness appear nowadays under an entirely new aspect. Before dealing, however, with this point, which shall be the subject of the next chapter, we must examine how modern Psychology looks at the fundamental functions of consciousness itself—viz. cognition, feeling, and will.

The ancient Greek and the mediæval philosophers had already noted that the soul is not wholly composed of homogeneous elements. Thus Plato and Aristotle distinguished the "rational" soul from the "vegetative" and "animal" soul, the first representing ideas, or the higher mental activities, and the two latter the physiological and sensory functions which are the lower activities of man.

The fundamental functions of the mind according to ancient ideas.

Here we have not only great uncertainty in the distinction of the various mental functions, but a fundamental confusion of the latter with physiological functions. In a like manner the scholastics distinguished the *appetitus sensitivus* from the *appetitus rationalis*. This distinction was extremely vague, and was almost entirely abandoned when, with Descartes and the Cartesians, the idea of the simplicity and indivisibility of the soul became generally accepted. According to Descartes's system, the various faculties of the soul depended on the relation in which the latter stands to the body; the "passions" are in this way the effect of the influence of the body on the soul, whereas the "internal emotions" are derived directly from the thoughts and judgments of the soul. Descartes endeavoured further to reduce the various feelings to a few elementary forms. A distinction of the mental faculties founded on metaphysical principles was given by Spinoza and Leibnitz, who may both be said to have followed the traditional idea of dividing the human soul into the higher and the lower. Leibnitz attributed to his monads the double faculty of representing and of striving after things (*Streben*); the former being considered the higher of the two and alone worthy to guide the actions of man; whereas the latter, which comprised the instincts and impulses of the senses, was entirely subordinate.

The more we advance in the history of philosophy, the greater we find the importance attributed to the so-called lower faculties. Christian Wolff, the disciple of Leibnitz, whose doctrines he made known to the world, and who was the first to introduce a methodical study of Psychology into the Universities, developed the ideas of his master in a classification of the mental faculties which was called after him, and which had a marked influence on the German Psychology of the eighteenth and part of the nineteenth century. Wolff, like his predecessors, maintains the Platonic division between the faculties of cognition and desire, each of which he subdivides into a higher and lower part. The lower cognitive faculty comprises imagination, the poetic faculty, and memory; the higher faculty comprises attention, reflection, and the reasoning power. The lower part of the faculty of desire embraces pleasure and displeasure (*Unlust*), desire and repugnance (*Abscheu*) and the emotions; the higher part embraces willing and not willing and liberty. The Wolffian school subsequently modified this division, giving increasing importance to feeling, which was finally separated from desire and recognised as an independent faculty between the other two. This was the origin of the classical triple distinction, subsequently accepted by Kant, of the three faculties of knowledge, feeling, and willing.[1] Kant exercised a great influence also upon the development of the conception of the faculties, and was, one may say, the first to attribute a proper importance to feeling. The seventeenth and eighteenth centuries, which affected great precision and clearness of ideas, were naturally inclined to consider these mental faculties, which impeded, or, at all events, did not favour, the development of the intelligence and of reason as lower in the scale. Wolff, for instance, notwithstanding his division of the mental activities into the faculties of knowledge and of desire, did not consider them of equal value, but placed the former far above the latter. In his *Psychologia Rationalis* he endeavours

Wolff and the theory of faculties.

Kant.

[1] See Wundt, *Grundzüge der physiologischen Psychologie*, Vol. I., p. 16 Dessoir, *Geschichte der neueren deutschen Psychologie*, Vol. I., pp. 196—301.

also to prove that they are all derived from one fundamental faculty of perception.[1] Kant, on the contrary (and herein lies his importance), was of opinion that the three faculties of knowing, feeling, and willing, had each an independent origin, and that it were vain to attempt any further reduction. On the other hand, he also was not entirely free from the intellectualistic prejudices of the time, and assigned a higher value to the faculty of knowledge, principally because it contains the element of liberty, the essential feature of the will. Kant divided knowledge into intelligence (*Verstand*), judgment, and reason (*Vernunft*), which constitute together the higher part, the lower part consisting in the sensations. In his opinion there is not only a difference of degree between the two, but the former is the active, the latter the passive, or receptive part, which furnishes the material for the other to work upon. Therefore, the faculty of knowledge, and more especially the reason, in Kant's estimation, is the sovereign faculty, which regulates and selects from the feelings and the desires.

This intellectualistic tendency was not confined to German philosophy, but was observable also in the English and French philosophies. Locke, Hume, Hartley, and the French sensationalists were pure intellectualists, the only difference between them and the Germans being that the connection between the senses and the higher intellectual activities was far better understood by the former. Locke having pointed out the great importance of experience in the formation of ideas, and how all ideas are the result of the combination of several sensations, English philosophy devoted itself to discovering the principle of the connection of ideas. This was eventually found to consist in the laws of association, to which feeling and willing, as derivative faculties, were both subject. David Hartley (1705—1757) and the subsequent English philosophers were of opinion that all thoughts and feelings, however elevated, are developed by means of association, and that the importance of the will in mental phenomena is also to be explained upon that principle.

English and French sensationalists.

The French sensationalists entertained similar ideas, and, following them to their extreme consequences, reached the point of denying all spontaneous energy to consciousness and of reducing the mental life to a mere combination of sensory phenomena. Intellectualism (which here ran into materialism) had thus cele-

[1] See Dessoir, *op. cit.*, p. 200.

brated its greatest triumph, by treating of consciousness as a mere reflection of the external world. Among the later sensationalists, such as Cabanis, we come across a novel idea, which was to be subsequently developed, that, namely, of the vital feeling, which included not only the sum-total of organic sensations of our body, but also our inherited instincts.

The intellectualist conception of consciousness which predominated during the eighteenth century is a natural one, for undoubtedly the first and simplest explanation which presents itself to us of mental phenomena is that they are the image of external phenomena. The latter forming what are psychologically called presentations, it follows that the whole mental life is considered under the aspect of presentation alone. It is thus also comprehensible how intellectualism may at times coincide with materialism, which denies all reality to consciousness. We shall, however, have occasion to see that other doctrines have had the same tendency towards materialism, although entirely opposed to intellectualism.

Meanwhile, during the first twenty years of the nineteenth century, in the schools and in philosophy in general, the foremost place was held by Wolff's theory of faculties as modified by his disciples, and accepted in this modified form by Kant. This theory distinguished, as we have seen, three fundamental faculties, knowledge, feeling, and willing, each being divided into a series of secondary faculties. Whilst each was independent of the others, with which it could be combined in different ways, greater importance was assigned to the faculties of knowledge, amongst which were imagination, attention, and memory. Thus, in the description of an individual character, it was thought possible to determine with a certain amount of precision his mnemonic, imaginative, volitional, or sensitive faculties, while owing to the higher value attributed to the cognitive faculty, judgment upon it was ultimately given in accordance with the relation in which cognition stood to the others. This exceedingly artificial and conventional system, in which the faculties were made to give an apparently plausible explanation of mental phenomena, was subsequently very properly condemned as " mythical Psychology." It was completed and rendered ridiculous at the same time by Gall's celebrated doctrine, which was its physiological counterpart. Just as the Wolffian psychologists divided consciousness into compartments, each performing its own function independently, Gall divided the brain into

Gall's phrenology.

various areas corresponding to the different mental activities.[1] Here, again, intellectualism coincided with materialism; the absence of any notion of the complexity of the mental processes with the absence of comprehension of the extraordinary complexity of the cerebral processes.

This artificial division and subdivision of consciousness into faculties found a strenuous adversary in Frederick Herbart. Though **Herbart's criticism of the theory of faculties.** Herbart did not succeed in substituting a more acceptable theory in its place, he possesses, nevertheless, the great merit of having been the first to demonstrate the vacuity of the Wolffian theory. The disciples of Wolff and Kant believed these faculties to be innate forces or energies, which necessarily produce corresponding mental acts, in the same way that physical forces produce certain given effects. Herbart, on the contrary, proved that those so-called "forces" are in reality no more than "possibilities," and that their effects are by no means as certain as the effects due to physical forces. In his opinion the theory of faculties is a fiction as void of sense as the *horror vacui* of the old physicists. There exists neither feeling nor knowledge nor willing; but only feelings, facts of knowledge, and acts of willing.[2] Instead of so many distinct sources of mental processes, there is only one—presentation. The mental life, according to Herbart, is made up of presentations, each of which, in tending to preserve itself, may be in harmony or at variance with the others. When a presentation is hindered by another, there arises a feeling; when there is a conflict between two presentations, there arises an impulse or act of willing by which one asserts itself against the other.

The metaphysical character of this theory is evident; we have no experiential proof of these hypotheses. The whole system, more- **Herbart's intellectualism.** over, is founded on a conception even more intellectualistic than the theories of the disciples of Wolff and Kant and of the English associationists, none of which had denied the originality of feeling and volition. It must be added that Herbart is in contradiction with himself when, on the one hand, he founds his doctrine upon the simplicity and indivisibility of the soul, and on the other reduces the mental life to a multiplicity of primitive elements or presentations, without establishing

---

[1] See Lange's *History of Materialism*, Vol. III., p. 113 foll. Gall's principal work is, as we have already noted, his *Anatomie et physiologie du système nerveux en général et du cerveau en particulier*, etc. (1810—1818).

[2] See Herbart, *Werke*, Vol. VII., p. 611.

any unity between them. In this way he only demolished one metaphysical theory to substitute for it another even more metaphysical. His criticisms consequently were excellent in a negative way by exposing the fallacy of the fictions upheld by the Wolffian school, but from a positive point of view they were entirely one-sided and hypothetical.

The excessively intellectualistic character of Herbart's Psychology (which his disciples endeavoured to correct) was in increasingly open contrast with the tendencies of European thought and literature at the beginning of the nineteenth century.

So-called "enlightment" (*Aufklärung*) had been opposed in France and Germany by "sentimentalism," represented principally by Rousseau. In a reaction against the logical and mathematical aridity which were then paramount, the sentimental school fought in the cause of feeling—that is to say, of the subjective part of consciousness, which is susceptible of no exact determination. This was the origin of the sentimental literature which contributed so largely to the Romanticism of the beginning of the nineteenth century, and is very important in the history of thought.[1] The preponderance attributed to the feelings was, nevertheless, insufficient to radically change the psychological ideas still dominant in philosophy, all the more that, with Hegel, the Romantic school had itself become entirely intellectualistic. It was necessary to shift the centre of gravity of the mental processes to a subjective element with more influence on the development of the mental life than the feelings have. This was to be found in the will; and the philosopher who has the merit of having been the first to point out the importance of the will is Schopenhauer.

Herbart and Schopenhauer. It is difficult to find two contemporary philosophers whose works were so nearly simultaneous,[2] and who are so different, as Herbart and Schopenhauer. Their only point of contact perhaps is the metaphysical tendency which was common at that time to all philosophers, and tempted them to overstep the limits of psychological observation in favour of cosmological systems. Another point of resemblance between them is the fact that Schopenhauer, in maintaining that will and knowledge are two distinct psychological factors, each governed by its own laws, was no less of an intellectualist than Herbart.

---

[1] See Höffding's *History of Modern Philosophy*.

[2] It must be remembered that Herbart wrote his principal works on Psychology between 1816 and 1825; and Schopenhauer published the first and most important part of his great work in 1819, and the second part in 1844.

The world of our consciousness is, in Schopenhauer's opinion, pure presentation; but the will, which is the inmost force of consciousness, though governing the moral conduct of man, has no power whatever to rule presentations. Nevertheless, there is no disputing Schopenhauer's merit in having pointed out the volitional element in consciousness. Neither Herbart nor Schopenhauer met with much success in their day, owing to the predominance of the absolute Idealism of Schelling and Hegel; but, although their efforts at founding a metaphysical science based on psychological observation were doomed to failure, they exercised no little influence on the philosophers and psychologists who came after them.[1] In our opinion, however, Schopenhauer has a greater sense of reality than Herbart, and, although he did not dedicate himself specially to psychological studies as the latter did, his influence on Psychology was none the less marked. It must be recognised that, in his conception of the will, he had been preceded by Kant, who, in his *Critique of Practical Reason*, had tempered his prevailing intellectualism with the doctrine that the real source of the moral imperative lies in no demonstrable knowledge of truth, but in the will; that, by its nature, it cannot be the result of logical reasonings, but is intuitively felt as a precept having a supernatural origin. Herbart also, though an intellectualist, considered that the primary source of all ethical principles lay in *Wohlwollen*, or the power of willing what is good. For Kant the "will" possesses an entirely spiritual and even transcendental character, being unconnected with any metaphysical principle. With Schopenhauer, on the other hand, the "will" is the basis of a speculative cosmological system. He starts from the empirical psychological observation that if we wish to find out what it is in ourselves which best expresses our inmost being, and which differentiates and singles us out amongst other human beings, we are obliged to recognise that it is not our intelligence, because not only is this common in different degrees to all men, but it is without power to regulate our moral conduct. For it is a fact, says Schopenhauer, that we never really conform our actions to our ideas. We may have the noblest moral

Schopenhauer against intellectualism.

[1] We have already mentioned the numerous followers of Herbart, some of whom are amongst the most eminent contemporary psychologists (such as Volkmann, Strümpell, and others). Schopenhauer's fame has increased of late years both in Germany, where there exists an extensive literature concerning him, and elsewhere.

principles regarding truth, justice, and humanity, and yet act entirely at variance with them. That which determines our actions, rules our whole life, and represents consequently better than any other mental activity our personality, is what we call our "character." When the latter coincides with our ideas, the mental life is harmonious, and we have the illusion that it is they which regulate our actions, whereas we are really only obeying our own nature. And of this we have an evident proof when there arises a discrepancy between our ideas and our character, for in that case it is always the character which conquers.[1] The intelligence is consequently a superadded element, or "epiphenomenon," and the real basis of our nature is the "will," which has its root in our innate instincts and organic tendencies. Within the term "will" Schopenhauer therefore comprises, not only the will commonly so-called, but feeling as well; in other words, the two most subjective elements of consciousness.

It is obvious that this theory lends itself to a materialistic interpretation, especially as Schopenhauer expressly says that the thinking faculty, or the intelligence or consciousness, by means of which we perceive the external world, as also the will itself, are simply products of our brain. On the other hand, Schopenhauer's doctrine has been modified and interpreted by some in an idealistic sense by retaining only that part of it which considers the will (or, better still, feeling) to be the inner and essential element of consciousness, around which the whole of our mental activity revolves.[2] The importance of Schopenhauer's theories reveals itself in all modern psychological works, which bear distinct traces of his influence. Nevertheless, in England amongst the associationists, and in Germany amongst the Herbartians, the contrary intellectualistic theory still possesses numerous adherents. It must not be forgotten that Schopenhauer's doctrine, notwithstanding an undoubted foundation of truth, possesses a markedly metaphysical character, which lends itself to nebulous speculations. This is also a reason why Schopenhauer's Psychology has had so much influence upon modern romantic literature, where the contrast between the intelligence and the blind instincts of the "will" has become a favourite theme.

[1] *The World as Will and Idea*, Vol. I., Part IV.
[2] For instance by Paulson, *Einleitung in die Philosophie*, p. 116 foll.; *System der Ethik* (3rd edit. 1894), Vol. I., p. 310 foll.; Ziegler, *Das Gefühl* (1893), p. 304 foll.; Riehl, *Das philosophische Criticismus* (1876—1877), Vol. III., p. 204 foll.

The later German psychologists, with the exception of the disciples of Herbart, have been obliged to renounce pure intellectualism, and to recognise the importance of feeling and volition. As instances, we may mention Beneke and Lotze. It is, nevertheless, a fact that all these psychologists are much in doubt as to the relation between the will and the intelligence. There is certainly a universal tendency amongst modern philosophers and psychologists to simplify and reduce the mental functions. Nevertheless, contemporary Psychology shows a strong inclination to consider the three mental functions of feeling, will, and intelligence as original, and yet so closely connected as to constitute an organism, whereof each part has to act in conjunction with the others.

Beneke, Lotze, Volkmann.

We shall now examine the ideas of the principal modern and contemporary psychologists with regard to each of these three functions. In Germany, and partly also in England, the ideas of Herbart as to their reciprocal relations retain a certain vogue. In Germany Volkmann, author of *Lehrbuch der Psychologie*, is one of the most popular authors of this school, and the same ideas are followed by Drobisch, Nahlowsky, Lipps, and others, who consider knowledge as the only primitive and independent faculty, of which feeling and willing are emanations. This theory, which is a product of metaphysical ideas, is in entire contradiction with the data of practical experience. We shall for the moment confine ourselves to examining if it can be made to agree with the fundamental principles of epistemology. The principal source of knowledge is perception, which the sciences which deal with the external world—*i.e.* the physical and natural sciences—are obliged to take as their starting-point. It is, however, also an undoubted fact that the objects which we perceive, or which we evoke out of our memory, produce in us certain feelings and awake in us certain impulses. It being manifestly impossible to arrive at an exact knowledge of those objects, unless we make abstraction from the aforesaid feelings and impulses, we may naturally ask how such abstraction is to be made if these feelings and impulses are really a necessary consequence of the combination of presentations. Moreover, if feeling is a secondary phenomenon, how does it come to have any influence upon the mental life and upon presentations? We ought to feel influenced by all external phenomena in an equal degree, or, in other words, to be entirely passive with regard to them. It would be quite incomprehensible why two persons

Intellectualism critically examined.

should behave in an entirely different manner in the presence of the same phenomenon, one, for instance, finding pleasure in a work of art or a landscape, and another being unmoved by either. A disciple of Herbart might answer that this is a consequence of the various intellectual qualities of each, or of their greater or lesser aptitude for discovering the real bearings of those phenomena. On the other hand, experience tells us that it is not difference in intellectual qualities, but different ways of feeling, which causes dissimilarity of behaviour. Again, why is it that two equally clever painters, in depicting the same landscape, will inevitably give it a distinctive character that enables you to tell the work of one from that of the other? Clearly their attention, or, let us say, their intelligence, has been attracted more especially towards one particular part or tint or outline, which has appealed more powerfully to one than to the other. And what is it that attracts the attention to one rather than the other direction? This is a point that the Herbartian and intellectualist theories cannot explain.

If we consider sensation, which is the most elementary form of cognition, we find that a certain tone of feeling is always **Sensation** connected with it. This "tone of feeling" is not, as **and feeling.** some think, inherent in sensation itself, nor does it vary in accordance with the variations of the latter. The mistake arises from not taking into consideration the peculiar character of feeling, which is not produced in us directly through an external impression, as is the case with sensation, but indirectly. The external impression causes a sensation, and the sensation awakens a certain "tone of feeling" which is entirely subjective, and depends greatly on the state of our consciousness, on our past mental states, and lastly on our individual character. This explains how the same perception may cause different and even contrary feelings in various individuals, and how different perceptions may, on the other hand, produce similar feelings. Feeling, therefore, is not a secondary formation sprung from presentations, which are complex facts and the outcome of a combination of sensations; it is in every case a "simple" phenomenon, expressing the unity of consciousness.[1] The subjective element of feeling and willing constitutes, in sooth, the personality whereby one individual differs from another; whereas the cognitive part, based on presentation, is an objective element common, in different measure, to all individuals and reducible to a general principle.

[1] Wundt, *Outlines of Psychology*, p. 41.

For this reason it must be admitted that the current of our thoughts is not regulated uniformly by the external element of presentation, but that we choose amongst presentations those most in unison with our mode of feeling. Feeling and willing are consequently primitive functions of consciousness, of fundamental importance for the development of the mental life. This will be more apparent after we have examined the various theories concerning these two mental functions.

The notion which inspired the older psychological theories was that the intellect was the dominant faculty. The lower faculties, designated by the comprehensive term of "appetites," comprised several mental functions which we now attribute to cognition, feeling, and willing. The English psychologists, followed by the French sensationalists, were the first to analyse the cognitive faculty, and, on the assumption that all knowledge originates in the senses, to make of the sensations the basis of the intellectual activities. German philosophy, on the contrary, although influenced, after Wolff, by the sensationalist and empirical theories of the French and English schools, did not for some time shake off the prejudice that the data of the senses, as regards the mental life, occupy a much lower place than those of reason and of intelligence, and even Kant was of the same opinion. For him the data of sense are the material of knowledge; intelligence and reason, its form.

Higher and lower faculties.

We find the same distinction applied to feeling. Just as there was no identity between sensation and idea, so a distinction was made between moral or æsthetic feelings and the feelings produced by the senses. Indeed, it was only later that so-called lower feelings were distinguished from sensations; and even to-day the two are frequently confused. According to a recent historian of philosophical terminology,[1] the first to draw a clear distinction between the two was Tetens, who defined sensation as the copy of an object, whereas feeling is something of which we only know that it brings about a change in ourselves. The distinction was of course more difficult with regard to those sensations which have no very decided qualitative character, such as organic or diffused sensations, where the feeling of pleasure or pain, which goes together with them, is in such preponderance that the "quality" of the sensation itself seems to disappear before it. Owing to the close affinity of feeling with volition, it also often

[1] Encken, *Geschichte der philosophischen Terminologie in Umriss*, p. 210 (quoted by Wundt, *Phil. Stud.*, Vol. VI., p. 339).

happened that the former was mistaken for phenomena connected with the latter. Thus the Wolffian school placed amongst the lower conative faculties pleasure and pain, appetite and passion; the higher consisting in free and independent will. In modern Psychology the term "feeling" embraces all those mental states which constitute a purely subjective modification of our consciousness, and are consequently not to be ascribed to any external fact. These states are rendered manifest in various forms, principally in pleasure and pain.

Passing now to the most salient theories concerning the nature of feeling, we have, first of all, the intellectualistic theories of Herbartians, such as Nahlowsky, Volkmann, Drobisch, and Lipps, who conceive feeling as a result of a reciprocal action of presentations, and reject the generally accepted opinion that it is an original activity of consciousness. Nahlowsky, for instance,[1] who endeavoured to modernise as far as possible the ideas of Herbart, maintains, in the first place, that sensations are the only primitive mental states, from which all other states (the feelings included) are derived; in the second place, that there are only two explanatory principles in Psychology —the reciprocal action between body and soul as regards primitive mental states, and the reciprocal action of presentations as regards states evolved from the former. It is an undoubted fact, which Kant has the merit of having been the first to point out, that no feeling exists which is not ascribable to some object, and consequently which is not connected with sensations and presentations. Those who deny this, base their view upon a confusion of terms arising from a not very clear understanding of the difference between elementary feelings and sensations. It is, however, impossible to infer therefrom that feeling is a mental state produced by the action upon one another of sensations and presentations. A fact which evidently contradicts this theory is that a simple sensation, unconnected with other sensations, can nevertheless produce in us a feeling of pleasure or pain. To explain this the Herbartians are obliged to distinguish the sensations possessing an affective tone (*betönte Empfindungen*) from feelings, in the proper sense of the word. In this way we have a repetition of the distinction between superior and inferior elements which we have already come across in the faculty theory. The affective or feeling tone with these psychologists stands for

The Herbartian theories concerning feeling.

[1] Nahlowsky, *Das Gefühlsleben in seinen wesentlichen Erscheinungen und Bezügen* (2nd edit., Leipsic, 1884), pp. 41, 42.

the manner of acting of the vital activity, and is merely an indication of purely physiological phenomena. For whereas sensations endowed with feeling can only have their origin in some nervous stimulus, the feelings themselves are elicited by the reciprocal action of presentations. But this distinction between sensations possessing an affective tone and feelings as such is entirely arbitrary and lacks confirmation in facts.[1] Pleasure and pain are *sui generis*, whether they accompany sensations or presentations and ideas; nor is there in reality any difference between the various degrees of feeling, beyond one of complexity and intensity. Any sensation, even the most simple, such as a tactile or olfactory sensation, is capable of causing very intense feelings of pleasure or pain, which may often constitute a potent stimulus of action. Who does not know the force of the pleasurable or painful feelings which accompany organic sensations? And yet these sensations act by themselves, directly, and possess only a very slight associative power. How can it be said that the feelings of pleasure or pain which attend such sensations are of an essentially different nature from the feelings produced by the more complex intellectual or æsthetic presentations?[2] Moreover, however differently we may combine sensations, they can never give us anything but an objective cognition, nor by themselves bring about an alteration of what we call our "state of mind."[3] Feeling, moreover, and sensation obey different laws. When the intensity of a sensation increases or diminishes, feeling also increases or diminishes, but only up to a certain point, for a moment arrives when its quality changes.[4]

The psychophysical materialistic school, which is generally entirely opposed to the Herbartian theories, agrees with them partly on this point, for, like the followers of Herbart, the followers of the psychophysical school also believe that simple feeling is as much a quality inherent in sensation as intensity. The more complex feelings, or emotions, these psychologists consider to be a result of the

The theories of the psychophysical materialistic school on feeling.

[1] See Alfred Lehmann's work *Die Hauptgesetze des menschlichen Gefühlslebens* (Danish tr., Leipsic, 1892). This work, which is the most complete of the kind on experimental Psychology, is remarkable for its clearness and excellent method. See also Höffding, *Outlines of Psychology*, p. 221 foll.

[2] It is necessary to remember the distinction to be made between the German and Herbartian intellectualists and the English associationists, for the latter admit the originality of feeling.

[3] See G. Croom Robertson, *Elements of Psychology*, p. 185 foll.

[4] See Wundt, *Outlines of Psychology*, p. 29; Höffding, *op. cit.*, p. 221 foll.

combination of elementary feelings, attending the sensations (generally of a muscular nature), which are a distinctive feature of the emotions. This theory, which is a mixture of intellectualism and materialism, lays itself open, however, to the same objections as the one we have just discussed, and as that other which affirms presentation to be the only primitive function. Feeling is an inner and subjective phenomenon which is caused by sensations and presentations, but depends also in a great measure on the general state of our consciousness, and on our "mental disposition."[1] This theory, which may be called that of the feeling-tone, gives an even more unsatisfactory explanation of the "emotions," as we shall have occasion to see when dealing with other theories on the same subject. All these systems, whether Herbartian or materialistic, aim at divesting feeling of its most characteristic quality, which is that of constituting an essentially inner state of our consciousness, and is, therefore, only to be explained through the latter. Münsterberg, who may be considered the most eminent representative of psychophysical materialism,[2] has followed the theories we have just discussed to their extreme consequences. As the subjective and spontaneous aspect of consciousness is undeniable, and it is also undoubtedly the source of our actions, Münsterberg, in accordance with his method of explaining the whole mental life by means of the sensations, contends that all that cannot be reduced to sensation exceeds the limits of psychological discussion. Consequently the will and feeling, considered in their psychological essence, as contrasted with their outer mechanism and the sensations that accompany them, can form no part of the object of Psychology, which should confine itself to the study of the intellectual aspect of consciousness. This theory, which, starting from experimental principles, arrives at conclusions closely resembling Schopenhauer's, is only tenable on the assumption that we are ready to give up the principle that Psychology should deal with the entire domain of mental phenomena.

On the other hand, there are psychologists who, as opposed to those who deny the originality of feeling, consider it the fundamental activity of consciousness, and the fountain-head

---

[1] See the neo-materialistic theory developed by Münsterberg, *Beiträge zur experimentellen Psychologie* (Heft. 4). Cf. Ziegler, *Das Gefühl* (Stuttgard, 1893), and F. de Sarlo, *Rivista Italiana di filosofia* (July and August, 1893).

[2] See Münsterberg, *Psychology and Life*, p. 93 foll. and p. 176 foll.; also *Grundzüge der Psychologie*, p. 180 foll. and p. 525 foll.

of all the others.[1] Various facts would seem to confirm this opinion. It is, for instance, not to be denied that, during the first period of infancy, feelings of pleasure or pain, caused especially by organic sensations, predominate over the clearness of perception and the determination of the will. The child is above all influenced by his general state of well-being or the reverse, all his mental world being circumscribed by his organic functions. Indistinct visceral, muscular, or thermal sensations continually affect his way of feeling, and consequently of acting. Even sensations of sight or hearing produce, during a certain period of an infant's life, certain impressions, which are closely connected with the whole organic feeling of well-being or the reverse. But, in spite of this, the above facts do not prove the existence of a pure state of feeling unaccompanied by any perceptive element. Even the most indistinct visceral sensations, which are difficult to localise with anything like exactness, remain nevertheless "sensations," and are distinguishable from the pleasurable or painful feeling which attends them, even though the latter may be so preponderatingly strong as to attract all our attention. Nor can we doubt that what *we* feel is also felt, even with greater intensity, by an infant. This theory is chiefly based, we think, upon the confusion which is very often made between organic sensation and feeling, owing in a certain degree to the preponderance of the latter in sensations of that kind.[2]

Feeling as a primitive activity.

By accepting this theory, the genesis of other mental activities is no less difficult of explanation, whether it be contended that they are potentially contained in feeling, or that they are evolved from the reciprocal action of various feelings. For it is necessary to make abstraction from the actual state of our consciousness,

[1] Thus Horwicz, *Psychologische Analysen auf physiologischen Grundlage* (1872). This theory was also maintained by Barratt; see his *Physical Ethics; or, the Science of Action* (1869). Horwicz's theory is discussed by Höffding, *op. cit.*, p. 96. See also Fouillée, *L'évolutionisme des idées forces*.

[2] See Lehmann, *op. cit.*, p. 47. The theory seems to be contradicted by the two phenomena of "anæsthesia" (insensibility) and "analgesia" (loss of the sense of pain). Thus Höffding contends that there may be abnormal states, in which the feeling of pain is unaccompanied by sensibility. But Lehmann denies (and, we think, with reason) that there can be a feeling of physical pain which has not at the same time a certain perceptive character (*op. cit.*, p. 48). Physiologists also refuse to admit such a state of absolute insensibility. See also Wundt (*Physiologische Psychologie*, Vols. I., III.). Lehmann, as opposed to Höffding, does not admit that there exists any interval of time between the sensation and the feeling which attends it (Lehmann, *op. cit.*, p. 46). See Max Frey, *Die Gefühle und ihre Verhältnisse zu den Empfindungen* (Leipsic, 1894).

which is composed of closely connected perceptive, emotional, and volitional elements, and to consider what are the properties which would remain to these elements, once they were isolated in this manner. Feeling is a purely subjective state of consciousness, so that by having recourse to a somewhat bold hypothesis we might say that if the world were purely " felt," and not perceived, it would be reduced to a continual alternation of pleasure and pain, without any knowledge being possible of its causes, or of the external relations of things, or of our own bodies.[1] This theory, of which Horwicz is the principal representative, is, moreover, as we shall have occasion to see, no less contrary to the laws of evolution than the intellectualistic theory or than the doctrine of the primordiality of reflex action.

Horwicz.

There is another theory of the feelings which has had some success of recent times, and is also remarkable for having put in doubt the very object of Psychology. A book by Ribot on the *Psychology of the Feelings*, which appeared some time ago, gave rise to an exhaustive discussion on the nature of the feelings and on their relation to other mental functions.[2] The author, following principally James and Lange, exaggerated some of the ideas of Spencer and Bain. The latter had especially noted the correspondence between states of pleasure or pain on the one hand, and the increase or decrease of the vital activity on the other, and had demonstrated the intimate and subjective character of feeling, which, both in mental and organic life, expresses, better than any other element of our consciousness, our personality in its physical and mental forms.[3] This principle is, of course, subject to restrictions. Thus a very strong physical pain may be, occasionally, only an indication of a slight vital affection, and, conversely, there may exist a deep-seated organic affection without proportionately painful outward symptoms.[4]

Physiological theory of feeling.

Ribot.

---

[1] See Fouillée, *L'évolutionisme des idées forces*, Book II., chap. i., p. 77. Fouillée, though admitting the primitive nature of the three principal functions of consciousness, holds nevertheless that the function of feeling and willing (which, by a somewhat antiquated term, he calls "appétition") is the most fundamental, and speaks of the " côté intellectuel, qui n'est pas encore dégagé du côté émotionnel" (*op. cit.*, p. 91-2).

[2] Th. Ribot, *La psychologie des sentiments* (Paris, 1896). See G. Villa's paper on that work in the *Rivista Italiana di filosofia* (November—December, 1896), and Tocco in the *Rivista d'Italia* (April, 1898).

[3] Bain, *The Emotions and the Will*, p. 11 foll.; *Mind and Body*, p. 59.

[4] See Carus, *Le problème de la conscience du moi*, and James's *Principles of Psychology*, Vol. I., p. 143.

Starting from this premise, which is open to serious question, it was not difficult for Lange and James to conclude that the feelings are solely the expression of the organic functions of the individual.[1] Following this hint, Ribot defines feeling as an *organic tendency*. The essence of feeling being placed in the vital functions, a very secondary position is thus assigned to the feelings which are dependent on the higher senses and connected with intellectual, æsthetic, and moral phenomena. The theory, moreover, asserts that feeling may exist " outside the intelligence " (as Ribot expresses it), so that it comes partly to coincide with the preceding theory of Horwicz.[2]

There is a close resemblance between this theory and Schopenhauer's idea of the "will" as embracing the whole of those "tendencies," desires, and instinctive necessities of the organism which manifest themselves externally, irresistibly, and independently of the intelligence. "In every animal," says Ribot, "you find at bottom the 'appetite' in the sense used by Spinoza, and the 'will' in the sense used by Schopenhauer—that is to say, feeling and acting, but not thinking."[3] Here we have the purely metaphysical contrast in which Schopenhauer placed the intelligence and the will, as opposed to intellectualism, which placed feeling in a subordinate position to knowledge. Let us examine more closely the above physiological interpretation of feeling.

Criticism of Ribot's theory.

If we wish to remain within the province of experience, it is clear that we can attribute a "tendency," or an impulse, only to beings endowed with a "will," and, further, that we can only make use of that term in the case of psychical, or rather psychophysical, phenomena. In other words, a tendency and a will can only belong to organisms endowed with consciousness. But even in a conscious organism, we cannot say that all functions have a "tendency," or an object. How can we, for instance, talk of "tendencies" in the functions of nutrition? It would be giving a teleological interpretation of natural processes not founded on

[1] Charles Lange, Professor of Pathological Anatomy at Copenhagen University, published in 1885 a short work on the *Emotions*, which gave rise to much discussion. [2] Ribot, *op. cit.*, Introd., Vol. I., p. 8.
[3] Ribot, *op. cit.*, p. 38 (see also " Conclusion," p. 434). Ribot, in the Introduction to his book, makes an entirely arbitrary distinction between psychologists on the ground of their manner of considering the feelings, dividing them into "physiologists" and "intellectualists." Wundt, Lehmann, Höffding, Sully, etc., are, in his opinion, "intellectualists." See G. Villa's paper before quoted (*Rivista Italiana di filosofia*, 1896).

fact. These physiological phenomena may have been originally conscious and voluntary, but they have long since become reflex and unconscious.

The foregoing theory could not logically be accepted by the believers in the physiological interpretation of feeling, who profess themselves positivists, and it must be recognised that the term "organic," as applied to the tendencies of a conscious being, is inexact. They might, with better reason, be called "psychophysical." Nor do we think that these hypotheses are necessary in order to prove that feeling is the most subjective part of our individuality. This notion has been accepted by contemporary philosophy and psychology, without any necessity of strengthening the data of empirical observation with metaphysical arguments borrowed from Schopenhauer and Hartmann. Those self-styled "physiological" psychologists are guilty of a misuse in psychological terms when they continually insist upon the omnipotence of feeling with respect to the intellect, which they consider of secondary importance and not expressive of the inmost nature of the individual. The term "intellect" is here used in the sense given to it by metaphysical philosophers such as Descartes, Spinoza, and Hegel—namely, of cognitive faculty in general, as distinguished from the faculty of desire, which was considered of a lower nature. In our view, on the contrary, the most indistinct sensation as well as the highest act of the intelligence represent the two extreme limits of one and the same order of mental facts which constitute knowledge, the only difference between them being a difference of degree. It is, therefore, erroneous to say that feeling can exist without the intelligence, for if intelligence stands for cognition in general, sensation, which always attends even the most elementary feeling, is indisputably an element of cognition. Feeling must consequently attend every cognitive element, whether it be a sensation, a perception, or an idea; for to admit the contrary would be tantamount to admitting a separation between the individual and the external world. Feeling, moreover, is necessarily a psychophysical activity, as are also knowledge and will; so that the two latter could with equal reason be called "organic tendencies," owing to their possessing an organic substratum.

One dominant idea underlies, more or less visibly, the metaphysical doctrines of the "physiological" psychologists. When Bain asserted that there is a constant correspondence between the feelings and the vital state, many jumped to the materialistic conclusion that feeling by itself as a mental state has a purely secondary value for the psychologist, and should be mainly looked upon as a "symptom" of the conditions of the organism, which alone constitute a worthy object of study.[1] Here we find the reappearance of the old materialistic idea that the only Real is the physically real, and that this alone lends itself to be studied with scientific method. The mentally real, on the contrary, even if it be not considered as the eighteenth-century materialists considered it, an utter illusion, is nevertheless held to be an aggregate of facts from which no certain data can be deduced, unless they be explained by means of physiological "causes," for which we must seek if we would avoid falling into metaphysical speculations.

These theories, as applied to the emotions, are a one-sided exaggeration of a true observation. An emotion is a complex product, comprising, besides feeling, two important factors, which are its principal characteristics—namely, presentations and certain physiological manifestations, such as gesture, facial expression, movements of the body, and peculiar phenomena of respiration and circulation. Formerly the emotions were mainly classified according to the element of presentation they contained, though some authorities, such as Bain, also took into account the physiological phenomena by which they were attended. More recently the latter have come to be considered *James's and C. Lange's theory on the emotions.* as the starting-point and as the only data to be relied upon, this idea being originally put forward by James,[2] followed later by Charles Lange, who developed it in a short treatise on the *Emotions* published in 1885. James's work, and especially Lange's little book, attracted the immediate attention of psychologists, Höffding and Wundt discussing the latter in the *Viertel-jahrschrift für Wissenschaftliche Philosophie*, Vol. XII., and in the *Philosophische Studien*, Vol. VI., p. 3, 1890, respectively. It is undeniable that these and similar works, such as Mosso's book on *Fear*, written with the object of explaining the physiological manifestations of the emotions, not only marked a considerable progress in the study of this part of Psychology, but did away with the old-fashioned intellectualistic theories, according to which the emotions were considered as an inferior form of cognition, or even as a malady of the mind. Formerly the emotions were

---

[1] See Ribot, *La psychologie des sentiments*, p. 32. Ribot says that the mental phenomena of feeling are only *des marques*.

[2] In an article published in *Mind* (1884), and entitled "What is an Emotion?" and subsequently reprinted in his *Principles of Psychology* (1891).

studied only from the point of view of their presentative content. Taking, for example, joy or anger, the object of Psychology was thought to be fulfilled by analysing the ideas, feelings, and desires connected with them. Amongst modern authors, on the contrary, Bain pointed out the double aspect—physical and mental—of the emotions; whilst Darwin, though not a professional psychologist, gave a capital description of the expressive movements of animals and children, which he explained by means of his theory of selection and heredity.[1] These authors, however, consider the external manifestations of an emotion as secondary, and not essential, phenomena. It has also been observed with truth that the notions which were formerly held concerning the emotions reduced the latter to the external phenomena, which are their manifestation; and it is only the fact that these ideas have been recently presented in more or less scientific shape that has given them a fictitious importance.[2] Although Lange and James differ on certain points, the former being more especially a psychologist and the latter a physiologist, they agree nevertheless in all essentials. James, in his psychological treatise, deals with the emotions immediately after the instincts, and not without reason, seeing that the movements and physical perturbations which characterise the emotions are neither more nor less than instinctive acts.[3] "Instinctive reactions," says James, "and emotional expressions shade imperceptibly into each other. Every object that excites our instinct excites an emotion as well."[4] These expressions are, in fact, reflex and automatic movements which take place when we are struck by some external impression. "The bodily changes follow directly the perception of the exciting fact, and our feeling of the same changes as they occur *is* the emotion." The general causes of the emotions, therefore, are without doubt physiological according to James.[5] When we are struck by some external impression, instead of the latter arousing, first of all, a feeling in us, it determines, on the contrary, various reflex phenomena, which in their turn produce a certain emotion, so that we must arrive at the

---

[1] Before Darwin, several attempts had been made at explaining the expressive movements of the emotions, by Bell (1806), Piderit (1859), Duchenne (1862), and Gratiolet (1865). See Lehmann, *op. cit.*, p. 64.
[2] See Lehmann, *op. cit.*, p. 64.
[3] W. James, *The Principles of Psychology*, Vol. II., p. 442.
[4] James, *op. cit.*, Vol. II., p. 442.
[5] *Ibid.*, p. 449.

paradoxical conclusion that "we feel sorry because we cry, angry because we strike, afraid because we tremble, and not that we cry, strike, or tremble, because we are sorry, angry, or fearful, as the case may be."[1] For "every one of the bodily changes, whatsoever it be, is *felt*, acutely or obscurely, the moment it occurs." So that the most important points to be considered in an emotion are these somatic phenomena, which are the most positive and indisputable facts observable in it.[2] "If we fancy some strong emotion, and then try to abstract from our consciousness of it all the feelings of its bodily symptoms, we find we have nothing left behind."[3]

Lange is even more explicit. He believes that while we limit ourselves to an entirely subjective notion of the emotions, considering them as something quite apart, such as the perceptions of red or green, no scientific analysis of their contents is possible. For this it is necessary to begin with the objective characteristics of the emotions, just as in the case of the study of colours, no really scientific result could be attained as long as one was only acquainted with the subjective effects they produced, whereas everything was changed from the time that Newton discovered an objective quality in the difference of refrangibility of coloured rays.[4] Lange considered the vaso-motor phenomena as the most important, and classifies the emotions accordingly under seven different forms. The first four of these are distinguished by the diminution of voluntary innervation, the first being simple, the second accompanied by vascular contraction, the third by the same contraction increased by spasms of the organic muscles, the fourth by inco-ordination. The other three forms are characterised by an increase of voluntary innervation, with spasms of the muscles in the first, vascular dilatation in the second and third, increased, in the last case, by inco-ordination. These seven physiological forms have as many corresponding emotions, in the following sequence: delusion, sorrow, fear, embarrassment, impatience, joy, anger.[5] The expla-

[1] James, *op. cit.*, Vol. II., p. 450.
[2] *Op. cit.*, p. 453. "The questions now are causal: 'Just what changes does this object, and what changes does that object, excite?' and 'How come they to excite these particular changes and not others?'" Bourdon has a somewhat similar theory in his *L'expression des émotions et des tendances dans le langage* (1892), p. 3 foll.
[3] James, *op. cit.*, Vol. II., p. 451.
[4] C. Lange, *Les émotions*, p. 27.
[5] C. Lange, *op. cit.*, p. 82. The physiological theory is also upheld by Sergi; see his work *Dolore e piacere, storia naturale dei sentimenti* (Milano, 1894).

nation of the manner of production of the emotions is mainly the same, both in Lange and in James—namely, a perception immediately determines a movement in the sensorial centres, which communicates itself directly to the vaso-motor centres, a process which is of course quicker in the case of a simple sensory impression than in the case of the association of various presentations.

Though acceptable in parts, many points of this theory must be rejected unless we are prepared to change entirely the character of Psychology. It is, first of all, undeniable that the sensations which accompany the reflex movement in an emotion have a great influence on the emotion itself. Therefore, although it is an exaggeration to say with James that we are sorry because we cry, it is, on the other hand, quite true that weeping increases the intensity of sorrow. Some very interesting observations upon these phenomena have been made by Lange, and more especially by James.[1] It is also necessary to note the contrary fact that whereas at first the external physiological manifestation increases the force of the emotion, it tends after a while to lessen it. There is consequently some truth in saying that sorrow is increased by crying, and that crying calms sorrow.[2] This last fact, indeed, might even be admitted by upholders of the physiological theories as a corroboration of their doctrine that physiological manifestations are the first cause of the emotions. There is also much truth in the observations of James and Lange regarding the action of certain external physical stimuli on the emotions. Every one, for instance, knows the effects that may be produced on an agitated spirit by music and especially by alcoholic stimulants. The emotion, considered from this point of view, presents itself in its completeness as a physical and psychical phenomenon.[3] The "physiological" school concerns itself only with the former aspect. Notwithstanding the close connection between the two, they possess, however, different importance according to the point of view from which they are studied. For the physiologist, who deals principally with purely organic phenomena, mental data are merely "symptoms"; while for the psychologist they are the principal part, physiological phenomena being symptoms and indications which are of use only when direct psychological observation is impossible. Thus, when studied from a psycho-

[1] See James, *op. cit.*, Vol. II., p. 442—486; Lange, *op. cit.*, p. 37—73.
[2] See Höffding, *Outlines*, p. 267; and Ziegler, *Das Gefühl*, p. 213.
[3] James, therefore, is right in saying that "a purely disembodied human emotion is a nonentity" (*op. cit.*, p. 452).

logical point of view, the psychical aspect of the emotion is the principal one, an emotion being essentially a process of consciousness, and the physical aspect has but a secondary importance. The conditions change entirely when the emotion is considered from the physiological point of view. In this case it is not the "emotion" which is the object under consideration, but certain special physiological processes of respiration and circulation which attend it. The distinction between the physical and psychical aspects is considered to be an artificial one by some, who hold that an emotion is in itself a phenomenon of a certain complexity because it consists of physical and psychical elements, but that these elements are inseparable. We also are of this opinion. The distinction is certainly artificial, and the result of a process of abstraction; but it must be borne in mind that science owes a great measure of its progress to the use of abstraction, by which the student can single out a certain group of phenomena, and apply his whole attention to it as if it were entirely isolated from any other. Science, however, avails itself also of another method, which may be called a process of combination, which consists in having recourse to the aid of other branches of investigation possessing some affinity to the subject under consideration, to which they are made to serve as auxiliary sciences. Every science can consequently be a principal and, at the same time, an auxiliary science. It is not, therefore, a case of re-establishing, as is feared by some, the dualism of the Cartesians, but only of finding a scientific method which shall commend itself by its precision. In conclusion, the psychologist should confine himself to the psychical aspect of emotions, the physical aspect being merely a concomitant to be studied in a subsidiary fashion. The one cannot be used to draw conclusions concerning the other. A mental phenomenon by itself has but a qualitative value, not to be expressed in quantities, nor to be understood by other means than direct psychological and individual observation; whereas a physical phenomenon, considered in itself alone, has no subjective value—it is neither good nor evil, beautiful nor ugly, but represents solely quantitative magnitudes.[1] Psychology, being obliged to have recourse to direct experience, must therefore consider both the objective and the subjective aspects—not separated, but in combination. When Lange says that no progress in science was

[1] See G. V. Dearborn's objections to the muscular theory of the emotions in his monograph "The Emotions of Joy" (Supplement to the *Psychological Review*, April, 1899).

possible before certain objective characteristics common to all individuals had been established, he makes a confusion between the physical sciences and science in general. The former may be, and are, hampered by the necessity to which Lange alludes ; but all human science is certainly not obliged to confine itself to one method of observation. The moral sciences, at least, are founded upon psychological phenomena, which Lange calls "subjective." The study of colours, quoted by Lange as an example, does not concern Psychology, which does not study them with respect to their causes, but only in so far as they present themselves to our consciousness—in other words, as "colours," and not as movements. One may even say that the progress of physical science, which reduces all external phenomena to movements, has widened the distance between these phenomena and their causes. Although physical science teaches, for instance, that black and white are not colours, and that the colour orange is the result of mixing red and yellow, from a psychological point of view, black, white, orange, red, and yellow are alike simple colours. The progress of Psychology on the one hand, and of physical science on the other, accentuates the difference between the qualitative facts which form the object of the former, and the quantitative facts which constitute the object of the latter. So likewise, in spite of all efforts to reduce the emotions solely to their external manifestations, they will always remain essentially qualitative processes.

When it is granted that a true psychological interpretation of composite processes of feeling must needs attribute a secondary importance to their concomitant physical phenomena, it is sometimes thought that contemporary experimental Psychology, in adopting the above method, endeavours to prove that the mental phenomenon is the cause of the corresponding external manifestation. This is an error. Mental and physical influence can only be accepted as the consequence of the dualistic hypothesis of the Cartesians. On the contrary, experimental Psychology with Fechner, and especially with Wundt and his disciples, rejects all theories concerning the relations of body and soul, except that of psychophysical parallelism, which, however, is to be understood in the purely empirical sense that a nervous or cerebral process corresponds to every process of consciousness. This principle suffices to establish the possibility of applying to elementary mental processes the methods of physiological research. To go beyond this and to inquire into the priority of the physical or the mental phenomenon is to enter a field of purely philosophical discussion, from which Psychology should hold aloof. In the case of the emotions, we are, and always shall be, unable to establish an even approximately constant relation between the intensity of the stimulus and the intensity of the emotion which it excites. A very feeble stimulus may cause in us a very powerful emotion, and *vice versa*.[1] In fact, the physiological phenomena which accompany an emotion can give us but a very uncertain and even erroneous notion concerning it. The very classification attempted by Lange, and based on purely physiological characteristics, is a manifest proof of the absolute insufficiency of his theory, placing, as it does, in the same category of physiological phenomena (those of increased voluntary innervation) two such very different emotions as joy and anger.[2] The intensity of an emotion, moreover, is not always proportioned to the strength of the physiological commotion. It is a well-known fact that the most deeply felt emotions are those which appear least outwardly, and it is a common saying that "great sorrows are dumb," though it does not follow that such emotions are not often accompanied by very violent physiological disturbances—a fact that should give upholders of psychophysical parallelism food for reflection.

The "physiological" theories are, however, forced to still more preposterous conclusions if they wish to be consistent. There being no doubt that outer expressions of emotion are much more lively in primitive man and in infants than in civilised man and in adults, the obvious deduction springing from the theory of absolute parallelism would be that the emotions are more powerful in the primitive than in the more advanced stages of the individual and of the species, and are, therefore fated in the long run to a gradual disappearance. It is a fact that the simple emotions, such as anger, joy, fear, sorrow, etc., preserve a notable amount of intensity and of expression in adults and in civilised man, whereas in the case of the more complex emotions (which are not determined by an actual or reproduced perception of a concrete object, but are the outcome of ideas), such as intellectual, moral, religious, and even æsthetic

---

[1] It might be possible to establish a comparatively constant relation between the emotions which are connected with the more general organic instincts, such as self-preservation, etc.

[2] Lange, *Les émotions*, p. 82. See Wundt, "Zur Lehre von den Gemüthsbewegungen" (*Philos. Stud.*, Vol. VI., p. 351). See also Bergson, *Essai sur les données immédiates de la conscience*, p. 6.

emotions, the explanation of their origin and development becomes exceedingly difficult, there being no very clearly marked physiological phenomena in their case. There consequently remains no choice but to deny that they are real emotions; and as these ideal emotions are increasingly prevalent in comparison to the simple ones, the only natural conclusion is that the emotional life is gradually becoming less vigorous. Indeed, Lange, who is the most logical amongst the "physiological" authors, says openly, at the conclusion of his work, that if our moral development continues at the present rate, we shall arrive at the realisation of Kant's ideal of a man endowed with pure intellect, for whom all the emotions, even supposing him to be still subject to such annoyances, will be nothing but a form of disease or mental perturbation unworthy of him. Ribot expresses very similar ideas.[1] In these authors we still find the contrast between feeling and intelligence, which we have already noted as wholly devoid of foundation.

Even from a general point of view there are other notable differences between the psychical and physical aspects of emotion which make it impossible to establish a perfect parallelism between them. The contents of our emotions vary continually during the life of the individual and that of the species, owing to the changes in the elements of presentation which produce them, and to the evolution of the mental life as a whole. On the other hand, the ways of expressing the emotions are susceptible of much slighter changes, and exhibit a character of greater fixity.[2] This difference is easily understood when we consider that the content of an emotion is a purely qualitative fact, which eludes all quantitative determination, whilst the external organic form is partly subservient to the rigidity of mechanical laws, and has consequently a much slower evolution. In this case there is a certain analogy with the relations which exist between linguistic symbols and their intellectual contents. The former remain for a very long time practically unaltered, whereas the latter may undergo very great modifications even during the course of a few centuries. In a more general sense we can even

---

[1] Ribot, *La psychologie des sentiments*, p. 19. See G. Villa's paper on this work, pp. 36, 37.

[2] This fact serves to corroborate the common theory that man is "always the same." Those who believe this do not stop to consider that in all human manifestations (religious, social, and especially linguistic) the outer form may be the same when the contents have already undergone radical changes.

find an analogy between the development of the mental life, which is comparatively rapid, and the evolution of the corresponding organic forms, such as the nervous system, and especially the brain, which remain for an indefinite length of time almost stationary. In all these cases we find ourselves face to face with the fact that there is an essential difference between the freedom of the life of consciousness and the rigid mechanism of physical phenomena.[1]

The physiological theory of the psychical functions. The "physiological" theory, unable as it is to explain not only the more complex emotions but also the psychological difference between two simple emotions, is also at fault with regard to the connection between knowledge, feeling, and willing, whose action does not harmonise with the principles which that school sets up as governing the emotions. In the case of the relation between feeling and the outward acts of willing the explanation is easy, for the expression of the emotions is in itself an elementary manifestation of such acts. But this is not enough; we have still to explain the relation of those outward acts to the presentations which cause them. In order to arrive even at the appearance of explanation, the theory must be followed to its extreme consequences—namely, that an act of willing is entirely mechanical, for otherwise the question of how a presentation can bring about an act of will, and what relation exists between the two, must remain unanswered. But in this case these two functions are left in isolation, to the total destruction of the unity of the mental processes, in place whereof we have a separation of the various activities, similar to that proposed by the theory of faculties, which the "physiological" theory takes every opportunity to criticise. According to this school the connection between the mental activities seems to be as follows: a presentation determines a series of reflex acts, which are the starting-point of acts of volition, which in their turn can only be reflex; these acts are then accompanied by muscular sensations, which constitute what is called an "emotion." But in this scheme of mental life there is no place either for inner acts of willing or for acts of conscious volition in general.

The most consistent in following this theory to its extreme conclusions is Lange. James, on the other hand, who is gifted with an uncommon degree of intuition, is often dissatisfied with it, and confines

[1] This analogy holds good only in the case of man; in animals, the mental and the organic appear to be equally stationary.

himself to facts as he finds them. Thus, in manifest contradiction to his own theory, he places the essence of the act of willing in the effort of attention, which is an inner phenomenon. Ribot, on the other hand, seeks to modify Lange's and James's theories in a metaphysical sense. In his opinion, emotion is above all the expression of unconscious organic tendencies arising out of the individual character and constituting its essence. We have already had occasion to observe the vagueness of such expressions, and how liable they are to the most different interpretations.

Most contemporary psychologists, when unprejudiced, hold a different theory as to the nature of feeling. Suffice it to quote Höffding, Wundt, Sully, Baldwin, Ladd, Külpe, Lehmann, and Ziegler. Feeling, in their opinion, is an autonomous mental function quite independent of cognition and of will, although closely connected with both. But although they hold that feeling and will represent the inmost part of consciousness, and are not consequently intellectualists, nevertheless they do not consider them solely as organic functions. As, however, the ideas of these psychologists with respect to feeling and to the connections between the various mental functions are closely connected, they will be better understood when we come to examine the latter.

We must now turn our attention to contemporary theories concerning the Will, which may be reduced to four, three negative and one positive. The first three respectively assimilate the fact of willing to perception (intellectualism), reflex motion (materialism), and feeling, each lending itself to modifications and to combinations with other theories, some psychologists of the intellectualistic school, for example, evincing a leaning towards materialistic ideas, whilst others follow a middle course [1]; the fourth and best attributes a specific character to the will.

Theories concerning the Will.

To begin with the intellectualistic theories, we find that they are nowadays almost solely followed by psychologists of the Herbartian school, such as Drobisch and Volkmann. Herbart's fundamental idea, subsequently modified by his disciples, is that the will is the result of an effort which a presentation makes in order to maintain itself and prevent other presentations from overcoming it. Will, like feeling, according

Intellectualistic theories.

[1] Regarding the ideas of modern pyschologists on the will, see O. Külpe's excellent paper "Die Lehre vom Willen der neueren Psychologie" (*Philos. Stud.*, Vol. V., Nos. 2 and 3, 1888—1889). We shall often have occasion to quote it.

to these doctrines, constitutes but a moment in the life of a presentation, which is the only simple element of the consciousness. This theory, which Drobisch and Volkmann endeavoured to render acceptable by pointing out the importance of impulse in the struggle between presentations, does not take into account the real nature of the act of willing, which is above all an inner activity, which we recognise owing to the special feeling which attends it. If we imagine presentations as existing by themselves, independently of will and of feeling, they would only afford us cognition of external objects and their relations, but not that peculiar feeling of activity which proves to us that we are doing something. This defect is implicitly recognised by the intellectualists themselves when they assert that presentations make an "effort" to overcome other presentations, and that they aspire after the preservation of their own existence. How could we perceive this "effort" and this "aspiration" if it were not that we ourselves "aspire" and "make an effort" towards some particular goal? If it were different—that is to say, if presentations were outside our consciousness, instead of forming a part of it—we should have to admit that it is the presentations and not we ourselves who perceive the "effort"; both of which notions are of course equally inadmissible. We must therefore recognise in the volitional impulse a phenomenon possessing peculiar characteristics of its own, which cannot be explained by means of other mental or physical facts. The "effort" which the Herbartians attribute to presentations we, on the contrary, attribute to the whole consciousness, of which they form but an element, and call it "volitional activity." A presentation, during the moment of making an effort, is no longer merely presentation, for, as such, it expresses only a cognitive phenomenon; but it becomes something more—viz. will.

Moreover, this theory only explains the act of inner volition, in which the activity is manifested with regard to presentations; but the outward act of willing remains unexplained. If with regard to attention the theory of the conflict of presentations may be admitted to have an analogical value, it has none whatever in the case of an outward act of willing, accomplished without any attention and attended by a feeling of activity, which has its origin in muscular sensations. Here it is necessary to have recourse to the far from intellectualistic theory, according to which external acts are merely reflex.

The hypothesis of a conflict between presentations is also contradicted by the fact, to which others have already drawn attention, that several presentations may exist simultaneously in consciousness, though not all possessing the same degree of clearness,[1] we ourselves being wholly unconscious of any struggle, and only perceiving a succession of various presentations attended by feelings and impulses, and nothing more. If we have recourse to the still more questionable theory that the struggle between presentations takes place beneath the threshold of the consciousness, we should be abandoning Psychology in favour of metaphysical speculations.

The fundamental defect of this doctrine consists in being based upon the spiritualistic principle that the soul is distinct from mental phenomena, and that presentations, consequently, can take place even beneath the threshold of consciousness, which becomes a phenomenon of purely secondary importance. There are, however, some psychologists who, with greater consistency, entirely deny the existence of the will. These may be divided into two categories: the first, though recognising that the will is distinct from presentation and feeling, are of opinion that it is not in itself a primitive phenomenon, but a derivative of the latter two; the second, which comprises the so-called "physiological" psychologists, deny the existence of the will as a mental phenomenon, affirming that it consists of nothing beyond the physiological processes which attend it.[2] Those who uphold the first of these theories, which may be called "genetic,"[3] are in their turn to be distinguished into three sections, according as they consider the will as a process resulting both from presentation and from feeling, as itself presentation, or as a developed form of feeling. The last two opinions deserve most attention. The first has few followers, amongst whom is the German pyschologist Th. Waitz. It is difficult to understand how the will can be derived from presentation and feeling. If one could imagine an individual endowed only with presentations and feelings of pleasure or pain, he would, in the presence of external impressions, remain entirely passive, for presentations by themselves only give us a notion of the external world, and feeling produces a state of pleasure or pain and nothing more. The impulse, the will, remains unexplained all

The will considered as a derivative function.

---

[1] Külpe, "Die Lehre vom Willen in der neueren Psychologie" (*Philos. Stud.*, Vol. V., Nos. 2 and 3, pp. 196—197).

[2] See Külpe, as above, p. 83. Külpe discusses minutely the theories of Lipps and Drobisch, both followers of Herbart, regarding the will.

[3] Külpe, as above, p. 214.

the same, because, however intense the feelings which presentations may arouse in us, they can never transform themselves into external or internal acts of volition without changing their nature entirely. Moreover, how could this theory explain those simple acts of willing which are not preceded by any feeling? It is particularly in the lower animals (in which, according to Waitz, the transforming of presentation and feeling into will is most observable) that examples of similar impulsive acts not preceded by any emotion [1] are most frequently met with.

We have said that the last two opinions on the genesis of the will are most important. Herbert Spencer is the most **Spencer's theory.** authoritative supporter of the theory that the will is nothing but a presentation transformed. Spencer draws his conclusions from general philosophical premises. All mental evolution consists, in his opinion, in the passage from a state of incoherent homogeneity to a state of coherent heterogeneity. The primitive state is that of a being who acts in a purely automatic way. Out of this homogeneous state, and owing to the necessity of the organism to adapt its inner to its outward actions, are evolved memory, feeling, will, reason, and so forth. Consequently these, which are the real mental phenomena, become, so to say, adjuncts of those primitive and automatic phenomena. This notion underlies Spencer's definition of the will as "a mental representation of the act, followed by a performance of it."[2] The fundamental and inmost essence of the will is, therefore, not mental but physical and mechanical. The presentation to which the act of volition is reduced, in this way, becomes a secondary element.

Objections may be made to Spencer's theory, on the one hand, from the point of view of the difficulty of explaining an act of willing as a presentation; on the other hand, more generally from the point of view of the transformation of automatic into mental processes. With respect to the former, we may refer to the arguments brought forward against the intellectualistic theories of the Herbartians, which are here equally valid. Presentation in itself is nothing but cognition of the outside world. We may perfectly well, of course, have cognition of our own acts; but this knowledge does not constitute an act of willing, whether it be a simple cognition, or whether a reflection concerning the act itself be added thereto. When I

[1] Külpe, as above, p. 215, etc.
[2] Spencer, *Principles of Psychology*, Vol. I., Part IV., chap. ix., p. 497.

wish to raise my arm, I see in imagination the action I wish to accomplish; but this image is by no means the action itself, which is accomplished only when I put in motion the muscles of the arm.[1] To imagine an act does not constitute an overt act of volition if it is not translated into an external action. Spencer, moreover, only admits acts of external willing: the inner volitional acts, which are unaccompanied by any external action, are not taken into consideration by him, unless he understands as such the representations of cerebral functions, which take place during the accomplishment of these inner acts. We do not, however, have these representations unless we endeavour expressly to evoke them, and even then they must necessarily be very imperfect and inadequate.[2] That a presentation may itself occasionally constitute an act of volition, Spencer naturally cannot admit. Therefore the mental connection which exists between the presentation of the movement and the external act remains unexplained; and there is nothing for it but to admit the existence of two parallel series: one of reflex and automatic acts, which constitute the real essence of the will; and one of mental processes of perception and of feeling. This theory is a logical consequence of Spencer's mode of understanding the genesis of mental life, according to which the primitive fact consists in the reflex mechanical act. His theory was therefore justly described as inspired by a "latent materialism."[3] Maudsley, who, on certain points, follows Spencer closely, affords an instance of how easy is the passage from these ideas to materialistic theories. According to him "the conception of the result or the design in the act of will constitute in fact the essential character of the particular volition."[4]

The theory propounded by Horwicz that the act of willing is the result of the development of feeling involves obvious difficulties. Feeling is in itself a purely passive process, whereas the act of willing is an active phenomenon, which, though generally determined by a state of pleasure or of

The theory of Horwicz.

---

[1] See James's *Principles of Psychology*, Vol. II., p. 522.

[2] See Külpe, as above, p. 223, etc.

[3] Külpe, as above, p. 223. "Wir erhalten hier, auf einer latent materialistischen Grundlage dieselbe Meinung, wie sie auf spiritualischen Boden bei Herbart und Lipps erkennbar wird, dass nämlich das Bewusstsein ein Luxus ist, den sich dort die Materie, hier die Seele erlaubt."

[4] See *The Physiology of Mind*, pp. 430, 431. This theory has recently been upheld by Titchener, who considers the will as an element derived from sensation and feeling. See *Outlines of Psychology*, pp. 134, 255 foll.

pain, may nevertheless occur without being preceded by either, and may follow immediately upon the stimulus. The act of volition is characterised by the change which it brings about, either in the external world or in the course of the presentations, whereas feeling alone does not produce any of these effects, and is merely the expression of a purely subjective state of our consciousness. How it can change into an active state, the theory of Horwicz does not explain.[1]

A yet more infelicitous attempt has been made by some contemporary psychologists who follow the physiological doctrine, and **Physiological** find the essence of the act of willing in reflex action. This **theories.** theory, mainly represented by Münsterberg,[2] is a development of Spencer's. Münsterberg considers volition under three **Münsterberg.** aspects—as pure movement, as a phenomenon of consciousness, and as a conscious movement. The act of willing can be entirely explained, in his opinion, on physical principles, without having recourse to any immaterial essence. Pyschology alone, on the other hand, cannot explain it in a satisfactory manner. As regards the psychical contents of the will, Münsterberg finds nothing beyond muscular sensations; and thus reduces the will to a mere conglomeration of sensations[3] grouped in a particular way. As to the psychophysical relations between the will considered as a psychical phenomenon and as a movement, Münsterberg is of opinion that psychical causality has no place whatever, and that the ultimate problem of the Psychology of the will consists in determining what stimuli of the cerebral centres are necessary in order that the sensations, which are produced by them, shall form the combination described as an act of volition.[4] We have, therefore, in Münsterberg's theory, two contradictory principles—one entirely materialistic, which places the essence of the act of willing in reflex movement, and one intellectualistic, which makes the

[1] Külpe, as above, p. 225 foll. Brentano also subordinates will to feeling, or rather to the feelings, which he calls "phenomena of love and hate." See his *Psychologie vom empirischen Standpunkt*, p. 260 foll. He divides consciousness into the three faculties of perceiving, of judging, and of love and hate.

[2] Hugo Münsterberg, *Die Willenshandlung; Ein Beitrag zur physiologischen Psychologie* (Freiburg, 1888), p. 100.

[3] Münsterberg, *op. cit.*, p. 62: "Der Wille ist nur ein Complex von Empfindungen"; p. 96: "Wir sahen, dass es einen allgemeinen konstanten Willen überhaupt nicht giebt, sondern nur zahllose einzelne Wollungen, und dass diese lediglich eine bestimmte Anordnung sind von Wahrnehmungsvorstellungen und Erinnerungsvorstellungen oder, da alle Vorstellungen aus Empfindungen bestehen, eine bestimmte Anordnung von Empfindungen."

[4] *Op. cit.*, p. 112. See Külpe, as above, p. 231 foll.

essence of the will consist in the presentation of the end which the volitional act has in view. If we explain the teleological character of reflex movements as a mere effect of a mechanical organisation, we are obliged to admit the metaphysical concept of natural teleology. If, on the contrary, we consider them as a transformation of originally voluntary movements, we cannot any longer admit that the reflex act is the initial phenomenon of the will.

No one can deny, as a matter of fact, that even the simplest voluntary acts produce in us a direct feeling of inner activity; we feel that we are willing something, and are not being guided by an external agency. This feeling accompanies all our voluntary actions, of which it forms the distinctive character. The whole mental contents of an act of willing is constituted, in Münsterberg's opinion, by the aggregate of organic sensations which attend the reflex movement. On a theory of this kind we could understand the exclusion from the will of the inner acts of volition, which manifest themselves in modifications of the stream of ideas. Münsterberg, nevertheless, takes into consideration also the inner acts of willing, affirming that they are composed solely of a series of presentations and of special feelings of "innervation" which accompany the muscular effort. The existence of internal mental processes possessing a minimum of external manifestation has ever been the stumbling-block of the so-called "physiological" psychologists when attempting to reduce the emotions and the acts of volition to simple sensory elements. When we endeavour, by means of an intense and continuous effort, to collect our thoughts upon a given object and to turn them towards a certain goal, we perceive principally a feeling of internal activity, and we have the consciousness of "willing" something; but we have no perception that the principal phenomena in our consciousness at that moment are the muscular and cutaneous sensations which are brought about by the act of thinking. After protracted intellectual work we may feel a sense of physical fatigue; but during the work itself, if our mental energies are really concentrated upon it, we have but a very feeble consciousness of the effort accomplished by our body. Nor even if we felt such sensations in a higher degree could they ever be considered essential to the act of willing. Moreover, it is difficult to understand how the "series of presentations" can be considered "elements" of the act of internal willing, which is in reality wholly constituted by them, the psychologist's aim being to ascertain the manner of their origin and development.

This "series of presentations" is put in order by means of a continual and persistent effort of the attention involving a number of acts of choice between the various presentations. These acts of choice are nothing but acts of internal volition, and we are made conscious of them by that peculiar sense of inner activity which Münsterberg holds as of no account. In outer acts of willing the most characteristic element is again the feeling we have of our inner activity, whereas Münsterberg believes it to be composed of two elements—the reflex physiological act, and the presentation of the act to be accomplished. When we are about to accomplish an outward act of willing, says Münsterberg, there arises in us the recollection of the muscular sensations which attended the same act on other occasions. These sensations make up a presentation of the act, which is also a presentation of the effect or purpose of the act itself. We find ourselves, however, here also confronted by the same difficulty we have noted in respect to inner acts of volition. The presentation, which is the effect as well as the purpose of the act which we wish to accomplish, does not arise within us without the intervention of our will, but is brought about by an inner act of willing, and chosen from amongst various others, or, in the case of simple or impulsive acts, where no choice takes place, is the product of an internal impulse which impels us to create it. Münsterberg, who in this agrees with Spencer, attributes to the presentation a purely passive part, thus making it difficult to understand what connection exists between it and the act of volition, the two most important elements of the given state of consciousness. Presentation consequently not only expresses the purpose of the act (as is thought by psychologists who mix up intellectualistic and materialistic ideas), but it is the result of an inner act of volition, or impulse, which is to be found in every case of inner or outer manifestation of consciousness.

Upon the psychophysical interpretation given by Münsterberg of the act of willing there is little to observe, for the materialistic principle on which it is founded has been discussed by us already. We must, however, note the extraordinary conclusion to which Münsterberg is logically driven. Not being able to deny the existence of moral "values" dependent on the will, nor consequently the whole world of action, he is obliged to separate these phenomena from all other mental phenomena, and to exclude them from psychological consideration. According to Münsterberg, they are "pure values," and cannot be scientifically determined in any way. It is manifest that this theory, which bears a close resemblance to Schopenhauer's, is untenable.

We have hitherto been discussing the negative theories concerning the will. We must now examine the positive theories which see in it a phenomenon *sui generis* originally distinct from presentation and feeling. Lotze was one of the first psychologists to assert the autonomy of the will, which he, however, limited to the very restricted field of mere resolve. A resolve is a choice made with full consciousness of one motive among many. Though representing the highest manifestation of volition, this nevertheless does not constitute in itself the entire will, which embraces also such so-called simple and impulsive acts as are not preceded by the feeling of hesitation proper to acts of free choice.[1]

Bain has a very interesting theory on the subject. He affirms that the will is an innate spontaneity of consciousness which manifests itself only when it is determined by a feeling of pleasure or pain, but which is accompanied by the presentation of the final effect of the act to be accomplished.[2] This meaning of the term "spontaneity" is not always very clear in Bain; for it sometimes appears as a purely mental impulse, and sometimes (or rather in the greater number of cases) as a physiological manifestation expressing itself in spontaneous movements determined by the exuberance of accumulated energy in the organism. It is also very difficult upon this theory to explain internal acts of volition, and, indeed, Bain shows great uncertainty when attempting to do so. Another objection to his theory is the fact that not every act of willing is preceded by an emotion or a feeling. In many cases the act follows immediately on the external stimulus, as in simple and impulsive acts, whether external or internal. Bain cannot explain this. The fact is that these simple acts are nothing but the result of a continual repetition of acts which were originally performed as the result of choice, and as such were attended by a peculiar sense of hesitation. The subsequent separation of the act of willing from feeling is the best proof that it can exist by itself, and is not necessarily preceded by the latter.

Bain's theory.

[1] Lotze, *Microcosmos*, Vol. I., p. 199, etc., 286 etc.; *Medicinische Psychologie*, p. 300, etc.
[2] Bain, *The Senses and the Intellect*, Vol. I.; *The Emotions and the Will*, etc.

A position intermediate between Bain and Spencer is occupied by Ribot. He also considers reflex movement as the starting-point of the will, which, through the different stages of impulse and ideo-motor actions develops into an act of choice, the real volition. But this act of choice is not of much value by itself, being merely an affirmative or negative judgment, and not the prime mover of an action, which, on the contrary, is the necessary consequence of feelings of pleasure or pain. The real activity resides, therefore, in the psychophysical organism. Here Ribot falls into the mistake already noticed with respect to the emotions when he recognises, on the one hand, that the will possesses a character of its own as a psychical phenomenon, and considers it, on the other hand, derived from reflex actions and dependent on feelings of pleasure and pain produced by organic impulses.[1] The theory of the evolution of will from reflex action, which Ribot has taken from Spencer, we have already refuted.

Ribot's theory.

Reflex action is purely mechanical, nor can one conceive how any mental act can have evolved itself from it. The entirely passive part that Ribot attributes to the intelligence in the act of choice is highly questionable. He makes no distinction between the mental phenomenon and the reflection upon the mental phenomenon, the latter of which may take place or not without changing the essence of the phenomenon. Thus, when we perform an act of choice, it remains such, even though we do not express a judgment in these terms: " I will and have willed thus and in no other way."[2] What is said of the will may be said with equal reason of presentation and of feeling. When we have an idea in our mind, that idea exists, even if we do not reflect upon the fact that it is in our minds; and when we feel a sense of pleasure or pain, it is not modified by our expressing the sentiment: " I feel this pleasure or this pain." Ribot, moreover, fails to explain internal acts of willing, or to indicate the nature of the connection between presentation and will, which is the great problem of modern Psychology. Briefly, we may say that he, more than others, inclines towards separating the intelligence

[1] The same error is to be noted in Maudsley, *The Physiology of Mind*, p. 409, etc.
[2] See Ribot, *Les maladies de la volonté* (1882; 10th edit. 1895), p. 29: " Considérée comme état de conscience, la volition n'est donc rien de plus qu'une affirmation ou une négation. . . . La volition, par elle même, à titre d'état de conscience, n'a plus d'efficacité pour produire un acte que le jugement pour produire la vérité. L'efficacité vient d'ailleurs " (that is to say, from organic impulses). See Külpe, *op. cit.*, p. 403.

from will and feeling, considering the latter two as organic tendencies, which are, as the most essential factors of our consciousness, responsible for all our mental actions.

Beneke was the first psychologist not only to attribute a character of autonomy to the will, but also to give it the importance of a fundamental factor in consciousness. Although his intention is to follow the empirical introspective method, he does not succeed in casting off certain metaphysical ideas. For instance, he does not reduce all mental phenomena to a few qualitatively simple facts, but to certain special aptitudes, which are virtually the "faculties," by means of which the old-fashioned psychologists explained the phenomena of consciousness.[1] Another proof of the metaphysical character of Beneke's Psychology is that, like Herbart, he makes frequent use of the concept of unconsciousness. The fundamental faculties or dispositions are, in Beneke's view, presentation, feeling, and conation (*Strebung*). The notion of will is broader in Beneke than in the preceding psychologists, whether because conation has its roots in the unconscious, or whether in every mental process there exists an element of effort.[2] The principal defect of this system is that it is founded not on facts, but on hypotheses, for Beneke's "primitive faculties" or "dispositions" can be called by no other name. Nevertheless, his attempt at amplifying the domain of the will, so as to comprise the other mental elements, is worthy of note as being the only way to find out the relation existing between them. Beneke was followed in this direction by others, who even surpassed him in their metaphysical tendencies.

Beneke's theory.

Occupying an intermediate position between these schools, metaphysical on the one hand (considering the will as a blind power, and having their most typical representative in Schopenhauer), empirical or intellectualistic on the other hand (denying the existence or originality of the will), there arose the theories now dominant in contemporary Psychology, amongst which the most notable and complete is that of Wundt. According to Wundt, as we have seen, consciousness consists of two principal elements—presentation (which is objective), and feeling and will (which is subjective). The first has a multiple character, and is susceptible of analysis into simple elements (sensations), which, however, appear always

Wundt's theory.

---

[1] E. Beneke, *Lehrbuch der Psychologie als Naturwissenschaft* (4th edit. 1877), p. 19.
[2] *Op. cit.*, p. 19; Külpe, as above, p. 409, etc.

associated in presentations. The second, on the contrary, has a character of unity, and expresses the subject, which is always "one" as compared to the object, which is manifold. Hence we have simple cognitive elements, but no simple elements of will or of feeling. This character of unity forms the most salient characteristic of the phenomena of consciousness as opposed to physical phenomena.[1] Consciousness is in itself a synthesis, for it collects that which is dispersed in the external world, and elaborates it in a special manner of its own. This synthesis could not be accomplished if our consciousness were only composed of presentations and feelings, for in that case it would have no activity of its own, but would be entirely passive. Its character is, on the contrary, to be *active*, and to react against external stimuli. Feeling is also a reaction against external stimuli, but only manifests itself in the form of pleasure or pain, excitement or depression, tension or relaxation, limited solely to the subject. The true reaction in which consciousness manifests its spontaneity is to be found in the act of volition. The simplest acts of willing are external, and consist in the movements of the body. These movements accompany the emotions when the latter attain a certain degree of intensity. The outward act requires two factors: the mental factor, consisting in consciousness, capable of "will"; and the physiological factor, consisting in the body, capable of executing a given movement. It cannot be said, therefore, that it is an originally reflex act, subsequently transformed into a conscious action, for, in the absence of a consciousness with a given purpose in view, we cannot imagine the accomplishment of an action directed towards that purpose. Experimental Psychology offers unmistakable evidence in favour of the theory that all movements which are now reflex were originally voluntary, in the fact that the continual repetition of certain acts, especially simple acts, tends to do away with the perception of the purpose for which they are performed, transforming them at last into purely mechanical acts, which can be performed unconsciously. The act of volition exhibits, however, a more important form in the internal act—without which it would be impossible to explain the relations between presentation and will.

<small>Active character of the will.</small>

---

[1] These general psychological ideas are expounded by Wundt in various of his works, and especially in his *System der Philosophie*, p. 373 foll., p. 579 foll.; in his *Grundzüge der physiologischen Psychologie*, p. 560 foll. ; and in his *Outlines of Psychology* (Eng. tr.), p. 28 foll., p. 169 foll., and p. 183 foll.

The old Psychology recognised only the overt acts of will, attributing all actions connected with the voluntary sequence of presentations to the faculty of cognition. Even modern psychologists, such as Spencer, Bain, and especially the physiological psychologists, are very much at fault when they attempt to explain the influence of will on presentation. The fact is that the notion of "presentation" has never been properly analysed. The habit still persists of regarding it as a fixed and immutable copy of external objects, without considering that it is the product of an inner activity which selects amongst internal objects, this selection being made by the "will." In presentation we have, consequently, always an act of will. But in our consciousness not all presentations have the same degree of clearness. Some, more than others, are placed in relief by a special effort of the will, called "attention." As in each moment of our mental life there is always some inner process which is more clearly defined than others, we are continually performing some act of volition even when no external action follows it. The will is consequently the fundamental principle of our consciousness, seeing that it determines all mental phenomena, and thus is the starting-point both of the outer and the inner acts of willing.[1]

Will and presentation.

The first use to which a conscious being applies his will naturally concerns those movements of his body which are indispensable to his vital functions and to his very existence. As a primary condition of existence the individual must, first of all, adjust himself to the surroundings in which he lives, and he is therefore obliged to perform a series of actions directed to that end.[2] In the second place (and only in man), we come across internal acts of will which are attended not by movements, but by modifications in the stream of presentations. It is in these actions that the connection between will and presentation manifests itself most clearly. Logical thought—that is to say, the chain of presentations and ideas—comes to be thus explained as a form of the will. It is necessary, however, to note a fact, the neglect of which may easily lead to erroneous conclusions. All acts of willing, whether

[1] See Wundt, *Grundzüge der physiologischen Psychologie*, p. 255 foll.
[2] See Wundt, *System der Philosophie*, p. 545. As the individual is a psychophysical being, the problems concerning the different action of organs and their functions, and therefore the origin of complex organic forms, are both psychological and biological.

external or internal, are divided into two great classes, the first comprising simple or impulsive acts; the second, complex acts, which imply freedom of choice. Simple or impulsive acts are determined by a single motive, whereas complex acts, though they may be determined by a single motive, imply a choice between several. An impulsive action, whether internal or external, is therefore quicker than an act of choice, which is preceded by a feeling of doubt and hesitation. The latter is also termed a free act, or an act of "free will," because it expresses more clearly than any other the freedom, spontaneity, and independence of the individual with regard to external stimuli. Impulsive acts are also acts of volition, though in a lesser degree than acts of free will, and possess the character of spontaneous consciousness, which distinguishes all manifestations of the will. The old Psychology, on the contrary, considered acts of free will as the only manifestations of volition, placing acts of impulse on a par with automatic actions. Impulsive acts have great importance in organic life; but they are not original, it being extremely probable that many actions which are at present impulsive were originally the outcome of choice.[1] The repetition of these actions, stimulated by a feeling of pleasure, which undoubtedly accompanies actions which favour the vital functions, must have gradually rendered impulsive all those acts which have as their object the preservation of the individual and of the species. Consequently, as the psychical life of animals is generally confined to those acts, it follows that it should be almost exclusively composed of simple impulses. The concatenation of these acts is what is called "instinct," which is common to man and animals alike, but is much stronger in the latter, the mental life in man being more independent of external stimuli. In the evolution of the species it is very probable that many of the external acts of volition, which were originally simple or impulsive, became subsequently habitual in the organism as vital and purely reflex functions. This would explain their teleological character. The problem of their origin is connected with the study of primary biological manifestations, concerning which there do not yet exist sufficient scientific data.

Internal acts, properly so-called, produce purely mental effects, with changes in the stream of presentations, and consequently in the feelings which accompany them. A stream of presentations

[1] Wundt, *op. cit.*, p. 545 foll.

means, therefore, a series of acts of volition, as also a series of emotions, seeing that during each single moment of its course we perform an "apperceptive" act. Internal acts may also be simple or complex, purely passive associations or associations guided by free will, and therefore acts of the logical intelligence. The will marks the highest degree of evolution, and it is at the root of all scientific discoveries and of creative art; for without a will to regulate the images which fill, for instance, the mind of an artist in accordance with some pre-established design, he could produce little more than fugitive impressions, and never a complete work of art.

Inner acts of volition.

This theory we owe to Wundt, and it is accepted by the majority of modern psychologists.[1] Its importance with regard to the general connection of psychological phenomena is great. It solves in a satisfactory fashion the problem of the relations between the various elements of the mind, and shows the peculiar character which distinguishes them from mechanical phenomena. Wundt's theory, moreover, has the additional merit of reconciling intellectualism with voluntarism.

The will is not a simple presentation, nor a transformed feeling, but a spontaneous impulse, something *sui generis* which cannot be compared to either of those mental activities. On the other hand, it is not a purely organic and mechanical impulse, manifesting itself in reflex movements, but a conscious phenomenon and a fundamental element of consciousness itself. Reflex movement comes, therefore, as a consequence, and is the transformation of a free and conscious act into an impulsive and mechanical one. This impulse, consequently, is not blind, as Schopenhauer would have it, but produced and guided by a presentation which becomes in this way its purpose, and is originally preceded by a feeling or an emotion, though the latter may be entirely wanting in the impulsive act itself. Will, feeling, and presentation are therefore closely connected, nor can they be separated, except by a process of abstraction. The first two represent the subjective and inmost side of consciousness, the last its objective aspect, but both aspects are closely connected, and not, as Schopenhauer believed, distinct. This connection is best shown in the phenomenon of attention, of which logical thought is the most complete expression.

Attention a fundamental fact.

---

[1] Wundt's theory is not to be found in his works in the above form, but we have attempted to condense it from the various passages in his work where he deals with the general connection of mental processes.

Feeling also necessarily accompanies every sensation and presentation, though not as an inherent quality, but as a subjective state which, though caused by them, is only partly dependent upon them, being in fact a consequence of all the psychical antecedents of the individual and of his character. Feeling, especially in the form of emotion, determines an act of volition (external or internal), which in its turn determines a presentation, by which new feelings and acts of willing are brought into being, and so on. There is thus formed what may be termed a "psychic circle,"[1] in which neither the beginning nor the end, neither the cause nor the effect, of a conscious process are discernible. The will is, however, the central point of all mental manifestations, forming, as it were, the substratum upon which they rest, and constituting the most characteristic of all mental factors. This explains why the new doctrine, which has its most eminent representative in Wundt, has been called *voluntarism*, as opposed to the older intellectualism.[2] It must not be supposed, however, that the will is here understood as Schopenhauer understood it, in the sense of a blind impulse in open contrast to the intelligence. Wundt, on the contrary, sees a close connection between will and intelligence, and considers them to be inseparable. It is not surprising, therefore, that he should have been occasionally accused of being an intellectualist, as well as of being a follower of Schopenhauer.[3]

Unity of the psychical functions. Psychology, after having passed through various phases like the physical sciences, has thus arrived at the notion of the indivisibility of primitive mental factors, which are not separate faculties, but properties of one and the same phenomenon. Old-fashioned physical science also believed that the various physical properties of bodies, such as

[1] Jodl (*Lehrbuch der Psychologie*, p. 136) calls it "der Kreislauf des psychischen Geschehens." See also Ward, *Encyclopædia Britannica*, Vol. XX., pp. 42, 43.

[2] See Paulsen, *Einleitung in die Philosophie*, Bk. I., chap. vi. ("Intellektualistische und voluntaristische Psychologie"). Paulsen was the first to apply the term *voluntaristic* to this new psychological doctrine. His own conception of the will is more metaphysical than Wundt's, and more like Schopenhauer's. The primitive form of the will is, in his opinion, the impulse (*der Trieb*), which appears to consciousness "als gefühlter Drang, auf höherer Stufe als Begierde zu bestimmter Lebensbethätigung" (p. 123). See Wundt, *op. cit.*, p. 579: "In dem Trieb, als dem auf allen Stufen des Psychischen Lebens Anzutreffenden Grundprocess, sind alle Elemente bereits enthalten, die in den höheren Bewusstseinsvorgängen wiederkehren, und diese sind vollständig aus der Verbindung und Differenzirung der Triebe abzuleiten."

[3] Külpe, *Einleitung in die Philosophie*, p. 188. Ladd, *Psychology: Descriptive and Explanatory*, pp. 50—51.

impenetrability, etc., were independent of each other, and that they could be found in opposition as well as in combination. Contemporary Psychology is unanimous in recognising that the three mental properties of cognition, feeling, and willing are inseparable. One of the most eminent modern psychologists, Höffding, attributes great significance to this fact, and, in one of the finest chapters of his work, conclusively proves that there cannot exist cognition unattended by feeling and will, nor feeling and will without presentation to govern them.[1] Höffding concludes that the will is the most fundamental mental phenomenon, and exercises a marked influence upon all the phenomena of consciousness.[2] The action which these elements reciprocally exercise upon each other is also noted by Sully,[3] Jodl, Baldwin, and other contemporary psychologists.[4]

In order, nevertheless, that the absurd notion of the division of the faculties (which is partly maintained by the division of the subject-matter of Psychology into the three sections of cognition, feeling, and will)[5] may be completely superseded, it is especially necessary to bear in mind the capital importance of the will as the foundation of all mental phenomena, in which all the activities of consciousness are concentrated, and whence they, so to say, radiate. The problem of the relation between will and cognition, with which metaphysicians had grappled to no avail, owing to their limitation of the will to mere external movements, is thus resolved by scientific Psychology. The metaphysical dissertations on the subject in Hartmann's *Philosophy of the Unconscious* are well known. As it was not possible to explain the relation of will to cognition with the ideas current amongst the old psychologists, Hartmann was obliged to have recourse to the hypothesis of unconscious ideas. Similarly,

---

[1] See Höffding, *Outlines of Psychology*, p. 87 foll., p. 298 foll., p. 321 foll.

[2] "If any one of the three species of conscious elements is to be regarded the original form of consciousness, it must evidently be the will" (Höffding, *op. cit.*, p. 99).

[3] Sully, *The Human Mind*, I., p. 67, etc. On the interdependence of sensation and movement, see Feré's interesting book *Sensation et mouvement*, (1887).

[4] Jodl, *Lehrbuch der Psychologie*, pp. 128—139 ("Grundfunctionen des Bewusstseins"): "Empfindung, Gefühl, Wille in untrennbarer Abhängigkeit von einander stehend, reguliren sich gegenseitig und führen sich wechselseitig immer neue Kraft zu." Baldwin, *Handbook of Psychology*, Vol. I., pp. 40—41 ("Unity of the Three Classes in Consciousness").

[5] See Ladd, *op. cit.*, p. 58; see also Stout's chapter on "Faulty Psychology" (*Manual of Psychology*, p. 103 foll.).

the explanation given by Spencer, followed by Bain, Ribot, and others of the ideo-motor impulses, is insufficient—in the first place, because the act of willing is restricted to the outer act, considered as a reflex movement; and in the second place, because it does not explain the relation between presentation and will. No course, consequently, is left but to consider the outer act of volition simply as the natural continuation of the inner act, which consists in apperception, and is essential to determine it. It may be objected that not even this theory explains how the corporeal movement can so combine itself with the mental impulse as to constitute a single phenomenon. This, however, is a question of much more general import than that of the genesis of the will, inasmuch as it is connected with the problem of the relations between mind and body, which has been already discussed. We have seen that the most acceptable hypothesis on that question is the theory of psychophysical parallelism. Psychology, moreover, must limit its investigations to the study of the formation and evolution of mental phenomena, and of the causal relations which connect them. Thus, with respect to the will, its object is to investigate its origin, and to ascertain its relations to presentation and feeling.

We have seen that the data of individual and experimental Psychology do not admit of a separation between the three elements of will, feeling, and cognition, which are not to be considered as entities, but as different properties of the same phenomenon. We must now inquire whether the history of the evolution of consciousness arrives at a different conclusion.

The greatest philosopher of the nineteenth century who has asserted and upheld the principle of evolution in all branches of existence—Herbert Spencer—fails to apply his general doctrine consistently to Psychology. According to his theory, evolution follows two parallel lines—from the homogeneous to the heterogeneous, and from the disconnected to the connected. According to Spencer, a confused mass with no differentiation nor connection of parts gradually becomes evolved into an organisation, the constituents of which assume little by little different functions, and become always more closely connected. Spencer applies this doctrine to general cosmology and individual organisms, as well as to social institutions and to all manifestations of the spirit. It would appear natural that he should admit the same with regard to the evolution of conscious-

Spencer's theory of evolution.

ness, from which social institutions spring, and, therefore, that from a homogeneous mass of mingled sensation, feeling, and will with no differentiation, there should gradually have evolved itself an increasingly complex whole with variously developed and connected constituent parts. Instead of this, Spencer is of opinion that the mental functions are derived solely from reflex movement. His preference for the conception of mechanical evolution as applied to Psychology is here especially patent. No mental function can be derived from a reflex movement, which is purely mechanical, nor a conscious act of willing from a presentation. If we consider micro-organisms, in which mental life is reduced to the most elementary functions, we find that they possess, though in an inconsiderable degree, the three activities which are found in a fully developed consciousness—namely, cognition in its most rudimentary form of pure sensation, feeling, consisting probably in a confused state of organic well-being, or the reverse, and, finally, volition in its impulsive form, and having for its object the preservation of the individual and of the species. As a consequence of the progressive differentiation of the organs and of the functions of the body, the mental life becomes also **Simultaneous** more complex. Sensation, from its primitive form of a **evolution of the psychical** feeling of confused and homogeneous motion or of tactile **faculties.** and organic sensation, becomes, owing to the formation of the various sensorial organs, split up into various kinds of sensations. The sensorial life becomes more varied, presentation gives place to memory and to associations, and, finally, all these elements, variously combined, constitute that web of mental phenomena which makes up the consciousness of the anatomically and physiologically highest and most differentiated animal—man. Mental evolution, understood in this fashion, runs perfectly parallel with biological evolution.

The fundamental activities of consciousness are thus developed by a progressive evolution, though remaining closely connected with each other, precisely as the various parts of the organism are developed in organic evolution.[1] The greater complexity of perceptive and ideational elements brings with it necessarily a greater wealth of feeling and a greater complication of the acts of volition. In the history of human thought and feeling—in other words, in the history of civilisation—we find abundant proof of

[1] See Külpe, *Einleitung in die Philosophie*, p. 195, and *Philos. Studien* (Vol. V., chap. ii. "Die Lehre vom Willen," etc., p. 221); Jodl, *op. cit.*, p. 137; Ladd, *op. cit.*, p. 58.

this. The contrast between intellect on the one hand, and feeling and will on the other, which Schopenhauer accepted as an incontrovertible fact, and which is a fundamental tenet of many contemporary novelists (who often pose as professional psychologists), is by no means confirmed by historical observation. According to Schopenhauer, man's innermost nature, constituted by innate, deeply rooted instincts, is not susceptible of change, in spite of the continual progress of his intelligence; for the latter has a purely cognitive mission, and does not influence the original character of the individual. The mind may consequently be endowed with acumen and culture, it may perceive what is wrong and disapprove of it; but if the character of the individual is inclined to wrongdoing, the intelligence cannot prevent or even correct his reprehensible inclinations. Well-doing or wrong-doing do not therefore depend upon the intellect, but on the character, on the "will." A certain affinity may be noticed between this theory and the well-known doctrine of Rousseau, according to which man is born with good qualities and spoilt by civilisation. Rousseau also lays stress on the contrast between intellectual culture and the primitive feelings, considering, however, that the good instincts alone are original. Schopenhauer goes further, and severs entirely cognition from volition.

Intellect and character.

Schopenhauer's theory.

Although this doctrine enjoys a certain amount of favour (especially among novelists), it is nevertheless certain that few psychological doctrines are so lacking in solid foundation. It is a fact that we do not always make our actions tally with our ideas, and that, in spite of the highest moral principles we profess, we do not always succeed in overcoming our bad inclinations and in getting the better of our foibles. There are even cases in which men of no common degree of intelligence and culture commit actions which reveal a low mind, and others in which learning, talent, and refinement of artistic taste are coupled with a total absence of moral sense, or even of the most elementary feelings of humanity. The latter cases are, however, so generally recognised as abnormal that they cannot be explained without admitting the presence of a serious disorder of the mental faculties, and are consequently to be considered by psychiatry. Yet even the more frequent cases, in which there exists a certain discord between ideas, feelings, and actions, cannot be adduced as a proof that there is no connection between will and knowledge. The connections between the various mental activities cannot be considered as physical relations, where a given cause invariably produces a certain effect, nor can they be considered only from the point of view of the individual consciousness; but they must, on the contrary, be studied from the point of view of historical evolution as a whole. As we shall see farther on, in respect to mental phenomena we cannot speak of effects which take place in a certain measure and in a given form, and consequently are easily determined beforehand. We cannot say in advance that a certain form and degree of feeling and a certain act of volition will follow on a given presentation. Moreover, these three manifestations are almost always combined into one single process, so that we cannot tell which of them is the cause and which the effect of the others. The relation between them is one of close interdependence, and must be understood as a connection existing between various parts of an organism, which are all closely connected and are all simultaneously and progressively evolved, but none of which can be fixed upon as the cause of the others. Similarly we find a simultaneous and progressive evolution of the mental activities, but, owing to their close connection, each has an influence on the development of the others, as is the case with the different parts of the organism.[1] It is thus natural that the growth and complication of the cognitive life should have an influence on the feelings and the volition. It must, however, be borne in mind that each of these two parts—objective and subjective—develops itself in accordance with its nature; the objective and cognitive element much earlier than the subjective,

Morality and Progress. for ideas travel much more rapidly than feelings, which are conservative by nature.[2] There have been moments in the life of humanity when, owing to some individual manifestation of genius, men have been too sanguine concerning the rate of progress attained, and such moments have generally been followed by periods of disillusion, when it has been perceived that the feelings and habits of humanity had not advanced at the same pace as its ideas. An apposite instance of this we have in the intellectualist and revolutionary period of the second half of the eighteenth century, which was followed by the clerical and romantic reaction of the beginning of the nineteenth. These facts,

---

[1] See Ladd, who speaks (*op. cit.*, p. 58) of all the so-called faculties as resulting from the development of mental life by the combination and elaboration of the simpler and more elementary psychical activities.

[2] This is shown, with his usual clearness and force, by Höffding in his *Psychology*, p. 240, and in his *Ethik*, p. 321.

however undeniable, do not destroy the principle by which mental elements are closely connected in their evolution. A fact generally admitted, even by those who deny the above principles, is that not only have moral ideas made great progress, but (although this is denied by many) that the moral feelings and habits which constitute morality have made great progress. If we have to notice a discord between our ideas and our actions, this springs from the fact that our moral standard has become higher, and that the effort which we constantly make to conform our actions to it is necessarily somewhat detrimental to the moral equilibrium.

This is well in one respect, for it indicates that certain habits, which we originally followed unhesitatingly, being out of harmony with our new ideas, are no longer satisfactory. The history of civilisation may be called a continual effort to adapt feelings and habits to new moral ideas. Many of the ideas which were once the prerogative of a chosen few have now entered into the popular mind and are sanctioned by usage and law. Likewise many actions which used to be habitual, and even considered natural, are now considered criminal and are universally stigmatised. In the same manner our own individual and social customs will in their turn some day be condemned as immoral, and others which we do not even think of, or only look upon as unattainable ideals, may some day be common. The morality of a country must consequently be judged not by the number of immoral facts which take place in that country, but by the reaction which such events cause on the moral consciousness of the majority of its inhabitants. When the moral consciousness is high, the moral standard will also be high, and the effort to reach it will be general.[1]

It is not the case, therefore, that mental culture leaves the foundation of individual character intact, for the character, though possessing a substratum of hereditary instincts and aptitudes, is nevertheless in a state of continual formation, and therefore susceptible to the influences and circumstances of the external world and of intellectual culture. In order to have a real, conscious morality, the mind must be free and aspire towards high ideals, and nothing favours such a state so much as intellectual culture. Primitive and ignorant man cannot have a very high degree of morality, owing to the fact that instinct alone is only capable of

---

[1] See Höffding, *Ethik*, p. 106 ("Ist die Kultur ein Weg zur allgemeinen Wohlfahrt"); J. H. Muirhead, *Elements of Ethics*, Bk. V.; and J. S. Mackenzie, *A Manual of Ethics*, Bk. III., chap. vii.

restricted moral ideas and feelings. Where instinct rules, there may exist, perhaps, a greater degree of harmony between the various psychical activities, but not a morality in the proper sense of the word. The theory, therefore, that culture spoils the original good instincts in man is entirely false, and finds no corroboration either in the study of individuals or in history.[1]

What is true in the historical evolution of civilisation is true in the case of individual Psychology. In the individual we always find the three fundamental properties of consciousness closely connected. None of them can exist by itself or be the cause of the other two. The mental factor most often neglected by modern as well as by the old Psychology is feeling. The poles of conscious life, according to some psychological theories, are the intelligence and the will, the latter expressing most clearly the distinctive character of liberty and spontaneous conscious activity. As regards feeling, we have seen how certain recent theories either eliminate it entirely or reduce it to a factor of secondary importance. Intellectual phenomena, according to these doctrines, are unaccompanied by feeling or emotion, so that we arrive thereby at a complete separation of the three psychical activities. Few theories have as little foundation. The notion of a will which should be set in motion by purely intellectual motives is an absurdity. What really gives the impulse to an act of volition is in every case a feeling or an emotion. Emotion and act constitute together the process of volition. Even the most abstract intellectual actions are determined by feelings, and men who consecrate their lives to purely scientific and intellectual objects, so far from being without any capacity for feeling, as is generally supposed, are, on the contrary, generally inspired by the most noble ideals and emotions.[2] Their indifference to everything which does not concern their ideal is what causes them commonly to be thought insensible. Hence the absurdity of the notion that feeling is destined to gradually dwindle away. It is enough to observe the immense, and often disinterested, work which goes on daily in every field of human activity, and especially in that

[1] Höffding (*Ethik*, p. 109) rightly says that it is as much a duty to remove the savage or the child from the state of restricted moral ideas in which he finds himself " as to awaken a sleeper from somnambulism dangerous to himself and others."

[2] See G. T. Ladd in his work on the *Philosophy of Knowledge* (New York, 1897), p. 165 : " No cognition at all is possible without the presence of affective and emotional factors in the very act of cognition, or without the influence of such factors over the nature of the cognitive process itself. To know is to feel as well as to think."

of science and that of art, to be convinced of that fact. Would such daring and noble endeavours be possible in a world without ideals and guided solely by intellect?[1]

Modern Psychology therefore no longer admits the division of consciousness into so many distinct and disconnected faculties. The notion of the unity of consciousness is now an accepted fact. Consciousness is not divided into higher and lower faculties, because it is composed of elements which mingle and separate in continually changing formations. These primary elements are reduced to two—sensations and simple feelings. From the former are evolved the various presentative and ideational complexes; from the latter, the emotions and volitional processes. The will is not, properly speaking, a mental factor, but something more. It is the primary impulse which sets in motion the development of conscious activity and regulates the formation and various combinations of psychical complexes. If the whole of consciousness is thus reduced to psychical elements, the theory of its division into higher and lower faculties, which was a relic of the Platonic and Aristotelian philosophy, falls to the ground. Between sensations and the higher forms of intelligence there is only a difference of degree of complexity. Nor can one talk of faculties of the mind, but only of properties, the psychical phenomena manifesting themselves in the three forms of cognition, feeling, and will.

[1] I have noted this in my paper above quoted on Ribot's *Psychology of the Feelings* (*Rivista Italiana di filosofia*, 1896).

CHAPTER VI

ON THE COMPOSITION AND DEVELOPMENT OF MENTAL LIFE

GRANTED that, as we have seen in the preceding chapter, the so-called mental "faculties" are nothing but properties or aspects of consciousness, closely connected among themselves in a united whole, there would seem to exist no longer any reason for dividing the subject-matter of Psychology into three classes, according as it refers to cognition, feeling, or will.

In accordance with this view, the best method to follow would be apparently that of considering the mental processes as a whole and as they present themselves immediately—that is, as a complex of presentations of actual objects and representations of the memory, of various kinds of feelings, desires, impulses, and so forth. Nor have there been wanting those amongst modern psychologists who have followed that method. Nevertheless, it cannot be called a scientific method. With equal reason, the physical and biological sciences might deal in the same way with the several phenomena which form their subject-matter, studying them as they present themselves to direct observation. Scientific observation, however, is not identical with empirical observation. The former is not content with taking phenomena as they come, and dealing with them according to the causal order in which they appear; but endeavours to establish a genetic sequence between them, and to show why a given phenomenon should result from one particular cause and not from another. This requires a process of analysis which has for its object the isolation and dissection of the various mental processes, and the reduction of the more complex to the simpler, so as to find a scientific explanation of the genesis and evolution of consciousness. This is what the experimental method has most successfully effected, and modern psychological treatises all keep more or less explicitly to this method of proceeding from the simpler to the more complex processes. Wundt has kept to it in his last work of general

Psychological analysis.

Psychology, and has followed it more systematically than other authors. Even such authors as Höffding (who still retain the threefold division as the basis of discussion) allow it to be plainly understood that such a distinction is purely formal and external.

The old Psychology, and especially that of Herbart, took presentations as the elements of mind, whereas it has now been proved that these are themselves compounded of simpler elements—viz. sensations. Considered as such, presentations are not immutable, as the external objects to which they refer, but are regulated by the laws of consciousness, which govern the mental factors, whereof they are compounded.[1]

The experimental method has enabled Psychology to make an accurate study of sensation, the result of which has been to add to the five classes known to the old Psychology (viz. the senses of touch, smell, sight, hearing, and taste) two important orders of sensations—namely, muscular or motor, and organic or diffused.[2]

Various kinds of sensations.

In order to produce a sensation a stimulus is necessary, and this is differently understood by Psychology and Physiology. A stimulus in physiology is that which produces a change in the nervous system. When the nervous excitation is not perceived by consciousness—*i.e.* when it fails to reach the "threshold" of the latter—it is a purely physiological excitation. We have, therefore,

---

[1] See W. E. Scripture's article "Zur Definition einer Vorstellung" (*Philosophische Studien*, Vol. VII., p. 213).

[2] The organic sensations (*Organempfindungen*) embrace, according to Külpe, the "muscular, tendinous, articular, and common sensations." The last he analyses with great ability. Külpe, moreover, believes in the existence of another sense, which he calls the "static," or the sense of the equilibrium of our body, connected with the semicircular canals of the inner aural apparatus. This opinion, however, is by no means generally accepted. Wundt comprises the sensations of motion (organic and tactile sensations) in one single class, which he calls that of the "general sense" (des allgemeinen Sinnes, *Outlines*, p. 46 ; *Grundzüge der physiologischen Psychologie*, Vol. I., p. 140 foll.). James (*Psychology*) distinguishes two classes—one of touch, temperature, pain, and muscular sensations, the other of sensations of motion. Baldwin adds to the seven classes we have quoted the sensation of temperature (*Handbook*, etc., Vol. I., p. 97). Sully (*Human Mind*, Vol. I.) divides the senses into six classes, putting together muscular and diffused sensations (p. 122 foll.). Jodl keeps to the division into seven classes. This part of Psychology possesses a very abundant literature. Amongst special works, suffice it to quote Mach's writings, Stumpf's on acoustic sensations, Kröner's on the corporeal sense, and Helmholtz's on visual sensations.

a stimulus in a psychological sense only in the case that it affects consciousness.[1] The stimulus may be external or internal, according as it is constituted by processes, which take place without or within the body. External stimuli are physical or chemical, the former being sometimes divided as follows: mechanical (pressure, collision, dragging); acoustic (aerial, periodical, and non-periodical vibrations); thermal (cold and heat); optical (homogeneous and mixed light); and electrical (galvanic, induction currents).[2] The process which precedes the nervous stimulus is likewise physical or chemical. Thus we have mechanical senses in the case of pressure and hearing, and chemical senses in the case of temperature, smell, taste, and sight. Physiological researches on the mechanical and chemical properties of the nerves are sufficiently familiar, as, for instance, the hypothesis (now generally rejected) that they possess a peculiar quality in virtue of which they are only capable of transmitting to the cerebral centres that particular form of stimulus and no other.[3] The internal stimuli are also called physiological, and may be distinguished into peripheral and central, according as they have their origin in the bodily organs or in the brain itself. A central stimulus is indispensable in order to bring about a sensation, whereas a peripheral or physical stimulus is not always necessary, and accordingly some psychologists divide the sensations into the two great categories of the external or peripheral and the reproduced.[4] While, however, the old Psychology believed that the processes of reproduction are purely psychical, and without any physiological substratum, modern Psychology, though recognising the great difference between perceived and reproduced sensations, does not admit that there exists any substantial difference of principle between them.

The sensations which are generally studied first are the cutaneous tactile, or general sensations. The term "general" is applied to them for two reasons: first, because the sense of touch is the one which offers the greatest sensitive surface to external stimuli; secondly, because it is the only sense common to all organic beings from which the other senses have been

---

[1] This is the definition given by Külpe, *Outlines*, p. 78.

[2] Külpe, *op. cit.* p. 80.

[3] See Wundt's ample treatment of the subject in his *Grundzüge der physiologischen Psychologie*, Vol. I., Part I., chap. vi.; Part II., chap. vii. See also his *Outlines*, p. 38.

[4] Külpe divides them into peripherally and centrally initiated.

evolved by a gradual process of differentiation.[1] Some psychologists (such as Wundt and James), taking rather the quality than the origin of the sensations into consideration, place the tactile together with the muscular and organic sensations, under the comprehensive term of "sensations of the general sense," dividing them subsequently into the four classes of sensations of pressure, of cold, of heat, and of pain. Those sometimes called muscular, which are the result of tension and movements of the muscles and of the joints, are thus reduced to simple sensations of pressure; while the so-called organic or diffused sensations, which are caused by the vital organic functions, are likewise reduced to sensations of pressure or of pain. The uncertainty and disagreement observable in the classifications given of these "general" sensations are an inevitable consequence of the difficulty of distinguishing them with precision, if one confines oneself to the "qualitative" aspect. On the other hand, the distinction becomes more marked when the emphasis is laid upon the intensity of feeling attending each class. It is a fact, for instance, that organic sensations exercise more influence upon the general disposition of the mind probably than any other order of sensations, owing especially to the intensity of the tone of feeling which is connected with them. There are also vivid feelings related to sensations of temperature, whereas those in connection with sensations of pressure and caused by the muscles are less intense.

Amongst these general sensations, the muscular and the organic or diffused have been the object of very careful study in recent times. Bain was the first to study the muscular sense and to draw attention to its importance in the evolution of mental life.[2] For it must be remembered that muscular sensations are associated with all kinds of complex mental functions, and contribute jointly with visual sensations to the formation of space-presentations. Some modern psychologists have even exaggerated their importance to the extent of considering them the only positive data we have for determining the character of most mental processes. Diffused and organic sensations have also been carefully studied, especially by physiologists, and as regards their relations with the physiological phenomena which cause them.[3] An attempt has also been made at classifying

[1] Wundt, *Grundzüge*, Vol. I., p. 410.
[2] Bain, *Senses and Intellect*, Part I., chap. ii.
[3] See Beaunis, *Les sensations internes* Paris, (1889). Under that name Beaunis studies organic and muscular sensations, sensations of pain, etc.

with precision gustatory sensations, which have been divided into four principal categories—acid, sweet, bitter, and salt. Acoustic sensations fall naturally into two classes—one of simple noise-sensations, which are homogeneous, and one of tone-sensations, which are complex. Visual sensations, lastly, are divided into achromatic and chromatic. The quality of the sensations once described, Psychology endeavours to establish their intensity by means of the methods enumerated in the preceding chapter.

After sensations it is necessary to consider the second of the two primary psychical elements—viz. simple feelings. Every **Psychical elements.** sensation is connected with a feeling-tone, which, however, is never found isolated in reality, but is the product of a twofold process of abstraction. It is necessary to separate it, in the first place, from its sensation, and, in the second place, to choose from among the various feelings which may accompany a sensation the one which is most constantly connected with it.

Simple feelings are an addition of modern experimental Psychology, for the old-fashioned intellectualist school, as well as modern English empirical Psychology, held as an undisputed dogma that the mental life reduces itself in the last analysis to sensations.[1] Even now this is not an uncommon mistake. Meantime we reserve it for consideration in the next chapter.

All writers, however, who follow modern scientific methods are not agreed in accepting these conclusions. Sully, in his chief work *The Human Mind* (1892), as well as in his shorter *Outlines of Psychology* (2nd edit. 1895), places amongst the "primitive psychical elements" not only the sensations and simple affective phenomena, but also the simple reactions and primary psychophysical complications—that is to say, reflex and instinctive acts. Sully, moreover, following herein the example of several contemporary psychologists, attributes to sensation, besides quality and intensity, also the character of massiveness or extensity. "Next to intensity and quality," says he, "the most important feature of sensation is massiveness or extensity . . . . Extensity is thus a new quantitative aspect or dimension of sensation. There is more or less of sensation according as a larger or smaller sensitive area is acted upon. In certain cases, especially that of sensations of touch and sight, this

[1] See Külpe, *Outlines*, p. 230 foll., on the "Investigation of the Feelings."

extensity, or extensive magnitude, becomes definitely appreciable or measurable."[1]

Thus also James maintains that "the element which is more or less discernible in every sensation is the original sensation of space, which, by means of processes of discrimination, association, and selection, gives us the exact knowledge of space we may subsequently possess."[2]

James Ward is likewise of opinion that just as intensity is as much an element of sensation as the sensible quality, so extension, being an entirely peculiar feeling inseparable from the sensational quality which accompanies it, must also be considered a sensational element.[3] Külpe, Jodl, and Titchener are also of the opinion that besides quality and intensity, extension and duration are characteristics of sensation.[4] Baldwin, on the contrary, besides quality and intensity (which he improperly calls "quantity"), adds duration, and the tone of feeling accompanying each sensation.[5]

These opinions of some of the best contemporary psychologists deserve notice, inasmuch as they furnish further proof of the fact which we have already touched upon—namely, that the experimental method has not yet succeeded in doing away with certain traditional ideas, which are an obstacle to the adoption by Psychology of a method similar to that of the physical sciences. The physical sciences, in their search after primary elements, must of necessity sever them by means of abstraction from all their surroundings, in order to subsequently examine the laws which govern their co-ordination and composition. This must also be done by Psychology. The experimental method, after a minute analysis of our perceptions, has succeeded in reducing them to two kinds of primitive and simple elements—that is, sensations

---

[1] Sully, *The Human Mind*, Vol. I., p. 94.

[2] James, *The Principles of Psychology*, Vol. II., p. 135. "In the sensations of hearing, touch, sight, and pain we are accustomed to distinguish from among the other elements the element of voluminousness" (p. 134).

[3] See *Encyclopædia Britannica*, 9th edit., art. "Psychology," pp. 46—53. See the same ideas in Stumpf, *Tonpyschologie*, pp. 207—211.

[4] Külpe, *Outlines*, p. 29: "Applying this criterion to sensation, we have to predicate of it four attributes: quality, intensity, duration, and extension." Extension is the property only of tactile and visual sensations; quality and duration are common to all sensations; intensity is excluded from visual sensations because every change in their intensity produces at the same time a change of quality. See also Jodl, *Lehrbuch*, p. 203.

[5] Baldwin, *Handbook of Psychology*, Vol. I., p. 85.

and elementary feelings. These are really and essentially psychical elements, as being purely qualities, the idea of quantity being excluded from them. It is true, as James notes, that a sensation cannot be separated from the particular point of space to which it refers; but Psychology is in no way concerned with the relations which hold between the internal and external orders of phenomena. Seeing that this is a question regarding the principles and conditions of our knowledge, it must be left to the science of epistemology. Psychology, on the contrary, has to consider sensations and elementary feelings by themselves, as qualitative and intensive states, and to ascertain the different modes in which they are organised and combined in order to form the various mental processes. Of the latter, the perception of space and that of time are the first and simplest, being the outcome of the relation between two or more sensations.

The sensations possess an essentially qualitative character.

In order, therefore, to form a true conception of what a sensation is, it is necessary not only to make abstraction from the other sensations which accompany it and are caused by sensorial impressions, but also from reproduced sensations which may easily become associated with them. Sensation, therefore, is a pure abstraction,[1] like the mathematical point or line, and as such is merely qualitative and intensive, for extension and duration, being the product of the combination of several sensations, are consequently not primitive properties.[2] For this reason the first instinctive actions of an infant cannot be counted, as Sully thinks, as primary psychical elements, for they imply a relation between several sensations, whether muscular, visual, or acoustic. Sully, moreover, treats of instinct immediately after instinctive action; whereas, as we know, instinct is a very complex process which can only be understood after the whole of human individual Psychology has been dealt with.

Amongst other errors that call for mention is that of considering sensations as physical phenomena, and thus of denying them the character of phenomena of consciousness.[3] That this is

---

[1] James also (*Principles of Psychology*, Vol. II., p. 3), maintains that a pure sensation is an abstraction, but attributes both duration and extension to it.

[2] The purely abstract quality of sensations is very well set forth by R. Ardigò in his work *L'unità della coscienza*, pp. 75, 76, 81, 82.

[3] Amongst the authors who are guilty of this mistake is Brentano. See his *Psychologie vom empirischen Standpunkte*, i. 103, etc. He offers as examples of physical phenomena, heat, cold, sound, etc. Cf. Külpe's *Outlines*, p. 25.

possible proves the uncertainty which still reigns concerning the most fundamental questions of psychological method.

This uncertainty appears also in the ambiguous use of the word "feeling," which is sometimes applied in the sense of sensation and sometimes in its true meaning. We admit with Ward and Baldwin that a special feeling always accompanies combinations of sensations in space or time; but that it is an inherent quality of sensation is inadmissible. Feeling is not, as we have said, a fact which varies with the varying of every sensation, so that each has a special tone of feeling of its own, but it is, on the contrary, a psychical phenomenon of a uniform nature, which, though it can vary with the varying of the sensations, is dependent principally upon the general dispositions of the psychophysical individual.[1] The first combinations of psychical elements, which Germans call *Gebilde*, are therefore those of space and of time, for we localise sensations first of all according to time and space. Experimental Psychology, however, instead of giving the first place to these simple forms of combination, gives priority to a still more simple form, called by some "intensive presentations" and by others "fusions." These occupy, so to say, a middle place between pure sensations and the presentations of time and space, for the sensations which make them up are arranged in such a way that the result is not an extensive property, but only a new intensive quality. Their constituent elements are not clearly distinguishable one from the other, but are mingled into a single comprehensive impression, and cannot be analysed except through the peculiar quality of each.[2] The best example of these intensive fusions is afforded by acoustic sensations. Külpe, in his *Outlines of Psychology*, devotes careful study to the fusion of sounds, considering it in relation to the quality, the intensity, the number of the component parts, and other special conditions, such as attention, practice, expectation,[3] etc. Similar fusions are also accomplished in the case of visual sensations and of the so-called general sense, and especially of organic or diffused sensations.[4]

Intensive and extensive presentations.

We have only hitherto considered the fusion which takes place between sensations of the same order; but, in the opinion

---

[1] S. H. Cornelius, *Psychologie*, p. 75.
[2] See Wundt, *Outlines*, p. 75 foll.
[3] Külpe, *Outlines*, p. 280 ("On Fusion.") Wundt, on the contrary, does not treat specially of it in his *Grundzüge*.
[4] *Op. cit.*, p. 308 foll.

of some (Külpe, for instance), it may also occur between different kinds of sensations, in which case the process takes place which Herbart termed "complication." Many of these cases, however, are cases of associations between one or several present sensations and other remembered sensations, and, moreover, a distinction has to be made between the attributes of the elements and those of the psychical compounds into which they enter.[1] Külpe, who lays great stress on the phenomenon of fusion, places under this category various emotional and volitional facts, such as emotions (*Affecte*), impulses, and the movements of expression.

Coming next to "extensive" presentations, these are divided into "space-" and "time-" presentations. Space-presentations, **Space- and time-presentations.** although they may be caused by any kind of sensation, are nevertheless originally peculiar to two senses —the sense of touch and the sense of sight. And here the oft-recurring problem of the localisation of the stimulus presents itself anew. This localisation is not the direct product of a single presentation, but the result of a relation between tactile and visual presentations, the sense of touch always producing a visualisation, though often but an obscure one, of the object which has been touched. By means of tactile sensation alone localisation could not be explained, except by admitting the theory (not founded on experience) that the property of space is, as some psychologists would have it, inherent in the sensation. Lotze's nativistic theory of local signs must consequently be modified in the sense of admitting a constant, though imperfect, fusion between the local signs and the visual images of the corresponding parts of the object. The local signs in both cases are merely subjective elements, which always stand in an identical relation to each other, however the external impressions may vary: hence the constancy of the properties of space, as compared with the various and changeable qualitative properties of the objects which it contains.[2]

Visual presentations of space are more complicated, and must be considered under a double aspect—that of the reciprocal

[1] Wundt, *Outlines*, p. 90 foll. Cf. Külpe, *op. cit.*, p. 276.

[2] The literature on the psychology of space is very abundant, and both the nativistic and empirical theories have a great number of supporters among physiologists and psychologists. Amongst the "nativists" we must quote Müller, Weber, and Stumpf; amongst the "empiricals" Helmholtz and Wundt. See Ribot in the *Psychologie allemande contemporaine*, chap. iv. See also Dunan's *La théorie psychologique de l'espace* (Paris, 1895).

relations of the elements of a presentation and that of their relations to the subject. Localisation is accomplished under very different conditions here and in the case of tactile presentations: first, because we do not refer the impression, as in the latter, to the corresponding point of the organ itself, but to a point outside ourselves in the "field of vision," placed at a certain distance from us; and secondly, because this distance is not given by a linear dimension to be measured on the sensitive surface itself, as in sensations of touch, but by an angle formed by two lines stretching from two points in the field of sight to two corresponding points of the image on the retina, passing through the lens.[1] The movements of the eyes have a very great importance, it being they alone which render possible the junction of the two separate monocular visions into one single monocular image. It is, moreover, in accordance with the laws of these movements (amongst which that of "correspondence between apperception and fixation" is here especially important) that a procedure takes place similar to that of tactile presentations, whereby the sensations of the retina mingle with those of touch and motion, and are referred as a whole to one single point.[2] The co-ordination of all these movements is naturally the result of physiological pre-formations, which the individual carries with him from his birth, the form which we give to the field of vision—*e.g.* the direction and position we attribute to each single object, as well as the measure of its dimensions, depending on the movements of the muscles of the eye. We must, however, make a distinction between the point of fixation, which is the middle point of the visual field, from the field itself. The objects placed in the middle of the field of vision are seen directly; those placed in the excentric parts are, on the contrary, seen indirectly. This theory of localisation, which is generally accepted by modern Psychology, is a modification of the theory first developed by Lotze. The latter was of opinion that local signs in the eye were not, as in the case of touch, concomitant sensations (*Mitempfindungen*), but sensations of motion, derived from reflex actions following upon stimuli acting on the retina. This theory, however, does not explain the relation between the visual perception and local signs; nor did Lotze exert himself to find an explanation, as he considered the intuition of space to be innate in us.[3]

---

[1] Wundt, *Grundzüge*, Vol. II., p. 96, etc.
[2] *Op. cit.*, p. 217.
[3] *Op. cit.*, Vol. II., p. 231; Külpe, *Outlines*, p. 337 foll.

Whereas space-presentations belong more especially to the senses of touch and of sight, time-presentations are characteristic of tactile sensations of motion and of sensations of hearing. Time-presentations, however, have the peculiarity of possessing a more general character than those of space, and, moreover, of being an accompaniment not only of sensations but of all the contents of consciousness. This more general character of the sense of time induces many philosophers to suppose that it is the form proper to consciousness as opposed to space, which they would consider as the form of the external world. It has, however, been rightly objected that we attribute the properties of time to subjective states only owing to the fact that they are connected with presentations, without which we do not know whether the subjective states would possess those properties. Time-presentations are primarily formed by means of sensations of touch, which sense is the starting-point, therefore, of time- as well as of space-presentations. The motor organs of our body are endowed with certain mechanical qualities which can occasion rhythmical movements, subject, as such, to the principle of the isochronism of pendulum oscillations, and are attended by peculiar feelings of expectation with regard to the movement to be accomplished, and of satisfaction with the movement accomplished. From this rhythmical succession of sensations and feelings combined we have the perception of time. Owing to these properties of the muscular sense some modern psychologists go even so far as to conclude that it is the only source of perceptions of time. But it has not been difficult to prove the insufficiency of such a theory, for the sense of touch, though a most important factor in space-presentations, cannot, owing to its peculiar nature, give us any very clear perception of a succession of sensations.[1] Greater precision, on the other hand, is attainable from the sense of hearing, for the sensations which make up acoustic perceptions do not form a continuous series, as in the case of tactile sensations, but are of an extremely short duration, and therefore mark much more distinctly than other sensations the intervals between each period of time, so that the relation between these periods is measured solely by their contents.

[1] One of the most eminent supporters of this theory is Münsterberg (see his *Beiträge zur experimentellen Psychologie*, Vol. IV.). His theory has been attacked by Menmann in the *Philosophische Studien*, Vol. VIII., p. 3, and Vol. IX., p. 2 (" Beiträge zur Psychologie des Zeitsinns "), and by Schumann (" *Zeitschrift für Psychologie und Physiologie der Sinnesorganen*," Vols. XVII. and XVIII.).

Of great and, we may say, of decisive importance with regard to time-duration generally is feeling. Every one has experienced that time seems to pass more or less slowly according to the feelings which are produced in us by various external or internal impressions. Time-perceptions, apart from their character of greater generality, differ finally from space-perceptions in the different manner in which we turn our attention to them.

From consideration of the part which feeling plays in the perceptions of time we naturally pass to the study of feeling in its composite form. Feelings also, as we have seen, can assume an intensive and an extensive form; that is to say, they can mingle together so as to produce an intense and momentary state of feeling, or they can extend themselves temporally in a continuous series. The former are termed compound feelings; the latter are termed emotions and volitional processes. We have, therefore, various partial feelings and a comprehensive feeling which is the result of their combination. Owing to its intensity, and consequently owing to the influence it exercises upon the whole mental life, great importance attaches to that so-called general or diffused feeling which is produced by the aggregate of other feelings attendant upon tactile, muscular, and organic sensations, and also upon sensations of smell and taste, and which represents our general state of well-being, or the reverse. This general feeling is twofold—of pleasure and of pain. The majority of psychologists distinguish all kinds of feeling alike into these two forms; but this generalisation is not quite justifiable, there being some which cannot be described either as feelings of pleasure or of pain, and among organic feelings themselves there are some which cannot be classed under the heading either of pleasure or pain, and might be called feelings of "contrast."[1] Thus Wundt divides feelings into the three classes of pleasure and pain, excitement and depression, tension and relief. Compound feelings, which are the result of visual and acoustic sensations together, are called elementary æsthetic feelings, and from them are evolved the more complex feelings—logical, moral, æsthetic, and so forth. They are subdivided according to their origin into two principal classes—namely, intensive and extensive, the former having their source in the qualitative properties of a perception, the latter in the order of their elements in time and space. The emotions (*Affecte*), on the other hand, differ from

Emotions and acts of volition.

[1] Wundt, *Outlines*, p. 163.

compound feelings, being constituted by a continuous series of feelings so connected as to form a distinct whole by themselves.

Emotions are consequently closely connected with volitional actions, which are external manifestations following upon the emotions themselves. We have, therefore, one form of volition which may be considered the most original—viz. the external; and another which is only encountered in a more perfect stage of psychical life—viz. the inner, consisting in a purely internal modification, in other words, in a variation of the current of presentations and feelings. An act of willing, whether external or internal, is always determined by some motive. These motives are the feelings or presentations which precede an action, and may be said to be the cause of the action itself. According to the different manner of their action we can distinguish acts of volition into two principal categories—simple and complex. The former, also termed impulsive, are caused by a single and immediate motive; the latter are determined by a motive which we choose amongst many. Impulsive acts are distinguished by the greater rapidity with which they are accomplished, and are naturally more spontaneous and common to all animals, whereas complex acts of volition require more time and belong to a more advanced state of mental evolution. Experimental Psychology has been successful in determining with increasing precision the exact time occupied by simple and complex reactions, and has collected a number of important data which may be of great service in the study of the evolution of voluntary action. Another important fact in general Psychology has also been studied experimentally—viz. the retrograde transformation which takes place when, owing to continued practice, acts of willing pass into simple impulsive acts.

The mental life, however, is not confined to these processes. Presentations, emotions, and acts of willing succeed each other continually, and become connected in the most complicated manner. Moreover, present states of consciousness recall past states, so that the entire psychic life constitutes a closely connected aggregate of elementary and compound factors, and the term consciousness must not be taken to signify something apart from the mental processes, but to stand for an abstract idea which comprises them all. When we are conscious of a mental content we say that it is "perceived" by us; when, on the contrary, besides perceiving it, we concentrate

Consciousness, attention, and apperception.

ourselves upon it so that it stands out as distinctly as possible, we say that it is "apperceived." The peculiar state, characterised by certain special feelings, which accompanies apperception is termed "attention." The mental life, therefore, consists in a continual succession of presentations, emotions, processes of willing—in other words, of psychical contents, some of which are apperceived, or perceived with attention, and others simply perceived. This idea might be graphically, though somewhat clumsily, expressed by imagining consciousness to be a circle, the centre of which represents the focus or point of apperception. The various stimuli which cross the threshold of consciousness (here represented by the circumference) might be depicted by lines entering the circle, some of which cross it without touching the centre, and others pass through the centre. The latter correspond to apperceived mental contents. There may even be others, which, after having remained some time at the circumference, subsequently pass through the centre, when they become apperceived.[1]

It is not to be thought, however, that all these processes take place without any modification of the subjective part of consciousness, that is, of feelings and impulses. On the contrary, it is to these that the continual changes in the mental life are due. Moreover, the entrance of a content into the centre of consciousness is characterised by peculiar feelings, which vary according as the content presents itself suddenly to our attention, or the latter has been attracted to it already before it has presented itself. These are two distinct cases, in the first of which we have a feeling of "passivity," because we are surprised and dominated immediately by a sudden impression; the second, on the contrary, causes a feeling of expectancy or "activity," which is afterwards attended and followed by stimulating feelings, or by feelings of pleasure or pain. In the first case we have the so-called *passive apperception*, in the second case the so-called *active apperception*. These forms of apperception correspond exactly to the two forms of volition already described, passive apperception being nothing but a form of simple internal, and active apperception a form of complex internal, act of will. By the old-fashioned Psychology these two forms of attention were termed involuntary and voluntary. This was erroneous, inasmuch as both the active and the passive forms are voluntary, just as impulsive

[1] Some psychologists, such as Baldwin, make frequent use of these comparisons. See Baldwin's *Handbook of Psychology*, Vol. I., p. 68.

action and acts of choice are both equally voluntary.[1] Passive attention is, therefore, an internal impulsive act; active attention, an internal act of choice. The will is thus the primary factor in mental processes, which are at bottom merely forms of volition. The importance of the attention, therefore, is manifest; for in it are closely combined the cognitive and the subjective aspects of the mental life. Attention reveals, moreover, better than any other mental phenomenon, the spontaneous and subjective character of consciousness. It is therefore natural that the old Psychology, being prevalently intellectualistic, should have attached little importance to it. German metaphysical Psychology, however, devoted much more study to attention than English Psychology, erroneously considering it either a metaphysical entity or a product of other psychical phenomena. The English empirical school, on the contrary, consistently disregarded the mental phenomenon of attention, and basing itself solely upon "experience," attributed almost exclusive importance to the cognitive element—that is, to sensations and perceptions, or, in other words, to that which comes to us from the outside and to which our minds passively submit.[2]

We have said that the psychic life is constituted by a complexity of processes which succeed and alternate with each other, continually changing their combinations and connections. One of the most important phenomena, in this series of processes, consists in what is called "association." English Psychology has always given it great prominence. Mill, for instance, compared it to the law of universal gravitation, because of its importance in regulating the phenomena of consciousness. This is a point in respect to which modern experimental Psychology is gradually effecting a radical transformation of the ideas which, as the result in a great measure of English Psychology, have hitherto prevailed. Naturally the question is much debated between ex-

Associations.

---

[1] It is a fact, however, that not a few modern text-books of Psychology maintain that mistaken distinction—*e.g.* Sully, Höffding, Baldwin. The same error is committed by J. C. Kreibig in a recent short work on the attention, *Die Aufmerksamkeit als Willenserscheinung* (Vienna, 1897).

[2] James, *The Principles of Psychology*, Vol. I., p. 402. Having pointed out that by Locke, Hume, Hartley, the two Mills, and Spencer, attention is either entirely left on one side or dealt with incidentally, he drily adds: "Attention, implying a degree of reactive spontaneity, would seem to break through the circle of pure receptivity which constitutes 'experiences,' and hence must not be spoken of under penalty of interfering with the smoothness of the tale."

perimental psychologists and so-called "empirical" psychologists, who still adhere to earlier ideas.

The English psychologists may claim without doubt the merit of having pointed out the importance of association in the evolution of the mental life, and of having endeavoured to reduce it to simple principles. It must be noted that Aristotle had already indicated similarity, contrast, and contiguity in time and place as different ways in which ideas became associated. English Psychology, and subsequently Herbart and Beneke, reduced resemblance and contrast to the single principle of "similarity." Association by similarity, referring as it does to the intrinsic part or contents of the presentation, may be called "internal." These two forms of association coincide exactly with Herbart's direct and indirect. Contemporary empirical Psychology, represented by Spencer, Bain, Höffding, Sully, Ladd, and others, adheres to these "laws of association," as being the only way of explaining the sequence of psychical processes. In those two principal forms of association numerous special forms have their origin. Thus external association may take place between simultaneous or successive presentations. In the first case we may have an association of a part with a whole, and *vice versa*, or an association between simultaneous but independent presentations; in the second case the association may take place between successive presentations of sound or of sight, or of the other senses. Internal association may take place by means of subordination, co-ordination, and relations of dependence. Recently the tendency has been to simplify these schemes as much as possible, and after having reduced them to the two principles of "similarity" and "contiguity," to attempt to derive all laws governing association from one of those principles alone. The majority of psychologists consider the fundamental law of association to be that of contiguity, whilst a few are in favour of the principle of similarity. Amongst the first we may quote Ladd and Sully[1]; amongst the second Höffding. Others, like Bain, do not attempt to reduce these laws to a single principle, and admit both principles, of "contiguity" and of "similarity," as fundamental.

<small>Similarity and contiguity.</small>

The first query which presents itself is whether these so-called "laws" of association are really and truly "laws," or simply schemes or forms, according to which association takes place.

[1] The first to attempt this reduction was James Mill. See Ribot, *La psychologie anglaise contemporaine*, p. 55 foll.

The term "law" means a rule which explains the inmost reason of certain facts, which suffers no exception, and verifies itself whenever certain given conditions exist. This cannot be said of the "laws" of association by contiguity and similarity.[1] The reason why a presentation recalls another which is either similar or has been found coexistent with it in space, eludes us. Thus Baldwin reduces all secondary laws to one, which he calls the law of correlation, and which is neither more nor less than a law of consciousness or of apperception, according to which "every association of psychical states is an integration."[2] But this does not explain much, merely referring us, as to a fundamental property of consciousness, to the fact that it unites in a synthesis the various contents which succeed each other in it. Other psychologists, such as Spencer and especially James, seek for an explanation in the physiological functions of the brain. "There are," says James, "mechanical conditions on which thought depends, and which, to say the least, determine the order in which is presented the content or material for comparisons, selections, and decisions."[3] For, he continues, "association, so far as the word stands for an effect, is between things thought of—it is things, not ideas, which are associated in the mind."[4] "There is no other elementary causal law of association than the law of neural habit. All the *materials* of our thought are due to the way in which one elementary process of the cerebral hemispheres tends to excite whatever other elementary process it may have excited at some former time, . . . so that *psychic* contiguity, similarity, etc., are derivatives of a single, profounder kind of fact."[5]

Is there one fundamental law of association?

Similar opinions are held by other contemporary psychologists, such as Ziehen,[6] who believes that the sensations we have experienced dispose themselves in special cells, which he calls memory-cells (*Erinnerungszellen*). It is, however, difficult to understand how such a "disposal" of impressions takes place, who is the disposing subject, and how the impression passes from the sensitive cells to the memory-cells.[7] James's explanation

Materialistic explanation.

---

[1] See Titchener, *Outline of Psychology*, p. 221.
[2] Baldwin, *Handbook of Psychology*, Vol. I., p. 201.
[3] *The Principles of Psychology*, Vol. I., p. 553.
[4] *Ibid.*, p. 554.
[5] *Ibid.*, p. 566.
[6] See *Introduction to the Study of Physiological Psychology*, p. 198 foll.
[7] See Wundt's criticism on these theories in the often-quoted paper published

is certainly of a much more general character, although it also is entirely arbitrary. It takes us back to the fundamental question whether psychical processes are a product of cerebral phenomena. Any combinations which may take place between the cells of the brain, however complicated they may be, belong to the order of physical phenomena, and are therefore subject to the laws of the latter. Now, the corresponding mental associations do not take place between physical phenomena and processes of the consciousness, but only between the latter, and the mental processes become associated and combined in accordance with laws of their own. These are the outcome of the specific equality of the mental processes, of the whole mass of the mental phenomena which have taken place in each individual consciousness, and of the inner nature of each individual character.

The primary defect of all the theories on association adopted by empirical Psychology consists in the fact that they are derived from intellectualistic notions, according to which the processes of consciousness are considered from the point of view of pure presentation, or of the external objects of which they are supposed to be copies. Thus it is believed that a mass of sensations is for ever attended by the same spatial properties which were the effect of their relative position when we perceived them for the first time, and that these properties are subsequently reproduced by us. This is the error committed by the associative theories of "contiguity." The theories of "similarity" commit an even more serious mistake, for the similarity we see between two presentations is in itself a very complicated psychical process which depends upon the operations of logical thought. Similarity and contiguity are therefore both very complicated psychical products, composed of many elements, and so far from giving an explanation of the associative processes, have need themselves of being explained. Consequently one should not speak of association of presentations, but of association of the elements of which the latter are composed—namely, of sensations.[1]

Association takes place between elements.

It is an important result achieved by experimental Psychology in the *Philos. Stud.* (Vol. X., Part I., p. 67, etc.), "Ueber Psychologische Causalität und Psychophysischen Parallelismus."

[1] See Wundt, *Grundzüge der physiologischen Psychologie*, Vol. II., p, 466 foll. The law of "similarity" is treated at great length by Bain, chap. ii. of *The Senses and the Intellect*; see also James, *op. cit.*, Vol. I., p. 591 foll. The whole question of associations is very well treated by Titchener, *Outline of Psychology*, chap. viii., p. 198 foll.

to have proved that in the so-called "reproduction" of presentations we never have a simple return to a past presentation. This is due to the circumstance that a new synthesis takes place between the elements of the old presentation and of the actual presentation by which it is recalled. Association, consequently, is merely a more developed form of certain psychical phenomena, which manifest themselves whenever there is a case of simple combination of two psychical elements. We have already seen that presentations are the result of an "association" of simple elements; thus the simple relation of space or time, which establishes itself between two sensations, is an "association." The only difference between these elementary associations and "associations" in the other sense of the word consists in the greater complexity of the latter, for in the case of the former the "association" takes place solely between elements which are supplied by present external impressions, whereas in the case of the latter it takes place between present elements, which have a peripheral origin, and reproduced elements, which have a central origin. In this way we establish a proper genetic order between the mental processes, which thus receive an explanation founded upon facts and not upon abstract ideas, as in the case of the laws of similarity and contiguity.

A proof that these so-called laws of association are not consistent with mental evolution in general, and cannot furnish a satisfactory explanation of the growth of complex processes, lies in the fact that they concern only so-called "successive" associations, in which the two presentations which recall each other can be clearly distinguished and placed in order of succession. The fact, moreover, **Simultaneous** was not taken into account that before arriving at **association and** this form of succession it is necessary to pass through **perception.** a form of simultaneousness, out of which the constituent elements become differentiated. The forms of simultaneous association would thus represent a more highly developed stage of the process of presentation, assuming, like the latter, an intensive and an extensive form. In the intensive form the elements are so closely connected that they disappear individually before the impression they produce as a whole. This form is consequently comprised in the general notion of *perception*, if by that term we understand the mental process whereby we become conscious of an aggregate of sensations, present or remembered, which constitute a distinct object. The perceptive process is therefore always more or less a process of integration. We could never, indeed, perceive an object in all its parts, if we had not the power of involuntarily completing the elements which we do perceive with others which we cannot actually perceive at the moment.[1] As regards the various ways in which this process of integration takes place, much allowance must be made for individual character, which reduces itself in this case to the greater or lesser quantity and to the quality of the sensations or perceptions which have been experienced, and are, so to say, accumulated in consciousness, and to the special mode in which each individual connects the various mental processes. The result is that around a nucleus of objective and actual sensations there may weave itself a more or less complicated system of subjective and remembered facts.[2]

In the extensive form, on the contrary, the elements can be better distinguished, and the passage is rendered easy to the "successive" form of association. Herbart had already applied the term "assimilation" to the combination of presentations of the same kind, and "complication" to the combination of different species of presentation. Although Herbart's fundamental notion that presentations are the primary elements of mental life must be considerably modified, it is possible, nevertheless, to retain the names above mentioned, provided they are applied not to presentations, but to the simple elements of which they are composed—that is, to sensations. Assimilation, in that case, is a simultaneous association of elements belonging to compounds of a like nature. This is a very common process, which we go through continually, without even being conscious of it. Thus, when reading a book, we often do not perceive the misprints it may contain; or when listening to a speech we seem to hear every word, though in reality many escape us, and instances of the kind might be multiplied indefinitely. What happens in these cases? Simply that we rapidly substitute for the wrong letters which we directly perceive, or for the words which we do not perceive, the images which present themselves immediately to our memory of the right letters and of the missing words, so that

Assimilation and complication.

[1] Sully is right in giving the following definition of perception (*Outlines of Psychology*, p. 153): "The process by which the mind, after discriminating and identifying a sense-impression, supplements it by an accompaniment or escort of revived sensations, the whole aggregate of actual and revived sensations being solidified or 'integrated' into the form of a percept." See also Höffding, *Outlines of Psychology*, p. 124 foll.

[2] See C. Lloyd Morgan's interesting observations in his *Introduction to Comparative Psychology* (1894), chap. iv., p. 63 *passim*. See also Dandolo, *Le integrazioni psichiche* (1898).

we seem to read or to hear everything correctly. This substitution is possible, owing to the fact that those same letters and words have been perceived by us on some other occasion jointly with those which we perceive actually, so that they are immediately recalled by them. Another instance of the associative process of assimilation is afforded by those illustrated puzzles, which consist in finding in a landscape or other picture the figure of a specified object. We have in our mind the vivid presentation of the object we are looking for, and while we are endeavouring to find it in the picture before us, we involuntarily transport our entirely subjective image of it into the picture itself, so that we momentarily think we see it, and require a certain amount of attention before we perceive our mistake.[1] When at last we find the figure we were looking for, there takes place a rapid assimilation between it and the image in our mind. Similar experiences are very frequent; for example, when we are looking for some one in a crowd, we continually mistake others for that person. This is a common illusion produced by the great vividness with which we reproduce the image of the person we are in search of, and which we erroneously assimilate with the features of other people.[2] Assimilation has also a great influence on visual perception. It is through its agency that we can perceive the perspective of objects, which are drawn or painted on the same plane. It is easy to understand that in this common process of assimilation there is to be found the germ of the pathological phenomenon of "illusion" and of "hallucination," which may be called an amplified and exaggerated form of illusion.

In the case of "complications" we can, on the contrary, more easily distinguish between present and reproduced perceptions. They are also of very common occurrence. Thus, when we hear the voice of a person we know, the image of that person presents itself immediately to our mind; when we hear the sound of a pianoforte, we represent its shape to ourselves, and so forth. Here we have an association of sensations of different kinds—acoustic and visual. Another example of complication of sensations is

[1] See Wundt's paper, in *Philosophische Studien*, Vol. VII. (p. 337, etc.), "Bemerkungen zur Associationslehre." See also Groos, *Einleitung in die Aesthetik* (Giessen, 1892), Part I. foll. (the first section is headed "Das Vexirbild"). See also Paulhan, *L'activité mentale et les éléments de l'esprit*, pp. 95-9; and James, *Psychology*, p. 322, etc., *Principles of Psychology*, Vol. II., p. 79, etc. See also Ardigò in the second part of his *L' unità della coscienza* ("La confluenza mentale") p. 157 foll.

[2] This is noted by Daudet in one of his best novels, *Le nabab*.

afforded by the gustatory and olfactory senses. When we smell a fruit, or some other edible object, we almost seem to taste it, so closely are the two sensations connected. The localisation of sensations is also achieved by means of a process of complication of the tactile and visual sensation of the part of our body which is touched. In such cases, however, the association is not so perfect as in cases of assimilation, in which we do not at once distinguish the elements that composed it; for here, on the contrary, owing to their diversity, they are more easily separated.[1]

Just as there is a gradual passage from perception, properly so-called, to simultaneous associations, so there is an almost insensible passage from simultaneous to successive associations. Complication is in itself more differentiated than assimilation, but there are other intermediate forms which prepare the way directly for successive associations. These cases have been made the subject of laboratory experiments, of which the simplest consists in "distinguishing" between impressions already experienced and a new impression of which we are in expectation. As soon as the new impression acts, it immediately recalls a passed presentation which resembles it, and the two become assimilated. The process of distinction here consists solely in the assimilation, which would not take place if the presentation did not correspond perfectly to the present impression.[2] The process is attended by

Recognition and memory. a peculiar feeling of "recognition," which is principally perceived when the immediate act of recognition, owing to some new and unlooked-for impression, is retarded or prevented.[3] From this it is but a step to a slightly more complicated form, called "act of recognition," which differs from the former solely in not being attended by a state of expectation, and also because the impression that is recalled is isolated from other objects in such a way that the assimilation shall take place solely between its own constituent elements and the new impression.[4] In the cases of assimilation already quoted the remembered elements belong not only to one particular impression

---

[1] See E. B. Titchener, *Outline of Psychology*, p. 201 foll. James (*Principles of Psychology*, Vol. II., p. 79 foll.) makes a detailed study of the various forms of perceptive illusions. See G. Croom-Robertson, *Elements of Psychology*, p. 115 foll.

[2] Wundt, *Grundzüge der physiologischen Psychologie*; Vol. II., p. 442.

[3] This peculiar feeling was first noted by Höffding, who calls it "Bekanntheit Gefühl" (see *loc. cit.*, and *Vierteljahrschrift für wissenschaftliche Philosophie*, Vol. XIII., p. 427.

[4] See Wundt, *op. cit.*, Vol. II., p. 444.

which has been experienced by us before, but to an indeterminate number of such impressions. In the case of the "act of recognition," on the contrary, the assimilation is limited to the present impression (which is the indispensable starting-point for all associative processes), and to the elements of a single past impression. We have thus between the present impression and the assimilation a short interval of time which is sufficient for the actual and the past presentation to appear distinct one from the other, and for the process to assume the character of a successive association. This characteristic stands out even more clearly in cases in which the assimilation takes place in an indirect way—that is to say, by means of accessory elements, recalling the other elements, which are alone susceptible of assimilation. We have in that case a series of three events divided by a certain interval of time—viz. the actual impression, the accessory presentation, and, lastly, the feeling of recognition. This process, and especially that of direct recognition, may take place so very rapidly that it is not always easy to know whether the recognition be simultaneous or successive, direct or indirect.[1] The division of a presentation into two parts, present and remembered, is more frequent where the obstacles which oppose themselves to assimilation are greater. Instances of this are very common. When we meet a person whom we are in the habit of seeing every day, we naturally have no difficulty in recognising him immediately; the actual impression at once assimilates itself with all the past impressions, and the result is a single new impression. If, on the contrary, we have only seen a man once or twice before, and he has not made much impression on our memory, we cannot effect an assimilation between the present and past impressions, but make an effort to recall his image to our memory, together with the time and place where we have met him

[1] There has been an interesting polemic on this question between Lehmann (who maintained the theory we have explained above) and Höffding (who does not admit this assimilation of elements, and considers that recognition is, instead, an immediate act of consciousness). The writings of Lehmann have appeared in *Philosophische Studien* (Vol. V., p. 69, and Vol. VII., p. 169 foll.), and those of Höffding in the *Vierteljahrschrift für wissenschaftliche Philosophie*, Vol. XIII., p. 420 foll., and Vol. XIV., p. 27 foll.; and in *Philos. Stud.*, Vol. VIII., p. 86 foll. Lehmann, in the first of the writings quoted (*Philos. Stud.*, Vol. V., p. 97), declares that he has directed his controversy against Höffding, whose ideas are in accordance with the English psychologists, because his work (*Psychologie in Umrissen*) "meines Wissens die vollständigste und durchsichtigste Darstellung der hier als unrichtig zu erweisenden Hypothese gibt."

before. The process which takes place in this case may serve as an illustration of the whole mode of association of presentations. As we search our memory and remember little by little the particulars we had noted in the person whom we now hardly recognise, an assimilation takes place between the similar elements to be found in the past and actual presentations. In these cases we have, so to say, a slow and imperfect assimilation. If past presentations did not contain some elements similar to those of presentations in the present, the former could never be recalled by the latter. Successive associations may all be embraced under the comprehensive term of " processes of the memory," which are characterised by an unmistakable succession of two presentations. These successive associations can take place, as we have seen, in two ways—directly and indirectly. The latter is the more frequent, which explains why some hold that certain presentations rise suddenly and spontaneously out of the " sombre depths of unconsciousness," as it is somewhat mystically described even by some " positivist " philosophers, without any noticeable connecting link with previous presentations. But this theory of " unconsciousness," though perhaps a convenient means of getting out of the difficulty, is not satisfactory as an explanation.[1] It often happens that a presentation, which had apparently arisen without any perceptible cause, is found to have been really occasioned by another presentation possessing some elements similar to its own, although it must be admitted that, considering the immense number of presentations we have experienced, and the multiplicity of similar elements which go to make them up, this is not always easy.

The fundamental cause of association consists, therefore, in an " affinity " of elements. This affinity is always of two kinds, internal and external—that is to say, of similarity and contiguity. Thus these two forms of relation, that used to be applied by empirical psychology to presentations—that is to say, to complex facts—have acquired a much more general character, and represent the primary causes of the association of elements. Association by similarity takes place immediately, is the most direct, and consists in an increase of intensity in the similar elements ; association by contiguity, on the contrary, takes place between different elements. But in order that it may do so, it is necessary that the

Affinity of psychological elements.

---

[1] See Jerusalem, " Ein Beispiel von Association durch unbewusste Mitglieder " (*Philosophische Studien*, No. X., chap. ii., p. 323 foll.), and Wundt, *ibid.*, p. 326 foll.

elements which are presented should recall other elements which we have perceived on other occasions as "contiguous" to the former—*i.e.* near to them in space or time; it is necessary, in other words, that the "intensive" action should become "extensive." If this holds good in the case of simple assimilation, it does so all the more in the case of complication, distinction, direct and indirect recognition, and especially of the processes of memory. An association by means of pure similarity, as admitted by some (Höffding), or of pure contiguity, as admitted by others (Morgan), is not possible, for those two processes complete each other reciprocally, and together can by themselves explain the mechanism of association, without having recourse to the metaphysical theory of unconsciousness.[1] Likewise it is only in this action, which takes place not between two different presentations, as the "empirical" school believes, but between the elements of two presentations that we can find the explanation of the continual process of synthesis and analysis which takes place in mental life. This disposes also of the theory which attributes a special quality to presentations which are perceived for the second time, and considers that they are always recognised in a direct manner.[2] Sensation, on the contrary, is responsible only for the two primitive characteristics of quality and intensity, the rest being nothing but a product of processes of combination and association.

The relations between the elements of a so-called "apperceptive association" are even more complicated. As the number of **Apperceptive** elements of a presentation may be very great, it is **association.** possible for them to coalesce with numbers of similar elements belonging to other presentations, and the association can thereby extend itself to an indefinite number of mental representative compounds. The association of elements, in this case, is governed only by relations of similarity and contiguity, which are determined on their part by the "mental disposition" of the moment.[3] In everyday life, though we generally guide more or less the current of our thoughts, yet it often happens that we abandon ourselves

---

[1] See Höffding, *op. cit.*, p. 152.

[2] As in the theory of Höffding already quoted. He gives to this act of immediate recognition the name of "Perception." See *op. cit.*, p. 124, and the paper already quoted in answer to Lehmann. See Lloyd Morgan, *op. cit.*, chap. iv. *passim.*

[3] As regards the action of feeling on associations, see Höffding, *op. cit.*, p. 298 foll. See also C. Lloyd Morgan, *op. cit.*, iv., 66 foll.

completely to what is commonly called "the spontaneous succession of ideas." Thus, in certain moments of semi-consciousness we allow representations to wander at their will, so that one recalls another, sometimes a very distant one ; this recalls a third and still more widely divergent one, and so on. Thought travels at a great rate without any fixed goal, and it is impossible to foresee where it may arrive. The facility with which these mental wanderings are indulged in varies, of course, greatly according to the individual, and is perhaps greater in women than in men. Above all, it is certain that it is in inverse ratio to what is called "mental force," and that it is greatly fostered by the absence of a system of methodical intellectual work. The most typical form of this primitive association of presentations is observed in dreams, which are nothing but a concatenation of impressions not under the control of the will, deprived therefore of all logical connection, and almost always of a most extravagant character.

But we all can, more or less, if we choose, regulate and direct our representations according to a given plan. To that end an act of inner volition is necessary, and the associations regulated in this way are attended by a particular feeling of activity. In that case there is a twofold process : first, a negative process, arresting the elements which, if left to themselves, would become associated ; secondly, a positive process, consisting in the choice we make of the elements to be associated with preceding presentations. These associations, which are governed by free will, are termed "apperceptive," although to be exact pure associations also are apperceptive and voluntary. Apperceptive associations, moreover, imply pure associations, which constitute the material upon which they operate. The English school, by considering logical associations as a form of simple associations, neglected the distinctive character of the former, which consists in being governed by the will, whereby a continual process of selection takes place between the various associations.[1]

Many theories have been, and are still, put forward with regard to the physiological phenomena attendant upon association. **Attendant physiological phenomena.** Although but little else is known about them, it is apparently certain that all such physiological processes are attributable to practice. The nervous substance, like any other substance, possesses the aptitude of performing actions which have already been performed with greater

[1] Bain was the first to note the great influence of the will on thought. See *The Emotions and the Will*, Part II., chap. iv.

facility than entirely new ones. The excitation caused in the cerebral centres by an external impression leaves in them a functional disposition towards the renewal of the same excitation. This disposition shows itself directly in the conjunction of the similar elements of the present and of the recalled impression, so that the former are, so to say, strengthened or intensified. In this case the cerebral excitation which is produced by the actual external stimulus is intensified by the disposition existing in the central parts to repeat the excitation already previously experienced. This causes immediately a diffusion of the excitation to the neighbouring parts, which had, conjointly with the central organs, experienced the previous stimulus, thus establishing a kind of physiological association, derived from repetition and analogous to the association of the psychical elements. It is certain, on the other hand, that physiology can yet give no definite judgment concerning the various modes of cerebral excitation that accompany the different forms of simple and apperceptive association.[1]

All forms of voluntary association of concepts—in other words, the forms of logical thought—naturally have their origin in the simpler mental processes, with which they are closely connected. Modern Psychology has proved that the higher logical forms are not the product of a special faculty other than the one which produces the simpler forms, but that they merely represent a more developed stage in the evolution of consciousness. Their origin is therefore better explained by means of the Psychology of infancy and of peoples than by experimental Psychology.

The "concept," which is the primary element of logical thought, used to be considered by the old Psychology as the result of a **Pyschological explanation of the "concept."** complicated operation of the intelligence, whereby the latter exercised a choice between the various characteristics possessed in common by different objects. This explanation, however, besides not being applicable to every form of concept, is not really in keeping with the evolution of consciousness, which cannot originally have had the qualities of a clear and precise intelligence required for such elaborate mental operations. English empirical Psychology, which was opposed to this theory, and endeavoured to explain the higher processes of consciousness empirically, held concepts to be merely presentations

---

[1] See Wundt, *Grundzüge der physiologischen Psychologie*, Vol. II., p. 473, etc.; Spencer, *Principles of Psychology*; James, *The Principles of Psychology*, Vol. I., chap. xiv. See also this last named author's historical epitome of the theories of association.

of a particular kind—that is to say, common presentations, referring to an indefinite number of objects. On the other hand, Berkeley contended that there exist only single and definite presentations, and that so-called " common perceptions " do not exist. Modern Psychology has also maintained the impossibility of this theory. A concept is distinguishable from a presentation merely by the representative value which we attribute to it, in consequence of which it can be referred not only to one special presentation, but to all similar presentations. In this case it loses its own particular, singular, and momentary character, and, acquiring the character of a general mental process, becomes a concept. It must not be forgotten, however, that this is ordinarily the product of a voluntary act of the mind; though the selection must have been originally guided, and is still, in the case of the spontaneous formation of concepts, partly guided, not by a clearly defined purpose, but by feeling, which causes the attention to turn to one presentation rather than to another, and to one element rather than another of the same presentation. Hence the diversity of concepts and, as a consequence, the different words which serve to express them in different languages, speech being the most faithful mirror of a people's character. Hence also the value of the history of language as a source of information on the subject.[1]

This act of selection implies a power of analysis and synthesis which we shall have occasion to examine later on, when we come to deal with instinct and its development, a subject closely related to the general problem of consciousness. Meantime, we turn to the question of the development of the intelligence in the individual and in the species.

The intelligence of animals has always been one of deep interest to philosophers, psychologists, and zoologists, and has given rise to the most widely divergent opinions. For some time Descartes' theory, that animals were merely unintelligent automatons, held the field. Recently a reaction has set in in an entirely opposite direction. Seeing that many actions of animals resemble our own, it has been maintained that animals possess an intelligence similar to ours, and it has become common to speak of the reasoning powers and of the language of animals. Modern Psychology has sifted these theories thoroughly, and has

Psychical evolution of animals.

---

[1] See, on the genesis of concepts, Höffding's *Psychology*, p. 226 foll. ; Wundt's *Logik*, Vol. I., p. 43 foll. ; Masci's *Logica*, pp. 85 and 195; Th. Lipp's *Grundzüge der Logik*, p. 124 foll. See also Ribot, *L'évolution des idées générales* (1897).

arrived at some tolerably trustworthy conclusions. That the actions of animals are purely mechanical and automatic is an absurd notion, in which no one any longer believes. On the other hand, the opposite opinion also encounters serious difficulties. Most of the so-called proofs of the intelligence of animals have been brought forward by observers not specially conversant with psychological analysis, and do not bear investigation. In most cases they merely prove that certain actions performed by animals have a general resemblance to actions which in the human species are the result of intelligence. We may admit that animals possess all the psychological conditions necessary for the development of logical thought, but they are wanting in that power of volition which directs and regulates presentations, and gives rise to generalisation, to concepts, and ultimately to thought proper. "It is probable, in fact," says Baldwin, "that this difference [that between the Generalisation which uses symbols, and mere Association] is the root of all the differences that follow later on, and give man the magnificent advantage over the animals which he has."[1] Thus abstraction, speech, and all that indicates the logical evolution of the mind, is too rudimentary in animals to deserve those names, and only outwardly resembles the processes of the human intelligence.[2] Although a child may be said to resemble animals in many points, nevertheless his intellectual activity shows itself occasionally at a very early stage, in an incomparably higher power of generalising and making use of linguistic symbols, of received impressions, and of shaping new psychical contents.

Some manifestations in animals are a fruitful subject of discussion, owing to a certain character of complication that does not allow of a simple explanation. We are not now alluding to instincts in general, but to a special manifestation, which may in a way be considered a variety of instinct—namely, the play of animals.[3]

Instinct.

The origin of instinct (which consists in a chain of impulsive acts) is not to be looked for in purely physical phenomena, or in reflex movements, for this would not in the least explain its teleological character ; but rather in acts of volition which have been caused in the individuals by the necessity of adaptation of the physical organism, and have thereafter slowly fixed themselves in

---

[1] Baldwin, *The Story of the Mind*, p. 54. See also his recent work on *Development and Evolution* (New York, 1902).

[2] See Ribot's *L'évolution des idées générales*.

[3] See Grosse, *Die Spiele der Thiere*.

the latter as dispositions of the nervous system. Instinct has therefore a biological origin.[1] Thus the play of animals is not to be explained simply as an excess of vitality, but as an essential part of their education, by means of which, encouraged by their parents, they develop the vital aptitudes which are necessary for their preservation in the struggle for existence.[2] This theory explains the variety of their play according to the various species; for play, as Baldwin says, illustrates both for the body and the soul the principle of organic selection, and renders the young animals flexible and adaptable to the conditions of life.[3]

The play of animals.

Real intelligence is only to be found in man, and it is interesting to follow its parallel development in the individual and in the species. The study of mental development must therefore include both.[4]

The most powerful instrument for the development of thought is language, which deserves a more profound study than has been accorded to it hitherto. It is a fact, notwithstanding assertions to the contrary, that animals only possess very rudimentary means of inter-communication. The language of animals, says Ribot in *L'évolution des idées générales*, bears testimony to a very rudimentary development, by no means proportionate to the development of mental images, and very inferior to that of analytical gestures. It is of no help whatever in the elucidation of the mystery of the origin of speech. The language of gestures, which very probably preceded phonetic language, as is proved by the importance of gestures as integral elements in the language of savage peoples, marks a great advance in the evolution of thought. It developed itself naturally as a consequence of the necessity felt by human beings of expressing their emotions and impulses, and subsequently served to represent things by means of the association of gestures with the object or the fact described.[5] But the greatest step in this development is

The origin and development of language.

---

[1] Lloyd Morgan, *Habit and Instinct*.
[2] Baldwin, *The Story of the Mind*, p. 55 foll.; *Development and Evolution*.
[3] *Ibid.*, pp. 60 foll.
[4] Romanes has an interesting work on *Mental Evolution in Man*; but Baldwin's *Mental Development in the Child and the Race* is of higher scientific value.
[5] Concerning language and its original evolution, besides Ribot, *op. cit.*, see Bourdon, *L'expression des émotions et des tendances dans le langage* (1892); Hermann Paul, *Principien der Sprachgeschichte* (3rd edit. 1898), and Wundt, *Völkerspsychologie*, Vol. I. A notable book is L. Noiré's *Der Ursprung der Sprache* (1877). See also A. Lefèvre's *Les races et les langues*, which contains a popular exposition of the subject.

marked by the transformation of generic and imperfectly expressive gestures and cries into the more precise and pliable form of articulate sounds. It must be borne in mind, however, that, contrary to what was believed by the idealists of the eighteenth century, language was not an invention, a voluntary and spontaneous creation of man to express his ideas, but the product of a slow evolution of expressions of primitive and rudimentary feelings, ideas, and impulses. The history of language furnishes us with numerous examples of this gradual development, and enables us to reconstruct the primitive history of human civilisation out of all the mass of embryonic ideas, feelings, and impulses from which the religions, the arts, the science, the philosophy, and the social institutions of humanity were slowly evolved. Syntax is gradually evolved from primitive sounds as mental development progresses, according to the laws of phonetic alteration (physiological law) and of analogy (psychological law), by which language becomes gradually differentiated into its several parts. This evolution resembles very closely that of natural organisms. A child, in order to learn articulate speech, is obliged to follow the same course as the species, though much abbreviated, commencing from the imperfect stage of cry and gesture. But the child, besides other physiological causes which assist him, has also the advantage of "imitating" the grown-up people amongst whom he lives.

The mental development in the child has lately been the object of diligent study; and an important work on the subject is Baldwin's often-quoted book. These studies are to be distinguished according as they concern the development of the senses, or of movement, or of the imitative processes, or of the intelligence properly so-called. It is probable that the primitive consciousness of the child is constituted by a confused aggregate of tactile and muscular sensations. Subsequently it begins to connect impressions and, at the end of the third month, to give evidences of memory; but during this period its consciousness is completely dominated by feelings of pleasure and pain. This stage must certainly have been common to primitive man. As regards *movements*, the first are naturally reflex, but during the first month they already begin to adapt themselves to the conditions of life. The child, meanwhile, acquires habits, and little by little, with the development of the nervous centres and of their connections, it develops the capacity of co-ordinating its own movements. During the second half-year of its life the child begins to imitate; movements first, then sounds,

[margin note: Importance of imitation in the mental development of the child.]

especially vocal, then complicated movements, such as drawing and writing. Motor suggestion is very potent with regard to imitation, and by its means the child forms habits which are of use in after-life.[1] An important advance is subsequently brought about by means of a process which has in all probability also taken place in the species—viz. the " suggestion of personality." One of the child's first tendencies is to distinguish the various personalities which surround him, beginning with his mother and his nurse. Gradually it ascribes greater importance to people than to objects, whilst amongst the latter it is principally attracted by those which are in motion. During this period the child begins to have a confused feeling of its own activity, owing to which it feels itself to be an acting agent, distinct from other persons and from surrounding objects. Herein lies the germ of social consciousness. Here imitation plays a great part, and is determined by emotions of sympathy towards fellow-creatures. Gradually the child's consciousness of self develops itself in conjunction with the general evolution of the mind, and more especially in connection with the sense of its own activity. Out of this, and out of the communion of knowledge which is the outcome of imitation, there arises sympathy, and lastly the transference by the child of its own feelings and ideas to other people, the so-called " ejective ego."[2]

Next we have to note the birth of social and ethical feelings. Social feeling may be defined, with Baldwin, as that " which arises in the child or man of the real identity, through its imitative origin, of all possible thoughts of self, whether yourself, myself, or someone else's self."[3]

After imitation comes invention—that is, personal creation—which varies according to the individual. As the child grows

Invention. amongst given social, moral, and intellectual surroundings, in a given historical epoch, he assimilates by means of imitation the ideas and feelings of his time, and afterwards brings his personal contribution in proportion to his forces. As far as ideas are concerned, it is an immense step from simple perceptions to the abstract concepts of science and philosophy. Philosophers, in discussing the origin of the concepts of number, space, time, cause, law, and species, have usually looked for it

---

[1] Baldwin, *Mental Development*, etc., chaps. iii. and v. See in these chapters his studies on the development of sensation and movement in the child.
[2] Baldwin, *ibid.*, chap. xi., § 3.
[3] *The Story of the Mind*, p. 106.

in sense or in intuition. Without entering into the question, we shall content ourselves with noting that the great primitive impulse to the development of thought has consisted in the practical necessity of making use of thought as an instrument of adaptation to the conditions of life and one's surroundings. Hence also the social origin of mathematics, astronomy, and physics. This stage has gradually given place to that of pure and disinterested observation.[1] If this holds good with regard to abstract thought, it is all the more applicable in the case of those social forms which are especially the expression of feeling and impulse, such as religion (considered from the moral point of view) and social institutions. The latter especially, born of the primitive impulse of sympathy amongst human beings, very soon felt the want of systematic discipline and regulation.[2]

The mainspring of the mental development of the individual and of the species thus consists in two great contrary forces, on whose equilibrium both individual and social progress depend. One— namely, " imitation "—is a conservative, the other—" invention "—is a progressive force. The former corresponds to biological heredity, and is responsible for social and individual habits and instincts; the latter corresponds to the biological law of variations, and finds its highest expression in " genius."[3] The naturalistic and positivist schools of the nineteenth century were too much inclined to consider social development as a purely natural and unconscious evolution, and omitted accordingly to take those two forces into consideration. Instead of considering social institutions, ideas, and phenomena as spontaneous products of the nameless multitude, modern Psychology rightly considers them the outcome of individual genius, subsequently consolidated, diffused, and preserved for the whole species by imitation. This idea, admirably developed by Tarde, on which Baldwin founds his studies of social Psychology, has transformed the theories which were current with regard to the evolution of the collective mind, which is thus presented in the light of a conscious, and not of an unconscious evolution, like that of geological phenomena. Genius, therefore, is not to be understood as a degeneration, a violation of the natural and conservative law of heredity, but

Genius.

---

[1] Ribot, *La psychologie de l'attention*, i. 39, etc. This idea has been well developed by positive philosophy and modern sociology.

[2] See Wundt, *Ethics*, § 104, etc.

[3] See Baldwin, *Social and Ethical Interpretations in Mental Development*, especially Bk. I.

as an integrating factor of the latter, expressive of variation, impulse, and motion, as a dynamic force, without which evolution itself would be impossible.[1]

[1] See Tarde, *Les lois de l'imitation*, *La logique sociale*, *L'opposition universelle*, especially the first. On genius, see Baldwin, *Social and Ethical Interpretations*, etc., Bk. I., Part II., chaps. iii., iv., and v.

CHAPTER VII

CONSCIOUSNESS

WE have now reached one of the most important points to be dealt with—namely, consciousness itself. Here we have a problem of a much more philosophical character than those we have treated hitherto, and one which serves as an introduction to the yet more general and philosophical questions concerning the laws of Psychology, which we shall have to discuss in the succeeding chapter. The question of consciousness is one that has furnished modern philosophers with ample food for debate, the data of empirical Psychology being made use of in support of *a priori* opinions and as a cloak for arguments of a purely theoretical nature. Contemporary experimental Psychology treats it from quite a different point of view, and tries to deduce a universal principle from the data of psychological observation in the widest sense of the word, both individual and historical. Psychology attributes to the term "consciousness" a somewhat wider meaning than that which it usually bears. "Consciousness" is commonly used to indicate full and complete apprehension. Thus we say that we are fully conscious of the end towards which we are tending, that we are conscious of our actions, and so forth. Likewise in the expressions "popular consciousness," "national consciousness," "human consciousness," the word is always used in the above-mentioned sense. Psychology, however, gives it a much more general and fundamental meaning, by which it is made to embrace the whole mass of psychical manifestations of the individual and of the species, which formerly was termed "soul," "spirit," or (more recently) "mind."

Various meanings of the term "consciousness."

Understood in a purely psychological sense, corresponding to what the Germans call "*Bewusstsein*," the term may be said to epitomise all that goes by the name of the "psychical world," as opposed to the "physical world" or phenomena of matter. "Consciousness" and "matter" consequently represent the sum-total of all that exists and can be an object of cognition. We give the name of conscious being

The physical and the psychical world.

where we have reason to suppose the existence of a soul, or Ego, and of unconscious being in the opposite case, from which it follows that we cannot attribute consciousness to all inorganic, or even to all organic, beings. To properly define consciousness is not possible, as it is not possible to give a good definition of matter. We must therefore rest satisfied with this general idea, and trust to the detailed study of its characteristics to enable us to understand it with greater clearness.

We have said that the notion of "consciousness" is equivalent to that of "soul" and of "spirit." Some explanation of this statement seems to be called for, for although those terms, if taken in the proper sense, are perfectly equivalent, they appear to differ somewhat in the use which has been made of them throughout the history of philosophy. "Soul" and "spirit" have been often taken in a wider sense than consciousness, many philosophers being of opinion that the soul processes may take place beneath the threshold of consciousness, and therefore quite unconsciously. We shall have occasion to return to this point later on.

The philosophical importance of the problem we are dealing with appears very clearly, even from the little we have said up to now. All psychical phenomena—that is, the so-called "psychical world," or world of consciousness—has so great an influence upon our ideas concerning all that may be the object of experience, that we cannot even imagine what the universe would be if no conscious being had ever existed. All that we can think, imagine, and perceive is thought, imagined, and perceived by our consciousness, so that it is impossible to entertain for one moment the idea of escaping from it. On the other hand, what our mind would be without the so-called "physical world" is equally unthinkable, for all that is in our consciousness refers, directly or indirectly, to the physical or external world.

Consciousness has, however, another and more characteristic aspect—viz. the subjective aspect, consisting in feeling and willing. Besides being capable of cognition, we are also subject to feelings and capable of accomplishing acts of volition. The will is indeed what more especially distinguishes the conscious from the inanimate being, and is more especially distinctive of the personality of man. All that constitutes history, literary, artistic, scientific productions, religious, social, and juridical institutions, is the product of human thought, mind, and will, and is that which raises man high above inanimate and even part of animate nature. The consciousness, which in the course of time has produced all those manifestations continues to be the source of new mental products. Indeed, its activity is on the increase. We owe to it the knowledge of our aim in life, and the conception of our moral responsibility, which, in its turn, is the basis of all the actions of the will.

Various theories concerning the consciousness. As the history of the concept of consciousness may easily be mistaken for that of Psychology, seeing that it often embraces all that is contained in the latter, we shall endeavour as far as possible, in order not to fall into useless repetition, to confine ourselves to the ideas held by the principal philosophers on the relations between consciousness (understood as the antithesis of matter) and so-called mental processes, which used for long to be considered as distinct from the consciousness itself.

Two historical theories as to the nature of consciousness deserve mention. The first, which has a pronounced metaphysical character, considers consciousness as a faculty *sui generis* which is added to the processes of consciousness. This notion may be called "rationalistic" or "intellectualistic," for it considers consciousness as a sort of idea we have or make to ourselves of our own Ego. According to the second theory, which is commonly accepted by modern Psychology, consciousness coincides with the mental processes, and is nothing but a collective concept denoting the latter as a whole. This doctrine, which is closely related to the theory of the actuality of mental processes, and with the "voluntaristic" conception of them, may be called empirical or psychological.[1] The concept of consciousness could not arise in philosophy before it had been understood that the phenomena of the mind form a group by themselves which cannot be reduced to the laws of quantity.

Rationalistic theories. This principle was first accepted as fundamental by Réné Descartes, who asserted that in all speculations on man and the universe the only certain principle is the affirmation of our own consciousness. But Descartes' Psychology is entirely intellectualistic. He can only conceive consciousness under the form of thought. Thought is for Descartes the essence of every psychical manifestation, in the same way

[1] See F. Bouiller, *De la conscience en psychologie et en morale* (Paris, 1872), chap. iv.; Wundt, *Grundzüge der physiologischen Psychologie*, Vol. II., p. 260, etc. On the notion of consciousness in ancient and mediæval philosophy, see Siebeck, *Geschichte der Psychologie*. See also G. Volkelt's *Das Unbewusste und der Pessimismus* (Berlin, 1873), which we shall have occasion to quote later on. The first part of this work deals with the history of the concept of unconsciousness, and necessarily contains much that also concerns the history of the conception of consciousness.

that extension is the property of external phenomena. Hence his distinction between " res extensa " and " res cogitans."[1] Descartes therefore understood by consciousness (or, as he expressed it, by " mens ") the main principle of the soul, which can manifest itself only in the shape of conscious phenomena. The same ideas were entertained by his followers, such as Malebranche and Arnauld. Leibnitz gave a wider meaning to the term consciousness. Descartes and his school, who started from the intellectualistic principle that the soul is pure thought, and that the latter not only is innate but is of supernatural origin, recognised its existence in its most distinctive form alone—that is, as it appears in man— and denied consciousness to animals, which they considered mere automatons. Leibnitz, on the contrary, held that there was no reason to refuse to extend the notion of consciousness to those dimmer perceptions which are themselves the elements of more distinct forms of perceptions. The latter Leibnitz called " apperceptions," a term which modern Psychology has again brought into use in a very similar sense.[2] Leibnitz is important in the history of Psychology in that he was the first to employ the conception of unconsciousness as an aid to understanding the phenomena of consciousness. In his opinion, as in that of Descartes, consciousness is not a special faculty, but the essence itself of mental facts, or, in other words, of the soul, seeing that conscious phenomena are nothing else than manifestations of the soul.

The same may be said of Locke, and in general of all the English associationist philosophers, who confined themselves in general to the facts of mental life which are beyond dispute. Even the French sensationalists and materialists, with Condillac at their head, although believing consciousness to be a product of cerebral activity,[3] understood consciousness in a sense very

---

[1] " Par le nom de pensée," wrote Descartes' " je comprends tout ce qui est tellement en nous que nous l'apercevons immédiatement par nous mêmes et en avonsune connaissance intérieure ; ainsi toutes les opérations de l'entendement, de la volonté, de l'imagination et des sens sont des pensées " (*Reponse aux deuxièmes objections*). " La pensée est une nature qui reçoit en soi tous ces modes, ainsi que l'extension est une nature qui reçoit en soi toute sorte de figures " (*Lettre à Arnauld*).

[2] Leibnitz, *Op. Philos.*, p. 706.

[3] In the first chapter of his *Traité des sensations*, Condillac says : " La perception et la conscience ne sont qu'une même opération sous deux noms. En tant qu'on ne la considère que comme une impression de l'âme, on peut lui conserver celui de perception ; en tant qu'elle avertit l'âme de sa présence on peut lui donner le nom de conscience."

similar to the meaning given by Leibnitz to "apperception"—viz. that of a "clear, distinct consciousness" of our own mental acts, therein differing widely from modern Psychology. Briefly, these philosophers of the seventeenth and eighteenth centuries inclined to understand consciousness as a "reflection" or deliberation upon our internal actions, a reflection which, consequently, is something more than consciousness in the simpler sense, and more also than the consciousness of our own Ego.

It is especially worthy of note that these philosophers distinguish a lower and a higher consciousness, the former of which they also call "perception" and referred to the senses; the latter they considered consciousness in the proper sense. This distinction is also to be found in Kant, who admitted the existence of an empirical consciousness connected with general sensibility, and a consciousness which attends the logical operations of the reasoning powers.[1]

Spiritualistic theories. The conception of consciousness as a distinct faculty was fostered especially by the "inner sense" school, which began with Locke, was developed by Wolff and his school in Germany, and pushed to its furthest consequences by the Scottish philosophy. Wolff did not admit that consciousness was different from perception and apperception, herein resembling Leibnitz.[2] The Scottish philosophers Reid and Stewart, who were spiritualistic in the extreme, maintained, on the contrary, that the soul not only is a spiritual substance which underlies the phenomena of consciousness, but that we can apprehend it only if we concentrate the whole of our attention upon the phenomena of our inner selves. Thus, when we are struck by an external impression, we do not limit ourselves to empirically perceiving the external properties of that impression, but we go beyond and seek to penetrate below it as into the very manifestation of our soul. As Reid says:[3] "Apprehension accompanied with belief and knowledge must go before simple

---

[1] Kant, *Kritik der reinen Vernunft*, § 16. "The 'I think,'" says Kant, "accompanies all our perceptions, for otherwise I should perceive things which I cannot think of—that is to say, perception would be impossible, or at any rate would be for me as if it did not exist."

[2] Wolff kept in general to comparatively empirical notions, even on the question of unconscious mental processes (which we shall examine further on). Although he admits the existence of the latter, he does not attribute much importance to them.

[3] *An Inquiry into the Human Mind on the Principles of Common Sense* (1764)

apprehension." These immediate, intuitive apprehensions, which come directly from the soul, are not subject to the control of any logical reasoning, but are derived simply from common sense. To quote Reid once more:[1] "They are judgments of nature—judgments not got by comparing ideas and perceiving agreements and disagreements but immediately inspired by our constitution." Here we come to the distinction between "consciousness" and "perception." The former is the faculty by means of which we apprehend internal phenomena; the latter regards the external world.[2] Stewart also assigns to consciousness the first place amongst our intellectual faculties.[3]

It is not surprising, therefore, if, given the habit of considering consciousness as a separate faculty, the quaint notion should have been entertained that it is unchangeable and independent of perception and other mental processes which belong to it. Consciousness has thus even been compared to a stage, where plays are acted, or to a person standing on the bank of a river and seeing the water flowing by. This idea is found in certain French spiritualistic philosophers of the beginning of the nineteenth century, such as Royer-Collard and Jouffroy, followers of the Scottish school. Royer-Collard, for example, developed the strange theory that "our sensations, acts, thoughts, pass before our consciousness as the waters of a river under the eyes of a spectator on its banks. Consciousness alone," he added, "observes them and gives an account of them to reflection, for which it must not be mistaken."[4]

The theories of the Scottish philosophers met with immediate opposition even in their own country from such writers as Thomas Brown, William Hamilton,[5] James Mill,[6] and John Stuart Mill,[7] who maintain with reason that there is no difference between consciousness and the mental processes. To experience a feeling,

[1] Reid, *Works*, p. 110. See, on Reid, Seth's *Scottish Philosophy* (2nd edit. 1890), especially chap. iii., p. 73; see also R. Falckenberg, *Geschichte der neueren Philosophie* (1886), p. 180 foll.
[2] Reid, *Essays on the Powers of the Human Mind*, chap. i.
[3] Dugald Stewart, *Philosophy of the Active and Moral Powers of Man*.
[4] *Fragments de Royer-Collard*, published by Jouffroy (see the end of the fourth volume of Reid's works). On the theories of Royer-Collard and on Jouffroy, see Taine's study in his *Les philosophes classiques du XIXme siècle*.
[5] W. Hamilton, *Lectures on Metaphysics*, Vols. XI., XII., XIII.
[6] J. Mill, *Analysis of the Phenomena of the Human Mind* (2nd edit., edited by Bain in 1878). Mill criticises strongly the confusion introduced by the philosophers who distinguish consciousness as a "feeling distinct of other feelings."
[7] J. Stuart Mill, *Examination of Sir W. Hamilton's Philosophy*, chap. viii.

says James Mill, is equivalent to being conscious, and to be conscious is equivalent to experiencing a feeling.[1]

This tendency to consider consciousness as the feeling of our own existence, of our Ego, appears even more marked in certain French philosophers of the beginning of the nineteenth century, such as Maine de Biran. By consciousness, the latter understands the feeling of individual existence.[2] "Il n'y a de fait pour nous," he says, "qu'autant que nous avons le sentiment de notre existence individuelle, et celui de quelque chose, objet ou modification, qui concourt avec cette existence et est distinct ou séparé d'elle. Sans ce sentiment d'existence individuelle (conscius sui, compos sui) que nous appelons en psychologie conscience, il n'y a point de fait qu'on puisse dire connu, point de connaissance d'aucune espèce ; car un fait n'est rien s'il n'est pas connu, c'est à dire s'il n'y a pas un sujet individuel et permanent qui connaisse." Cousin, on the other hand, had more definite ideas regarding consciousness, and was of an entirely different opinion from his master Royer-Collard, admitting no distinction either between consciousness and intelligence, or between consciousness and life itself.[3]

The Italian spiritualistic philosopher Rosmini, whose works belong to this period, adopted a similar point of view to that of the Scottish philosophers regarding consciousness. It may, however, be said that, notwithstanding certain metaphysical prejudices, the idea was gaining ground that the difference between consciousness and psychical phenomena is merely nominal, that they are in reality one and the same thing. The last obstacle which still opposed itself to this simple and natural conception consisted in the old-fashioned division of the mental life into two sections—a lower part, comprising the life of the senses, and a higher, corresponding to the rational life. This dualism, as we have had occasion to see, was most clearly apparent in Kant, and was only finally abolished by modern Psychology, which reduces all mental processes to simple elements, and conceives the life of consciousness as a

---

[1] The word "feeling" is often used by old-fashioned English philosophers in a not very exact sense as meaning something betwixt "feeling" and "sensation." The passage of James Mill above alluded to is an instance of this want of precision.

[2] Maine de Biran, *Fondements de la psychologie* (Introduction générale, Vol. I., p. 36).

[3] Cousin, *Fragments philosophiques*: "Une intelligence sans conscience est une intelligence sans intelligence, une contradiction radicale, une chimère." And elsewhere: "La conscience de la vie est la vie même, car il n'y a vraiment de vie qu'autant qu'elle se manifeste et s'aperçoit."

progressive evolution from simpler to more complex forms. This simple, and at the same time profoundly scientific, conception of the conscious life was successively developed by Herbart, Lotze, Fechner, Bain, and Wundt.

In Herbart we find a definition of consciousness which, though it is at bottom a tautology defining nothing, shows clearly that the author identifies consciousness with the mental processes as a whole, and does not consider it either a peculiar feeling of our Ego or a reflection upon our own mental acts. Consciousness is for Herbart the "sum-total of all real or simultaneous perceptions."[1] Lotze and Fechner also consider the mental life as consisting in a complexity of elements; but they attribute a much greater importance than Herbart does to the unity in which those elements are bound together.[2] The empirical conception of consciousness was developed and maintained by Wundt more resolutely than by his predecessors. He holds that consciousness is equivalent to the mental processes taken as a whole in their coexistence and continuity. Wundt, moreover, makes a sharp distinction between consciousness understood in this general sense and the consciousness of our own Ego, which is a later development, having for its principal foundation a peculiar and characteristic feeling.[3]

Empirical and scientific contemporary Psychology, as represented by Spencer, Bain, Höffding, Sully, James, Baldwin, Ladd, Külpe, and others we have quoted, agree entirely in holding this empirical conception of consciousness.[4] The phenomenon which we describe specifically as consciousness does not consist in the so-called "consciousness of the second degree," but in the "consciousness of self." This higher form of

Modern empirical theories.

[1] *Werke*, Vol. V., p. 208: "Die Summe aller wirklichen oder gleichzeitig gegenwärtigen Vorstellungen." Herbart distinguished real perceptions—that is to say, those which are above the threshold of the consciousness—from "potential" perceptions, (*Strebungen*), which are beneath the threshold of the consciousness.

[2] See especially Lotze, *Medicinische Psychologie*, p. 15 foll. On the relations between Lotze's and Herbart's Psychology, see Max Nath, *Die Psychologie Hermann Lotze's in ihrem Verhältniss zu Herbart* (Halle, 1892). On Fechner's general psychological ideas, see his *Elemente der Psychophysik*, Vol. I., pp. 13, 14, and Vol. II., p. 452 foll.

[3] Wundt, *Grundzüge der physiologischen Psychologie*, Vol. II., p. 25 foll., p. 302 foll.; *Human and Animal Psychology*, p. 235 foll.; *Outlines*, p. 221 foll.

[4] James, in his *Principles of Psychology* (Vol. I., chaps. ix. and x.), and Höffding in his *Outlines of Psychology* (p. 71 foll.), have some notable passages on this subject.

consciousness is the product of a more perfect mental evolution, and is very probably wanting in the higher animals and in the first stages of childhood, evolving itself gradually and *pari passu* with the evolution of all the mental processes in the individual, and especially with the definite localisation of the sensations of the body. This consciousness of self is characterised by the fact that its perceptive content is very restricted, though vivid, consisting of organic and muscular sensations,[1] together with a particular feeling of activity, owing to which we "feel" that we are a spontaneously acting personality. It is, moreover, susceptible of improvement, for as the complexity of our mental processes increases, the consciousness of our personality also becomes clearer, and extends itself to a greater number of phenomena. Hence the gradual formation of individual moral consciousness, as well as of social, civil, religious, artistic, and scientific consciousness.

Consciousness in a general sense is different, for it consists of the mental processes of the individual or of the species taken as a whole, as distinguished from the processes of the physical world, which are unconscious. The notion of consciousness is consequently a natural postulate from which all psychological studies must start, and which eludes all attempts at a more exact definition. One may describe its properties, but not define it; just as one cannot define sensation, feeling, or willing.[2] It is therefore natural that contemporary Psychology, which deals especially with the experimental analysis of those processes, should have thrown new light upon the concept of consciousness. Another doctrine has also contributed towards an almost complete modification of the old theories on the subject, and that is the doctrine of evolution.

The notion that biological phenomena, as we find them in the higher organisms, are the result of a gradual evolution, has introduced an entirely new mode of looking upon the formation of organisms. Organic evolution is now universally admitted ; the idea having gradually been introduced into all branches of human knowledge, and applied finally to the phenomena of consciousness. The

Natural genesis of consciousness.

---

[1] The importance of muscular and organic sensations as the foundation of consciousness of self has been very much studied in recent times. See, for example, Ribot's *Maladies de la personnalité*, chap. i. ; James, *Principles of Psychology*, Vol. I., chap. x. ; Wundt, *Grundzüge*, Vol. II., p. 302 foll. ; Külpe, *Outlines*, p. 445 foll.

[2] All definitions based on the conception that consciousness is different from mental processes resolve themselves into mere tautologies.

older Psychology, on the contrary, concerned itself only with the fully developed consciousness as it appears in the adult, neglecting the fact that it is the product of a lengthy evolution, which should be studied in the individual as well as in the species. The old-fashioned prejudice that consciousness is something supernatural, not to be apprehended except through the help of a species of mystical intuition, was in like manner an insurmountable obstacle to a scientific study of its phenomena. As a consequence of this view, all psychical manifestations in animals were excluded, seeing that animals were not credited with the possession of a "soul." Even when their instincts ceased to be considered as of a miraculous and almost incomprehensible character, no one thought of bringing them into connection with psychical phenomena in man, nor of trying to find out what there was in common between them, such a course running counter to traditional, metaphysical, and religious ideas. As with the species, so with the individual. Not only was the formation and development of mental activity in childhood neglected by the older Psychology, but, as regards grown-up man, only the highest logical or ideational activities, which are the last to become perfect, were considered. The whole substratum of simpler psychical faculties, sensations, simple feelings, sensible perceptions, impulsive actions, were neglected because they did not possess a marked character of "spirituality," but resembled the psychic manifestations in animals. It was consequently impossible to arrive at a really scientific knowledge of the nature of consciousness, for while Psychology neglected to study the formation of the simpler mental processes, their subsequent combination into more complicated processes, and their evolution in the individual and in the species from the very lowest possible degree in the animal scale where symptoms of conscious life are first observable, it was condemned to remain shackled by metaphysical prejudices and empty generalities.

The merit of having pointed out the progressive evolution of consciousness in the species belongs to Spencer. Spencer's work, in conjunction with that of Fechner and Bain on individual Psychology, marks the beginning of a new conception of consciousness.[1]

The first question which here presents itself is : When and how does mental life begin, and what are the characteristics which prove that a certain phenomenon is connected with conscious processes? The importance of this question, both from a scientific and from a philosophic point of view, is easily understood; and although

[1] See above, chap. i.

Origin of the mental life.
Psychology should confine itself to problems of which there is some probability of an exact solution, it nevertheless cannot abstain from touching upon certain philosophical questions which necessarily present themselves when the utmost limit of empirical research has been reached. It is now a universally accepted fact that mental life is not an exclusive appanage of man, but is shared by all living animals. The difficulty nevertheless remains. The special sciences and the philosophy of nature rest upon a much broader foundation than the idea of mere " animal organism " (which is confined to only one of the domains into which natural objects are divided), and that is the concept of " organism " in general. Plants and animals are both organisms, endowed with different properties but with the same fundamental elements. From the vegetable to the animal kingdom there is only a step marked by greater complexity and differentiation. But this is not all. The mechanical theory of life, which is almost universally accepted, teaches that the primary elements which constitute animal and vegetable organisms are to be found in the inorganic world in the shape of chemical elements.[1] What we call "life," or biological organisation, is the result of a peculiar combination of these elements. If we admit this continuity of evolution of matter, at what moment of that evolution do we meet with signs of consciousness and of mental processes?

Ancient and modern hylozoism.
Primitive man believed that there existed in the physical world a soul similar to the one which he felt within himself; children likewise are inclined to endow all objects which surround them with life. This mode of feeling, elevated to a philosophical system by the so-called "hylozoists"— philosophers who believed in universal animation—was not the result of scientific reflection, but merely the spontaneous manifestation of an ingenuous and immediate feeling.

The most marked contrast to these hylozoistic systems, ancient and modern, is to be found in Descartes' philosophy, which limited consciousness to man alone. Philosophy wavered for long between these two extremes; but Descartes' rationalism continued to lose ground, whilst hylozoism in the nineteenth century found a new support in the natural sciences and in the doctrine of physical and biological evolution, and gave rise to the philosophic systems of Schelling and Hartmann.[2]

[1] See, amongst many, Höffding, *op. cit.*, p. 35 foll.; Z. Bernstein, *Die mechanistische Theorie des Lebens*, p. 25.
[2] See on Hartmann, Lange's *History of Materialism*, Vol. III., p. 71 foll.

Ernest Haeckel is the most popular and enthusiastic modern upholder of the doctrine of universal animation. In his estimation mind is a primitive element of the world, which manifests itself in extremely different degrees, from the soul of an atom or of a cell to that of the higher organisms. This theory, it will be seen, extends indefinitely the domain of consciousness and has a markedly mystic character.[1]

In order to ascertain how much truth there may be in this theory, we must not discuss it solely from the standpoint of general philosophical principles concerning matter and spirit, but we must have recourse to the more exact *data* afforded by the science of mental processes. We have already seen that the most salient characteristic of psychic phenomena consists in an independent, spontaneous volition which has a purely qualitative value. What marks the independent character of the will is the fact that it is directed towards a purpose; a blind will is unthinkable, and the term could only be used (and that with not much propriety) to indicate a purely mechanical physical force.[2] The will manifests itself, first of all, by means of certain movements, which are indispensable to the preservation of the individual and of the species, and from this point upwards, wherever we find movements which we can reasonably suppose to be caused and governed by a will, we maintain that there exists mental life and consciousness.

As a general rule, we may say that voluntary movements are only to be found in animal organisms, certain movements which are met with in plants being merely an effect of mechanical causes. But as the line of demarcation between the vegetable and the animal worlds is not very sharply defined, it is not always easy to distinguish a voluntary from a mechanical movement.

Biological and mental evolution.

Contractility, for example, is a property of living matter; and certain movements which owe their origin to this property may easily be taken for voluntary ones. Thus, in vegetable protoplasm, movements connected with nutrition have a somewhat voluntary character; while, on the other hand, the movements of certain elementary organisms, which perform their nutritive functions

---

[1] E. Haeckel, *Generelle Morphologie* (1862—1866), and *Welträtsel* (1900). See Tanzi's criticism of Haeckel's panpsychical notion in his lecture on *I limiti della psicologia* (Florence, 1897), p. 10. See also Mosso, "Materialismo e misticismo" (*Nuova Antologia*, December 1st, 1895, p. 445).

[2] Regarding the limitations of the mental life, see the chapter "Merkmale und Grenzen des psychischen Lebens" in Vol. I., Part II., p. 21 foll., of Wundt's *Grundzüge der physiologischen Psychologie*.

through absorption, appear to be the product of mechanical actions.[1] It is only in the case of organisms which have attained a certain degree of biological development that we can have the certainty that the movements we perceive are voluntary and that there is consciousness behind them. But how does this mental life begin? Does it spring up by enchantment, out of nothing, or does it arise from something which was pre-existent to it? This is the point where, *data* being scarce, hypotheses begin.

Apparently the simplest explanation would be that psychical phenomena are derived from matter itself, and that they constitute a novel property, which matter acquires at a given moment of its evolution. This is the materialistic theory, which is also entertained by some "positivist" philosophers. It is well known indeed that Spencer derives consciousness from reflex acts.[2] The first movements, which tend to the preservation of the individual and of the species are purely mechanical adaptations. As soon as the individual is not absolutely and completely in harmony with his surroundings, a hiatus is formed which awakens him to a consciousness of self. But this hypothesis, whilst seeking to explain the evolution of consciousness by that of the organism, fails to show how the first psychical phenomenon has its origin. For, even admitting (which is untenable) that the first movements of primeval organisms are mechanical, it is not possible to comprehend in what manner a discord between those organisms and their surroundings, and consequently an antagonism between purely physical forces, can engender a phenomenon of such an entirely different nature as the phenomenon of consciousness. Some modern psychologists go even further than Spencer, and are of opinion that the physical necessities of the biological organism manifest themselves in a real want, in which the mind (which is the necessary instrument for satisfying the more complex wants of the fully developed organism) has its germ. But the objection naturally presents itself that a *want* is a psychical fact, and, as such, implies the pre-existence of consciousness. Instead of explaining the origin of mind, a want has itself to find its explanation in the mind. It is a vicious circle from which there is no escape.[3]

[1] Wundt, *Physiologische Psychologie*, Vol. I., p. 23.
[2] Spencer, *Principles of Psychology*, Vol. I., Part IV., chap. iv.
[3] This theory is strenuously upheld by Sergi. See his book *La psiche nei fenomeni della vita* (Torina, 1901). It is confuted with great ability by E. Regalia in a short paper published in the *Rivista di filosofia, pedagogia e scienze affini* (Bologna, Maggio-Guiguo, 1902), entitled "La psiche ha origine da bisogni?"

The attempts of the materialists to derive consciousness from chemical combination (as was done, for instance, by Lewes) have been even less successful.[1] No combination of chemical elements suffices to explain life ; and although we may recognise that life is the effect of a peculiar combination of those elements, we are obliged to admit that its origin is a mystery. Nor can we better explain the fact that as soon as we find an animal organisation we find a consciousness.

Materialist theories concerning the origin of consciousness.

However far we may go back in the scale of organic evolution, we can never reach a point where physical and mental phenomena cease to be governed by their respective laws. There can consequently be no other explanation than to suppose that the primary elements which constitute life themselves contain psychical elements, and that mind is therefore as universal as matter. This is the conclusion arrived at by Haeckel. Thus, from materialism we seem to arrive at the novel form of hylozoism which goes by the name of panpsychism. If we reject the materialistic explanations, can we accept the latter theory? We have already seen that the primary characteristic of conscious phenomena is " freedom," and of this freedom there is no trace in the physical world, where all phenomena are determined and regulated in a fixed and unchangeable way by laws of motion. How, then, can we suppose that they possess "consciousness" as we understand it—that is, free and spontaneous power of determination? The theory of panpsychism must, therefore, also be rejected.

The problem, however, remains how to formulate a theory compatible with the principle of psycho-physical parallelism. Modern scientific ideas can accept no theory which is not founded upon the continuity of phenomena, whether physical or psychical. The idea, therefore, that consciousness may have arisen *ex nihilo*, or out of something entirely different from itself, must be at once rejected. If, on the other hand, we do not meet with mental life outside animal organism, it is reasonable to suppose that, like life itself, it is the result of a peculiar organisation and combination of elements which already pre-exist along with the primitive elements which constitute life. On the other hand, these primitive mental elements are not themselves consciousness, as we understand it, any more than

Psycho-physical parallelism and consciousness.

---

[1] Lewes, *Problems of Life and Mind* (" The Physical Basis of Mind "). See also Sergi, *L' origine dei fenomeni psichici e la loro significazione biologica* (1885) See the confutation of Lewes's doctrine in L. Carrau's *La conscience psychologique et morale dans l'individu et dans l'histoire* (Paris, 1887), p. 4 foll.

inorganic elements in themselves are life. It is therefore just as out of place to apply the term " soul " to the psychical elements which may exist in inorganic matter, as it would be to speak of the life of inorganic matter itself. The psychical life of universal matter is not, therefore, a real and actual life, but merely a "latent life," which manifests itself under certain determinate conditions.[1] These conditions do not appear to tally with those of life itself, for plants, which are living organisms, are endowed with no real psychical life. This theory does not run counter to any scientific postulate, since, owing to its comprehensiveness, it does not profess to offer a conclusive and final explanation, but, on the contrary, leaves room for any new discoveries which Psychology and biology may eventually make concerning the vexed question of primitive organic manifestations.

The fact therefore remains that the pyschic life presents in primitive organisms the same elements which are to be found in the fully developed consciousness, the sole difference being that they appear in the former in an extremely simple form. It may easily be imagined to what an infinitesimal degree the psychic life must be reduced in those beings in which hardly any differentiation of organs and functions exists,[2] though we already find in them, in an extremely simple form, the three fundamental elements of psychical life—to wit, sensation, feeling, and will. The evolution of consciousness proceeds *pari passu* with that of biological organisation. In both cases a homogeneous and incoherent whole becomes gradually complex and differentiated. This is the sense in which the evolution of conscious life should be understood, and not as Spencer understands it. Indeed, it can be shown that in deriving the whole mental life from reflex mechanical acts, Spencer is guilty of misapplying the principles he had so ably formulated and applied to organic evolution.

Primitive psychical elements.

We have, on the contrary, every reason for believing that the acts of lower organisms are, like our own, determined by feelings and presentations, though of an extremely simple and uniform nature. "In the lower and simpler forms of life," says Binet, "are to be found manifestations of an intelligence which far surpasses the phenomena of cellular irritability." The psychical activities of micro-organisms may form

Psychical life of micro-organisms.

---

[1] Wundt, *Grundzüge der physiologischen Psychologie*, Vol. I., pp. 25, 26.

[2] See a minute description of the evolution of physiological organisation, especially with regard to the nervous system, in *Grundzüge der physiologischen Psychologie* (Vol. I., Part I., p. 26 foll).

the object of a very interesting though difficult study, which will be of invaluable help to comparative Psychology. Two eminent observers, Max Verworn from the side of physiology, and Binet from that of Psychology, have recently given detailed accounts,[1] from which it appears that micro-organisms, from a psychological point of view, are far from being semi-automatic creatures, as was for a long time supposed.[2] Some of these elementary beings, such as the infusoria ciliata, have, according to Binet, some very interesting habits and peculiarities. Seen through the microscope, certain movements are observable, which are by no means simple, for they swim avoiding obstacles, and sometimes go round them after several attempts, all these movements having seemingly a purpose, which is generally the search for food. " The infusoria," says Binet, "approach certain particles which are suspended in the liquid, feel them with their cilia, then retreat, only to return, describing a zig-zag course similar to that of fish in an aquarium; in fact, the movements of free infusoria present all the characteristics of voluntary movements."[3]

In the acts of micro-organisms we can, therefore, distinguish various stages: the perception of the external object, the choice between several objects, the perception of their position in space, and the movements directed either towards the object with a view to seizing it, or from the object in order to escape from it. The acts which these micro-organisms perform with a view to fecundation and the preservation of the species are also very complicated, and imply a certain development of psychical activities. From all this it is fair to conclude that as soon as there exists a biological organisation which presents a certain complexity (the existence of unicellular organisms is very much discussed), we find psychical functions possessing in rudimentary form all the elements to be met with in higher forms of consciousness. For it is likewise certain that there exists in them, besides perception and will, also an elementary form of pain or pleasure, the first being probably the principal stimulus to the satisfaction of organic wants, and the second the natural consequence of the fulfilment of the want. We cannot

---

[1] A. Binet, *Etudes de psychologie expérimentale* (Paris, 1888); *La vie psychique des micro-organismes*, pp. 87—239. The passage quoted is on page 90. Max Verworn, *Psycho-physiologische Protistenstudien*; *Experimentellen Untersuchungen* (Jena, 1889).
[2] Amongst those who consider that micro-organisms are endowed solely with an unconscious physiological life. see Romanes and Richet.
[3] Binet, *op. cit.*, pp. 145—146.

imagine, indeed, a psychical activity unaccompanied by feeling, nor have we any reason to suppose that the lower forms of life are an exception to this rule. It is the more necessary to assume it, seeing that otherwise we should have no means of explaining the origin of feeling, which cannot certainly be derived from sensation, nor volition, nor from both combined.[1]

The evolution of consciousness takes place in the same way as the general evolution of biological organisation. In man, who pre-sents the utmost differentiation of organic and vital func-tions, we also find the greatest differentiation as regards psychical functions. Sensations, owing to the differ-entiation of the sensory organs, become more numerous; likewise they become associated in various combinations, which in their turn become associated and recall each other in an ever-increasing variety of ways, as the capacity for retaining and reproducing impressions increases, until finally we reach the power of forming abstract and general ideas.

Progressive evolution of mental life.

The same evolution is to be noted in the feelings. Out of the rudimentary primitive forms of pleasure and pain, which are solely caused by organic sensations, are gradually evolved new feelings, which owe their being to the differentiation of the sensitive qualities, are, like them, associated, and thus tend to recall each other, becoming in the end independent of external impressions so as to constitute a whole network of psychic processes which express the inmost and most subjective aspect of consciousness.

Finally the will, which is the most fundamental of all the psychic activities, offers in its evolution an image of the evolution of the whole consciousness. Primitive movements are all impulsive, and aim at the preservation of the individual and of the species. But it must not be supposed that this impulsiveness is always the same, or that the individual always responds in an identical manner to every impression received, seeing that the surrounding con-ditions of life are not in every case identical. Individual and spontaneous variation, brought about by the necessity of self-preservation, must therefore be admitted, even though in general the field of impulsive, or, as they are called, instinctive, acts remains unchanged. These variations have sometimes left traces upon the physical organisation of certain species, whilst in some cases other changes have supervened to modify them in their turn.[2]

[1] See chap. v. of the present work.

[2] See Baldwin's often-quoted *Mental Development in the Child and the Race*, chap. vii. This theory, which is opposed to that of natural selection, is known

We have consequently two forces, which tend to balance each other: an external force, given by the physical conditions of the surroundings, and an internal force, consisting in the psychophysical organism with which the individual reacts upon external agencies. This inner force, which is the real psychical activity, is therefore a very potent factor of biological evolution, seeing that the organism is by no means passive with respect to its surroundings, nor does it merely adapt itself mechanically to them (as in Spencer's opinion). On the contrary, in the regulation of its actions inspired by a certain purpose, of which the organism may be conscious, it is frequently obliged to modify these actions, and, consequently, the vital functions, which are an essential part of them.[1] The mere mechanical transformation of organisms does not, in fact, always explain the transformation of the functions, for we can see in ourselves that, although we are at our birth possessed of a corporeal organism, the latter becomes gradually modified and developed under the control of consciousness. In other words, the conscious movements which we are continually making tend to modify our way of living, and, consequently, in a long series of generations, bring about a gradual modification of the organism itself.[2] We have, therefore, in the first conscious movements of organisms the germ of that double form of will which appears so distinctly in man—viz. external and internal will.

Importance of the attention. What characterises, in fact, more than anything else the evolution of psychic life, is the progressive increase of the force of attention, or of the internal will. As the attention becomes more capable of intensity and duration it becomes more possible for presentations to become associated at will, so that we can form to ourselves an inner world of ideas, feelings, and impulses which belongs to ourselves and is, to a certain point, independent of the impressions of the physical world. As we have often remarked, this evolution of the will is accompanied by increasingly varied and intense feelings, the three fundamental psychic activities being so thoroughly interwoven that each is simultaneously the effect and the cause of the others.

as the theory of *organic selection*, and is upheld by many eminent modern psychologists and biologists, such as Wundt, C. Lloyd Morgan (*Introduction to Comparative Psychology*, and especially *Habit and Instinct*), James, Stout, Groos, Osborn, Wallace, Poulton, Habrecht. See also Fouillée, *L'évolutionisme des idées forces*.

[1] See *System der Philosophie* of Wundt, p. 545 foll., on "Selbstregulirungen im entwickelten Organismus; Mechanisirung der Lebensvorgänge."

[2] See Fouillée, *L'évolutionisme des idées forces*, Bk. III., chap. i.

The above view, however, is by no means unanimously accepted. As a reaction against the metaphysical spiritualistic theories of the old Psychology, there has arisen in recent times a theory which has gone to the opposite extreme, considering consciousness a secondary phenomenon in the mechanism of mental life. The origin of this doctrine is twofold, for it is related on the one hand to the materialistic systems of the eighteenth and nineteenth centuries, and to modern biological ideas founded on the principle of evolution; on the other hand, it has various points of contact with the metaphysical philosophy of Schopenhauer. It was originally brought forward by Maudsley, the alienist, and by Lewes, the physiologist, but was popularised and further developed by Ribot. In examining it, we shall therefore follow the work of the last named on *The Diseases of Personality*.[1]

Theory of Maudsley and Ribot.

In Ribot's opinion, consciousness is very different from what it appeared to be in the eyes of the old psychologists, for whom it was a metaphysical entity, existing independently of the biological organism to which it is in reality united, and forming therefore an absolutely simple, self-identical unit. The term "consciousness," which in the higher and concrete sense means the human "personality," is taken, on the contrary, to mean an aggregate to be analysed and studied in its constituent elements, which are of three kinds—organic, affective, and intellectual. Consciousness in itself is an abstract conception, the practical manifestations of which are a series of concrete phenomena. Granting the fact demonstrated by physiology, that for consciousness to exist the nervous system must be active, Ribot holds that the converse is not the case, seeing that nervous activity extends much further than mental activity. Consciousness is therefore something superadded (*surajouté*), from which Ribot concludes that "every state of consciousness is a complex event, which implies a particular state of the nervous system"; that "this nervous process is not an accessory, but an essential part of the event—in fact, its basis and fundamental condition"; that "finally consciousness completes and finishes it, but does not constitute it." Therefore all manifestations of psychic life, sensations, desires, feelings, volitions, recollections, reasonings,

---

[1] See Maudsley's *Physiology of Mind* (2nd edit., London, 1876), especially chap. iv., p. 186 foll.; and Lewes's *The Physical Basis of Mind* (1877), Problem III., chap. iv., p. 353 foll. Ribot's work on *Les maladies de la personnalité*, which reached its fifth edition in 1894, appeared in 1884. This theory is also upheld by Sergi, Despine, Richel, and generally by physiologists and alienists.

may be conscious or unconscious.[1] Consciousness becomes in this way what Maudsley considers it—namely, an epiphenomenon added to physiological phenomena, but not necessary to the psychic life, which is included in those phenomena.

The confusion of ideas revealed by this theory is remarkable. Consciousness is confused on the one hand with the consciousness of self, and on the other with physiological functions. There can be no doubt that the physiological life extends much further than the psychical, but neither Ribot nor others have yet succeeded in proving that they are identical. To affirm that ideas, feelings, desires, recollections, and volitions can exist both in the conscious and the unconscious states is a contradiction in terms, for, as psychical phenomena, they can only belong to consciousness. On the other hand, a confusion arises not only between consciousness (which we hold to be the aggregate of psychic processes) and the consciousness of self (which, as we have seen, implies an advanced form of mental development), but also between the former and the affirmation, or outer expression, of consciousness in action.[2] This is an error that Ribot also commits, as we have had occasion to observe, in the case of the will.[3] Consciousness, moreover, and consequently the acts of willing, together with all the other mental processes, exist independently of the reflections we may make regarding them; in other words, they have an independent value of their own.[4] Further, what are we to understand by that "super-added" phenomenon which crowns the physiological action? If it is distinct from organic phenomena, it must have a value and laws of its own, and cannot be determined by the latter. Biological phenomena can be reduced to the laws of general physics, and are

---

[1] Ribot, *op. cit.*, Introduction, pp. 6—7. See, on the theory of consciousness as an epiphenomenon, H. Bergson's *Matière et Mémoire* (2nd edit. 1900).

[2] Maudsley (*Physiology of Mind*, p. 245): "It can hardly be doubted that too much has been made of consciousness in times past, and that instead of mental phenomena revolving round it as the sun of the system, it is rather a sort of satellite of mind—the indicator which makes known what is being done, not the agent in doing it."

[3] Ribot, *op. cit.*, p. 16: "Lorsque un état physiologique est devenu un état de conscience, il a acquis par la même un caractère particulier . . . il a pris une position dans le temps : il s'est produit après ceci et avant cela, tandis que, pour l'état inconscient, il n'y a ni avant ni après. Il devient susceptible d'être rappelé, c'est à dire reconnu comme ayant occupé une position précise entre d'autres états de conscience." Ribot then quotes volition as an instance of a state of consciousness, stating that "La volition est toujours un état de conscience, l'affirmation qu'une chose doit être faite ou empêchée."

[4] See chap. v. above.

ultimately to be considered as phenomena of motion, whereas psychical processes are qualitative facts which elude this law. How, then, can we place the two side by side and assign to the latter a secondary part in comparison to the former? And, if this be granted, how can we speak of psychic phenomena when there exist only mechanical phenomena? There would be no other way out of the difficulty but to admit with the hylozoists that consciousness is also to be found in the latter order of phenomena, which would be an odd result for positivist philosophers to arrive at!

The neo-materialists have been much struck by the phenomenon of reflex movement, in which some have thought they saw the connecting-link between the mental and physical life. Thus the psychic life has been conceived by some as a series of reflex movements, in which case it is difficult to understand how they explain the teleological character of those movements. In their view consciousness might be compared to the lights of a locomotive, which have no action on the engine itself, and serve only to illuminate it.[1] The term "psychical reflexes" has even been used by some without considering that "reflex" and "psychic" are contradictory terms.[2] For the most difficult point, which defies the subtlest arguments of the materialists, is to prove how a reflex mechanical act, performed by organic beings, can possess a voluntary character and be directed towards a determinate purpose. If one does not wish to fall into the metaphysical improbabilities of hylozoism, it must be recognised that no sooner does organic life manifest itself than there is to be found a beginning of consciousness, with its fundamental characteristics of volition and finality—*i.e.* of feeling and impulse; and this is confirmed by introspection, which shows that all our psychic

The theory of biological determinism.

---

[1] Among the supporters of these extreme theories we must quote Despine *Psychologie naturelle*, 1868), Sergi (*L' origine dei fenomeni psichici e la loro significazione biologica*, 1885). See Fouillée's criticism in his *Evolutionisme des idées forces*, p. 158 foll., and Masci, *Il materialismo psicofisico e la dottrina del parallelismo in psicologia*, p. 171 foll. It is to be noted, however, that Ribot does not arrive at the extreme consequences reached by contemporary materialists. He is of opinion that consciousness, though derived from a reflex act, becomes subsequently a new factor and does not merely play a passive part. "La conscience," he says, "quelles qu'en soient l'origine et la nature, ne perd rien de sa valeur: c'est en elle-même qu'elle doit être appréciée; et pour qui se place au point de vue de l'évolution, ce n'est pas l'origine qui importe, mais la hauteur atteinte" (*op. cit.*, pp. 14 and 15).

[2] For example, Richet, *Essai de psychologie générale* (2nd edit. 1891), p. 75.

actions are attended by a peculiar feeling of activity—a feeling which is the surest index of the spontaneity of our psychic life.[1] The attempt has recently been made (*e.g.* by Delage and Dantec)[2] to prove the existence of an absolute biological determinism by which the individual organism develops itself in a purely mechanical fashion, in accordance with a scheme which is to be found pre-existent in the primitive and elementary organism—*i.e.* in the cell. This theory does away with all action of the consciousness in the evolution of organic forms, consciousness being again reduced to an "epiphenomenon." The metaphysical character of this theory is palpable. The neo-determinists fall into the same error as the spiritualists, for both schools sever the psychophysical individual into two abstract entities—psychic or spiritual, and physical.[3]

From this absolutely mechanical determinism to what may be called a *Teleological* determinism there is but a step. In order to explain how consciousness in the course of progressive biological evolution adapts itself to novel external conditions, some modern psychologists have no hesitation in accepting the theory that this progressive evolution is not only mechanically but also psychically preordained. Such a theory, however, must rest on one of the following hypotheses: either (1) that general biological development is directed by an extraneous and supernatural power; or (2) that the variations to

[1] This feeling was noted by Wundt and Fouillée (see *L'évolutionisme des idées-forces*). James calls it "the feeling of tendency" (*The Principles of Psychology*, Vol. I., p. 249).

[2] Yves Delage (professor at the University of Paris), *La structure des protoplasma et les théories sur l'hérédité et les grands problèmes de la biologie générale* (1895); Dantec, *Théorie nouvelle de la vie*; *Le déterminisme biologique* (1897); *L'individualité* (1898). See, on this theory, a short but interesting paper by Professor Tito Vignoli (*Rendiconti del R. Istituto Lombardo di scienze e lettere*, Ser. II., Vol. XXX., 1897), "Il determinismo biologico e gli epifenomeni psichici, a proposito di recenti publicazioni." Vignoli, who opposes the theories of Delage and Dantec, very aptly quotes the words of an eminent Italian zoologist, Professor B. Grassi, of the University of Rome: "There is no possibility of throwing light upon the living being according to purely mechanical principles, because we are always obliged to take as a base of the living being an organisation which makes use of this mechanism."

[3] Wundt, *System der Philosophie*, p. 545 foll.; *Logik*, Vol. II., chap. i. ("Logik der Biologie," p. 550 foll.) "Mit der Anerkennung dass psychische Ursachen auf die Ausbildung der organischen Formen bestimmend einwirken, ja für die Anfänge aller organischen Entwicklung vielleicht unerlässlich sind, ist nun aber zugleich ausgesprochen dass das Problem der Entwicklung überhaupt kein rein physiologisches, sondern zu einem wesentlichen Theile zugleich ein psychologisches Problem ist."

which the organism is subjected, and consequently the means by which it can preserve and protect itself, exist in the primitive organism as *idea*. The first of these suppositions cannot be entertained, owing to its eminently metaphysical character, which eludes all positive demonstration; but the second is no less arbitrary and inadmissible. It is indeed absurd to believe that the primitive organism is capable of such prevision as to foresee all future wants and the means to satisfy them. Consequently this theory, with the notion of a universal mind diffused amongst the biological and cosmic elements, is tainted by the same defect as mysticism.[1] The individual is a psychophysical being, and his biological and psychological evolution run always on parallel lines. Reflex movement, which is considered by some as the starting-point of evolution, is, on the contrary, a derivative fact.[2] These theories, therefore, mark a return to the concept of a " substance " underlying conscious phenomena.

The hypothesis of unconscious mental life is the necessary complement of these, as of the spiritualistic theories. This has been a favourite subject of discussion for philosophers and psychologists. The psychological problem, which gave rise to the various theories and hypotheses concerning unconscious psychical activity, consisted in the necessity of explaining how it happens that a presentation can pass the threshold of our consciousness, rise above it, and finally fall again beneath it. It was difficult to understand why a presentation disappears in order to make room for another, and it was still harder to explain why that presentation reappears after a longer or shorter interval, sometimes under entirely changed circumstances and in an unforeseen manner.

The concept of an unconscious pyschic life.

The earliest metaphysical theory is the Cartesian one of " ideæ innatæ." Man, according to this school, is born with ready-formed

---

[1] Richet, for instance, explains the finality of organic processes in a somewhat mystical fashion (see *Révue scientifique*, July 2nd, 1898, " L'effort vers la vie et la théorie des causes finales "). See, on the influence of the mental factor on organic evolution, C. Lloyd Morgan, *Habit and Instinct*, chap. xii.

[2] Fouillée (*L'évolutionisme des idées forces*, p. 168) calls these mechanical theories " de la tendance matérialiste, que le psychologue comme tel doit s'interdire. Il n'y a pas de 'transformation' possible du pur automatisme en conscience. Le rapport du conscient au mécanisme n'est dont pas le rapport d'un phénomène à un autre phénomène du genre mécanique, qui serait seulement moins complexe: c'est un rapport de tout autre nature. On peut concevoir ce rapport de plusieurs façons, mais jamais à la façon d'un mouvement qui en suit et en prolonge un autre."

ideas on God, the world, and other cosmological and ontological concepts, which could never be acquired by experience. This **Descartes.** was an entirely spiritualistic notion, a remnant of scholastic philosophy, kept alive principally by moral and religious prejudices. Locke, on the contrary, who was an empiricist, rejected this metaphysical conception in favour of a more probable one, according to which all the ideas we possess have their origin in experience, which, taking the sensations as a starting-point, gradually arrives at more complex presentations, and finally at the formation of abstract ideas. But the metaphysical conceptions regarding the origin of ideas and presentations **Leibnitz.** reappeared under a different shape with Leibnitz, who was of opinion that both in its lower and higher degrees consciousness is always spontaneous and active. According to Leibnitz, the soul is never purely passive, as Locke believed it to be, though he, nevertheless, admitted the existence of a thinking substance. The great merit of Leibnitz is that of having first pointed out these obscure phenomena of the mental life and noted their importance from the point of view of the continuity of the consciousness. The latter is a continuous and connected whole; but it often happens, as Leibnitz justly observes, that we are not aware of the continuity: we perceive the clearer and more distinct mental states, whilst the smaller perceptions and confused feelings which connect one state with another often escape us.

These views, though undoubtedly profound, and entirely in keeping with the ideas of modern Psychology, lent themselves nevertheless to very different interpretations. While rejecting the Cartesian innate ideas, Leibnitz believed in certain innate "dispositions" or aptitudes of the soul (interpreted as a spontaneous activity), aptitudes which, however, are in need of the help of experience to develop themselves.[1] These two concepts of "obscure perceptions" and of innate "dispositions" of the soul can be perfectly well accepted without admitting the existence of a mental life beneath the threshold of consciousness; but the **Wolff.** followers of Leibnitz, and especially Wolff, based upon them their belief not only that there are, as Leibnitz maintained, various degrees of clearness in the consciousness, but also unconscious mental states which we can only apprehend in an indirect manner by induction, taking the psychical phenomena of the conscious states as a starting-point. Wolff's successors were

---

[1] See Leibnitz, *Principes de la nature et de la grâce*, § 4; "Monadologia," § 14 (Latta's *Leibnitz*, p. 420).

guilty of exaggeration in this sense, bringing forward metaphysical theories on the nature of unconsciousness, and even going the length of constructing thereon a whole system of philosophy, as in the case of Edward von Hartmann.[1]

Besides this, which we may call the purely metaphysical school, and which extends from Leibnitz to Hartmann,[2] there exists a more recent one, which, starting from different premises, arrives at the same idea of an unconscious mental life, and may be called the physiological and evolutionist school. Modern physiology and Psychology having satisfactorily proved that every state of consciousness is connected with a certain number of more or less properly understood cerebral phenomena, it was believed by many that a real explanation of the psychical processes had been arrived at and was to be found in the nervous mechanism, which is also responsible for the unconscious mental states. Unconsciousness would be therefore reduced to a physiological *datum*. Ribot, we have seen, follows this opinion, which is accepted by Lewes, Maudsley, and in general by all the followers of the so-called "physiological" school.[3] This process, which takes place inside the brain, has, indeed, received the special name of "unconscious cerebration."

The modern evolutionist school.

Both the spiritualists and the materialists thus agree as to the existence of unconscious mental states, but the concept of unconsciousness meets with scant favour on the part of the greater number of contemporary psychologists. James, Sully, Baldwin, Wundt, are entirely opposed to it; Höffding is only partly in favour of it. Only the "physiologists" and Herbartians,

[1] Hartmann's *Philosophie des Unbewussten* (published in 1869, Eng. tr. by Coupland), has reached a tenth edition. It must be noted that the success of this work is greatly due to the literary form in which it is written.

[2] A history of the doctrines of unconsciousness is to be found in the first volume of Hartmann's work above quoted and in G. Volkelt's *Das Unbewusste und der Pessimismus* (Berlin, 1873), Part I., pp. 1—103. Volkelt divides the history of the doctrine into two periods, negative and positive : the first embraces the Middle Ages, Descartes, Spinoza, Locke, the materialists, and Berkeley ; the second, Leibnitz, Kant, Hegel, Carus, and Hartmann.

[3] The writers who especially insist upon this notion of what they call "unconscious cerebration" are Colsenet, *La vie inconsciente de l'esprit* (1880); Laycock, *Mind and Brain*, Vol. I. (1860) ; W. B. Carpenter, *Mental Physiology*, chap. xiii. ; F. P. Cobbe, *Darwinism in Morals, and Other Essays*, essay xi., Unconscious Cerebration (1872) ; G. H. Lewes's *Problems of Life and Mind*, Series III., Problem II., chap. x., and Problem III., chap. ii. See also D. G. Thompson, *A System of Psychology*, chap. xxxiii. ; J. M. Baldwin, *Handbook of Psychology*, chap. iv.

with a few metaphysicians of the school of Hartmann, are favourable to it. In Germany until quite recently it has been better received than in England;[1] and Wundt himself, in the first edition of his *Lectures on the Soul of Man and Animals* (published in 1862), attributed a much greater importance to unconsciousness than he has done in his later works. This theory had, nevertheless, been hotly opposed as early as 1874 by Franz Brentano,[2] who dedicates a lengthy chapter of his *Psychology* to its confutation from every point of view. The same may be said of Theodor Lipps.[3]

The principal arguments brought forward by the partisans of the theory of unconscious mental phenomena are the same as proposed by Leibnitz, with additions derived from the data of experimental Psychology. The first is that we do not perceive all the elements which make up a sensation separately, but as a whole, the sensation appearing, therefore, as a unity, whereas it is in reality composed of many constituents. Indeed, if we make an effort to attentively observe a sensation as it arises within us, we are able gradually to discern them, which means that they penetrate to our consciousness one by one. Our not having perceived them sooner is therefore a proof that they were beneath the threshold of consciousness, or, in other words, unconscious, but were nevertheless in existence as elements of sensations. The reply to this is not difficult. A pyschical state cannot be called such unless it has at least touched the threshold of consciousness. As long as a physical impression or a nervous stimulus has not attained a degree of intensity sufficient to produce a sensation or to pass the threshold of excitation, it remains a purely physical or physiological fact unattended by phenomena of consciousness.[4] If by an increased effort of our attention we are enabled to perceive certain elements in a sensation which we did not at first perceive, it signifies that the threshold of consciousness during the state of attention

Critique of the arguments in favour of unconscious cerebration.

---

[1] Amongst English philosophers, the only one of authority in favour of the notion of unconsciousness (apart from physiologists) is Hamilton, who has been energetically confuted by Mill in his well-known *Examination of Sir William Hamilton's Philosophy.* Bain is also opposed to it.

[2] F. Brentano, *Psychologie vom empirischen Standpunkte*, Bk. II., chap. ii., p. 131 foll.

[3] Th. Lipps, *Grundthatsachen des Seelenlebens.*

[4] This theory, which is connected with that of psychical "Atomism," is ably confuted by James in his *Principles of Psychology*, Vol. I., p. 158 foll., and by Baldwin, *Handbook of Psychology*, Vol. I., p. 46 foll.

is lowered, so that the same degree of intensity in the stimulus produces a new sensation, which was previously absent.

An observation is here necessary in order to properly understand the inmost nature of mental phenomena. The expression "to perceive the elements of a sensation" is improperly used by analogy with physical phenomena. A sensation is a simple phenomenon of psychic life, which cannot be separated into other constituents; so that, instead of saying that we perceive new elements, we ought rather to say that we perceive new sensations. It is impossible to penetrate further than these and to perceive other simpler elements. The mistake of believing that a sensation consists of various elements is mainly due to the mistaken use of the word "sensation" instead of "presentation," which is itself an aggregate of sensations. This confusion of terms is especially to be guarded against in the case of so-called "intensive" presentations, in which the various sensations which make them up are confined to the smallest possible extension of space and time; so that it is not always easy to distinguish the various parts. As long as a phenomenon is beneath the threshold of consciousness, it cannot be termed psychical, but only physical or physiological; nor should the nervous stimuli which produce a sensation be mistaken for the sensation itself, which is a purely psychical phenomenon.

Once this notion is clearly established, the remaining arguments brought forward in favour of the theory of "unconscious psychic life" fall of themselves. The strongest of these arguments is one which used to be a favourite weapon of the metaphysical spiritualistic schools, and appears now to find confirmation in the theory of evolution. This is the intellectualistic theory of "immortal" presentations. We have often had occasion to remark that one of the most generally accepted notions in Psychology is that presentations are unities, and consequently when they *re*present themselves to consciousness after having disappeared, they return in a form identical with that in which in the first instance they appeared. As a corollary of this principle, it was natural for the question to present itself whither presentations withdraw themselves when they fall below the threshold of consciousness, how they continue to exist, and by what laws they are governed during this latent condition? The Herbartians pushed this principle to its utmost limit. When a presentation falls below the threshold of consciousness, said Herbart, it continues to live a latent life and aspires to return above the threshold and to expel other presentations. Upon such a basis, unchecked by any observation of facts, it became possible to formulate all sorts of theories concerning the subconscious life. It was thought, for instance, that all the forms of conscious mental life were also to be found in the unconscious life whence the expressions " unconscious reasoning," " unconscious feeling," " unconscious will," and so forth, gained a footing. As several simple phenomena of the mental life, such as space-presentations, instinctive actions, and others of the same kind, all possess a marked character of adaptability to certain ends, it was supposed by many that they are the result of unconscious reasoning, similar to that which takes place consciously according to the rules of logic. One writer has even gone so far as to use the phrase " unconscious logic." [1]

These ideas, which all centred around the principle of the unity and immortality of presentations, found a powerful ally in the theory of evolution. When it had been ascertained that we inherit from our parents and ancestors a physical structure, and with it certain mental aptitudes which show themselves in the individual character, it was thought by some that we not only inherit certain sensible presentations, but social, moral, and æsthetic ideas into the bargain. Thus what individual Psychology could not explain, was explained by the Psychology of the species. It is, however, a moot point whether this theory were not the old doctrine of innate ideas presented in a new form, for, when all is said, the problem of the formation of presentations comes to be simply shifted and not explained. Moreover, the explanations given by Spencer of the transmission of such complex mental phenomena as abstract ideas are very unsatisfactory and based upon physiological hypotheses, which are very far from having an experiential confirmation.[2] It was thought, in fact, that such phenomena are transmitted with the cells, and that the latter are in a reciprocal state of connection, which is also transmissible.

These ideas are all founded upon a very imperfect notion of the nature of psychical phenomena. A presentation is not a fixed unity, like a physical phenomenon, but an aggregate of unities—that is

---

[1] The first to introduce these expressions into philosophy was Schopenhauer in his well-known thesis concerning the quadruple root of the principle of sufficient reason. A similar abuse of language is also noticeable in Colsenet (*La vie inconsciente de l'esprit*) and Binet (*La psychologie du raisonnement*, 1886). Binet, for instance (*op. cit.*, p. 75), calls perception " unconscious reasoning."

[2] Spencer, *Principles of Psychology*, Vol. I., p. 432 foll. On instinct, see Schneider, *Der thierische Wille* (1880), chap. iii., p. 55 foll., where there is an able confutation of the spiritualistic theories on instinct. See also Wundt, *Lectures in Human and Animal Psychology*, p. 388 foll.

to say, an aggregate of sensations, which are the only veritable "psychical atoms." When the mental life is considered not only from the point of view of presentation, as by the intellectualists, but from its three aspects of presentation, feeling, and volition, it no longer appears immutable in its substance, like the physical world, but in the light of a continuous sequence of processes entirely devoid of any unchangeable substratum. It will then be seen that a presentation never occurs a second time in the same form, seeing that its constituent elements never come together in exactly the same way twice over. When a presentation recurs to our consciousness through association, without knowing it, we add to, or change, some of its elements, putting in their place others belonging to the presentation which has recalled the previous one, or to other past presentations, so that the result must perforce be different from the original presentation. It may be also that we concentrate more [1] attention upon one or other of the constituent elements of a presentation, according to the state of mind we happen to be in. The whole hypothetical fabric, constructed upon the basis of a latent mental life, existing beneath the threshold of consciousness, falls, therefore, to pieces like a house of cards. When a presentation disappears from consciousness, its elements separate, and consequently do not exist any more as psychical facts comparable to those which make up consciousness.

Psychologists, nevertheless, must not be denied the right of seeking to pry a little beyond actual facts and of trying to make out which is the most reasonable hypothesis concerning the origin of "actual" mental life, and how psychical elements can return to consciousness under the guise of new mental images. This question is similar to that of the origin of mental life in the species, and must be resolved in a similar way. It is a moot point whether the psychic elements, which, in a developed organism, are connected in a chain of conscious functions, are to be found dispersed in inorganic matter, or whether they exist in the latter in the form of "dispositions," or latent aptitudes. Seeing that it is impossible to suppose that mental life begins *ex novo*, at a certain stage of organic evolution it seems necessary to have recourse to some theory of latent "dispositions" which, by steering a middle course between absolute empiricism (admitting of none but conscious mental phenomena) and hylozoism (the theory of universal animation), may, up to a certain point, explain the origin of mental phenomena. The same may be said

The theory of "mental dispositions."

[1] See above, chap. vi.

of the conscious life of the individual. The most probable theory here seems to be that all the mental elements of a presentation which has vanished remain beneath consciousness in a latent state, and may be called to life again by a fresh stimulus. Harald Höffding discusses this theory with great ability in his *Psychology*,[1] adopting the philosophical rather than the empirical conception of the continuity of the mental life, which Leibnitz had been the first to affirm. " It cannot be admitted," observes Höffding, " that whereas the series of physical phenomena does not stop short, but continues|in the shape of cerebral phenomena, the series of mental phenomena should suddenly cease, or otherwise begin as if by magic, without being determined by a preceding phenomenon of similar nature."[2] Cerebral activity indeed continues in an attenuated form when presentations and other mental phenomena have ceased ; and this activity, which is not strong enough to evoke conscious processes, is nevertheless identical with that by which the latter are occasionally attended. How can it be explained that when the nervous and cerebral stimulus has reached a certain degree of intensity, there should suddenly arise processes of consciousness ? If we accept the theory of psychophysical parellelism, we cannot mix up the physical and mental series of phenomena, and, even though admitting their indissoluble connection, we must bear in mind that they each follow rules and principles of their own, each forming a continuous chain, the origin of which loses itself in the beginning of life and of the world.

These reasons have induced some modern psychologists [3] to invoke psychophysical parallelism as a proof of the existence of an unconscious mental life. Consciousness, constituted as it is at present in man, being connected with a nervous system which is the product of a lengthy evolution, during which some of the organs which are now a part of that nervous system without any conscious nervous activity, used to be organs of greater importance and centres of psychical importance, Lewes concludes that it is inadmissible to limit human consciousness to the more complicated parts of the cerebro-spinal system. It is more probable, on the

---

[1] See the excellent chapter on " Consciousness and Unconsciousness." See also Masci, *op. cit.*, p. 233 foll., and *La formazione naturale dell' istinto*.

[2] *Op. cit.*, p. 81. Höffding quotes the words of Leibnitz : " Rien ne saurait naître tout d'un coup, la pensée non plus que le mouvement."

[3] *E.g.* Lewes. See *Problems of Life and Mind* (" The Physical Basis of Mind "). See Sully's confutation in *Pessimism*, Appendix A.

contrary, that the inferior centres also possess a consciousness of their own, a subconsciousness, of which we are not aware. The brain in that case would be the supreme ruler of all this hierarchy of lower degrees of consciousness.[1] The theory of Lewes arouses a scientifically and philosophically important question as to the physiological seat of consciousness. If consciousness be considered a faculty by itself, it is natural to ask in what part of the body it has its seat. The most universally accepted theory places the seat of the soul in the brain. It is therefore natural that the doctrine of organic evolution should have cast doubts upon a theory according to which consciousness resides only in the most complex part of the cerebro-spinal system, the brain, and should have wished to examine whether the so-called lower parts of the system do not also participate in the mental life. The problem concerns both physiology and Psychology.

Subconsciousness of the lower centres.

The seat of the consciousness.

The growing differentiation and complexity of the organs of the nervous system proceeds *pari passu* in the mental life. Through the process of evolution, not only is the number of conscious phenomena increased, but their connection becomes always closer, so that in man, in addition to a great multitude of psychic elements, we find a notable power of connection and co-ordination, which reaches its acme in apperceptive activity and in logical thought. This psychical co-ordination finds its parallel in the co-ordination of the nerve-centres, which form a species of hierarchy of organs and functions governed by the brain, and more especially by the cortex cerebri and the frontal lobes. The nervous system, therefore, like consciousness, is a unity at the same time that it is multiple, as Höffding has very aptly noted in his interesting comparison between consciousness and the body.[2] Accordingly, if consciousness is to be considered as the sum-total of mental processes co-ordinated for a certain purpose, and finding their clearest expression in apperceptive activity, it cannot have its seat in one particular portion of the nervous system, but in the whole of it. Just as consciousness shows a connection of mental phenomena, the nervous system displays a connection of organs and functions. Organic evolution,

---

[1] See *Physiology of Everyday Life*, Vol. II., chap. ix., p. 58 foll. On this imaginary lower consciousness see Lange, *History of Materialism*, Vol. III., Part III., chap. ii., and Schmid, *Les sciences naturelles et la philosophie de l'inconscient* (French tr. 1879). See the able refutation of the doctrine of subconsciousness in Lotze's *Medizinische Psychologie*, p. 18.

[2] *Op. cit.*, p. 85 foll.

we know, consists in an increase of differentiation and complexity, with the effect that, as the elements of an organism become more numerous, they gather round one particular organ which assumes the direction and co-ordination of the actions performed by the whole organism. As the power of this central activity increases, it naturally follows that, on the one hand, the other functions should give up a portion of their own, and on the other that, as an effect of the continual differentiation and division of organic labour, they should acquire an increased independence. It is, indeed, very probable that many functions which in the human organism are performed in a purely mechanical fashion, and consequently without any mental strain, such as respiration, digestion, and so forth, should, on the contrary, absorb the whole mental activity of primitive organisms, and that, as the nervous system increases in complexity and the sphere of activity of the higher centres develops itself, those functions should gradually be abandoned to the lower centres while remaining to some extent dependent upon the higher centres. On any other hypothesis it would be impossible to explain the purposeful character of many reflex actions.[1] It must not be supposed, however, that the lower centres possess a psychic life of their own, for the nervous system forms a closely connected whole, the elements of which cannot be severed from the others, but constitute integral parts of the whole. To suppose a will in the lower centres is to imagine two or more different degrees of consciousness in man, and to destroy all connection between them. Our personality would be cut up into several parts, and the consciousness we have of forming a unity would be an illusion only. The proof of these different degrees of consciousness could only be afforded to us by direct and immediate experience. Experience, however, so far from giving us a feeling of the subdivision of our personality, fills us with an immediate sense of the unity and connection of all our conscious actions. We feel that we have only one, and not several personalities. Latent mental life is therefore reduced to dispositions or aptitudes of the psychical elements to return to consciousness and become freshly combined into complex forms more or less resembling those which they had previously assumed. Beyond this, hypothesis will not carry us. Many of the older psychological treatises indeed complacently quote numberless cases of presentations suddenly returning to consciousness without any apparent cause, of ideas newly improvised by the mind, and so forth, which were supposed to be inexplicable otherwise than by

[1] See Wundt, *System der Philosophie*, p. 545 foll.

admitting an unconscious working of the mind.[1] This latent elaboration of ideas is supposed to be particularly evident in the work of artists and scientists, in whom the impressions, data, and ideas, accumulated through observation and study, require (though in a different manner in the case of artists and in that of scientists) to be co-ordinated and amalgamated, so as to constitute a harmonious and organic whole, without which there can be no art or science. It is true that many famous artists have described their impressions concerning this latent working of the mind, and as their observations have not met with any effective criticism, they have indulged in descriptions of this unconscious elaboration as of a fact which really takes place. The fact remains, however, that we have no direct perception of any such unconscious working of the mind; although it must be admitted that the results are there and claim notice. The fundamental principle, which governs the development and reproduction of mental processes, as we have often had occasion to notice, is that of association, not in the sense given to it by the intellectualists—that is, as an association of presentations and consequently only of psychical compounds—but in the wider sense given to it nowadays by experimental Psychology. Association, in the latter sense, is a process which takes place between mental elements. It is already to be found in the formation of simpler presentations, and occurs in the case of more complicated associations of presentations and ideas. All reproductions of past mental impressions are explicable by means of the association of some element they contained with others belonging to mental phenomena which are actually occurring in consciousness. The obsolete intellectualistic notion that a presentation can be reproduced exactly as it was before is responsible also for the idea that a presentation may reappear suddenly without being recalled by some other cause. On closer examination it is easily ascertained that a past presentation cannot be recalled to mind except by another actual presentation with which it has some element in common.

Association and combination of mental elements.

The theory of latent mental life finds an even stronger argument in the apparently unconscious elaboration of ideas and images. In this case also, however, it is necessary to have recourse to the law of association of psychical elements, which is the one rule of any value in Psychology. This elaboration of ideas ultimately reduces

[1] See Beneke, *Psychologische Skizzen* (1825—1827); Taine, *L'intelligence* (1870); and Colsenet, *op. cit.* This theory is especially affected by men of letters and by literary philosophers.

itself to a process of combination of mental elements, which consists in the elimination of some and the substitution of others, so as to form mental compounds, which, whether composed of presentations or ideas, appear entirely new. The new form assumed by psychical compounds depends upon several circumstances, but principally upon the various capacity of each individual to assimilate and combine past and present impressions or ideas; in other words, upon the aptitude and promptness with which the elements of the present and of a past impression or idea can be combined.

Absolute novelty in science or art is impossible: what we call "new" is, generally, in reality nothing but a new combination of known elements. This synthetic power of amalgamating different elements constitutes a psychological law, of which the inner nature escapes us, just as the first cause of any physical law escapes us. What we can say is that this combination and elaboration of elements takes place, in all probability, within consciousness, for it is a fact that, by following up the chain of our thoughts and imaginings, we can often find a sufficient explanation of how certain new ideas or concepts occurred to us. This operation, moreover, is often attended by a feeling of effort, which is the most marked characteristic of conscious and voluntary elaboration. What, however, throws more light than anything else upon this so-called "unconscious" elaboration is the psychological fact (which must be always before us) that a presentation is never represented to consciousness in exactly the same form as on the first occasion.[1]

Other facts adduced in favour of the theory of unconscious mental life, such as the purposiveness of reflex movements and of instincts, and the actions performed during somnambulism, natural or artificial, are even better explained by means of the common laws of Psychology. Reflex movements have, it is true, a character of finality which is, at first sight, in contrast with the fact that they can occur without any participation in consciousness. Experimental Psychology has, however, proved that the law according to which habit facilitates action is applicable also to consciousness, experiments in reaction having shown that the reaction follows all the quicker upon the stimulus when the experiment has been often repeated, so that the act of choice becomes simple and impulsive.

[1] This elaboration or synthesis, which takes place beneath the threshold of consciousness, may be called "unconscious." For this reason Volkelt (*Das Unbewusste und der Pessimismus*, p. 44 foll.) places Kant amongst the supporters of the theory of unconsciousness.

These simple acts of volition, therefore, are not original, but derivative, and are to be found as much in the individual as in the species.

Instinct. The same fact furnishes an explanation of instinct, which has furnished so many arguments to the metaphysical supporters of the theory of "unconscious mind." We no longer believe that instincts are limited to animals. Man also is endowed with instincts, and indeed certain inferior individuals and races are almost exclusively governed by them. In man, however, they form generally a secondary element of his psychic life, which is more independent, and therefore susceptible of new developments. In animals, on the contrary, especially in the lower animals, instinct embraces almost the whole of their psychic life, and leaves but an inconsiderable part to the spontaneous action of the individual. If we inquire into the formation of instincts, much light is thrown upon the question by individual human Psychology. Instincts are merely a chain of impulsive acts which have become simplified and connected through continual repetition of the same actions following upon the same stimuli, so as to become finally fixed into the physiological organisation. This process has, of course, required a lengthy series of generations, each adding an imperceptible contribution to the hereditary aptitudes of the organism.[1] The formation of the instincts may even be said to proceed *pari passu* with that of the various species, so that a complicated instinct, which in a given species of animals (*e.g.* in bees or ants) may have attained great perfection, is to be found in a gradually simpler form in the lower species, not unlike the sketches of a picture, which becomes always more perfect as the attempts are repeated.[2] In this way instinct may be said to have completed its evolution in each species, restricting itself to a series of impulsive actions, to which each higher species has added some fresh element. The result is oftentimes so complicated that it seems *prima facie* impossible to explain it satisfactorily by means of the ordinary laws of psychological and biological evolution.

Other facts closely connected with instinct and with impulsive acts are the actions performed during a state of natural or of artificial sleep. In neither case does the individual will disappear;

---

[1] See Ribot, *L'hérédité psychologique* (5th edit. 1894, especially Part I., chap. i.); the works already quoted of Wundt and Schneider; and F. Masci's *Formazione naturale dell' istinto*.

[2] This process is very well explained by Wundt in his *Outlines of Psychology*, p. 276 foll.

in both it remains in the form of simple impulse, subservient to external suggestions, amongst which it is incapable of making a choice. Artificial sleep or hypnotism, about which much that is fantastic (*e.g.* the so-called "transmission of will") has been imagined, may be perfectly well explained in accordance with the ordinary laws of normal Psychology.[1]

We now pass to reflex movements, though between them and the instincts a clearly defined distinction is not always discernible.

Reflex movements. In the case of instincts, which are nothing but a series— at times a complicated series—of simple or impulsive acts, consciousness has not disappeared, but is limited to each single act as it comes to be performed, without any perception of its purpose. In the case of reflex movement, on the contrary, every form of consciousness has entirely disappeared. The study of reflex actions consequently belongs no longer to Psychology, but to physiology, though they play an important part in the formation of many simple or complex psychical acts. Every individual, indeed, is born with certain organic aptitudes (as of moving his limbs, of emitting cries, and so forth) which manifest themselves in the formation of presentations of space, in the development of articulate speech, etc. But the reflex act is in itself purely mechanical and does not belong to the series of mental processes. Its origin explains the character of purposiveness which it possesses in that it is the result of the gradual transformation of originally independent adaptive movements which have subsequently become simple and impulsive, and ultimately mechanical. Reflex movement is, consequently, not original, as some think, but derivative. The formation of these reflex acts is, indeed, one of the most important phenomena of psychic and organic life; we may even say that it is the real link between consciousness and the physical organism, as well as a phenomenon perfectly consonant with the laws of evolution and of functional differentiation. Thus the organic functions, which in primitive organisms probably absorbed the whole psychical activity, became gradually reflex and mechanical, and were entrusted to the practically spontaneous action of the vegetative organs, thus enabling consciousness to enlarge the sphere of its activity and develop increasingly complex forms. We have, therefore, a continual interchange of processes between the organic and the psychic life. On the one hand there is the fact that out of purely organic life sensations or mental

[1] This is what Wundt has done for the first time in his interesting study on *Hypnotism and Suggestion.*

elements are revived and form themselves into representations or other psychic compounds; and on the other hand there are the mental functions, which formerly were performed with full consciousness, but have become gradually simpler, and finally, entirely unconscious. The ultimate explanation of this fact, connected as it is with the problem of the origin of organic and of psychic life, escapes us, nor will it be known as long as the reason why consciousness is never found except in conjunction with an organic body remains a mystery. We must, however, observe that the two forms in which the passage between mental and physiological phenomena takes place present some very marked differences. The first of these differences concerns the production and reproduction of elementary mental processes and their combination into more complicated processes. The only positive *datum* of which we can be cognisant before the production of the mental phenomenon, and which remains after its disappearance, is that of the concomitant cerebral processes of that phenomenon, which continue even after it has passed beneath the threshold of consciousness. But we are by no means justified in concluding therefrom (as the materialists do more or less explicitly) that the mental processes are a transformation of the cerebral processes, nor that, when they disappear from consciousness, they resume the form of the latter, like steam which returns to the shape of water when it cools. This conception, which had some success in the eighteenth and during the first half of the nineteenth centuries, and even now has a few supporters, does not bear a critical investigation, cerebral phenomena being only a more complex form of the general phenomena of motion, between which and the mental processes no comparison is possible.

The process, on the other hand, whereby certain mental acts which used to be accomplished with full consciousness and volition become gradually impulsive and finally mechanical and divested of all psychical quality, has enabled the materialists, as well as the spiritualists, to say that either that process is a proof of the physiological origin of mental processes, or else that it is set in motion by an unconscious volition, of which we are not aware. We have, however, already seen that these theories, which have been upheld by Münsterberg, Ziehen, Maudsley, and Lewes (not to mention others who do not properly belong to the same school, such as Ribot and James) are untenable.[1] The contention that

[1] We do not count those psychologists who are really and truly physiologists (such as Richet and Setchenoff), or those who aim at reducing Psychology

consciousness is nothing but an epiphenomenon, or unnecessary adjunct, and that life might very well evolve itself without its help, is entirely without corroboration.

Another fact to which psychologists have justly attributed great importance is the persistence of certain general dispositions of feeling in the individual and the species, forming a kind of substratum (unconscious at times) to our mental life, and constituting the real cause of our actions. This substratum of feeling is an essential element peculiar to the psychical constitution of each individual and race, and forms the individual or national "ethos." It is, indeed, a fact that feelings are the innermost part of our being, and that they have a much longer duration than ideas, not only in the individual, but also in the species, notwithstanding that intellectual energy varies immensely in different individuals.[1] This is, however, another case in which the very vague and indefinite concept of "unconsciousness" is used to explain what cannot be explained, in that it refers to the primary sources of mental life. How explain the peculiar attitude of the individual before an external stimulus? or, again, individual inclinations? Moreover, it has to be remembered that unconscious feelings are incomprehensible: under whatever shape they may present themselves, whether of pleasure or pain, tension or relaxation, exhilaration or depression, they are facts of consciousness, and therefore directly perceived by us. The determining motive may be "unconscious," but in that case the term "unconsciousness" is improperly used; it would be better to speak of it as "undistinguished."

Character.

Having examined the more general and important questions connected with the concept of consciousness, we must next proceed to investigate the concrete forms which it assumes, and the characteristics which it presents during that stage of the mental life of an adult man, when the fundamental psychic activities have arrived at their complete development.

to physiology (such as Sergi and Despine). James's participation in these theories is confined chiefly to his theory of emotions, which we dealt with in the preceding chapter; Ribot, on the other hand, notwithstanding his many concessions to materialism, remains a true psychologist.

[1] This fact is demonstrated by Höffding, *Outlines of Pyschology*, p. 96 foll., p. 298 foll. See also Ribot, *L'hérédité psychologique*, p. 86 foll.; *La psychologie des sentiments*, p. 171 foll.; and Paulhan, *Les phénomènes affectifs et les lois de leur apparition.*

CHAPTER VIII

CONSCIOUSNESS (Continued)

WE have seen in the preceding chapters that, in order to produce a sensation, which, apart from certain organic conditions of the individual, is the simplest psychical phenomenon, an external stimulus of a certain degree of intensity is required. The point at which a stimulus attains the necessary intensity is called "the threshold of consciousness or of excitation," according as the consciousness or its external conditions are considered. If, then, the intensity of the stimulus goes on increasing, the sensation may also increase up to a certain point, beyond which no difference is perceived in the sensation; this point is called the "upper limit of sensibility." On the other hand, beneath the threshold of consciousness we do not perceive any further stimulus; it is as if it did not exist. Are we, therefore, to limit the concept of consciousness to the point at which a psychical phenomenon is produced? In that case we ought to make a distinction between the moment when the mental phenomenon "arises" and all the other moments during which it "is developed." We have seen, however, that consciousness is indistinguishable from mental processes or phenomena, a mental phenomenon being equivalent to a conscious phenomenon, precisely in the same manner that a physical phenomenon is equivalent to a mechanical or unconscious phenomenon. In this sense consciousness presents itself to us as a continuous stream of mental phenomena, each of which is closely connected with the preceding, succeeding, and simultaneous ones. These different moments of conscious life can only be separated by means of a process of abstraction, for they really form a continuous whole. Modern Psychology, as opposed to the old spiritualistic Psychology, with its metaphysical conception of consciousness as of an entity entirely separate from our real personality, has laid special stress upon this continuity, which Leibnitz was the first to point out.

Spencer had already defined mind and consciousness as a series of successive facts, and Bain gives an almost identical definition of it.[1] Consciousness without this character of continuity would not be consciousness. If our mental life of to-day were not connected with that of yesterday and previous days and years, we should not constitute a conscious personality. Each one of our mental states tends to connect itself with previous states. Thus, when we awake we immediately connect the mesh of our thoughts and feelings with that of the day before, our consciousness immediately resuming its unity and continuity. Even hysterical attacks, which used to be thought purely reflex movements, have been proved by modern research to be attended by a confused feeling or glimmering of consciousness.[2] Briefly, continuity is an essential characteristic of consciousness. Of this we have a proof in mental pathology, seeing that the most salient fact which distinguishes abnormal mental life is the disintegration of the personality, which shows itself at first in the weakening of the memory.

A contemporary psychologist noted for the expressiveness of his style aptly speaks of "the stream of consciousness." That which we especially notice in ourselves, he adds, is that without intermission "consciousness of some sort goes on." The mental states succeed one another in such a manner that "if we could say in English 'it thinks,' as we say 'it rains,' or 'it blows,' we should be stating the fact most simply and with the minimum of assumption. As we cannot, we must simply say that 'thought goes on.'"[3] Consciousness, therefore, presents, according to James, the following four characteristics: each state tends to become part of an individual consciousness; the states of each personal consciousness are continually changing; each personal consciousness is sensibly continuous, and, fourthly, takes an interest in some part of its object to the exclusion of other parts, and is continually making choice between them. James thus indicates in the clearest manner possible the true, distinctive characteristics of consciousness. Amongst the four, the second and fourth are the most important, and we shall therefore investigate them more closely.

The characteristics of the consciousness according to James.

[1] Spencer, *Principles of Psychology*; Bain, *The Senses and the Intellect* (Introduction).

[2] This has been ably demonstrated by Pierre Janet in his very interesting book, *L'automatisme psychologique* (2nd edit. 1894), p. 316 foll. See also James, *The Principles of Psychology*, Vol. I., p. 299, quoted above; and Ardigò, *L' unità della coscienza*.

[3] See W. James, *The Principles of Psychology*, Vol. I., p. 224 foll.; also his *Psychology*, p. 152.

Psychical processes belong, in the first instance, to a personal consciousness. Every individual has a special mental organisation, as he has a special physical constitution, the former corresponding to what is commonly called the "character." The character is, however, made up of inherited dispositions, which develop themselves and, within certain limits, transform themselves, owing to all the new mental facts which occur, and which mingle with and become connected with those already existent. This connection of mental facts is a peculiarity of our own person, and constitutes our "self." Events which have been lived through, feelings which have been undergone, things thought of and seen, actions performed by ourselves, belong to ourselves and not to others, so that each of us forms a small personal world, or microcosm. This is self-evident, and requires no demonstration.

The most important points to note, and those which require a more careful investigation, as they do not present themselves directly to our observation, are the last three mentioned by James, which, however, might be reduced to two, the third being but a corollary of the second. "Within each personal consciousness states are always changing."[1] This is one of the most remarkable characteristics of mental phenomena which more especially distinguishes them from matter. Psychic states are processes, not objects, and consequently never the same. The gravest obstacle to pure introspection is the fact that a state of consciousness never reproduces itself in the identical form in which it appeared the first time. The continual change and succession of different states of consciousness is one of the most notable facts of the mental world. One may object that physical phenomena also are not always immutable, and that when they happen to be purely processes they also are liable to continual change. There is, indeed, a certain analogy between physical and mental processes, neither of which reproduce themselves in exactly the same conditions, and cannot therefore be properly studied but with the help of the experimental method. There is, however, the following important difference between them: that physical processes can be reduced to relations of quantities, can be determined with exactitude beforehand, and rest upon a fixed substratum—matter—which is quantitatively invariable; whereas psychical processes are not to be measured quantitatively, nor do they rest upon an unchanging substratum. One might say that physical processes represent relative changes, whereas

[1] *The Principles of Psychology*, Vol. I., pp. 225 and 229.

the processes of consciousness represent absolute changes. So soon as we realise that there is no absolute criterion for calculating and measuring mental processes, as there is in the case of physical phenomena, we realise also that their value can only be relative. A fact of consciousness has therefore no value in itself, but acquires it only in virtue of the relations in which it stands to previous, simultaneous, or successive facts.

The law of relativity consequently is, as we shall see in the following chapter, the one fundamental law of consciousness. English psychologists have the merit of having first pointed out this state of continual change in mental phenomena. Hume, Spencer, and Bain have even tried to show that change is the first condition of consciousness, without which it would be unthinkable. This has been a much-debated question, and is of too metaphysical a character to allow of any positive conclusions. It is a fact that when a sensation or a feeling is repeated or has a long duration, our sensibility with regard to it becomes blunted, and similarly an act of willing, if often repeated, tends to become impulsive and even mechanical. Are these facts sufficient to induce us to conclude that consciousness cannot exist unless there be changes in the external conditions which produce changes in the internal?[1] This question takes us back to the discussion of the essential characteristics of consciousness. We have seen that the principal fact which distinguishes a mental process from a physical phenomenon is that the former expresses itself by means of a free impulse directed towards a certain purpose. The above theory of Spencer and Bain, on the contrary, seems to deny this spontaneity of consciousness, and to consider the latter entirely dependent upon external conditions; so that, failing a change in these conditions, consciousness, which consists principally in a change of states, cannot exist. This property of continual change must not, however, be taken too exclusively into consideration, for, by itself, it cannot suffice to represent the character of consciousness, and has to be supplemented by another, which James places last.

Consciousness, he says, " is interested in some parts of its objects to the exclusion of others, and welcomes or rejects; chooses from among them, in a word, all the while," [2] going on to

---

[1] See Spencer, *Principles of Psychology*, Vol. I., Part II., chap. i., and Part IV., chap. ii. See the confutation of Spencer's and Bain's theory in Fouillée, *L'évolutionisme des idées forces*, p. 30 foll., and Baldwin, *Handbook of Psychology*, Vol. I., p. 59 foll.

[2] *The Principles of Psychology*, Vol. I., p. 284 foll.; *Psychology*, p. 170 foll.

make some very interesting observations upon this property of consciousness, the nature of which he has apprehended with great precision. With numerous examples he shows how, from the simpler functions of perception up to the higher and more complex processes of scientific and artistic creation, we have a continual process of selection. Every individual acts in a certain way when brought face to face with external impressions, and this originality is all the more marked when consciousness is more complex and the mental capacity higher. This particular mode of reacting against external impressions is a consequence of the mental constitution of each individual, of his character, his education, his tastes, and of an aggregate of elements partly inherited, partly acquired, which it is often rather difficult to sever. " Let four men," says James, " make a tour in Europe. One will bring home only picturesque impressions—costumes and colours, parks and views and works of architecture, pictures and statues. To another all this will be non-existent, and distances and prices, population and drainage arrangements, door- and window-fastenings, and other useful statistics will take their place. A third will give a rich account of the theatres, restaurants, and public halls, and naught beside; whilst the fourth will perhaps have been so wrapped in his own subjective broodings as to tell little more than a few names of places through which he passed. Each has selected, out of the same mass of presented objects, those which suited his private interest, and has made his experience thereby."[1] In the case of logical thought we always find an active choice; indeed, the fact of placing a series of conceptions and judgments in logical sequence consists in choosing from amongst them those which are of use, and in rejecting the others. Scientific production, as well as artistic creation, consists in a methodically continuous choice. It is not enough for an artist to have his mind replete with pictorial, sculptural, poetical, or musical ideas and images, but he must know how to arrange and co-ordinate them so that the result may be a complete and magnificent whole: fragmentary and disconnected artistic work cannot be considered of a high order, even though it may present many particular merits. Similarly, ethical life is based upon choice, for, amongst the many impulses which may dictate our actions, we have continually to be making a choice in accordance with the principles of morality.

Consciousness, therefore, is a perpetual choice between the several impressions which offer themselves to us. The impression

[1] *The Principles of Psychology*, Vol. I., p. 286 foll.; *Psychology*, p. 172.

which strikes us most strongly, to which we turn our attention more especially, and which we perceive, therefore, with greater distinctness, forms in that given moment the central point of our consciousness. The other elements, which are perceived in different degrees of lesser intensity, form a species of frame, which James picturesquely describes as a "halo" or "fringe." When the impression which we perceive most distinctly is perceived with the effort of will called "attention," it is said to be "apperceived" (a term introduced into modern Psychology by Wundt, though Leibnitz was the first to use it); whereas other impressions, which appear to us less clearly and require a lesser degree of attention, are simply "perceived." Consciousness and will are therefore inseparable, seeing that the will forms the central point of every moment of the mental life, and is thus one of the most fundamental and general of the psychical activities.[1] Contemporary psychologists are therefore right in treating of consciousness and attention together, for they are two inseparable facts.

Attention has been much studied by modern Psychology, and the ideas current on the subject are very different from what they used to be. To begin with, it is no longer considered a purely intellectual phenomenon, but its complexity has been realised, as well as the hitherto neglected circumstance of the part played by the feelings, both in producing it and in keeping it alive. One of the most notable works on the subject is Ribot's *La psychologie de l'attention* (1st edit. 1889, 2nd edit. 1894). In this work, as in all his others, Ribot takes his inspiration from modern English Psychology, and especially from Maudsley. His fundamental idea, taken from Maudsley, is that attention is an abnormal state of consciousness, the natural condition of the latter being the continual change of its content—"polyideism," or multiplicity of ideas, as opposed to "monoideism," or singleness of idea, in other words, attention.[2] Attention, according to Ribot, is the mental expression of a physical state, which consists in the convergence of all the organs of the body towards an object: it is, in other words, "an exclusive or predominating intellectual state which goes together with a spontaneous or voluntary adaptation of the individual."[3] Ribot therefore distinguishes spontaneous from voluntary consciousness: the first being solely caused by the *affective* states; the second, which is an artificial product of education,

Attention or apperception.

---
[1] See above, chap. v.
[2] *La psychologie de l'attention* (Introduction), p. 6.
[3] *Op. cit.*, p. 6.

being attended by a special sense of effort caused by the muscular sensations produced by the state of attention.

This theory, however, does not explain how attention begins. Even if we admit, as we must, that voluntary attention is a transformation of spontaneous attention, we have still to explain how the latter arises. To say, with Ribot, that it is solely determined by affective states, gives no idea of its peculiar nature; for the same may be said of any other manifestation of the will. Moreover, it has also been noted[1] that the will itself may awaken a feeling of interest. But what, in our opinion, reveals even in a greater degree Ribot's misconception of the nature of attention is his assertion that, change being an essential characteristic of consciousness, the state of attention is consequently an abnormal condition. It must, on the contrary, be borne in mind that change is not the only essential condition of consciousness. It is now universally accepted that in each moment of our conscious life there is a central point round which our presentations, feelings, ideas, and impulses appear more intense and clearly defined, and a background in which the other elements of our consciousness show themselves less distinctly; there is, in other words, a part of the content of our consciousness upon which we centre most of our attention. The motives which determine this are various. In the elementary forms, as Ribot noted, they are constituted by affective states; in the more complex forms they are made up of chains of ideas; but whether simple or complex, a state of attention always exists in every moment of our mental life. Experimental Psychology has proved this fact to be of such common occurrence that it is now generally accepted without controversy.

Ribot's other theory, that voluntary attention is only to be distinguished from spontaneous attention by the accompanying feeling of effort caused by muscular contraction, is also inadmissible, and, though upheld recently by Münsterberg and others, has no serious foundation.[2] It is impossible to maintain that the principal feeling attendant upon the intellectual, logical, and direct work of the attention is purely muscular, unless we are prepared to deny the existence of any other form of feeling other than bodily sensation. What, on the contrary, distinguishes simple or impulsive attention (which is also voluntary) from complex and independent attention is that in the latter there is a choice of motive, whereas the former

---

[1] Ladd, *Psychology, Descriptive and Explanatory*, pp. 80—81.

[2] Besides Külpe's and Wundt's confutations, see also Fouillée's in *L'évolutionisme des idées forces*, p. 157 foll.

comes into existence immediately, from a single motive, apart from any choice. The complex form is, therefore, preceded and attended by peculiar feelings of hesitation or exhilaration.

This divergence of opinion concerning the nature of attention resolves itself ultimately into a disparity of views concerning the nature of mental life. The notion of the capital importance of attention as a foundation for the entire conscious life has not penetrated into the minds of all contemporary psychologists, but there is every probability that, being the result of positive and experimental research, and not the fruit of philosophical speculations, it will end by being generally accepted.[1] This divergence of view (as frequently happens in Psychology) arises from a divergence in the philosophical schools. Consciousness has been conceived in two different ways by the two dominating schools of philosophy—English and German. The former, more empirical, has attributed special importance to the external conditions of consciousness—that is, to the continual change of presentations and of states of consciousness in general. The German school, on the contrary, more inclined by nature towards profound speculations, has laid emphasis on the subjective side, the inner and spontaneous force of consciousness, which comprises and concentrates in itself all that lies dispersed in the external world, and thus constitutes the primary fact whence the originality of personal character springs.[2] Although both these doctrines are right up to a certain point, it is easy to see to what extreme consequences their exaggeration would lead. The first, or empirical point of view, leads to materialism; the second, to spiritualism—both metaphysical theories. For the materialists, external succession became the principal fact of mental life; for the spiritualists (who followed the purely introspective method), consciousness cast off all external conditions and became a metaphysical entity. Consciousness is, therefore, as Höffding says, a unity and a multiplicity. It is a unity in so far as we can embrace in a single mental act objects which in space are far removed one

Various modes of considering the unity and multiplicity of the consciousness.

---

[1] In most modern treatises of Psychology the study of consciousness is closely connected with that of attention. See Sully's *The Human Mind*, Vol. I., p. 74, p. 163 foll., and Ladd's *Psychology, Descriptive and Explanatory*, chap. v., p. 70 foll., where it is pointed out that "primary attention is a necessary accompaniment of every truly psychic fact." Almost all contemporary psychologists further recognise that attention is a manifestation of the will. See J. C. Kreibig's recent work *Die Aufmerksamkeit als Willenserscheinung* (Vienna, 1897).

[2] See Höffding's *Outlines of Psychology*, p. 99, where he develops this twofold conception of consciousness.

from the other, and this quality manifests itself principally in the "energy" with which the contents of consciousness, in the beginning disconnected and dispersed, become gradually comprised in a united and connected whole. In memory, in the recognition of a presentation which has been once before in our consciousness, in the process of comparison, says Höffding, the same unifying principle manifests itself, which may be called the *active* character of consciousness, and finds its highest expression in the will. A corresponding passive side of consciousness is found in the variety and multiplicity of facts which form the content of consciousness itself.[1] This variety and multiplicity is due, as we have seen, to the presentative content of the consciousness—that is, to the sum-total of facts which, considered from another point of view, are termed objects, and were generally known to the old psychologists as "external" facts. The other elements which make up the content of consciousness—namely, feelings and impulses—are, on the contrary, subjective, and give to consciousness its most characteristic quality of being, as Kant said, a synthetic activity. Indeed, if we are able to combine in one single moment widely divergent presentations, to compare them and unite them into concepts, and so forth, it is owing to this subjective activity of consciousness, which finds its most characteristic expression in the will. The conclusion at which Höffding arrives is that will is the most fundamental element of the mind.[2]

The relativity of mental processes. The spiritualistic doctrines which consider consciousness as a purely metaphysical entity, untrammelled by any dependence upon the external world, are nowadays almost entirely abandoned. The idea that the whole content of our consciousness is necessarily determined by its relations with the physical surroundings of the individual has come to be so generally admitted that even the most obdurate idealists are obliged to accept it. The idealism of the Hegelians, who consider the external world as a mere means for the realisation of the aims of spirit, must give way, in all branches of the moral sciences, to the principle (which may be said to be definitely established) that spirit and the physical world are so intimately connected that the

---

[1] Höffding, *op cit.*

[2] "The unity and intimacy which distinguish consciousness," says Höffding, "however varied and changeable its contents may be, are closely connected with the capacity of feeling *pleasure* and *pain*. . . . The feelings of pleasure and of pain imply a certain concentration. The 'active' side of consciousness is closely connected with its character of 'oneness' (consciousness understood as will)." Cf. *op cit.*, p. 49.

development of the former is subordinate to the conditions of the latter.[1] On the other hand, the materialistic theories, according to which consciousness is nothing but illusion, the only reality being cerebral phenomena, are entirely rejected (in this crude shape, at least) by psychologists and philosophers alike.[2] We have seen, indeed, that materialism has not yet declared itself vanquished, and that it ever and anon reappears, under the auspices of experimental Psychology; but the concessions which it is obliged to make, and the contradictions into which it falls, deprive it of any philosophic value as a scientific movement. Nevertheless, there are certain doctrines concerning the nature of consciousness which have had their origin in positivist philosophy, especially in England, and which are still of some importance.

We refer to those theories which have two closely connected aims in views: namely, that of assigning a preponderant importance amongst all psychical phenomena to the variability of the states of consciousness; and the even more remarkable one of considering consciousness as a mass of mental elements, mostly presentations, which, owing to their exact correspondence with external physical and physiological impressions, are capable of reproducing within consciousness an exact image of the external world. Positivist philosophers are enthusiastic supporters of this theory. " The first and fundamental property of mind," says Bain, " is the consciousness of difference or discrimination. To be distinctively affected by two or more successive impressions is the most general fact of consciousness. We are never conscious at all without experiencing transition or change."[3] And Spencer also is of opinion that consciousness is but a succession of changes.[4] Consciousness is thus reduced to a sense of difference. It is certain that if the states of consciousness did not change, we could not have the feeling of the continuity of the mental life, for if conscious-

---

[1] Some remains of this idealism may be found still amongst the neo-scholastics, though they also have partially adapted themselves to the new scientific exigencies.

[2] Fouillée is right when he says: " Parmi les philosophes de quelque valeur, où sont les matérialistes? C'est une espèce disparue. Les derniers survivants ne se rencontrent plus que chez quelques savants de profession peu au courant du progrès philosophique" (*Le mouvement idéaliste et la réaction contre la science positive*, Introduction, p. xlvi.).

[3] Bain, *Senses and Intellect*, 3rd edit., p. 321.

[4] *Principles of Psychology*, Vol. I., Part IV., chap. i., p. 395 foll. Another supporter of this theory is George W. Hagen. These doctrines are all discussed by Baldwin, *Handbook of Psychology*, Vol. I., p. 59 foll.

ness never varied its content, it would appear as a single state, without a beginning or a course. Considering, moreover, as Spencer has been the first to note, that a state of consciousness is unthinkable unless it be separated from preceding and successive states,[1] it follows that if there existed no difference between its various states, consciousness itself would be non-existent. It must be borne in mind, however, that this is an essentially metaphysical question. In order to imagine mental processes totally devoid of variety, consciousness has to be thought of as so entirely different from what it really is that such an investigation is entirely vain and profitless.

Lotze[2] has objected that this theory of "relativity" mistakes consciousness for its contents—namely, what we are conscious of. This distinction, as we have seen, is inadmissible, consciousness and its contents being the same thing. A more serious objection is founded upon the fact that the supporters of this theory, starting from the intellectualistic principle that consciousness reproduces external impressions, think to find the laws of consciousness in these impressions and their changes. But we have seen in the case of Weber's law that the changes of consciousness depend only partly upon external agents, the relation between various states of consciousness being a predominantly subjective fact.[3] If, therefore, the relativity of mental states is a mainly subjective fact, this means that it refers not to external impressions, but to an inner cause, which is the spontaneity, the internal energy, of volition. This point is neglected by the upholders of relativity and by positivists alike, but it is nevertheless the central point around which all psychical facts revolve. This neglect was the source of an intellectualistic conception of the mental life, in which

[1] *Principles of Psychology*, Vol. I., Part II., chap. ii., p. 164.

[2] See Lotze's *Logik*, Vol. II., p. 256 foll. Baldwin makes use of the same argument (*op. cit.*, p. 60).

[3] "A real difference," says Baldwin, "is not the same as a perceived difference" (*op. cit.*, Vol. I., p. 60). The word "real" is here used in the sense of "physical"; improperly, it would seem, for reality is not confined to the physical world, but embraces also the whole moral world. The distinction between "real" and "perceived" difference is also partly recognised by Spencer (*Principles of Psychology*, Vol. I., Part II., chap. ii., p. 154 foll.). Baldwin's observation that "the feeling of difference is the 'content' of consciousness, not consciousness itself" (*op. cit.*, pp. 60—61) is inadmissible. What difference is there between consciousness and its content? Consciousness is the sum-total of all the mental states of the individual, and as such presents a succession of changes. On this point the positivist theory is unassailable; it is, however, one-sided in almost wholly neglecting the spontaneous energy of consciousness.

its subjective elements had hardly any place, whereas it ought to be remembered that though consciousness may be a succession of changes, as Bain and Spencer define it, it is itself also an energy which gives rise to those very changes.

Another variety of this theory which is supported by philosophers rather than by psychologists reduces consciousness to a feeling of relation between subject and object.[1] It is easy to see that a confusion is here made between "simple" consciousness and the consciousness of "self," and no confutation is, consequently, necessary.

Closely connected with the theory of the absolute relativity of mental processes is the doctrine which has been called "psychical atomism." A contemporary psychologist we have often quoted examines it exhaustively and enters into a minute confutation of it.[2] Briefly, we can say with him, that this theory conceives our mental states as "compounds."[3] The importance of this doctrine, however, is so great that we must treat of it in some detail. It is as well to note, in the first place, that it comes as a natural consequence of the theory of evolution, according to which all that exists in the universe is nothing but the product of various combinations of the same primitive elements. Every thing is, therefore, reduced to combinations of atoms. But can consciousness be explained in this way? In spite of every effort to do so, it will never be possible to explain how a fact of consciousness can be derived from matter and movement.[4] Spencer himself and other positivists are obliged to admit as much.[5] But Spencer falls into contradiction with himself, as we

Psychical atomism.

---

[1] Mansel is one of the philosophers who uphold this theory (*Metaphysics*, pp. 33—66 and p. 183), which has been confuted by Spencer and Rénouvier.

[2] See James's *Principles of Psychology*, Vol. I., chap. vi., p. 145 foll. James calls this a "mind-stuff theory," and chap. vi., which deals with it, is very interesting reading.

[3] James, *op. cit.*, Vol. I., p. 145.

[4] James says, with reason (*op. cit.*, Vol. I., p. 146): "A motion become a feeling! No phrase that our lips can frame is so devoid of apprehensible meaning."

[5] *Principles of Psychology*, Vol. I., § 62, p. 158: "Can the oscillations of a molecule be represented, side by side, with a nervous shock, and the two be recognised as one? No effort enables us to assimilate them. That a unit of feeling has nothing in common with a unit of motion becomes more than ever manifest when we bring the two into juxtaposition." James rightly notes that by "nervous shock" Spencer meant to say "mental shock." It happens very frequently that positivists fall into the mistake of taking cerebral phenomena for mental processes. James quotes also a famous passage from Tyndall's *Fragments of Science*, p. 420: "The passage from the physics of the brain to the

have seen, when he proceeds to derive consciousness from reflex movement.[1] In fact, the problem of consciousness is the rock on which all the systems of philosophers who endeavour to explain everything by means of the evolution of matter have foundered. In order to get out of the difficulty, it was thought possible, as we have had occasion to see, to assimilate consciousness and matter, and it was maintained that every material atom is joined to a physical atom. Thus human and animal consciousness would be the result of a combination of all these mental atoms, which are a perfect reproduction of the physical world. Positivist philosophers, Spencer and Taine especially, thought they had the proof of this, and maintained that sensations, emotions, and all other mental states which, at first sight, appear simple, will be seen upon attentive examination to be composed of various elements.[2] A sensation, however, is, as we have seen, a simple process of consciousness with a certain "qualitative" character, and endowed with a certain degree of "intensity"; this and nothing more. It is a simple fact, and is of value in so far as it exists in consciousness at a given moment. It is thus impossible to dissect a sensation into its constituents, for if a stimulus which at first produced in us a single sensation, subsequently, owing to an increased effort of attention, produces several, these cannot be considered by any means "elements" of the former, but new sensations endowed with

corresponding facts of consciousness is unthinkable. Granted that a definite thought and a definite molecular action in the brain occur simultaneously, we do not possess the intellectual organ, nor apparently any rudiment of the organ, which would enable us to pass, by a process of reasoning, from one to the other."

[1] The contradiction in Spencer is concealed by an ambiguity which James has very ably exposed. Spencer speaks of "nascent" consciousness, upon which James observes (*op. cit.*, Vol. I., Part II., chap. ii.): " It is true that the word signifies not yet 'quite' born, and so seems to form a sort of bridge between existence and nonentity. But that is a verbal quibble. The fact is that discontinuity comes in if a new nature comes in at all. The quantity of the latter is quite immaterial." He adds : " The girl in *Midshipman Easy* could not excuse the illegitimacy of her child by saying, 'It was a very little one.' And consciousness, however little, is an illegitimate birth in any philosophy that starts without it, and yet professes to explain all facts by continuous evolution."

[2] Spencer, *Principles of Psychology*, Vol. I., Part II., chap. i., p. 148 foll. ; Taine, *De l'intelligence*, Book III. Psychical atomism is also defended by Haeckel, Barratt, Clifford, Morton Prince (*The Nature of Mind and Human Automatism*, 1885), Riehl (*Der philosophische Kriticismus*, Vol. II., Part II., chap. ii., § 2). The theory has been keenly opposed by Lotze (see *Microcosmus*, Book II., chap. i., § 5; *Metaphysik*, §§ 242, 260); also by Bonatelli (*Il meccanismo interiore e la coscienza*).

an autonomous existence. The threshold of the consciousness, indeed, may vary—that is, rise and fall in accordance with the general state of our consciousness—and, as a consequence, our sensibility may increase or diminish. But psychological analysis has nothing whatever in common with physical analysis; for the latter deals with facts dispersed in space, whereas the former deals always with unities.[1] The first property of consciousness is that of always presenting single states. A notable part of consciousness, indeed, is made up of presentations, which are multiple; but the most characteristic aspect of consciousness consists in its subjective elements of feeling and will, and these are eminently "*unities.*"

All mental phenomena being concentrated in the spontaneous and volitional activity of consciousness, the principal characteristic of consciousness is, therefore, that of being "synthetical." That which in the physical world, whether in the shape of external and purely physical phenomena, or in that of physiological, nervous, and cerebral phenomena, is extended and multiple, appears to consciousness as a unit. The spiritualistic philosopher Rosmini has a well-known passage referring to the distinction between external physical phenomena and consciousness, which contains an able criticism of the intellectualistic theories. "And, indeed, if it is the property of an extended body that every part assignable in it is outside of every other and independent of every other—and we never succeed in assigning to a body any part to which others and yet others cannot be assigned—it necessarily follows that, if the parts are not united and held together by a simple principle, it becomes an absurdity, seeing that that is absurd which cannot be thought, and in a body the first parts are not found existing in themselves, since in every assignable part there is still a smaller part outside of all the others, and there remains no extended part that is wholly in the whole of itself. These remain, therefore, only simple points existing in themselves. But such points are not a body, nor are they parts of an extended body. Consequently they cannot form a continuity, however much they may be multiplied. Even an infinite sum of beings, each having an extension equal to zero, can give no result but an extension = 0, hence the extended either does not

Rosmini's critique of the intellectualistic theories.

---

[1] See Fechner (*Elemente der Psychophysik*, Vol. II., p. 526): "Das psychisch Einheitliche und Einfache knüpft sich an ein physisch Mannichfaltiges, das physisch Mannichfaltige zieht sich psychisch ins Einheitliche, Einfache oder doch Einfachere zusammen." See also Höffding, *Outlines of Psychology*, p. 47.

exist, or, if it does, it does so only in a simple principle which holds it together."[1]

It must be borne in mind, however, that Rosmini's demonstration is entirely based upon the inadmissible principle of the distinction between the inner and outer worlds, the former of which embraces the phenomena which take place in time, the latter those which occur in space. It holds good, nevertheless, when it attacks intellectualism with regard to the principle of absolute parallelism between external phenomena and facts of consciousness. A presentation, a complex perceptive phenomenon, is not merely the "sum-total" of its constituents, but it is the result of a particular synthesis, and therefore it is a new and consequently single fact. If this holds good for the perceptive facts of consciousness, it is all the more applicable in the case of feelings and volition. How can we imagine an emotion composed of several elementary emotions? An emotion is a single fact, a "unit" into which the whole consciousness is concentrated, and which expresses the whole individual personality. The same may be said of an act of volition. We may either be moved by an emotion or by several in succession; but we cannot be under the influence of an emotion, which is in its turn made up of several. If several emotions combine to form a single one, they disappear and give place to the latter, which, therefore, is a new fact distinct from its predecessors.

To find a solution of all these difficulties, the "atomists" have had recourse to the convenient hypothesis of unconscious mental elaboration. But this theory, as we have seen, has no value for psychological interpretation; for a psychical fact exists only in so far as it is conscious. Physical and physiological phenomena have nothing in common with a process of consciousness, and are in no way sufficient to explain it. The theory of psychic atomism, in spite of contrary opinions, must therefore be judged lacking in scientific value. It not only does not explain scientifically the processes of consciousness; but it is based upon an entirely erroneous conception of them.[2]

[1] *Psychology*, by Antonio Rosmini Serbati (London, 1884—1888), Vol. I., Book IV., p. 238. "This," he adds, "was the irrefragable argument of the Platonists of Alexandria." And his opinion is that those who feel its force will do well to apply themselves to philosophy; but those who do not had better abandon its study.

[2] Marillier, in a lengthy review of James's *Psychology* (*Revue Philosophique*, November and December, 1892, January and February, 1893), does not agree with his criticism of the associationist psychologists, and maintains that

To recapitulate what we have said concerning the properties of consciousness, the latter consists in a series of processes, which are not merely reproductions of external phenomena, but apperceptive and therefore volitional acts. It thus has its root in the fundamental and most characteristic process of mental life—viz. the will. The will manifests itself in the course of mental life not only in each of the apperceptive acts of which consciousness in general consists, but in the general synthetic connection of them which form individual consciousness.

Consciousness is above all individual; by historical, social, religious consciousness, and so forth, we therefore understand that aggregate of feelings, ideas, and impulses by which every individual living in social intercourse feels himself drawn towards his fellow-men in the present and in the past. These higher forms of consciousness are a product of social life and of the stimuli by which individuals act and react upon one another.[1] Simultaneously, however, with this collective consciousness, the consciousness of self evolves itself in the individual, taking various more or less complex forms, according to the greater or lesser complexity of conditions in which the individual finds himself.[2] The consciousness of self is based upon the sensations of our own body, which form the real substratum of our Ego. Spiritualistic Psychology, in affirming the absolute simplicity of consciousness, could not admit this multiple origin. Modern Psychology, on the other hand, has proved the complexity of the feeling of personality, which consists in a quantity of elements not always perfectly harmonised. Pathological Psychology has, on its part, contributed largely towards establishing this fact, by exhibiting the numerous cases of disintegration of the personality, and showing how they always have their root in a derangement of the general sense—that is, of tactile, muscular, and organic sensations. Following upon these derangements, we find aberrations of the reasoning power, of the higher emotions, and of the will. From this it follows that, although consciousness considered in itself during a single moment may appear to be simple, when considered, on the contrary, from the

---

"psychical atomism" is the only scientific explanation of the processes of consciousness.

[1] On the individual character of consciousness, see Ladd, *Psychology: Descriptive and Explanatory*, p. 5. See also Baldwin's fine study on *Sociological and Ethical Interpretations in Mental Development*.

[2] See James's analysis of these forms of consciousness in *The Principles of Psychology*, Vol. I., chap. x., p. 291 foll.

side of succession, it reveals itself as a more or less complete aggregate of elements, a complicated and delicately balanced structure.[1]

The problem we have now to investigate is whether there exists any constant law governing this consecutive series of acts, and what general principles may be applied to it.

[1] See Ribot's interesting work *Les maladies de la personnalité*, and Binet's *Les alterations de la personnalité* (1893).

CHAPTER IX

THE LAWS OF PSYCHOLOGY

WE have reserved this subject for the last, as a fitting conclusion to the subjects we have already discussed.

It is now universally recognised that as long as a group or series of facts have not been subjected to fixed and constant rules, they cannot be said to constitute an object of science. That which is fortuitous or casual does not enter into the domain of science: it may enter into other provinces of human activity, such as religion or art; but science deals only with that which can be reduced to general and constant principles.

A constant rule to which a given order of facts is subservient is called a "law." The idea of law has its origin in the rules voluntarily laid down by men—that is, in so-called political laws, which are the most evident and easily apprehended of any. To grasp the meaning of natural law a greater effort of mind is required, it being necessary to abstract the permanent part of phenomena from their varying concomitants. It is to be noted, however, that the inclination to conceive the mass of cosmological phenomena as occurring with definite regularity is very ancient. One of the first endeavours of human beings, as the stimulus of material wants made itself less urgently felt, was to find an explanation of the phenomena which were taking place around them and upon which their very existence in a great measure depended, and also to comprehend the nature of the relations existing between those phenomena and their own lives. These early suggestions of a natural philosophy presented themselves in a mythological form, and were the starting-point of ethical religions on the one hand, and of science and philosophy on the other. Mythology is probably the first manifestation of philosophical activity in man, and may be said to have passed through two distinct phases. The first comprises the period in which man conceives natural phenomena

Meaning of the term "law."

Two phases of philosophical activity.

as produced by animated beings not in human form but as fantastic beasts or monsters, with which he identifies the power of cosmic forces; this may be called the phase of "primitive naturalism." The second phase is more human. The monsters gradually assume a less terrible form, and at last become neither more nor less than men, though with the qualities and the defects of human beings accentuated to an exaggerated degree.[1] This form of mythology, which affords such a wealth of material for artistic treatment, is the one which we find amongst the Greeks, and has almost entirely lost its cosmological character.

Primitive naturalism.

During this period in which the myths have almost entirely lost their naturalistic form, attempts are made, quite irrespective of religion, to find a scientific explanation of the universe, and we have the first philosophic systems. It is a well-known fact that Greek philosophy down to Socrates is essentially cosmological, concerning itself solely with the search for a single physical principle, as the origin of all natural phenomena. In most of these primitive philosophies, however, law is conceived of on the analogy of human law, the world being imagined as animated by a will similar to that of man.[2]

The philosophic system of Democritus has therefore an extraordinary importance in the history of human thought, that philosopher being the first to conceive the connection of physical phenomena as determined by a fatal necessity, and even to extend this determinism to human phenomena.[3] The concept of human and political law and that of natural law, however, continued for a long time to be confounded, philosophy during the Middle Ages being almost exclusively dominated by the notion of a divine providence governing physical as well as human events.

Democritus.

---

[1] This process of evolution in religion is ably depicted by Wundt in his *Ethics* (Part I., chap. ii., p. 39 foll.).

[2] On the evolution of the concept of law, see F. de Sarlo, *Saggi filosofici*, Vols. I. and II. See also Wundt, " Ueber den Begriff des Gesetzes " (*Phil. Stud.*, Vol. III., p. 191 foll.

[3] See Lange, *History of Materialism.* The naturalistic systems, which arose much later, in the sixteenth century, are closely connected with that of Democritus. The first materialist philosopher of the Renaissance of any importance is Gassendi, who is closely connected with Epicurus. In England the first is Boyle. See Lange, *op. cit.* Materialism had subsequently numerous followers in France.

A clear conception of the inevitableness of natural facts is not to be found before the sixteenth and seventeenth centuries, which witnessed those great physical and mathematical discoveries that have since opened up new horizons to human thought. Then only do we come across a clear conception of the meaning of physical law, Descartes being the first to make a proper distinction between the "extended" and the "mental" world. The first is subject to a physical and immutable law; the other is, on the contrary, much more independent. The freedom of the processes of consciousness, as compared to the inevitableness of natural phenomena, was accentuated even more by the spiritualistic philosophers, followers of Descartes, in whose opinion the former found their sole limitation in divine will.

Descartes.

The problem of human freedom, which had already occupied the ancients, thus began again to be discussed, and the question was asked whether human facts, individual and collective, are not subject to some governing law. The importance of this problem, related as it is to morals and religion, is obvious. The continual aspiration of philosophy was to sever itself from religion and to establish for itself independent ethical principles; but a long time was still to elapse before this ideal could be realised. There were only two ways out of the difficulty: either to discover moral laws possessing the same character of absolute inevitableness as physical laws; or to admit a certain amount of individual liberty, only limited by the will of other individuals. Spinoza's system, in which physical and psychical phenomena constitute two parallel series which merge themselves in God, established a universal determinism of all natural and moral facts. The conception thus introduced was placed upon a basis more consonant with psychological data by Leibnitz, whose philosophy contains many germs of truth which have been developed in recent times. As opposed to Spinoza, Leibnitz is of opinion that there exists no single substance, but an indefinite number of substances, of individual beings, each of which possesses an activity and a life of its own, all being held together by a pre-established harmony.[1] Substance, however, resolves itself into "force," which is the only real existence. Force or energy is, however, inseparable from law, seeing that it is the cause of the changes that take place in any

Spinoza.

Leibnitz.

[1] On the relations between the philosophies of Leibnitz and Spinoza, see L. Stein, *Leibnitz and Spinoza* (Berlin, 1890).

given state.[1] Hence the important principle which we owe to Leibnitz, and which he called the principle of "sufficient reason," whereby every fact is determined by another which precedes it. Thus between the various physical and psychical states there is a continuity, which does not, however, detract from the individuality of the several substances, which in their turn, though independent, act and react upon each other. The principles of reason and of the continuity of facts give, therefore, the determining tone to the philosophy of Leibnitz. The fundamental principle of natural phenomena is the law of the conservation of energy; that of moral phenomena is the conservation and continuity of psychic activity. All this was of the greatest importance, and gave a wholly new direction to the study of moral facts.

Whilst German philosophy is, so to speak, in a great measure founded upon internal intuition and upon the metaphysical concept of substance, English philosophy is, on the contrary, entirely based upon experience. From Bacon, Hobbes, and Locke, down to contemporary philosophers, the latter has such a markedly empirical character that it cannot be mistaken for any other philosophic school, even when, as happens with Spencer, it rises to broad and elevated metaphysical views. Associationist Psychology is, as we know, a product of the English school of philosophy.

The psychological problem which, in modern philosophy, is becoming the centre of all philosophical conceptions, has been discussed by English philosophers from a much more empirical point of view than that of the Germans; and John Locke may not only be called one of the greatest philosophers, but also one of the founders of Psychology, which he placed upon the road of exact investigation. Locke, however, turned his attention more especially to the epistemological question, putting an end for ever to the concept of "innate ideas" which had enjoyed such favour in the metaphysical Cartesian systems. The vicissitudes of epistemological doctrines in English philosophy are well known. From purely empirical beginnings with Locke, they arrived at an absolute idealism with Berkeley, who admitted of no other form of existence in the external world but that which consists in sensations and presentations; a principle which was concisely and clearly expressed by him in the formula that the "esse" of external objects is their "percipi."[2]

[1] See Höffding, *History of Modern Philosophy*, Vol. I., p. 346. Co. Latta's *Leibnitz*, p. 89 foll.
[2] Höffding, *op. cit.*, Vol. I., p. 422.

In David Hume the problem of cognition made another important step, for Hume, starting from the same empirical principles as Bacon and Locke, arrived at the conclusion that all our knowledge is founded upon the acquaintance we have with the causal relations between phenomena. We cannot, however, according to Hume, know the inmost nature of this causal relation, we cannot even know whether it really exists; for we only know different forms of phenomena, without being able to affirm that one is caused by the other. This is an absolutely empirical deduction. What is, however, of greater importance in Hume is that whilst rejecting the inner necessity of phenomenal causality, he attempted to explain the belief we have in this causality by means of a succession or chain of ideas or presentations—in other words, by means of a purely psychological fact. Every disposition of the mind, when highly excited, has, according to Hume, a tendency to last and to have an influence upon succeeding presentations. Moreover (and this is very important), our presentations have a tendency to recall one another; every presentation has an associative power, a "gentle force" leading from one to the other. The conditions under which associations take place are, in Hume's opinion, similarity, co-existence in time and space and causality. There exists in the internal world as potent a force of attraction as that of physical attraction in the external world. But the ultimate cause of this also escapes us, for it is probably the outcome of properties of human nature of which we are ignorant; the link which connects our presentations is as inexplicable as that which connects external objects, and it is only through experience that we may understand it. This link is so inexplicable for Hume that he considers that it even contradicts the other principle, according to which our mind consists only of isolated sensations and presentations, a contradiction which he finds it impossible to explain.[1]

In Hume, however, there is a real attempt at finding a psychological law which should explain the association of presentations. These ideas were developed in his *Treatise on Human Nature* (1739—1740) and in his *Inquiry concerning Human Understanding* (1749). The year in which this last work was published saw the publication of David Hartley's *Observations on Man, his Frame, his Duty, and his Expectations*, which contained ideas on psychical association very similar to Hume's. Hume was, however, more

[1] Höffding, *op. cit.*, Vol. I., p. 430.

especially a philosopher and Hartley a psychologist, so that the latter's researches are more empirical, and consequently also more exact. Hartley's efforts aimed at proving that complicated psychical phenomena, such as thought and feeling in their most ideal and abstract forms, and even the force of will which manifests itself in presentations, feelings, and actions, are all derived from associations of psychical elements—that is, of sensations and simple presentations.[1] Association is thus the highest psychological law, and reduces itself to the two forms of association between synchronous presentations and of association between immediately successive presentations. Those two forms take the place of the laws which by Hume and others have been called "laws of contiguity and similarity." Moreover, the fundamental law of association manifests itself according to three constant principles, which might be called secondary or derivative laws. The first is that the psychic life evolves itself gradually from simpler to more complex forms, producing new forms which, it is important to note, present characters different from their constituents; the second is that psychical actions, which are performed at first with full consciousness, become by degrees and by dint of continual practice automatic activities (as Hartley calls them); and the third is that the vividness and force with which certain ideas present themselves can subsequently be transferred to other presentations connected with the former through association. The importance of this theory, which was afterwards expounded and defended by Priestley, is clear: it may be said that the whole problem of psychological laws revolves round it, and it can but increase in importance in modern philosophical systems.

At the close of the eighteenth century, therefore, the following two principal schools held the field in philosophy and Psychology: the German school, following Leibnitz's system, variously modified by his successors, according to which consciousness is a unity, the laws of which reside in its inner nature, its manifestations having their source in unconsciousness; and the English school of Hume, Hartley, and Priestley, going by the name of the "associationist" school, according to which the whole mental life is an aggregate of elementary psychic facts, which have gradually developed and been combined through association into broader and more complicated psychical compounds, with a progression from the simple to the complex and from the concrete to the abstract. The first

The two dominant schools at the close of the eighteenth century.

[1] Höffding, *op. cit.*, Vol. I., p. 447.

of these systems gave a greater importance to the subjective and inner element which unifies all mental facts; the second, on the contrary, gave more importance to the several elements of consciousness—that is, to presentations.

The defect of both systems, and more especially of the latter, was that of being founded upon a purely intellectualistic conception of consciousness, which attributed too much importance to presentation, and not enough to the subjective elements of feeling and volition.

Immanuel Kant, whose name is famous in the history of thought, especially in connection with epistemology, occupies a foremost place also in the history of Psychology, owing to his profound conception of psychological synthesis, by which he reconciled the ideas of Leibnitz with those of the English school. Kant was of opinion that external elements, or sensations, are as necessary to the psychical life as the inner subjective element which combines them; the former constitute the matter of consciousness, the latter the form.[1] This conception lies at the foundation of all subsequent psychological progress, although Kant and his followers differed considerably in their way of developing it. Kant, moreover, was also an intellectualistic in his Psychology, although his *Critique of Pure Reason* has opened up new horizons by pointing out the importance of the inner and more subjective element of consciousness. These views, however, were not developed by him into a methodical psychological system.

Kant.

Kant's successors of the idealistic school, Fichte, Schelling, and especially Hegel, followed the intellectualistic doctrine to its extreme limits, to such an extent that, according to Hegel, the evolution of things was nothing but a necessary consequence of the logical development of thought. These philosophers, however, did not concern themselves specially with Psychology, considering it rather as an offshoot of their metaphysical speculations. The first who attempted to make of Psychology an exact science on intellectualistic lines was Frederick Herbart, in whom the intellectualistic bias reached its culminating point.

Kant's successors.

F. Herbart.

This school found an adversary in Schopenhauer, who, as often happens in the reaction against current ideas, attributed an exaggerated influence to the will in mental life. His ideas, however, were to bear fruit, and, reduced within reasonable limits,

---

[1] See Edward Caird, *Critical Philosophy of Kant*, Vol. I., p. 309 foll., and p. 373 foll. and C. Cantoni: *Emanuele Kant*, Vol. I., p. 155 and p. 208 foll.

have been found by modern Psychology to harmonise with the results of experience. It is a common illusion to believe that our actions follow as consequences of our ideas, whereas, on the contrary, they cannot be guided by any law, but solely by the will, which resides in our inmost nature and eludes all determination. The series of moral facts, therefore, cannot be regulated by precise laws, as are the series of natural phenomena. Schopenhauer consequently did not admit that history could be called a science, for we cannot foresee historical events with that certainty and precision which are the characteristics of scientific knowledge. Art alone can penetrate into the inmost recesses of the universal will.[1]

Between these two extremes of Hegel's and Herbart's intellectualism and Schopenhauer's volitionalism what path was Psychology to follow? Was it to endeavour to find psychological laws of the same value as physical laws, or was it to give up the search, and to treat moral facts as free from all law and solely dependent upon chance, on the ground that we must reckon as casual all those facts of which we do not understand the origin, the evolution, or the ending? Was all that constitutes the domain of moral and psychical facts—for example, historical events, social, religious, and political institutions, the works of literature and of art—to be excluded from the field of scientific study and from the influence of ruling principles?

This is a problem of capital importance, upon which all the efforts of Psychology and the moral sciences are at present concentrated. The first question which a naturalist, and, indeed, anyone, is impelled to ask, when confronted with the different historical, psychological, social, and philological branches of learning, is this: What *positive* results have all these studies attained? What laws have they established? What conclusions have the researches on the psychical nature of man rendered possible? And as these questions are not always easily answered with precision, naturalists and all those who place the study of physical and biological science before all others look with a certain scepticism, not unmixed with irony, upon these so-called "moral" sciences, being quite persuaded within themselves that such studies will never obtain any positive results, and that they are destined to remain always in the condition of vague and hypothetical speculation. It may therefore be worth while stating the principal views that have been held upon the subject.

[1] See Schopenhauer, *The World as Will and Idea*.

The philosophers of the positivist school, such as Comte, and some modern English thinkers, such as Mill and Spencer, are **Comte.** intellectualist at bottom, and cling to the idea of arriving in time at the discovery of laws of psychical life as exact as those which govern natural phenomena. Auguste Comte's "classification of the sciences" is a very important document for the history of this question.[1] Comte did not concern himself particularly with Psychology, but his notion of "sociology" (of which he is universally recognised as the founder) was so broad, that the principles which we apply to Psychology can be perfectly well applied to it. It is well known that, with regard to individual Psychology, Comte quoted as an example and a model the phrenological speculations of Gall! For him the real Psychology was not individual Psychology, but social Psychology, or "sociology."

His classification of the sciences was on the principle of decreasing generality and of increasing complexity. In his opinion, the science possessing the maximum of generality and the minimum of complexity was mathematics; the most complex and least general sciences being, on the other hand, biology and sociology.[2] For us the latter is clearly distinguishable from the former in that it is a moral science, whereas the others are physical or natural sciences. Comte, on the contrary, saw no difference between them but one of complexity and generality, sociology being a science which has for its object phenomena of a more complex nature than biological phenomena, which in their turn are more complex than chemical, and so on.

The same theory, with modifications in certain particulars, was professed by Mill, who in his *Logic* has the merit of having been **Mill.** the first to treat somewhat extensively the question of the logic of the moral sciences.[3] Mill also places the difference between historical and social and physical phenomena in the greater complexity of the two former, as compared with the latter. Although gifted with great critical acumen, he sees no difference of principle in these two orders of phenomena, and the profound observations he makes concerning them are generally purely empirical and rather inspired by common sense than

---

[1] Comte expounded his celebrated classification in his *Cours de philosophie positive* between 1830 and 1842.
[2] See *Cours de philosophie positive*, Vol. I., lec. 2ième. See also Höffding, *History of Modern Philosophy*, Vol. II., p. 340.
[3] Mill's *System of Logic* appeared in 1843.

rigorously scientific. Mill asserts, for example, that Psychology, or, as he calls it, the "general science of human nature," is still confronted by the same kind of difficulties which prevent meteorology from becoming an exact science. Like the latter, it deals with highly complicated phenomena, which are extremely difficult to subject to hard-and-fast general rules.[1] Mill also thinks that as the study of the human character progresses it will be possible to predict with certainty historical and social events, at least (he cautiously adds) in their general lines. Mill, however, never alludes to the possibility of founding a really scientific Psychology on the methods of the natural sciences. On the contrary, he is satisfied with introspection and with the study of the more complex psychical processes. Briefly, Mill is a logician rather than a psychologist.

After Mill others attempted in various ways to solve the difficult problem of the laws of moral phenomena, under the guidance of the idea that the latter are to be studied after the fashion of biological phenomena. The attempts made during the past century to introduce the idea of law into sociology and history likewise betray the influence of biological principles, as may also be said of the philosophical system which is without doubt the clearest profoundest expression of the general culture of the second half of the nineteenth century—

Spencer.

i.e. the philosophy of Spencer.

The most notable essays in this direction are, in sociology those of Herbert Spencer himself, of Schäffle, and of Lilienfeld, in statistics that of Quetelet, in history that of Buckle.[2]

Taine.

Taine's studies concerning the history of art and literature in various countries (and especially of English literature) were

[1] J. Stuart Mill, *A System of Logic, Ratiocinative and Inductive*, Vol. II., Bk. VI., pp. 401, 527. It is well to note that Mill does not admit the possibility of applying the deductive method to historical facts, but only the inductive and the "inverse" deductive method. The latter consists in following up the causal series of historical and social facts (by means of an inductive process) with the view of explaining the chain of events thereby disclosed by means of a process of deduction. The ideas of Mill, Comte, and their contemporaries concerning the moral sciences have been studied by Professor Guido Villa in two papers dealing with the modern development of historical and social sciences, and on the moral sciences and Psychology (*Rivista Italiana di sociologia*, July and October, 1898).

[2] H. Spencer, *The Principles of Sociology* (1876); F. Schäffle, *Bau und Leben des socialen Körpers* (1875—1878); P. von Lilienfeld, *Gedanken über die Socialwissenschaft der Zukunft* (1873). On these authors see L. Gumplowitz in his *Grundriss der Sociologie* (1885), Part I. Quetelet's celebrated work *Sur l'homme* appeared in 1835; his *Physique sociale* in 1869. Buckle's *History of Civilisation*

also directed towards the discovery of certain primary elements which should prove to contain in themselves the reason why one course of evolution had been followed instead of another.[1] Taine's idea was the same as Mill's, that if we follow backwards the series of historical or social phenomena, we are obliged to recognise that they could not have occurred in a different manner. In Taine, however, the artistic temperament and (especially in his later works) the extraordinary wealth of his erudition contributed largely to temper these principles, and to admit of the consideration of historical facts as a whole, so that rather than being subordinate to general ideas (as in the *Philosophie de l'art*), it was the latter which adapted themselves, so to speak, to the former. Thus, in the *Origines de la France contemporaine* Taine makes able use of general psychological principles to explain the chain of historical events; but they do not any longer play exclusively the part of governing principles.[2] If, however, the scientific principles of the positivist school were tempered in the works of isolated individuals, they were accepted without discussion by the majority of students.

Despite the asseverations and hopes of philosophers and sociologists of the above persuasion, it was clear to dispassionate minds that the accurate methods of the physical sciences could not be applied with the same precise results to the moral sciences. Accordingly, it is not surprising to find a certain amount of scepticism with regard to those methods, nor that an open reaction set in against them. In Germany the principles of the positivist school never met with much favour, that country being always averse to empiricism. The pretension, therefore, of guiding moral studies by the light of laws similar to those which govern physical phenomena could not but find in Germany a strenuous opposition.

Rümelin. A very palpable sign of this reaction against the pretensions of sociologists and statisticians is to be found in 1875 in two lectures of the eminent economist Gustav Rümelin upon social and historical laws.[3] In these Rümelin shows the

in England appeared in 1857—1861. See, concerning it, Bernheim's *Lehrbuch der historischen Methode* (*passim*), and especially p. 535 foll.

[1] Taine's *Philosophie de l'art* appeared in 1865: his *Histoire de la littérature anglaise* in 1864. See G. Barzellotti, *La philosophie de H. Taine* (French edit., Paris, Alcan, 1900), Part III., § 1.

[2] *Les origines de la France contemporaine* was published between 1875 and 1884.

[3] Rümelin's two discourses, "Ueber den Begriff eines sozialen Gesetzes" (pp. 1—32) and "Ueber Gesetze der Geschichte," are contained, the first in

impossibility of applying any rule to historical and social facts, seeing that they are the product of so many individual and psychological factors, and moreover that the phenomena of consciousness are the emanation of a free and spontaneous will which eludes all laws.

To this freedom and spontaneity of moral phenomena, which positivists omitted to take into account, the Germans, who had always attributed great importance to the "inner world," assigned once again the weight which it deserved. Rümelin's lectures, nevertheless, are an index to the state of uncertainty which generally reigned at that time concerning the question of the moral sciences and of their laws. The only way of escape from this state of uncertainty was by individual and ethnical Psychology. But the beginnings of these two psychological methods, which for some little time were considered as two distinct sciences, were still too much mixed up with philosophy on the one side, and with physiology and sociology on the other, to afford any hope that they would become independent and strike out a line of their own.

And yet, at its very beginning, physiological Psychology discovered a law—the "Weber-Fechner law"—by means of which it was sought to establish an exact relation between the intensity of physical impression and of the resultant sensation. This discovery, which became thenceforth the basis of the majority of psychological experiments, roused great hopes amongst psychologists; being even interpreted by many as a proof that the processes of consciousness may, like physical phenomena, be subjected to mathematical law, and are therefore really another form of the latter. Moreover, the progress made by the study of the general physiological phenomena attendant upon certain states of mind, such as emotion, processes of volition, etc., encouraged psychologists to consider objective observation as the only possible way of arriving at any positive result.

The "physiological" philosophers had now ceased to recognise any value in introspection, the observation of external phenomena being the only means, in their estimation, to elevate Psychology to the same scientific level as physiology. This extreme opinion, however, was not generally professed, except by those who,

---

Vol. I. of his *Reden und Aufsätze* (1875), the second in Vol. II. (New Series, 1881), pp. 118—148. See also Rümelin's essay "Ueber den Begriff der Gesellschaft und einer Gesellschaftslehre" (*Reden und Aufsätze*, Third Series, 1894). See also Wundt, "Ueber den Begriff des Gesetzes" in *Philosophische Studien* 1886), Vol. III., p. 195 foll. See also G. Villa's paper above quoted.

neglecting empirical research and the independent observation of psychical facts, gave themselves up to metaphysical speculations upon the relations between body and soul, the origin of consciousness, and so forth. Those, on the contrary, who studied dispassionately the formation and development of psychical processes, and made use of experiment in investigating the simpler mental phenomena, as was the case with psychologists, or else considered, as did the students of the various moral sciences, the more complex psychical manifestations of history, society, and literature, could not but recognise that these processes presented, even in their simplest forms, a mode of formation and connection distinguishable in many ways from physical causality.

Almost all the psychologists who (inspired partly by Bain) flourished about 1880, and whom we may describe as empiricists, such as Wundt (in his earlier works), Höffding, Sully, James, Baldwin, Ladd, and others, were of one accord in recognising that mental causality has laws of its own not to be confounded with physical. In our day both the scepticism of "libertarians" (who, like Rümelin, denied the possibility of the existence of historical and social laws) and the identification of mental and physical causality (upheld by the materialists and by some positivists) have been abandoned in favour of a middle course, which aims at finding out what are the laws of the mind and how they differ from mechanical laws. Before examining the results of this quest, it will be well to investigate what attempts have been made in the history of philosophy to explain the inner essence of mental processes, and to subject them to scientific laws.

And first of the concept of "soul," which was for a long time of common acceptance in philosophic language, and is by many still considered indispensable in the study of the phenomena of consciousness. Two principal tendencies are traceable in the history of philosophy, with regard to the nature of consciousness. One, which prevailed until the rise of modern Psychology, and is not even now without supporters, is the principle of the "substantiality" of the soul; the other, which is recent, but answers much more closely to the requirements of modern empirical and scientific methods, is the principle of the "actuality" of mental facts. The "soul" was long considered the substratum of the phenomena of consciousness, in the same way as "matter" is the substratum of physical phenomena. The ingenuous materialism of the ancients represented it as an ethereal substance, a shadow or pallid copy of the body;

The concept of "soul."

The "substantiality" and "actuality" theories.

and this concept, so familiar to the ancient religious traditions of the East, remained throughout the Middle Ages as a doctrine of the Christian religion.[1]

Amongst ancient philosophers, Plato, the great spiritualistic philosopher, was the first to conceive the soul as something absolutely immaterial, but for a long time his idea remained without a following. The concept of spirit or soul continued to be confounded, even by Aristotle, with that of organic activity. The first philosopher to establish the absolutely independent character of the spirit, as opposed to matter, was Descartes. This Cartesian idea, which is of so great an importance in the history of thought that it is often considered the starting-point of modern philosophy, was the result of the scientific revolution which did away with the interpretation of nature according to subjective and fantastic criteria, and explained it in accordance with the general laws of motion. René Descartes, who was a mathematician before he was a philosopher, laid the foundation of the new philosophy by distinguishing the " res extensa " from the " res cogitans." Here therefore we find formulated for the first time the concept of psychic substance. Just as it was proved by natural science, after Galilei, that we only perceive the manifestations, the outward phenomena, of natural facts, whereas their inner essence—*i.e.* matter—eludes our senses ; so it was believed that the facts of consciousness were only manifestations of an essence, which underlies them, and which remains immutable throughout their continual changes. This essence, this fixed and immutable something, from which all thoughts, feelings, and acts of volition emanate, was naturally the " soul," the conception of which thus took shape by analogy with the notion of matter, and was indeed the counterpart of it. The ultimate aim of the philosophy of mind was accordingly conceived of by many philosophers as that of penetrating through the changeable mass of phenomena of consciousness to the innermost precincts of the soul itself. It was natural, therefore, that this " science of the soul " should be different from the empirical study of mental facts, as we understand it.

But there is another no less important point to notice in Descartes and the Cartesian school. The conception of consciousness was, for that philosopher and for his followers, restricted to the higher mental, and, in fact, to logical, processes. It was natural that this exaggerated intellectualism should have had to give way, and that the domain of consciousness should subse-

[1] See Lange, *History of Materialism*.

quently be extended so as to embrace other mental facts of a less salient character than the phenomena of the intellect. The merit of this change undoubtedly belongs to Leibnitz, who was the first to call attention to those dim psychical phenomena which go to make up presentations, and which he called "petites perceptions." He believed that beneath the threshold of consciousness a synthesis of the "petites perceptions" takes place, and that they consequently appear to us as a single "sensation." Leibnitz thus introduced into philosophy the concept of "unconsciousness," which was a logical consequence of the universally accepted concept of "psychical substance." The dissertations of the Wolffian school concerning the "Psychologia rationalis" had all of them, more or less, the "substantiality of the soul" for their theme. But the metaphysical explanations of the spiritualists did not satisfy those who desired rather to keep to facts than to empty abstractions. English associationists followed the empirical method of describing the phenomena of consciousness, and gave up searching after their original causes. Some (like Hume) explicitly declared this to be an insoluble problem. Hume, indeed, may be considered the first philosopher who denied the principle of substance, which was upheld, at the time, not only by the spiritualists, but by the materialists as well. The former maintained that the mental processes are manifestations of a spiritual essence which underlies them ; the latter, on the contrary, were of opinion that those processes are nothing but a manifestation of the corporeal substance—that is, of the brain. "It is sufficient for us to know," wrote Holbach in his *Système de la nature*, "that the soul is moved and modified by the corporeal causes acting upon it. We have the right to conclude, therefore, that it must be itself corporeal."[1] The materialists of the past century (who added nothing to the results obtained by their predecessors of the eighteenth) upheld the no less metaphysical hypothesis that the only Real is the material, and that the so-called processes of consciousness should be referred to it.

These theories of substantiality, and especially the Wolffian "Psychologia rationalis," were opposed by Immanuel Kant. Kant maintained that all the efforts of rational Psychology to prove the existence of a simple thinking substance, ever identical with itself, underlying the phenomena of consciousness (which form the object

[1] Holbach, *Système de la nature*, Vol. I., p. 118. See Höffding, *Psychology*, p. 15. Broussais (quoted by Höffding, *ibid.*) defined the soul as "un cerveau agissant et rien de plus."

of empirical Psychology) are vain, for we can only have cognition of phenomena. We must therefore rest satisfied with examining the mental processes as they present themselves to our consciousness, nor can we go beyond them. The same may be said of external phenomena, of which we cannot apprehend the inmost essence. But neither can external phenomena be reduced to internal, nor the latter to the former. Thus Kant is neither a spiritualist nor a materialist. Kant's *Critique* had an extraordinary importance in the history of philosophy, because it placed scientific research, psychological and natural, upon a safe road, to which it must always return if, instead of indulging in metaphysical speculation, it wishes to obtain practical results.

The idealist philosophers, however, who succeeded Kant did not keep to his critical method, and abandoned themselves, on the contrary, to metaphysical speculations upon Reality. The philosophical systems of Fichte, Schelling, Hegel, are all founded upon the principle that thought only, considered as a continual evolution, represents the absolute Real. These philosophers, however, were not properly psychologists. On the contrary, they professed to hold Psychology of small account, on the ground that it was unable to afford any explanation of the universal laws of thought. Psychological questions only recovered the importance they had lost after the Wolffian period on the return of philosophy to the critical method indicated by Kant.

Frederic Herbart, the founder of realistic or critical idealism, in spite of his opinion that Psychology should be merely an application of general philosophical principles, had, nevertheless, the great merit not only of having replaced it upon the footing to which it has a right, but also of having first attempted to conduct its investigations on rigorous scientific lines. Herbart also entertained the idea of a psychical substance, which, however, assumes in his system a very different significance from that which it had amongst the preceding spiritualistic philosophers. Herbart's principle is closely connected with his whole system. In the place of the concept of the old spiritualistic philosophy, according to which the soul was a simple essence manifesting itself in the various phenomena of consciousness, the highest aim of Psychology consisting therefore in penetrating to its inmost essence, Herbart substitutes the notion that we are only able to apprehend the forms in which the soul manifests itself, in other words, presentations, and not the soul itself, whose qualities, as they are in reality, are unknown to us.

Spiritualistic philosophy made a last attempt at reconciling the doctrine of psychical substance with the data of scientific experience in the person of Hermann Lotze, a professional physiologist and psychologist possessed of a vast amount of culture in all branches of philosophical and natural science. Lotze, though he entertained various general philosophical ideas of an even more decidedly spiritualistic tendency than Herbart's, did away with a great deal of the metaphysical character which still adhered to the concept of substance. "The fact of the unity of consciousness proves 'eo ipso' the fact of the existence of a substance." The "soul" reduces itself, therefore, in Lotze's estimation, to a "unity living in determined presentations, feelings, and aspirations," and the psychic substance is nothing but the inner connection of all the contents of experience.[1]

Lotze may be called the last authoritative representative of the concept of a psychical "substance." Contemporary philosophy and Psychology generally repudiate this principle, keeping solely to the data of experience.[2] English psychologists, indeed, without having theoretically formulated the empirical principle that we must consider the data of consciousness and nothing more, had, nevertheless, admitted it implicitly and followed it in practice. Contemporary German philosophy, of which Wundt and Paulsen are the most eminent representatives, openly uphold the theory of the "actuality of psychic facts," as the contrary of the theory of substantiality.

This concept of the "actuality" of psychic facts was familiar to the moral sciences before it was introduced into Philosophy and Psychology. These sciences have developed on a foundation of purely empirical facts, a very important part being played in this empirical progress by the so-called "historical school." Whilst amongst philosophers discussion was rife concerning the great problems of cognition and morality, and Psychology was attempting to divest itself of transcendental ideas in order to adopt an independent empirical method, History, Political Economy, and Law were accumulating a great quantity of data which they interpreted empirically, without having

[1] This was well noted by Külpe (*Einleitung in die Philosophie*, p. 189). "Thereby," he adds, "its conception approaches very near to the theory of actuality—is, indeed, removed from it, one may say, only in name."

[2] The concept of substantiality, however, has still some eminent supporters. A defence of that principle was lately undertaken by Professor F. de Sarlo in a lecture *On the Conception of the Soul in Modern Psychology* (Florence, 1900).

recourse to the notion of a psychical substance. The results arrived at by the moral sciences have therefore contributed largely to the development of Psychology by freeing it from the metaphysical concept of a "mind-substance."[1] According to the theory of "actuality," the processes of consciousness have an "actual," independent value apart from any connection with a hypothetical psychical or material substratum. The word "consciousness," according to the "actuality" theory, should be understood to mean the whole aggregate of psychical facts pertaining to the individual. It is, therefore, a collective concept, which excludes everything outside those processes.[2] Kant, who was the first to point out and maintain that we must rest satisfied with a science of phenomena, seeing that we cannot arrive at a knowledge of the essence of things, admitted nevertheless that this substratum, if not determinable, is at least thinkable. Contemporary philosophy goes even further, Wundt, among others, maintaining that though we have the right to think that a fixed and immutable substance underlies physical phenomena, we are not to suppose the same with regard to the mental processes. The reason adduced for this difference is that the phenomena of the physical world are governed by the law of the conservation of energy, and are consequently immutable in quantity. Moreover, as those phenomena considered by themselves do not possess any other fundamentally distinguishing characteristic beyond that of quantity, they possess a character of immutability which induces the belief in a permanent substratum underlying the continual variation of physical phenomena, to which we give the name of "matter."[3] The

[1] Wundt, *Outlines of Psychology*, pp. 312—313.
[2] Wundt, *System der Philosophie*, Part III., chap. iii. ("Psychologische Anwendung des Substanzbegriffs"), p. 289 foll., and Part IV., chap. ii., especially p. 391; Paulsen, *Einleitung in die Philosophie*, p. 133 foll. See also Jodl, *Lehrbuch der Psychologie*, p. 70 foll.
[3] There has been a recent attempt at substituting the concept of pure energy for that of "matter." This idea was upheld by Ostwald in a lecture which made a great impression at the time (*Die Ueberwindung des wissenschaftlichen Materialismus*, lecture delivered before the Society of German Materialists at Lübeck on September 20th, 1895). But in reality the advantage of this substitution is not clear. The concept of "matter" is purely hypothetical, and corresponds to the abstract idea of pure "quantity." One cannot indeed conceive a physical energy which is not at the same time material— that is to say, which does not manifest itself by means of movement in space and is therefore reducible to a quantity. Wundt believes, as we have already noted, that the primary origin of consciousness is to be sought for in the psychical

same cannot, however, be said of the psychic processes, which having a value of their own, cannot be reduced to a fixed quantity, and are in a state of continual increase (if the term "increase" or growth may be used to indicate a purely qualitative fact).

This view of the subject-matter of Psychology, which is far from meeting with universal acceptance, was named by Lange a "Psychology without soul." It has lately found its clearest expression in the works of Wundt, who defines the theory upon which it is founded as the theory of actuality, because it considers psychic facts just as they present themselves and as they are "actually," without seeking for a hypothetical substratum or substance, as was done by the old Psychology.[1] This theory of actuality is closely connected with the theory of "volitionism," whilst the doctrine of "substantiality" is connected with intellectualistic theories. Indeed, whereas the latter gives preponderating if not exclusive importance to the intellectual and cognitive aspect of psychical phenomena, and supposes consciousness and the mind to be fashioned in the image of the physical world, as an aggregate of variable phenomena with a permanent and unchangeable substratum, the theory of "volitionism," on the contrary, selects the will as the fundamental element in mental processes, and arrives at the conclusion that they, like the will, are purely "actual," and not to be referred to anything fixed and immutable ; that they are, in fact, entirely *sui generis*, obeying laws and assuming forms of their own, not comparable in any way to those of matter and physical energy.[2] Contemporary and empirical Psychology, as represented by the majority of the authors we have hitherto quoted, such as Wundt, Höffding, Sully, James, Jodl, Ladd, Baldwin, identifies consciousness with mental process.[3]

phenomena of direct experience, from which objective and natural observation has been evolved by means of abstraction. In our opinion, therefore, it is a mistake to place Wundt amongst the spiritualistic philosophers, as Külpe, for instance, does in his *Einleitung in die Philosophie*, p. 140, although he admits that Wundt is only " in a certain sense " a spiritualist.

[1] It is not long ago that Professor Bonatelli, of Padua University, in a lecture at the Venetian Institute of Sciences, Letters, and Arts (Tome VIII., 1896—1897), entered a strong protest against this empirical tendency of Psychology. Bonatelli's point of view is very similar to Lotze's.

[2] See Wundt, *Logik*, Vol. II., p. 156 foll., p. 164 foll., p. 259 foll. ; *Philosophische Studien*, Vol. X., Part I. (1894), p. 101 foll. ; Vol. XII., Part I. (1895), p, 36 foll.

[3] See James, *The Principles of Psychology*, Vol. I., p. 182. James professes to follow purely empirical principles.

The theory of "substantiality," as well as the doctrine which considers consciousness as a separate faculty distinguishable from psychical processes, has had numerous supporters amongst eminent philosophers and psychologists, and enjoys even now a certain repute, so that it will be well to examine it somewhat minutely. This theory has reappeared in connection with the experimental school, though in a different form from that of the old-fashioned doctrines of substantiality, for contemporary supporters of the concept of "substance" do not have recourse to the mystical arguments which appealed to psychologists such as Jouffroy. Modern spiritualists may all be said to follow the lead of Lotze in finding the proof of the existence of a mental substance in the unity of the conscious processes. The principal argument they adduce in favour of a permanent substratum underlying all psychical facts, which must consequently be considered only as "phenomena," is that every individual during the whole course of his mental life and through the continual succession of presentations, feelings, and acts of volition, feels himself nevertheless always the same and identical with himself, feels, in fact, that he has a distinct individuality, which is persistent, and which, in the normal development of consciousness, becomes more fully aware of its own existence.

But there is here an evident confusion between the two widely different meanings attaching to the word "consciousness," which may stand for "consciousness" properly so-called, and for the "consciousness of self." In the first acceptation, consciousness is nothing but an aggregate of mental processes; in the second, on the contrary, it is the feeling we have that these processes belong to us and constitute our personality. In the former there is no mental fact in addition to or resulting from those which go to make up mental life; we have nothing in this case but psychical processes, simultaneous or successive, connected with each other in a causal series. What, in any given moment of our mental life, do we perceive directly in ourselves, besides the purely psychical processes of presentation, feeling, or impulse? Doubtless we are conscious that these processes belong to us and not to others; but this is no proof that what may be called "simple" consciousness is connected with a special inner sense, which enables us to perceive our own Ego. This theory arose by analogy from the concept of Matter, and has recently found some authoritative supporters, not amongst metaphysical philosophers, but amongst psychologists of the experimental school, who are devoted to the physiological method as applied to psychological research. One of these, Oswald Külpe, in his *Introduction to the Study of Philosophy*, when dealing with the psychological tendencies in metaphysics, examines the theory of substantiality, which he attempts to defend on the ground that although it may be a fact that the psychical substance is not the direct object of our perception, and although we cannot say what the atoms are, yet we believe that they exist.[1] This analogy has, however, no foundation in fact, the physical and psychical orders of phenomena having no point of comparison, and the causality of each being entirely different. In the physical world a fact is a pure "quantity," and, considered in itself, can only be appraised on the assumption that this quantity is unchangeable—*i.e.* that there is conservation of energy. In order to explain this immutability, it is necessary to have recourse to the notion of a permanent substratum. Atoms and matter are not, however, an object of sense-perception—they cannot even be imagined; they are merely an indispensable hypothesis in the natural sciences, which can only deal with phenomena. Without some such integrating concept, such phenomena are inexplicable. In the mental world it is different, for facts here are not appraised according to their quantity, but according to their "qualitative" value. This, however, not only cannot be said to remain the same, but we see, on the contrary, that it increases continually both as regards the individual and the species. Wherefore we have no reason to suppose the existence of a substratum of any kind underlying the psychical processes.

Theory of the "unity of consciousness." The "unity of consciousness" is, we have seen, the principle upon which the modern upholders of the concept of substance base their theory. Thus Külpe contends that, since we cannot admit the multiplicity of the facts of consciousness to be itself the substratum (*der Träger*) of each of them, we must admit the existence of a thinking subject, or of a psychical substance.[2] This concept of multiplicity is, however, itself entirely a metaphysical one, for it implies that the multiplicity exists as something apart from the psychical

---

[1] Külpe, *Einleitung in die Philosophie*, p. 191 foll. It is well to note that on p. 193 of the same work Külpe maintains that empirical Psychology should hold aloof from the concept of "psychical substance" in the description and explanation of the facts. See Wundt's statement of Külpe's theory in his paper on the "Definition of Psychology" (*Philosophische Studien*, Vol. XII., Part I., 1895, p. 38 foll.).

[2] Külpe, *Einleitung in die Philosophie*, p. 191.

processes which constitute it, whereas it consists of the continual stream of the mental processes, and itself constitutes consciousness, so that if it is done away with, consciousness comes to an end.[1]

These are the only arguments to be adduced in a purely psychological question like the present, and once rejected, there remain only reasons of a moral or philosophical nature in favour of the theory of psychical substantiality. These reasons, however, can have no more weight in this connection than when they are made use of against certain physical or biological theories, such as the theory of descent and heredity. A purely explicative science like biology or Psychology can only aim at establishing facts as they really are, without any concern as to the philosophic or moral consequences which may accrue from them. Moreover, it is not for the special sciences to submit to the rule of philosophy ; on the contrary, philosophy should be a product of the special sciences.

We have already noted that the theory of consciousness considered as a separate faculty, besides being purely metaphysical, had its origin in the intellectualistic theory which assimilates mental processes and phenomena to physical facts. The view which identifies psychical processes with consciousness, on the contrary, assigns to these processes a character entirely their own and absolutely different from that of natural phenomena, accentuating this difference in contrast to the old spiritualistic theories, which, being based upon intellectualistic prejudices, approached nearer to materialism than they were aware of. Contemporary Psychology, on the contrary, in determining the mode of formation, evolution, and association of psychical facts and of their laws, aims rather at proving their specific quality, and thus divesting them of all resemblance to natural phenomena. Thus not only does it completely destroy the materialistic hypothesis, but it considers volition and spontaneity the most salient characteristic of mental life. But as freedom of will is the first condition of moral life, it is difficult to see how the theory of the identity of psychical processes with consciousness can be detrimental to an elevated morality, the essence of which is that it should be entirely free from fatalistic or mechanical concepts. As to general philosophy, it can only gain by these new psychological ideas, which afford it the means of progress in the comprehension of the general laws of the mental world to which these researches afford an increasingly

[1] Wundt, *Philosophische Studien*, Vol. XII., Part I., p. 40.

extended sphere. Contemporary empirical Psychology may thus be said to be unanimous in denying the existence of a "psychic substance," and in considering psychical processes by themselves, according to their "actual" value. It will therefore be interesting to examine in another chapter how the evolution of mental facts is regarded by it and what are the laws which it deduces therefrom.

CHAPTER X

THE LAWS OF PSYCHOLOGY (Continued)

IN spite of the consensus of opinion described in the last chapter, there remain several essential discrepancies between the various contemporary psychological schools concerning the essence of mental processes. We have, on the one hand, what we may call "intellectualistic" empiricism, connected with the associationist philosophers and psychologists who reject the concept of a "psychic substance," and give almost exclusive importance to the succession of cognitive processes, sensations, presentations, and ideas. They are the representatives of what we have called "psychical atomism." On the other hand, we have the so-called volitional school, which, though also rejecting the notion of a "psychic substance," gives a preponderating weight to the subjective processes of consciousness—that is, to feeling and willing. The intellectualistic school had reached its highest development with Frederic Herbart and his followers, Herbart having attempted to found a veritable statical and mechanical science of the mind by taking presentations as units and applying to them the mathematical method.[1] But the intellectualistic doctrine has assumed a different form in modern Psychology, the philosopher who has developed it with most originality being Herbert Spencer.[2] In his *Principles of Psychology* Spencer deals with this question at great length, more especially in the chapter on the "Law of Intelligence." The psychic life consists, in his estimation, of a continual succession and change of mental states. He recognises that it is by no means easy to formulate the law which governs all these changes. The surroundings in which consciousness exists contain a very great number of simultaneous

(margin note: Modern notions concerning the "psychic substance.")

---

[1] See Herbart, *Psychologie als Wissenschaft neu gegründet auf Erfahrung, Metaphysik und Mathematik.* Cf. Volkmann, *Lehrbuch der Psychologie*, Vol. I., Part III.
[2] See *The Principles of Psychology*, Vol. I., p. 407.

facts, whereas psychical phenomena succeed each other in time. Apart from this, there is also the fact that the surrounding physical world is unlimited in extent, and that the phenomena it contains are not only infinite in number, but sink insensibly into a relative non-existence the farther removed they are from the organism. The difficulties of finding an exact formula are consequently such that it seems almost hopeless to succeed. Nevertheless, if we carefully examine how the internal and the external world stand to each other, we find that the relation existing between any two states of consciousness corresponds to the relation existing between the two external phenomena which produce them. This relation consists in the fact that the "persistence" of the connection between the two states of consciousness is proportionate to the "persistence" of the connection between the external phenomena to which they correspond.[1] When the correspondence becomes complete—that is, when the intelligence attains a higher degree of development—the different degrees of the one series show an increasingly marked parallelism with the degrees of the other. It will be asked how a series of states of consciousness, which occur successively, can represent relations between external objects, which exist simultaneously? The answer is, that it is owing to a process of association, whereby, when an external object causes a state of consciousness, this state recalls another state of consciousness, which corresponds to a second object coexisting with the first. In its turn the second state recalls the first, so that the relation between the two remains the object of the conscious process. This relation subsists also when it is purely casual. It may, therefore, be said that the tendency which the antecedent of any psychical variation has to be followed by its consequent is proportionate to the coexistence of the connection between the external objects they represent.[2] Only in virtue of this law can that adaptation of internal to external relations take place without which life is impossible; and it is only upon this assumption that we can explain the facts: first, that relations which are absolute in the physical world are also absolute in ourselves; secondly, that relations which are probable in the physical world are also probable in ourselves; thirdly and lastly, that relations which are casual in the physical world are casual in ourselves.

Upon this principle Spencer seeks to explain the development

[1] Spencer, *op. cit.*, Vol. I., p. 408 (3rd edit.).
[2] *Ibid.*, pp. 411, 412.

of the intelligence, which, according to him, exhibits three phases. At first there is an increase of the exactitude with which internal tendencies correspond to external persistencies; secondly, there is an increasing number of cases in which the same result is attained; and thirdly, there is an increase of "complexity" of connected states of consciousness, corresponding to the connected complexities in the environment.[1] All this may, however, be explained in accordance with the same general principle, namely, that one state of consciousness will recall another the more easily the oftener those states have previously been connected together; for the harmony between the internal and external relations is derived from the fact that the former are a product of the latter. As to the facts which cannot find an explanation in individual experience, such as reflex and instinctive actions, they can find it in the experience of the race.[2]

Spencer's explanation of the development of the intelligence.

Such is the theory which Spencer deduced from the general principles of biological evolution and applied to the processes of consciousness. The first thing which is apparent in it all is that Spencer only considers the intellectual part of the consciousness. In this, as in everything, he adheres strictly to the intellectualistic principles of English philosophy. External objects and their relations translate themselves in consciousness into presentations of objects and of relations. Consciousness is thus a mirror which faithfully reflects external objects and the relations in which they stand to each other.

The first question suggested by these assertions is very simple : To what external fact do the feelings which attend presentations correspond? To what object or relation can they be compared? Spencer admits that feelings are inseparable from intellectual processes, but nevertheless gives them no very important place as elements of psychical activity.[3] The will also, which, as we have seen, is the most characteristic element of mental life, plays a very subordinate part in Spencer's system, being considered by him a transformation of reflex movement.[4] His conception is therefore one-sided and lends itself to grave objections from an epistemological point of view. What are the internal and the

[1] Spencer, *op. cit.*, Vol. I., p. 417, in the chapter on the "Development of the Intelligence."
[2] *Op. cit.*, p. 418.
[3] *Op. cit.*, p. 472.
[4] *Op. cit.*, pp. 427 and 495.

external world but a repetition of the old metaphysical definitions, scarcely disguised under the novel terms adopted by Spencer of inner and outer relations? Spencer intends by them to place the psychophysical individual in juxtaposition to his environment. It is certainly a fact that the individual is both body and mind—that is to say, a psychophysical being; but it is no less true that the organism, considered merely as an aggregate of physical energies (abstraction being made from psychical activity), is itself of the same nature as the external physical environment, the only difference being that physical phenomena in the organism present themselves in a much more complicated form. A cerebral phenomenon is of a physical nature as much as a geological or as any external chemical phenomenon. When the physical impression strikes the terminations of the peripheral nerves, and possesses a certain degree of intensity, it is transmitted by means of the nerves to the brain, and causes a state of consciousness composed of a sensation (which can recall other sensations and make up a presentation) and of feelings and impulses. But, until the impression is communicated to the brain, though it transforms itself into a physiological phenomenon, it remains a purely physical fact. These phenomena must therefore be also considered as external. Indeed, as compared with consciousness, the relation between any two cells of the brain is as much an external fact as the relation between two objects in space, and it is an error to consider the psychophysical organism as standing in sharp contrast to its environment.

But there is another yet more important question to be considered. In what way are these presentations, which, as Spencer says, correspond in a successive series to the successive and simultaneous objects and relations of the outer world, really distinguishable from these same objects and relations? Is not the distinction we make between objects and presentations rather the result of a process of abstraction? Spencer attributes to the external object a much greater importance than to presentation: the former is "real," the latter is but a copy of it. But the one is as real as the other. How can we truly distinguish a presentation from the object to which it refers? and how can we, on the other hand, distinguish the latter from the presentation which it evokes within us, and without which we could not have any knowledge of it? There can be no objects which are not objects of a presentation or of an idea. For, even when we imagine that they can exist independently, we always have to refer to them by means of our thoughts, either making up new presentations out of elements of other real presentations, or else thinking of them in the abstract as pure concepts. In every case there is a necessary correspondence between object and presentation. This fact Spencer himself fully recognises, and consequently refuses to admit of any other psychical law but the law of association of presentations. This "psychical law," however, resolves itself ultimately into a secondary form of physical law, for Spencer is of opinion that its causes lie in the connections and external, physical relations, which produce the internal relations. And here once again we may notice the artificiality of the distinction he makes between the object and its relations on the one hand, and presentation and internal relations on the other. We have seen that Spencer explains the manner in which the internal series, which is purely successive, can represent external simultaneous relations, by means of a "reversing" of the association: A recalls B, and B recalls A. How can this fact be explained? If the internal series is purely successive, when one state recalls another, the former must necessarily yield its place to the latter, which means that they cannot coexist. This elaborate theory, devised to explain a very simple fact, is a natural consequence of the distinction made by Spencer between the external and internal world, which he considered as entirely detached. He seeks to establish a distinction between two series of facts, in order, on the one hand, to avoid the conclusions of the materialists, for whom consciousness is an illusion; and on the other hand, because he desires to limit reality to external objects, of which he considers presentations and the inner world but copies.

Spencer's theory of the reproduction and association of presentations is in open conflict with the data of empirical experimental Psychology. He speaks of objects and presentations as if they had an equal value, and as if the latter were a faithful copy of the former. And yet experience teaches that, when a presentation evoked by several external impressions returns to consciousness, in spite of our efforts to reproduce it exactly, it reappears in each case profoundly modified—new elements are added to it, others disappear; so that a so-called "reproduced" presentation is in reality a new psychic fact comparable to, but never identical with, some past fact. How does this take place? Simply owing to the fact that the mental life is not a reproduction of the physical external world, but that it takes a quantity of simple elements from the latter, which are subsequently elaborated and combined in different ways and according to certain principles and laws of its own. A presentation, considered by Spencer and other intellectualists as a unity, is, on the contrary, an aggregate of units, or of simple elements, continually becoming associated and disassociated. It is here that the divergence between the mental and the physical world shows itself most clearly. The psychic life is not only composed of presentations, but of other facts as well which have nothing to do with the external world, and are purely subjective (viz. feelings and impulses), to whose influence presentations, considered merely as mental facts, are subject, and upon which these in turn react. As, moreover, the objective aspect of mental life changes continually, the will, which represents the centre of the subjective part and of the whole mental life, brings about new combinations of psychic elements, and consequently new presentations. The mental life, or consciousness, constitutes, we repeat, a series of acts of volition, or apperceptive acts, in which the central point of the attention is continually changing, and thus itself represents a continual series of changes.

Considered from this point of view, it seems much more complicated than would at first sight appear when considered merely as a reproduction of the external life; and the necessity therefore arises of discovering the laws which govern the formation and evolution of mental processes and of ascertaining how they differ from physical laws.

We have often had occasion to remark that the facts of consciousness have a purely "actual" value—that is to say, have a value only inasmuch as they exist at a given moment—and cannot be referred to any fixed substratum. There is, therefore, no psychical "substance," but only "psychical processes." These processes, however, are not fragmentary and isolated, but linked together, thereby disclosing a certain unity, which the upholders of the concept of "substance" miss in the "actuality" theory. The psychical processes therefore stand in a certain "relation" to each other—a fact which constitutes the first and most general psychical law, "the law of relativity."

This law of relativity has been considered very important by modern psychologists, who herein follow the idea first propounded *The law of* by Leibnitz—that the world of the spirit forms a con-
relativity. tinuous stream. This conception might perhaps have been arrived at by the English associationists, had they not given

an almost exclusive importance to the intellectual part of consciousness.[1] Other philosophers had already noted that, with regard to moral facts, and especially with regard to pleasure and pain, there is no means of determining their "absolute" value, but that their value depends upon the relation in which each fact stands to other simultaneous or preceding ones. Thus Gerolamo Cardano believed that the pleasure or displeasure we may experience from external stimuli depends exclusively upon our state of mind, the desires and wants of the moment, and consequently on preceding psychical states. Good things, he said, please all the more if they follow upon bad things, and *vice versa*; thus light after darkness, a sweet flavour after a bitter, and so forth. Every sensation, according to Cardano, supposes a change, and every change fluctuates between opposites.[2] Some mathematicians also, such as Bernouilli and Laplace, have made a distinction between absolute possessions, which are purely external (*fortune physique*), and relative possessions (*fortune morale*), which are dependent upon the subjective state of the individual.[3] Fechner, in his *Elements of Psychophysics*, develops the same idea. The physical things which we possess, he says, have no value and meaning for us as lifeless masses, but only inasmuch as they are external means for producing sensations having a certain value (*werthvoller Empfindungen*), and in reference to which they play the part of stimuli. A dollar, continues Fechner, has consequently a much smaller value from this point of view for a rich man than for a poor, as it can bring happiness to the latter for a whole day, whereas the former does not even notice whether he possesses one more or less. This fact, says Fechner in conclusion, may also be placed under the operation of Weber's law.[4]

The "law of relativity" has been most extensively employed amongst modern Psychologists by Bain in his work on *The Emotions and the Will*, published in 1859, and in his little book on the *Mind and Body*, published in 1873. We have seen that Bain, in his various works, and especially in that upon *The Senses and the Intelligence* (1856), considers change an essential condition of

[1] See the fine chapter we have already quoted from W. James's *Principles of Psychology* on "The Stream of Thought," Vol. I., p. 224 foll.
[2] Cardano, *De Subtilitate*, Book XIII. See L. Dumont, *Théorie scientifique de la sensibilité* (4th edit. 1890), pp. 28, 29.
[3] Bernouilli, *Specimen theoriæ novæ de mensura sortis* (1738); Laplace, *Théorie analytique des probabilités* (1847). See Höffding, *Psychology*, pp. 314, 329.
[4] Fechner, *Elemente der Psychophysik*, Vol. I., p. 236.

mental life. Without the perception of a change there can be no consciousness; the primitive fact which characterises the life of the spirit is, therefore, the act of *discrimination*. Upon this original mental activity the whole of consciousness is based. There is, however, over and above this primitive characteristic of mind, which concerns the cognitive part, the intelligence and the laws of association, another general law which more especially concerns the feelings, or subjective part of consciousness—viz. the law of relativity.[1] Thus our feelings are all related to our state of mind at the moment, so that something which gives us great pleasure one day may be indifferent to us on the morrow, or a pain which at first appeared unbearable, through habit makes itself less and less felt, and at last disappears entirely.[2] Bain gives numerous examples of the relativity of our pleasures and pains, which he takes from everyday life, from the history of letters and philosophy, thus elevating the principle of change to the level of a general law of the mind.[3]

Spencer also, in obedience to his general concept of mental life, attributes much importance to the principle of relativity,[4] and the same has been done by subsequent psychologists. Thus Höffding, in his *Psychology*, studies the law of relativity both from the point of view of sensations and from that of feeling.[5] What he says on the subject deserves to be noted. "The study of sensations," says Höffding, "thus corroborates the general account of consciousness given in an earlier chapter. It is impossible to resolve consciousness into a series of simple and self-existent sensations, absolutely independent of one another." The several sensations are determined by the relations of the various states or of parts of the same state, and this, which holds good also for other elements of consciousness, may be called the *law of relativity*. The distinction or relation may be simultaneous or successive, or it may be a relation between the parts of the same state or between two states which are reciprocally determined by each other. Simultaneous

---

[1] Bain, *The Emotions and the Will*, Part II., chap. xi., p. 549 foll. Cf. *Mind and Body*; Höffding, *Einleitung in die Englische Philosophie unserer Zeit* (Leipsic, 1889), p. 86 foll.; Ribot, *La psychologie anglaise contemporaine*, p. 274 foll.

[2] *Mind and Body*, p. 45 foll.

[3] See also *The Emotions and the Will*, Part I., chap. iv., p. 78 foll.

[4] See E. Pace, "Das Relativität-Princip in H. Spencer's psychologischen Entwicklungslehre" (*Philosophische Studien*, Vol. VII., 1892, p. 487 foll.).

[5] *Psychology*, p. 114 foll., p. 314 foll. See also Ladd, *Psychology: Descriptive and Explanatory*, p. 661 foll.

sensations have a tendency to merge into one (especially those of touch, taste, and smell), which means that successive sensations are more clearly separated."[1]

These considerations naturally lead to the study of Weber's or Fechner's law, which aims at establishing, with mathematical accuracy, the relation existing between the various sensations and the strength of the corresponding physical impressions by which they are produced. Höffding goes on to note how, in obedience to the law of relativity, no sharp distinction can be drawn between sensible perception and its recollection, nor between sensible perception and thought. As we are aware, in the case of successive states the preceding state influences the following.[2] Here, therefore, we have an elementary recollection, in its simplest form, showing the influence of the preceding state upon the following, with an absence of consciousness of the influence. Here also we have what Bain was the first to note as a fundamental characteristic of consciousness—viz. the power of drawing a comparison between two states, and so discriminating between them, showing itself already in the case of simple sensation, and in the higher grades of mental life becoming what is commonly called the thinking power. The law of relativity shows itself also in the close connection between sensations, which are to consciousness as the parts to a whole. Finally, concludes Höffding, the law of relativity proves the truth of one of the most important points of the Kantian philosophy. Kant made a distinction between the matter and the form of our knowledge. The sensations were considered by him as passive matter, which is fashioned by an activity derived from a separate source. On Kant's view, sensations, which are the matter of consciousness, are data, whereas the forms, according to which this matter is put in order and fashioned, exist *a priori* in our consciousness. Kant adds that what puts in order and gives shape to the sensations cannot itself be a sensation. According to the law of relativity, says Höffding, consciousness has its origin in a comprehensive activity, for which there exists no matter without form; to deny this would be tantamount to believing that there can exist purely independent sensations. The difference between matter and form is only one of degree. Psychical experience shows us facts resembling purely passive sensations, but these facts have also points of contact with consciousness. We are never absolutely passive and receptive, for the influence to which each

[1] Höffding, *op. cit.*, p. 114.   [2] *Ibid.*, p. 116.

new stimulus is subjected is determined by some preceding or simultaneous fact within ourselves.[1]

Similar observations are also to be found in Sully.[2] Similarly James and Ladd assign great importance amongst psychical facts to the continuity of the states of consciousness, which they call the "stream of consciousness."[3] This continuous stream, however, is not to be taken in an absolute sense. Consciousness, says James, is distinguished by two fundamental properties—conception and discrimination. By the help of the former we recognise that an object remains permanently the same, notwithstanding the continual changes occurring in our states of consciousness. On the other hand, in order to become acquainted with any given fact it is necessary to discriminate between its elements, though to outward appearance it may appear as a compound with no differentiation.[4] This process of discrimination may take place in various ways, according to the conditions under which percepts present themselves. Thus the differences may be directly felt or inferred or singled out in a compound. In the first case the perceptions must have a difference either of time or space or quality; they must, that is to say, present themselves in immediate succession, or else be of different quality. In the second case we have no direct perception of differences existing between two things, but an idea of difference, obtained by means of a reasoning or logical process. Lastly, we have that process of discrimination which consists in analysing or singling out the constituent elements of a mental compound.[5] These two fundamental properties of "conception" and "discrimination" established by James, correspond more or less to the two properties which Kant, followed by modern psychologists, recognised in consciousness—viz. the "unity" and the "multiplicity" of its elements. James's distinction has, however, a more logical character, the properties of conception and discrimination referring to the higher and more complex forms of mental activity rather than to the more fundamental and primitive.

The stream of consciousness: conception and discrimination.

The most difficult task for the psychologist who wishes to give a clear summary of the most constant and general facts of con-

---

[1] Höffding, *op. cit.*, p. 118.
[2] Sully, *The Human Mind*, Vol. I., p. 175.
[3] James, *The Principles of Psychology*, p. 224 foll.; *Psychology*, p. 151 foll.; Ladd, *Psychology: Descriptive and Explanatory*, p. 659.
[4] James, *Psychology*, p. 244; *The Principles of Psychology*, Vol. I., p. 483.
[5] *Psychology*, p. 248; *The Principles of Psychology*, Vol. I., p. 449 foll.

sciousness is that of choosing out of the complex and varied mass of mental phenomena a limited number of governing principles. The general tendency is, with James, to pay especial attention to the psychological laws observable in the higher processes of logical thought and imagination, for in these processes the working of mental laws is most evidently discernible. The simpler phenomena, such as perception or presentation, are neglected even when they are not considered subservient rather to physical than to mental laws. It is certainly one of the most important results of experimental Psychology to have demonstrated upon a basis of facts, and not only on philosophic grounds, that mental life forms a continuous stream, and that between primitive and complex psychical phenomena there is but a difference of degree. As, moreover, the simpler mental phenomena are more easily subjected to scientific observation and to experimentation, the laws and principles which are to be met with in all the stages of mental life can thus be determined and verified with accuracy and precision.

We have seen that modern psychologists place the principle of "relativity" foremost among psychological principles. This principle, though ably developed by Bain and better still by Höffding, has not been examined by them in all its forms and varieties, nor applied to all aspects of the phenomena of consciousness. While asserting that the law of relativity is a constant factor in psychic life, those psychologists have studied it with regard to the reciprocal bearings rather of successive mental states than of simultaneous ones. This question, which is, one may say, the focus of contemporary psychological research, is analysed with the greatest completeness and ability by Wundt, whose work deserves, therefore, to be dealt with at some length.

When one mentions *relations* between psychical states, the only possible meaning which can be attributed to the word is that of "causal" relations. Those who are accustomed to hear the term "cause" used only in connection with natural, physical, chemical, or biological sciences will naturally ask what relation subsists between the notion of psychical and that of physical causality. The idea is very widely spread at the present time that the only form of causality is connected with energy and matter, and that the facts of consciousness are to be considered objects for scientific investigation only when it is possible to refer them to that form of causality, as in any other case they elude all laws. And yet, if one considers the question of causality not with reference to a particular order of science, but from a broader and more philosophic point of view, it will be seen that we find within ourselves the idea that every fact, every phenomenon, is an effect of a preceding, and in its turn the cause of a following phenomenon, for it is primarily within ourselves that we follow the succession and connection of our states of consciousness.[1] This causal principle, which was first formulated by Leibnitz as the "principle of sufficient reason," is one of the most general logical principles upon which scientific knowledge rests.[2] It assumes, however, two different forms, according as we apply it to direct or indirect experience. The first, which is the psychological form, is also the most primitive; the second is obtained by means of a process of abstraction. In the case of psychical causality, which we directly perceive within our consciousness, we have a series of states of consciousness related to each other as cause to effect and composed of various elements — presentations, feelings, impulses. It is not possible to doubt the existence of this causal chain of psychical processes, for both experience and observation unmistakably declare that every fact of our consciousness, whether it be a presentation or a feeling, an emotion or an act of volition, is always connected with a preceding fact by which it is determined. The question whether mental facts are completely autonomous (one might even say autochthonous) or whether they are, like all natural phenomena, determined by other facts, is one of the most important, not only in Psychology, but also in philosophy. The question of "free will" with respect to our moral actions, so much discussed in ancient and in modern philosophy, is one of the gravest problems concerning the individual and the community, and upon its solution depends our conception of the real character of mental activity as compared with natural phenomena. This question has mostly been treated from erroneous points of view, and is only to be answered by Psychology.

Most writers have identified "determinism" with mechanical necessity, without taking into consideration that psychical facts are determined in quite a different way from physical phenomena, and this confusion of ideas has been the cause of much misunderstanding. The result has been that, on the one hand, it was not possible to be a "determinist" without

---

[1] See, in Sigwart's *Kleine Schriften*, the essay "Der Begriff des Wollens und sein Verhältniss zum Begriff der Ursache" (Series II., 2nd edit. 1889).
[2] See Wundt, Vol. I. of his *Logik*, p. 567 foll.

being accused of wishing to assimilate mental facts to those of matter, and of denying the freedom of conscious action. On the other hand, owing to a distrust of this fatalistic notion of mechanical determinism, many resorted to the opposite extreme, maintaining that the phenomena of consciousness (conceived of usually from the spiritualistic point of view as "phenomena," or manifestations of an inner substance) are not determined by other phenomena, but have their root in the recesses of the soul, and rise out of the depth of our substance, so that their origin, their course, and their disappearance are wholly inexplicable to us. At the present time we witness a revival of spiritualism, which, in part following up the ideas of Lotze, endeavours to conceive the whole universe, and therefore even physical phenomena, as freed from all subjection to constant laws. This system, which we think erroneous, tends to destroy the basis upon which modern science is reared.[1] There are also not wanting those who, in assimilating completely the facts of consciousness to natural phenomena, or discovering a perfect parallelism between psychical and cerebral phenomena, hope to arrive somehow at a complete subordination of conscious processes to physical laws. The former, who are few in number, are materialists in the old sense of the word; the latter are the modern self-styled psychophysical materialists.[2] Every age has a special point of view in the consideration of fundamental philosophic questions. Thus half a century ago the two extremes in Psychology were materialism and spiritualism; now the point of view has changed. Experimental Psychology has introduced new views, so that the same degree of divergence is no longer possible and there is a tendency on both sides to come to an agreement. On less debateable ground experimental Psychology has definitely established some fundamental facts, upon which discussion is no longer possible, whereas the metaphysical foundation which underlay both the materialistic and spiritualistic systems prevented them from arriving at any satisfactory conclusion.

Allied to this there is an important question agitating psychologists

---

[1] The most notable philosophers of this school are French, such as Renouvier and Boutroux. See the confutation by Fouillée in his book on the *Mouvement idéaliste et la réaction contre la science positive* and Masci's lectures already quoted on *L' idéalismo indeterminista* (Atti della R. Accad. di Napoli, 1898), especially the second, "L' indeterminismo metafisico e l' indeterminismo critico."

[2] See chap. iv. of the present work, where the theories of these neo-materialists are discussed.

at the present time. On the one hand, the psychophysical materialists, though admitting that primitive psychical elements,
such as sensations, cannot be reduced to a physical fact,
maintain that between the facts of consciousness and
the cerebral phenomena which attend them there is so
close a parallelism that, when we succeed in accurately
determining the latter, we may claim fully to understand
the former. But we have already seen that this is a mistaken
principle, as there can be no comparison between cerebral
phenomena and conscious processes, the former being physical
and having a value solely as "quantities" ("quantitative values of
magnitude," as Wundt calls them), whereas the latter possess a
value only inasmuch as they express a "quality" ("qualitative
magnitudes of value").[1] The circumstance which has induced
many to believe that it will some day be possible to arrive at an
objective measurement of the relations between the conscious
processes is Weber's and Fechner's discovery of a constant relation
existing between the intensity of external stimuli and that of
corresponding sensations. It is an undeniable fact that this
discovery placed Psychology upon an entirely new footing, and
rendered it possible to investigate experimentally the behaviour
of mental processes in their reciprocal relations. But Weber's law
should be interpreted according to its true bearings, from which
it cannot be inferred that there exists any absolute parallelism
between two totally different orders of phenomena. If the
constant relation existing between stimuli and sensations presents
facts which, at the same time that they are susceptible of objective
measurement, are also of value with regard to psychological
research, that is because sensations are the simplest of psychical
processes, and the qualitative character being less conspicuous in
them than in the more complicated processes, they may be
subjected, up to a certain point, to the quantitative rules of the
physical sciences. Yet even in the case of these simpler phenomena of consciousness there is no absolute parallelism, for every
sensation has a "quality" of its own, which distinguishes it from
other sensations and from the stimulus by which it is determined,
and which is an inner psychical fact not to be explained by, or
reduced to, any form of motion or of mechanical phenomena.

Discussions as to the possibility of measuring mental processes.

---

[1] The contrary error is committed by the spiritualists (pure philosophers most of them) who endeavour to introduce into the series of quantities qualitative values, and thus to break the chain of mechanical causality. See the above-quoted lecture by Masci, *op. cit.*, p. 37 foll.

Moreover, the "intensity" of the sensation can only be perceived by ourselves, and it is only by means of our own perceptive power that we can distinguish between sensations of varying intensity. The perception of the various qualities and of the differences of intensity of sensations are therefore purely psychical facts. But though it may be possible to establish, in the case of sensations, a certain constant relation between the physical and psychical series, it is impossible to extend it to more complicated mental phenomena, in which, in comparison with the actual stimulus, the preponderating part is played by associative processes, recollections, or abstract processes of the mind. It is thus impossible to point to any constant relation between external stimuli and the higher intellectual processes, or emotions, or acts of free will. The progression of sensations established by Fechner is, moreover, itself a confirmation of the law of relativity, which governs all processes of consciousness, of which more hereafter.

There can, therefore, be no doubt that the processes of consciousness stand to one another in a relation of cause and effect, and that there is a "psychical causality," but that this form of it cannot be subjected to the accurate measurements applicable to physical causality. We cannot, in fact, establish any standard of measurement for ideas, feelings, emotions, and acts of volition; our judgments can never assume, with regard to these facts, an "absolute" form, as in the case of mathematical judgments; they must always be "relative."[1]

A feeling, an emotion, an idea, or an act of volition has no value, except as compared with other feelings, emotions, ideas, or acts of volition. In saying, for example, that an emotion is exciting, the comparison with one which is depressing is evident; and so in the case of emotions of pleasure or pain, of simple and complex ideas. In all these cases there can be no absolute measurement. But in order to properly understand all the characteristics of psychical causation, it is necessary to see how it manifests itself and acts in the various moments of the life of consciousness. Wundt, **Wundt's fundamental psychological principles.** after a long and accurate study of the subject, has succeeded in establishing some fundamental principles of Psychology, which, though differently grouped in his *Logic*, in his *Outlines of Psychology*, and in his other writings, fall into two principal classes, each of which comprises three

[1] Bain also recognises that the difficulty of reducing the mental processes to quantitative measurements will always prevent Psychology from becoming an exact science. See *The Emotions and the Will*, p. 23 foll.

laws.[1] Wundt's two great classes comprise the "laws of relation" (*Beziehungsgesetze*) and the "laws of evolution"; the former being subdivided into laws of psychical "resultants," "relations," and "contrasts," the latter into the laws of "psychical increase," of the "heterogeneity of purposes," and of "evolution by means of contrast." The laws of the first class correspond respectively to each of those of the second in the order in which they are mentioned. We have now to note the great difference which exists between these laws and the laws of physical causality, notwithstanding the apparent points of contact, or, indeed (according to some), the apparent identity between them.

The law of "psychical resultants" is the one which apparently resembles most a physical law—such as is observable, for instance, in the case of "chemical synthesis," when the combination of two substances gives birth to a new one possessing quite different properties. In the same way there is a "psychical synthesis"; for every complicated psychological fact is the result of the combination of several psychical elements, or, in other words, is the result of a synthesis. Since the whole psychic life, in the individual as well as in the species, consists in a stream of psychical facts which steadily increase in complexity, "psychical synthesis" may be said to be the most important factor of consciousness. The forms in which this "synthesis" manifests itself naturally vary according to the degree of complexity of the processes between which it takes place. The simplest form is the elementary combination which occurs between two sensations, and produces a "psychical compound" or "formation." When the synthesis takes place between compounds, it is called "association," which may be simultaneous and successive. Simultaneous association may be, as we have seen, either a simple "assimilation" or a "complication," according as it occurs between compounds of the same kind or of a different kind. Successive association may occur either in the processes of sense ("recognition or cognition"), or in the processes of "memory." We have had frequent occasion to point out that an association is never an exact

Laws of relation. The law of resultants.

---

[1] In his *Logik* (Vol. II., Part II., p. 241 foll.) Wundt distinguishes eight psychological principles—the concept of soul, the principle of psychophysical parallelism, of psychic actuality, of creative synthesis, of intensification by contrast, of the analysis of relation, the fundamental law of psychical causality, and the concept of psychical community. In the *Philosophische Studien* (Vol. X., Part I., 1894, p. 101 foll.) he only distinguishes three general principles —that of the pure actuality of psychic facts, that of the creative synthesis, and that of the analysis of relation.

reproduction of a past presentation or idea, but is in all cases a mixture of elements belonging to a past and to a present psychical compound. As such, association necessarily resolves itself into a synthetic act, giving birth consequently to a novel fact, different from those which have gone before. It is here that those who desire to reduce psychical to physical causality, or (like the positivists) to a copy of the latter, find themselves at fault in explaining the action of consciousness, for even the simplest psychical combination which occurs between two sensations cannot be explained without admitting a special form of causality for the processes of consciousness. Why does consciousness make a "selection" from the mass of physical impressions which affect it, and also from the elements of past presentations, in order to make up new ones? Why has each individual consciousness a method of its own for making this selection?[1] The difference of sensibility, and consequently of "reactivity," of sense-impressions in different individuals is not sufficient to explain this originality of consciousness, for amongst the multitude of received impressions every one makes a selection and a synthesis according to his own special method, almost entirely independent of external conditions. This originality of individual consciousness shows itself most clearly in the complex productions of science and art, which are the highest expression of individual "psychical synthesis," and consist in the elaboration and combination of a great number of physical or concrete elements in the case of artistic productions, and of abstract elements in the case of scientific productions. Nevertheless, this aptitude for original creation, the rudiments of which may be possessed by any one, and which reaches its acme in the artistic, scientific, social, and religious creations of the man of genius, has its origin in the power which all beings endowed with consciousness have in common to combine several psychical elements into new compounds. It is this which gives its importance to experimental Psychology (which deals mostly with the simpler psychical manifestations), for the explanation of what is meant by psychical causality. Those who hope, like the materialists, or fear, like the spiritualists, that experimental Psychology will prove an ally of theories which endeavour to reduce the processes of consciousness to the laws of mechanical causation can perceive that it accentuates, on the contrary, the originality and spontaneity of those processes. We find, for example,

[1] See James, *Principles of Psychology*, Vol. I., p. 225 foll., already quoted.

that space-presentations are the result of different (tactile or visual) sensations, but that they also possess properties which these have not. It is thus seen that the formation of these presentations, which are certainly the simplest and most primitive, cannot be otherwise explained except by the action of the synthetic power of consciousness, the explanation given by some (Spencer, for instance) that it takes place owing to a double association itself requiring an explanation. Psychophysical materialists can only attempt to explain the formation of these presentations by having resort to the hypothesis (not substantiated either by observation or experiment) that sensations have an inherent " spatial " property, just as they possess a certain quality and degree of intensity.

The same may be said, and with greater reason, of time-presentations, which contain also elements of feeling which we know are entirely subjective. The old and simple theory that space- and time-presentations are a copy of the external relations of objects can no longer be entertained, seeing that the properties of time and space are not inherent in the primitive psychical elements, but are the result of their combination.

The fundamental difference between psychical and chemical synthesis is that the properties belonging to a chemical compound are assumed to be discoverable in the elements, so that the result is equal to the sum-total of the properties of the several elements, which remain comparatively independent of each other, like the parts of a sum. There is consequently nothing new and unforeseen in the final result, the properties of which were pre-existent in its elements, the difference between them being only one of quantity.[1] As chemical combinations, moreover, may be ultimately reduced to the general laws of mechanics, the members in any causal equation are assumed to be magnitudes or functions of magnitudes of the same kind, and to be mathematically deducible from them.[2] In the case of these equations, however, we have only quantitative values, the quality of the various phenomena having but a secondary importance for the

---

[1] The objection might be made that the chemical compounds, which are the result of a chemical synthesis, possess not only a " quantitative " but also a " qualitative " difference. But quality is not here the proper term if the quality is considered as inherent in matter. It is, on the contrary, a property which we ourselves attribute to it, seeing that " quality " is a psychological fact which depends upon the impression which the quantitative physical energies produce upon our senses.

[2] See Wundt, *Philosophische Studien*, Vol. XII., Part I., p. 216; *Logik*, Vol. II., pp. 269 and 270.

physicist or naturalist. This principle, which mechanical science establishes in its general forms, is assumed to hold also in the most complex natural phenomena, such as biological phenomena. The fact that these have not yet been reduced to the general laws of dynamics is not due to any inherent obstacle in the phenomena themselves, but to the insufficiency of the means of research at our disposal.

This law of psychical resultants is observable in all the domains of mental life. Thus, setting aside the simpler cases of space- and time-perceptions, which require a finer analysis and consequently a more highly developed power of abstraction, it is easily understood how, in the case of emotions, even a very small variation of the feelings which compose them may give rise to completely different results. In the same way a novel idea which is introduced into a series of other ideas may completely change their course and give rise to entirely new ones, the elements of which, however, existed in the former. The clearest example of such psychical synthesis is to be found in the case of scientific or artistic productions. A poetic fancy, a painting, a melody, an architectural outline, or an original scientific idea are indeed composed of elements contained in other presentations or ideas which the artist or the scientist already possesses; but in the shape they have assumed, after a synthetical associative process, they are entirely new—they are, in fact, creations which present themselves at times in the character of revelations, so suddenly do they dawn upon the mind. Numerous examples may be adduced of the constant correspondence between forms of mental processes of different complexity; but, in order to be more easily understood, we shall merely quote those which refer to simultaneous associations occurring between present and recollected images. This kind of association is one of the most evident forms of "psychical synthesis." It can, as we have seen, take the form either of "association" or of "complication," according as the association occurs between elements of the same kind or of different kinds. The same process is exemplified in numberless cases of intellectual and moral facts. The impressions of all sorts which we receive from the physical and social environment in which we are living, whether moral, æsthetic, religious, or intellectual, produce different effects according to our state of mind. If we happen to be in a state of mind made up of ideas and feelings possessing an affinity with the impression we have received, the latter is immediately accepted with enthusiasm, amplified, beautified, enlarged—in other words, a synthesis immediately takes place, of which we are not even always aware. If, on the other hand, we happen to be in a contrary disposition of mind, the same impression leaves us unmoved, and may not even be apperceived by us. The history of politics and art can furnish us with numerous examples of this. It explains the wherefore of certain ideas, of certain books, of certain works of art, the reason of the existence of certain men in a given moment of history, and why, that moment past, they no longer retain their influence. When they make their appearance, public feeling happens to be favourable and collective opinion is in unison with their individual ideas; whereas subsequently this harmony may have disappeared, and in that case the individual manifestation remains isolated and of no account. The public always adds something to the man or the work of art, or to the idea which happens to correspond with its tastes and tendencies, endowing them with qualities which only exist in its imagination. The success of an idea or of a work of art depends, therefore, on its correspondence with the ideas and tastes of the community, which may show themselves immediately or after a lapse of time. Thus it has often happened that ideas and artistic creations have remained for a long time unappreciated, acquiring only later a hold upon the public consciousness. Social consciousness, as well as individual consciousness, is thus always the product of a synthesis, of a merging of actual excitations and of the images and ideas previously possessed. Round the elements, which are the product of real sensations, there forms itself, so to speak, a fringe of subjective elements.

"Psychical synthesis" is therefore distinguishable from physical in that it is "creative," as Wundt calls it—a principle of fundamental importance, as it explains the difference between the phenomena of nature and moral facts. We shall come upon it again when we treat of the laws of psychological evolution.[1]

The other psychological law we have quoted is the law of "psychical relations,"[2] which may be called an integration of the preceding one. The law of creative synthesis, in fact, refers to

---

[1] See, concerning the principle of "creative synthesis," Tönnies in his paper "La synthèse créatrice," in the first volume of the *Bibliothèque du congrès international de philosophie* (Paris, Colin, 1900), pp. 415—434. The author studies the action of this law in the progressive evolution of philosophic thought.

[2] Wundt, *Outlines of Psychology*, p. 323 foll.

the mode of formation of a single psychical process, whereas the other regards the relations which exist between the various elements of a process. Thus, whilst it is an integration of the law of psychical "resultants," it is also its natural counterpart, for the latter concerns the synthetic processes of consciousness—that is, those processes by means of which compounds are formed out of existing psychical elements; whereas the law of "relativity" concerns the analytical processes of consciousness, by means of which the various psychical elements are examined one by one, and, as it were, momentarily isolated from the compound to which they belong. Like the synthetic process, the analytical process plays an essential part in the formation of consciousness. Both correspond exactly to the two constituent factors of consciousness which a contemporary psychologist calls the "unity" and the "multiplicity" of psychic facts, and which Kant called the "form" and the "matter" of conscious life.[1] They are two simultaneous processes, each of which implies the other, for we cannot imagine an analysis without a previous synthesis, nor a synthesis without a previous analysis.[2] How does this law of relativity, which has been noted as regards the sum-total of psychic facts, but has been always neglected with regard to each separate moment of psychic life, manifest itself?

The law of relations.

Analysis is one of the primary functions of consciousness, for the latter has always before it a content of various facts and processes, perceptions, recollections, associations, and so forth, amongst which it is constantly called upon to make a choice. How does this choice take place? It is here that the fundamentally spontaneous character of consciousness shows itself. Every act of consciousness is an act of volition, or, better still, of apperception—that is, an act by means of which consciousness fastens upon a given part of its contents, to the momentary or partial exclusion of the others. This is the root of the analytical process of consciousness, which becomes clearer and better defined as the mental life becomes more complex, and reaches the highest degree of clearness in the logical processes of thought. These processes manifest themselves in those acts of comparison and relation which by some are considered to lie at the very foundation of mental life, whereas they are in reality to be met with only when

[1] Höffding, *Outlines of Psychology*, p. 48 foll.
[2] These are the laws which English psychologists (Sully, James, etc.) call "discrimination" (analysis) and "assimilation" (synthesis.)

the latter has attained a high degree of development. The faculty of discovering the identity and difference of external phenomena is the basis of all logical operations, and consequently of all knowledge.[1] The relation, which we establish between two facts of our consciousness, implies therefore a certain degree of reflection upon those facts themselves. When the relation takes place between two successive states of consciousness, it assumes a different character from that which it has between simultaneous contents. As all these states are connected, it follows that they are to be measured, not only by the impression which causes them, but also by the preceding psychic fact with which they are related. This relation between successive psychic facts was accurately determined, as regards sensations, by Fechner with his famous "Weber's Law." The working of this law is more noticeable, though not so accurately determinable, in the higher and more complex forms of psychic life, so that the most notable feature of moral facts is commonly supposed to be that of "relativity," as opposed to the character of absolute reality pertaining to natural phenomena. It is this law of "relativity," which, whilst lending to the processes of consciousness a certain regularity and constancy, forms, on the other hand, an obstacle to the recognition of Psychology and moral and philosophic studies in general as sciences, for many think that there can be no science without a foundation of data possessing an absolute and objective value. It is this consideration which impels psychophysical materialists to attempt to measure the facts of consciousness with the quantitative standards of physical forces. It is certain that the moral sciences cannot give us the same degree of accuracy and certainty as the physical sciences; but between this absolute scientific rigour and the opposite extreme of complete relativity and subjectivity the margin is wide, and it may be possible to reconcile a certain precision of research with the peculiar character of the psychical processes. It is, nevertheless, undeniable that the value of any particular moral fact, especially of those in which the subjective element of feeling predominates, is in a high degree relative. A thing, an event, may on one occasion produce in us a pleasurable emotion, and in other circumstances

---

[1] James rightly says, concerning the principle of "conception" (*The Principles of Psychology*, Vol. I., p. 460): "Without the psychological sense of identity, sameness might rain down upon us from the outer world for ever and we be none the wiser. With the psychological sense, on the other hand, the outer world might be an unbroken flux, and yet we should perceive a repeated experience."

leave us quite unmoved, or even cause us pain ; an object we once desired intensely may subsequently appear of no value, and we may, on the other hand, wish very much for that which a short time ago we held as of no account. Moreover, as every individual has a psychical content of his own, made up of the experiences he has had, of the "facts he has lived through," and of his own individual character, every new impression may produce a different effect according to the different individuals upon which it acts, owing to the more or less complicated psychic processes it gives rise to through association. It is this fact which induces many to believe that both as regards moral and æsthetic appreciations every individual has in himself a subjective rule of his own, and that, therefore, with regard to such facts we can never arrive at any reliable judgments which hold good for all men and all ages. This opinion is, however, losing ground even amongst those who are unacquainted with the most recent results in Psychology and the moral sciences, while in scientific circles very different ideas are finding favour.

The law of "relativity" is closely connected with the last of the laws of psychical relations, which is that of "contrast." This law refers also to the relation between various psychical contents, but it refers more especially to the subjective part of consciousness, whereas the law of "relativity" particularly concerns the objective and cognitive elements. It is a well-known fact that feelings act always by contrast, so that when they have arrived at a certain point in one direction they tend subsequently to pass to the opposite extreme, the different forms of feelings, such as pleasure and pain, tension and relief, excitement and depression, being correlative states. Whereas the intensity of sensations may increase up to the extreme degree of sensibility, beyond which no further sensation is perceptible, the intensity of a pleasurable feeling is not always on the same level as the force of the sensations which gives rise to it, but, arrived at a certain limit, variable according to the quality of the feeling, it changes suddenly into the opposite feeling of pain.[1] As feeling constitutes the inmost part of the psychic life, and has a direct effect upon our actions, whereas cognition has only an indirect effect, it is clear that the principle of "contrast" is exceedingly important, both in the life of the individual and in general history. The effect of these psychic contrasts is noticeable at every stage of conscious life, from the simplest to the most complex. Thus it is a fact commonly

The law of contrasts.

[1] Wundt, *Outlines of Psychology*, p. 31.

observed and carefully noted by contemporary psychologists, following Bain's example, that pleasure and pain, or any other form of feeling, vary greatly in intensity, according to the state of mind in which we happen to be, and that "contrast" is the most essential condition for throwing into relief a feeling of any kind.[1] Thus pleasure will be all the greater when it follows upon pain, whereas if it succeeds a more intense pleasure, it loses a great deal of its intensity. As Dante says:

> . . . Nessun maggior dolore
> Che ricordarsi del tempo felice nella miseria,

present misery being intensified by the recollection of the past happiness.

As feelings and acts of volition are closely interwoven with sensations, presentations, and ideas—or, in other words, with the intellectual and cognitive side of consciousness—it is certain that the law of contrast exercises an influence also upon the latter. This explains how we may at times turn particular attention to objects which we previously neglected. The new direction taken by our mind is not always due to associative processes, being, on the contrary, often the effect of a reaction against ideas or facts which had at first occupied us exclusively, and which had subsequently caused a feeling of boredom, rendering necessary something different by way of contrast. Attention is an act of will, and is always directly determined and attended by a feeling. This principle of contrast has given rise to the widespread belief that it is impossible to find any law governing the evolution of the phenomena of consciousness, but this extreme opinion is now giving way to ideas more consonant with the exigencies of modern science.

The laws of "resultants," of "relativity," and of "contrast" are therefore, according to Wundt, the laws of "psychical relations." **Laws of evolution.** They lie at the root of other laws, which may be considered as applications of them to psychical facts of wider range, and which may be called the "psychological laws development."[2] Just as individual Psychology is more adapted to studying the former, the latter are more particularly the object of the Psychology of peoples, and have therefore a more direct bearing upon moral and æsthetical problems.

[1] See the fine chapter on the value of the law of relativity as regards feeling in Höffding, *op. cit.*, p. 275 foll.
[2] See Wundt, *op. cit.*, p. 325 foll.

A deduction from the law of "resultants" is to be found in the psychological principle of the "increase of psychic energy." This law, which was first established by Wundt, marks the most fundamental difference between physical and psychical energy, and is founded on a survey of the whole intellectual and moral history of man. Whilst the physical world is formed of an aggregate of energies, which vary in form but not in quantity, and can be reduced to the invariable substratum of "matter" which underlies it; the moral world, on the contrary, is, so to speak, in continual formation.[1] We have seen that every psychic fact is in itself a new fact, formed of pre-existing elements differently combined. Physical phenomena are best studied by analysing them into their first elements; the latter once known, the complex phenomena resulting from them are also necessarily understood; in the case of conscious processes, on the contrary, an essential requisite is to understand the "manner" of their combination and formation, seeing that out of the various combinations entirely new properties come into being which did not belong to the elements as such. A confirmation of this law is to be found in the transformations brought about by man in his physical environment. The varied uses to which he applies the natural energies, which have existed since the universe came into existence, is nothing but the result of the continual progress of the human mind, adding continually new ideas and feelings and actions to the ideas, feelings, and actions of preceding generations. Whereas there is no justification for saying that a physical energy is "new" merely because we were not acquainted with it, every "new idea" is rightly described as such, because it really constitutes a novel fact which is added to pre-existing ones. In the former case the only novelty consists in the idea which led to its discovery. Therefore, while the physical world presents an immutable rigidity in all its mechanism, the moral world presents a continual increase of energy.

This concept of "energy" in the psychical sense requires however, an explanation, for it may lead to fallacious analogies with physical energy. It is true that the notion of "psychical" energy is taken from that of physical energy; for it seems well adapted to indicate an aggregate of connected facts producing important effects in various directions. But the analogy between

[1] It is natural that this law should have been studied especially by German philosophy, which has devoted more attention than English to the consideration of the laws of the moral world.

these two forms of energy is only apparent, for they have in reality little or nothing in common, the one being a material and quantitative phenomenon, and the other a series of conscious qualitative processes. In speaking, therefore, of "psychical energy," it must be borne in mind that the term is used only to indicate briefly the aggregate of psychical processes, and not that it is comparable with material energy, still less (as the materialists believe) that it is a form of the latter. Nor is it to be supposed (with the spiritualists) that the term refers to a fixed psychical substratum, or spiritual "substance" which remains immutable through the continual changing of conscious processes.[1] In conclusion, it ought to be noted that the "increase of psychical energy" is merely to be taken as meaning that every process of consciousness, whether in the individual or in history, is to be considered as the product of a "new" synthesis, and therefore as a new fact or "event." The Germans make use of a felicitous expression to indicate a moral fact as distinguished from natural phenomena—viz. *Erlebniss*, or that which has been lived through by the individual, in contrast to physical facts, which are *Gegenstände*, or "objects." The former, when they have once disappeared, never return in the same form; and this, which we have already noted with regard to the psychical processes of the individual, holds good also in history, where a series of events may bear a resemblance to other events, but contains always a greater or lesser number of different elements.

These considerations lead to various reflections which prove the confusion of existing ideas with regard to the evolution of moral facts. Thus, whilst on the one hand much stress is laid upon the instability of conscious processes, individual and collective, and the conclusion drawn that they cannot be subject to any law, on the other hand it is believed by many that history presents a series of recurrences, in which the same facts, ideas, and passions repeat themselves, and that there is, therefore, nothing new under the sun. It is necessary, therefore, that science should investigate the question of the relative amount of truth contained in each of these opinions. The theory of "historical recurrence" cannot, however, be properly investigated until we shall have had occasion to speak of the law of "contrast in psychical evolution," which, in a certain manner, completes the law of "increase of energy." We can, nevertheless, even

[1] See Jodl, *Lehrbuch der Psychologie*, p. 88.

now note some of the arguments in favour of and against that theory.[1]

It is a fact that in political history, in the history of social and religious institutions, of literature and art, and in that of science and philosophy, periods occur now and then the circumstances of which are so similar to those of preceding periods as to induce the belief that they are repetitions. Savants, historians, and philologists, who are generally the most convinced upholders of the theory that *nihil sub sole novi*, are fond of making these comparisons and of noting the points in common between different historical, social, or literary periods; and they often succeed in making them appear worthy of serious consideration. Nevertheless, an unbiassed examination will prove that such comparisons are mostly superficial, and fail to penetrate to the spirit which animates the historical or artistic phenomena which they happen to have under consideration. Language itself, which preserves for us the most exact record of past events, is often a cause of error; for the words which compose it, though apparently unchanged as to their external form, may, in the course of time, have become radically changed as to their inner meaning and psychological content, whilst of course the same phonetic form, passing from one language to another, may have assumed an entirely new sense.[2] Language here resembles social institutions, which may, especially amongst certain peoples, preserve their original outward forms, while the spirit that animates them is entirely transformed.[3] What has been said of language holds also of the other means of expression used by man, such as monuments, works of art, and so forth, of which the historical interpretation is even more difficult. Thus, when in historical memoirs we come across phrases similar to those with which we are in the habit of expressing certain ideas and feelings, we are easily led to attribute to them a meaning approaching much closer to the one with which we are familiar than to that which they originally bore.

Psychological interpretation, which should constitute the highest part of historical and philological research, is consequently very

---

[1] In Italy this theory was formulated by Giuseppe Ferrari in his work *La teoria dei periodi politici* (1874). See C. Cantoni, *G. Ferrari* (1878).

[2] See Paul, *Principien der Sprachgeschichte* (2nd edit. 1886), already quoted.

[3] It is well known how the English people are tenacious of the traditional external forms of their public life, whereas its spirit is continually being renewed.

difficult, and this difficulty not unfrequently gives rise to superficial or inexact historical comparisons, though the slightest consideration will enable us to see the extreme improbability of the same circumstances repeating themselves in politics or in the history of civilisation. For science, history and society are two abstract notions which serve to indicate an aggregate of human events or a more or less numerous conglomeration of individuals living together and related in certain ways to one another. In reality, however, we only have individuals and facts produced by individuals alone; so that all the phenomena which go by the name of historical or social phenomena are really nothing but psychical manifestations of individuals. Now, if we consider how consciousness is constituted, we shall easily be convinced that it is never to be found exactly alike in different individuals, for its component factors are highly complex, and every individual has his own psychical aptitudes which differentiate him more or less profoundly from other individuals. And if this is the case with individuals living in the same epoch and belonging to a certain form of society, the differences will be all the greater in individuals belonging to different periods and different social conditions. For, besides the primitive, original energy to be found in every individual, there are other elements connected with the environment in which he lives which vary naturally from age to age.

The objection might perhaps be made that this is a vicious circle; for if individuals vary with changing historical and social conditions, and, on the other hand, these conditions are said to be ultimately produced by the individuals, no proof is afforded thereby that these conditions must necessarily be subject to change. This objection, however, is easily answered. Society being composed of individuals, the latter originate conditions which must necessarily react not only upon the individuals of a given period, but also upon those who come after, so that as mankind progresses, intellectual and moral conditions become more complex, and the repetition of a given fact more difficult. Thus if we compare, for example, England of to-day with the Roman Empire, the analogy is very imperfect, for the state of culture and the character of mind of the English people are entirely different from those of the ancient Romans. The same may be said of the analogies that are sometimes pointed out between the present social movement and the origin of Christianity; or between the so-called anti-materialistic, or idealistic, reaction and the clerical and legitimist reaction of the beginning of the nineteenth century. These are all very superficial comparisons, which do not go beyond certain formal and external resemblances. If we examine the consciousness of an individual of the present day, we find a number of elements which either did not exist at all in the consciousness of one living a century ago, or only existed potentially. Scientific progress and the continual evolution of moral tendencies and of the less important factors which concern individuals forming a community, react upon the individuals, and are the reason why every generation is, as to the average of its components, different from its predecessors. It must be noted, moreover, that the continual growth of the general patrimony of ideas, feelings, and experiences renders the individual psychic life more complex, and endows it with a multitude of elements variously associated and combined, and that as a consequence there is an increase of individual differentiation, which is the result of diversity of aptitude to combine and associate those elements. It is notorious, indeed, that where there is less complexity of elements, individual character is also less marked; so that the higher one rises in the organic and consequently in the psychic scale, the more individualities are accentuated. This fact precludes still more effectively the probability that an aggregate of historical and social phenomena will repeat itself with any degree of approximation to the form in which it first appeared. The theory of recurrence is the product of an entirely intellectualistic point of view, which assigns very little importance to the subjective elements of consciousness, considering psychical processes merely in the light of natural phenomena, of which the distinctive mark is the equivalence of energy. But the Psychology of to-day proves that even the simplest psychical compounds never present themselves twice in the same way, but are in all cases the product of a new synthesis. *A fortiori* may this be said of the complicated processes represented by historical and social facts.

Every manifestation of the individual and of the community is therefore a novel fact, which increases the number of facts which have occurred.[1] The term "increase of psychic energy" must not lead one to suppose that this increase is absolute and continual, for it is necessary to bear in mind the difficulties it encounters during the evolution of consciousness. A continual increase of psychical energy would imply a mental life proceeding in a continual chain

[1] Wundt, in his *Ethik*, § 424 (Eng. tr., Vol. II., p. 181), ably confutes the theory of evolutionist utilitarianism, according to which we inherit moral presentations together with the dispositions of the nervous system.

without interruptions, so that all new facts form an addition to existing consciousness. But we have seen that the formation of new psychic processes involves the dissection of previous processes into their elements and their disappearance from consciousness. This disappearance of psychical facts from consciousness is what gives to the concept of psychical increase a very relative character. What we have, therefore, is not an increasing series of original ideas, feelings, and acts of volition, but mainly new combinations of old elements. This is the sense in which the gradual increase of psychic life is to be understood. Thus, when a novel idea is acquired by science, it remains subject to continual transformations, and may become associated with other elements, and consequently produce new ideas in its turn; but the combinations are always between psychic elements, or compounds, so that the novelty is limited in all cases to a certain number of the former. Hence the circumstance observable in the individual as well as in the history of humanity, which is in marked contrast to the originality of individual, mental processes—viz. that even if a man be endowed with exceptional abilities, his work always contains a number of psychic elements and compounds, which existed before him and had already been elaborated and combined in the same way by others. Both in history and in the evolution of the individual there takes place a continual arrangement and rearrangement of the elements of culture. Though a given epoch continues, on the whole, the work of the preceding one, it often happens that many elements of the latter are lost, and that an apparent retrogression occurs. This was the case, for instance, in the passage from Antiquity to the Middle Ages. These transition periods, however, are always very slowly evolved, and are not noticed as such at the time; it is only in the eyes of posterity that there seems to have occurred an abrupt change, to which they assign a given date. In the aggregate, however, the sum-total of ideas and tendencies may be considered to represent a real progress. On the other hand, facts, once divided into their elements, may never be combined again except in quite a different form, nor is it ever possible to reconstruct a harmonious concourse of circumstances exactly as it has been.[1] Thus, the Middle Ages compared to Antiquity mark an undoubted progress, owing to such elements as the broader feeling of humanity and of social

---

[1] Carducci has a fine essay on the subject as applied to the history of letters, "Sullo svolgimento della letteratura nazionale" (see *Opere di G. Carducci: Discorsi storici e letterari*").

equality, and the participation of a greater number of peoples in political life, which either did not previously exist or did not make themselves felt. From several other points of view, on the other hand, the Middle Ages lay far behind Antiquity, witness, for instance, the falling off in serenity and freedom of thought, and in the artistic sense. " Indefinite" progress, therefore, as the humanists of the eighteenth and nineteenth centuries imagined it, must be understood with these restrictions. The evolution of civilisation follows a most irregular course, with interruptions, apparent retrogressions, and sudden reactions, which are all caused by the continual work of elaboration, combination of existing elements, formation of new facts, etc., the whole constituting what is properly termed "progress." As the difficulties which it has to surmount increase, the more numerous and complex are the facts to be collected and combined.

One of the most important factors in the progress of civilisation is indicated by the second law of evolution, corresponding to that of relativity—*i.e.* the law of the "heterogony of ends." This law, which is of the greatest psychological and ethical importance, is closely connected not only with that of relativity, but also necessarily with that of " psychical resultants." Every creative synthesis brings about a change in the relations between its constituent elements, for it produces a new fact not formerly contained in the latter which naturally becomes related to those primitive components. The relations between the various contents of a psychical process are consequently continually changing. It is this which constitutes the " heterogony of ends or purposes." As every psychical content consists of subjective and objective elements—that is, of feelings and impulses and of presentations—the latter constitute the " purpose " or object towards which the former are directed. This " purpose " is not always clear to consciousness. For example, in the case of the simple associations of presentations, or of certain particular feelings, we do not distinguish the motive or purpose of mental action. Yet such ultimate purpose always exists. In many instances it rises out of the relations of the psychical elements, in which case the relation of the several constituents of the presentation is that of a correlated compound of means, for which the product of the connection appears as the end.[1] Just as new

The law of "heterogony of ends."

---

[1] Wundt, *Outlines of Psychology*, p. 326 foll.; *Ethik*, § 265 foll. (Eng. tr., Vol. I., p. 265 foll.). The principle of heterogony of ends is amply expounded in the latter work.

psychic facts are always the product of a new synthesis, so there are continually appearing new purposes, which are formed in the same way as resultants—*i.e.* by means of the addition of new elements to those which existed before. A fact, therefore, which in a given psychical combination had only a secondary importance as a means, may under different circumstances become itself an end.

This law, which may appear abstruse when formulated in psychological terms, is very simple if expressed in ordinary language. It may, for instance, be enunciated as follows : the end does not always produce the means, but the means oftener originate the end. Any object, idea, or fact, which may be of little or no importance for our present purposes, may subsequently become the object upon which, owing to the fact that new circumstances have wrought a change in our state of mind, we concentrate all our desires and efforts. We cannot, in the region of moral facts, keep a given end in view without ever deviating from it. They are not like physical phenomena, in which we can always (in theory) foresee with certainty the final effects of a given cause ; with moral, æsthetic, historical, and psychical facts in general we foresee, on the contrary, only the general lines of their future development, and nothing more. Who can pretend to have accomplished any complicated series of actions according to a pre-established plan in which all these actions were present and fixed beforehand ?

The manner in which our actions are developed and connected is oftenest fortuitous, very different effects being attributed to the same cause, according to circumstances which we are seldom in a position to foresee or to control. Our actions are severally inspired by a certain purpose, which we endeavour to effect. But in order to do so we have to employ a series of means, and must therefore accomplish a series of psychic processes, seeing that it is as such that means as well as the presentation of the end in view appear. These processes are so many psychic syntheses, and it constantly occurs that other presentations of new purposes arise out of these syntheses, so that the primitive object is modified or even changed entirely.[1] In the case of a politician, an artist, a scientist, or a merchant, of all those, in fact, who aim at a given end, this substitution or modification of purpose takes place very frequently. Indeed, given a certain kind of psychic process, it may be said to occur always, though in a different

[1] Wundt, *Ethik*, § 446—447. See also Fouillée, *L'évolution des idées forces*, Introduction, p. lxxxvi. foll.

measure according to the greater or less complexity of the volitional acts. Thus in the evolution of the mental life in general, and especially of the moral life, there occurs a continual differentiation of purposes, which renders its study extremely complicated.

This law of the heterogony of ends, which is accepted by all who consider that ethics should be founded upon psychological, and not purely biological principles, affords also a solution of the vexed question of free-will. Though every one of our moral actions is determined by another moral action, it cannot be said that they are predetermined for all time, and that given a particular moral cause or motive, certain effects must necessarily and inevitably follow. "In order to prove," says Alfred Fouillée,[1] "that the future can neither be deduced from nor limited by the past, we may quote the law formulated by Wundt, which is of the greatest importance both as regards ethics and metaphysics: the "unforeseen" and "heterogonous" character of real effects as contrasted with expected effects. This is what Wundt calls the "law of heterogony" as applied to acts of volition and their results. Every voluntary act produces consequences which are more or less in excess of the motives which have caused it. A man who has acted purely in accordance with his own personal ambition may bring about results which are useful not only to himself but to his country; whilst another who has thought to render service to his country may do quite the contrary. Hence the law, recognised also by Schopenhauer and Hartmann, that the ultimate result of our actions has never in any case been the motive which has actuated them. Our power of prevision being so limited, we have no right to assign any limit to evolution. Moreover, seeing that neither the future effects of moral facts can be "deduced" from the causes with which they are connected, nor the ultimate effects of our volitional actions from the immediate effects, the result is a twofold character of indefiniteness in the future as compared with the present, which is actually known. This indeterminateness renders possible an intellectual and moral progress which no one can anticipate. Briefly, neither the annihilation nor the limitation of the world's moral progress can be the object of demonstration or even of clear conception. From which it follows that intellectual perfectibility will be, in one shape or the other, always indefinite, the fecundity of the mental universe, the world of ideas, being for us illimitable."

[1] *Ibid.*

Man is thus intellectually and morally free in the sense that no one can set a limit to, nor establish a precise direction for, his actions; nor again, assuming that these actions are all caused by motives, is there anything to prevent his forming to himself new ones, with which to regulate his acts in the future. The formation of motives is indeed the most important fact of moral education, and no deterministic or materialistic theory will ever be able to prove that (subject to certain limitations, which are set by the wills of other individuals, the physical environment, individual physiological conditions, and other circumstances) the individual is not free to propose to himself certain ends, which, it is to be observed, are themselves the outcome of psychological syntheses. The only way to solve the question of "free will" is therefore to make a sharp distinction between mechanical and psychical causality, and to have a clear notion of the nature and limits of the latter.[1]

The last of the laws of psychical evolution is the one which corresponds to the law of "psychical contrast," and which Wundt calls the law of "evolution by means of contrast."[2] It has reference especially to feelings, and consequently to the volitional processes which issue directly from them, seeing that those psychical facts, which are mainly subjective in character, depend chiefly upon contrast. This law is also an application of the corresponding psychical law of relativity to historical and social phenomena. When our actions are dominated by certain motives and we endeavour to attain a particular end, the prolonged effort may gradually change the feelings which accompany our actions in such a way as to cause us to do something of a totally different character from what we have been doing hitherto. As, however, this law is connected with the laws of the increase of psychical energy and of the heterogony of ends, it is not to be supposed that it has an unconditional value and that it can absolutely govern the development of conscious life. On the contrary, it has a special value only in the case of certain elements of consciousness, seeing that, taken as a whole, the psychic life does not present a succession of contrasts but of similar phases. The law of evolution by contrast, says Wundt, "shows itself in the

The law of "evolution by contrast."

---

[1] See Wundt, *Ethik*, p. 467 foll. As regards the law of heterogony of purposes, see Masci, *Logica*, p. 506 foll., and *Il materialismo psicofisico e la dottrina del parallelismo in psicologia*, p. 126 foll. See the instances brought forward by Tarde in his book *Les lois de l'imitation*, p. 174 foll.

[2] Wundt, *Outlines of Psychology*, p. 327.

mental development of the individual, partly in a purely individual way within shorter periods of time, and partly in certain universal regularities in the relation of various periods of life." Hence it has been often observed that the temperaments which predominate in the various stages of life present certain contrasts. Thus the facile excitability of infancy changes into the sentimental and often melancholy disposition of youth, when impressions are slowly elaborated and tenaciously retained ; and this again changes into the frame of mind of manhood, which is generally prone to quick and energetic resolutions and actions ; finally and by gradual steps passing into that of old age, with its inclination towards contemplative repose. The principle of contrast is, however, more apparent in history and in social life than in the individual, and manifests itself in the sequence of mental tendencies and in the effect they have on social and political evolution, civilisation, and customs. As the principle of the heterogony of purposes has a particular value for ethical life, so evolution by contrast has its main importance in the province of history.[1]

Many examples might be adduced of this succession of historical periods, dominated by contrasting modes of feeling. One which is very well known and is comparatively recent is the period of reaction, monarchical and clerical in politics, romantic in literature, and idealistic in philosophy, which took place at the beginning of the nineteenth century, against the Jacobinical and Revolutionary ideas, and the classic and academic style of the eighteenth. Another reactionary period which is especially remarkable in the history of philosophy, but which had its effects on art, literature, and politics, is the materialistic and naturalistic reaction which followed upon the period of the great German philosophic systems, and has been called by some the "period of philosophic romanticism." This school has produced in our day an idealistic reaction which is making itself increasingly felt in philosophy, art, politics, and social questions, among those to whom purely materialistic and economic theories are beginning to prove themselves unsatisfactory.

Thus, if we go back along the course of history, we come across frequent examples of such contrasts : the humanistic period which follows upon the Middle Ages, the Middle Ages which follow upon Paganism, and so forth. As Wundt says, these changes do not occur all at once, but go through a gradual preparation, until, having arrived at a certain maturity, they manifest themselves with

[1] Wundt, *loc. cit.* Also *Logik*, Vol. II., chap. ii., p. 282 foll.

such suddenness that superficial observers are induced to believe them to be spontaneously generated, an error closely connected with the other of subdividing history into periods limited by certain dates corresponding to the events which most clearly distinguish one era from another. This law of "psychical contrast" further furnishes an explanation of the limitations of the laws of "increase of psychical energy" and of "indefinite progress." The reactions towards certain ideas noticeable during given historical periods are like stoppages in the continual evolution of history, and are often interpreted as an absolute retrogression, a fact which originated, as we have seen, the theory of "historical recurrences." The law of "psychical contrast," however, as already said, is not to be considered alone, but in connection with that of the "increase of psychical energy" and that of the "heterogony of ends."

Seeing that these principles are mental laws, they cannot possess the same character of precision as physical laws. They may rather be said to be general forms of psychical evolution, and as a natural consequence they are not formulated alike by all contemporary psychologists. An instance of this diversity of nomenclature may be seen in the case of the law of relativity, which Wundt has endeavoured to determine with great precision in its various bearings. Similarly, two contemporary writers, Tarde and Baldwin, assign great importance to the laws of imitation and invention, which in psychical evolution correspond to the biological laws of heredity and of variations. Mankind receives from preceding generations a heritage of ideas, feelings, and impulses, which it preserves and hands on, not by acts of conscious volition, but through imitation, which acts continually upon the mental growth of individuals. This is, in our opinion, only a different way of formulating the law by which the increase of psychic energy finds its limit in the necessity for old forms of consciousness to disappear before new ones come upon the scene. It is therefore a law of limitation. On the other hand, imitation is itself always a relative fact. Absolute psychical imitation is not possible, not even in the form of animal instinct, which is the nearest approach to mechanical repetition.[1] Again, imitation has its contrast in invention, which corresponds to creative synthesis. For invention represents originality, spontaneity, individual variation, and manifests itself, like the creative synthesis, in simple forms of perception and feeling, finding its highest expression in the creations of artistic, scientific, religious, and social genius. Genius, therefore, marks the

[1] See Ardigò, *L' unità della coscienza*, chap. vi., p. 131 foll.

extreme point of psychical evolution, which has its beginning in simple impulses and instinct. Tarde and Baldwin, on the other hand, have some profound and original observations concerning this psychical evolution, which, in conjunction with the laws formulated by Wundt, throw a strong light upon the peculiar character of psychical laws.[1]

[1] See Baldwin's works often quoted above, also Tarde, *Les lois de l'imitation*, etc. The laws of imitation may, in a manner, be considered connected with what Ladd (*Psychology*, p. 664 foll.) calls the "Principle of Solidarity," which expresses the unification and conservation of psychic processes in the individual consciousness.

CHAPTER XI

THE LAWS OF PSYCHOLOGY (Concluded)

OUR survey of the opinions of modern psychologists, such as Bain, Wundt, James, Höffding, Stout, Baldwin, and Ladd, on the meaning of psychological laws, proves conclusively that they all agree upon one point—namely, that to determine and define the true character of conscious life, it is necessary to pay special attention to its inner and subjective aspect, consisting in feeling and volition. Psychology, which was formerly intellectualistic, may now be said to be decidedly "volitionist." The laws of consciousness are substantially the laws of feeling and of volition. Is it possible, one may ask, to find a psychological principle to express the fundamental and typical qualities of this most characteristic portion of consciousness? The attempt to find such a principle may be compared to that made by some mathematical physicists to reduce all mechanical laws to the law of "least action."

On a close examination of the above-mentioned psychological laws, we shall find that they all point to the purposeful character of consciousness. In other words, that which distinguishes them from mechanical principles is that they are always "teleological." This requires explanation. It would be a grave error to believe (as many have done) that in all our individual or social actions we always aim at the ultimate end which those actions are fitted to fulfil. The examples we have adduced in the case of the law of "heterogony of ends" have proved the contrary. Man, together with other conscious beings, has primarily in view the proximate end, which concerns him more closely, his life, like that of conscious beings in general, consisting of a continuous series of these proximate ends. Now, the inner or subjective aspect of this series of ends consists in a series of acts of attention upon which the individual concentrates all his will and his intelligence, but the prime motor of which is feeling. The individual always turns instinctively to that to which feeling attracts him,

[marginal note:] Teleological character of psychological principles.

whatever form or degree this may assume. In this sense we may speak of a psychical law of least action, which has nothing to do with the corresponding physical law, which contemplates only the fundamental fact of mechanical resistance, into which no conscious element enters. Consequently it is a mistake on the part of some psychologists to attempt to reduce this law to the principle of nervous resistance. According to these psychologists, the brain and the nervous system are normally in a state of inertness, and require to be roused by the action of outer stimuli, to which they are naturally inclined to oppose a resistance.[1] This theory is erroneous, because it takes no account of the subjective and spontaneous elements of consciousness. The law of least action, it has been observed, would be, in this sense, purely negative; whereas it is a law of unification and intensification, and at the same time also of limitation of consciousness, for the latter becomes absorbed in a determined object, to the exclusion of all others, except those most closely related to the one which occupies it at the moment.[2] This explains a number of very remarkable facts in the history of thought and of human intercourse. The history of language and of the formation of concepts is a clear proof of it. Mankind all over the world has not indicated the same things by the same terms, because, according to their different mode of feeling, different peoples have given more weight to one element than to another. A similar explanation may be given of the differences of individual and social manners and customs, and of the progressive changes of the various languages, in all of which there is a constant law of economy. The form varies much less than the substance, and the latter may be radically transformed, while the former remains almost the same. The reason is that both the individual and the species follow involuntarily a method consonant with their feelings of repugnance towards any effort not directly connected with the issue at stake.[3] In all cases, in fact, the primary source of intellectual and moral evolution is

---

[1] This idea is, amongst others, upheld by G. Ferrero, "L'inertie mentale et la loi du moindre effort" (*Revue philosophique*, February, 1894); but it was originated by C. Lombroso).

[2] See W. R. Boyce-Gibson's interesting article "The Principle of Least Action as a Psychological Principle" (*Mind*, October, 1900).

[3] See, concerning the law of economy, James, *The Principles of Psychology*, pp. 188, 239—240; and *Psychology*, p. 345; Cornelius, *Psychologie als Erfahrungswissenschaft*, p. 84. It was more amply expounded, though in a somewhat intellectualistic sense, by R. Avenarius, in his *Philosophie als Denken der Welt nach dem Princip des kleinsten Kraftmasses* (Leipsic, 1876).

feeling, governed by the law of least action, which might be more aptly called the law of "greatest advantage."

Now that we have examined the "laws of Psychology," it is natural to ask what value they possess, in what sense they should be understood, and what are their points of contact and similarity with, and also of divergence from, physical laws? It is an indisputable fact that the consideration in which the physical and natural sciences are held in our time has, little by little, brought about the conviction that there is no science but natural science, and that the latter, in its various manifestations of physical, chemical, and biological science, represents the acme of scientific knowledge. This opinion has gained ground, notwithstanding that biology in general and physiology in particular are still very far from having attained that degree of accuracy and certainty which has been reached by pure physics and chemistry. Physiologists, however, exhibit generally an absolute faith in the future result of their researches, so that they often take hypotheses for proven facts, and do not hesitate to explain by means of physiological laws the inmost nature of psychical processes. Nevertheless, if it is desirable for physiologists and histologists in general to observe greater caution in their methods, it cannot be denied that there exists no theoretical difficulty in reducing even the most complex biological phenomena to the same general laws as all other physical phenomena; and though the time for this may still be remote, it is no less to be hoped that the continual progress of physiology and histology may bring this about, and that the notion of the mechanism of life may, from a theoretical proposition become an accepted fact. Briefly, all that constitutes a natural phenomenon, whether it be a physical, or a chemical, or a vital process, is dominated by the same laws of physical energy, and this uniformity of laws is becoming daily more apparent, the whole natural world appearing as a connected whole, governed by fixed and immutable mechanical laws.[1]

It is therefore natural that this marvellous unity of conception attained by natural philosophy should have brought about a widespread conviction that, taking science for certain and demonstrable knowledge, having an absolute value for all men in all ages, no form of science is possible without it. But the nineteenth century

---

[1] This mechanical conception of the physical world is not to be shaken by the attempt of certain contemporary spiritualistic philosophers (such as Boutroux, Renouvier, and others above quoted), who wish per contra to introduce the notion of liberty into physical phenomena.

has seen the rise of new branches of study, which have made themselves independent of the philosophical sciences from which they sprang, and have led to results which are not to be confounded with those of the physical sciences. This has taken place simultaneously with and under the influence of the progress of physical and biological science, and those new sciences, which have come to be added to Philosophy, Art, and Religion, have been termed "moral," or, according to a German expression, which makes the antithesis to the science of nature more apparent, "sciences of the mind" (*Geisteswissenschaften*). It is needless to insist upon the development during the nineteenth century of History, Philology, and the social sciences in general, such as Political Economy, Statistics, Law, and Sociology. All these sciences now form a complete system which is distinct from the natural sciences, principally owing to the fact that their object is not physical phenomena, but the creations of human consciousness, such as history, works of art and literature, social institutions, the production and circulation of wealth, and the principles of jurisprudence.[1] What is the nature of all these branches of study, and how do they differ from the sciences of physical phenomena, of art, philosophy, or religion? For a long time it was not easy to give an answer to this question, owing to the confusion between some of the moral sciences and art or philosophy. A solution appears more possible when we consider the moral sciences in their relation to Psychology, which may be considered the most general and fundamental science of the mind, the others being special forms of it. What, in fact, are the phenomena which form the object of the moral sciences but products of consciousness? And what other science than Psychology studies the products of consciousness? Psychology, therefore, should be to the sciences of the mind's phenomena—*e.g.* history and sociology—what general physics

---

[1] The most complete study of this system of sciences under certain general principles is that of Wundt, in the second part of the second volume of his *Logik*, entitled "Die Logik der Geisteswissenschaften" (1895). In the first edition of this work (1883) the portion dedicated to the moral sciences was much smaller. See also Sigwart, *Logic* (Vol. II., Part III.); and W. Dilthey, *Einleitung in die Geisteswissenschaften* (1883, of which only the first volume has appeared). As regards the social sciences more especially, see Ludwig Stein, *Die Soziale Frage im Lichte der Philosophie* (Stuttgart, 1897), which contains an exhaustive discussion of the character and methods of the social sciences in relation to Psychology. On the development of these sciences, see my paper "Sull odierno sviluppo delle scienze storiche e sociali" (*Rivista Ital. di sociol.*, July, 1898).

or mechanics is to those of nature. This truth was a long time in forcing itself upon philosophy, for, on the one hand, the moral sciences had not yet attained their present degree of development, so that the necessity of a synthesis was not yet felt; and, on the other hand, Psychology has only lately emerged from a state of uncertainty concerning its objects and its methods and the place it ought to occupy in the general system of sciences. Now, however, that our ideas have undergone a change, philosophers and students of the sciences of mind are endeavouring to place the latter upon a sound psychological basis, though it must be remembered that this "psychological" tendency of the moral sciences meets still with no little opposition. The principal argument brought forward against it is that the object of Psychology is the study of the processes of consciousness in the individual, whereas the facts which are studied by the moral sciences generally, and by the historical and social sciences in particular, are manifestations possessing primarily a collective and social character. This argument, however, is of little value in that it neglects that very important branch of Psychology which studies the first manifestations of social consciousness, such as language, myths, manners and customs, æsthetic efforts, etc., and which is a combination of the individual and comparative method. There is, moreover, a circumstance which, however self-evident it may appear, is sometimes lost sight of—viz. that the community is composed of individuals, and can therefore contain no psychical elements which do not exist in the individuals of which it is composed. It may, however, be argued that the same holds good in the case of biological phenomena, which, though made up of the same elements as are found in inorganic phenomena, present, nevertheless, entirely different characteristics. This is indeed the case, but it is also argued that biological phenomena may be reduced to the same laws as chemical and physical phenomena; and in the same way the processes of social consciousness may be traced back to the laws of individual processes. Moreover, whilst physical and chemical phenomena may occur in a simple form, entirely distinct from the complex form they assume in the organism, there exist no purely individual processes of consciousness. Psychical evolution in an individual, considered as severed from all connection with other individuals, is a mere abstraction which has no foundation in fact. Man has always lived in communion with his kind, and his intellectual and moral evolution has always been accomplished, and is still accomplishing itself by means of his binding relations with other human beings. The individual consciousness of to-day is consequently the result of a lengthy social evolution, nor can we even imagine that it could have developed itself, in defiance of all biological necessities, in a state of perfect isolation. The social instinct, moreover, is to be found also in animals, and is one of the strongest in man.

Individual Psychology is therefore the product of an "abstraction," by means of which the student considers the psychical individual, as existing by himself, irrespective of the real conditions of life, and adapts the real contents of consciousness to the requirements of a general scheme. A great part of the contents of our consciousness consists of facts, which come within the domain of the moral sciences, being either social, or historical, or æsthetic, or juridical, or economic. Psychology, by an abstraction, is able to sever these psychical processes from their concrete manifestations and to form them into concepts, such as the concept of logical thought, of emotion, of will, and so forth. It proceeds, in fact, like the science of mechanics, which, taking the concrete forms of the phenomena of matter as a starting-point, arrives at a conception of motion in the abstract. Without the help of such a process of abstraction the moral sciences could never have existed. How could the historian, for instance, study political and civil events by themselves, if he could not make abstraction from all the other social, economic, artistic, religious events, with which they are always connected in real life? By a similar abstraction the political economist considers only economic facts, and so with all the moral sciences.[1]

The objection taken to the psychological school is consequently of little value, resting as it does on the assumption that individual Psychology as a science has for its object concrete facts, distinct from social facts; whereas it is the latter which form its real starting-point. This cuts the ground from all the theories which separate individual Psychology from the sociological study of mankind, and aim at exempting the historical and moral sciences from all dependence on psychological laws, either reducing them to the biological method, or denying them all power to give a causal explanation of the facts which they study, and considering

[1] One of the most pronounced adversaries of the psychological school amongst modern sociologists, is Durkheim. See his book *Les règles de la méthode sociologique* (especially Vol. II., chap. v.). The dependence of sociological upon psychological laws and the importance of abstraction in the scientific study of moral facts is well expounded by Simmel in a paper "Le problème de la sociologie," which appeared in the *Revue de métaphysique* (1894) and other works.

them "sciences of mere fact." Nothing is to be observed in historical and social facts which has not its precise counterpart in individual Psychology, as was illustrated by the complete parallelism which we found to exist between the psychical laws of the individual and those of the community. Thus the argument brought forward by these authors to prove that historical facts cannot be reduced to the laws of Psychology, seeing that they have a character of continual novelty and can never be foreseen, appears to be of little value when we consider that all psychic facts, even the simplest, possess that same character, and that the law of "creative synthesis" and of "invention" rules all the productions of consciousness.[1]

The importance of psychological laws is palpable, for upon them depends the solution of numerous problems of capital importance in life, and they form the basis of the philosophy of the mind—*i.e.* of Ethics, Æsthetics, Law, and Religion. So long as we are unable to give to the philosophy of the mind a foundation of precise law, such as exists for natural philosophy, it cannot be said to form a solid branch of learning, independent of the fluctuations and vicissitudes of individual opinions. It cannot, indeed, be denied that the laws of morality and æsthetics are incapable of demonstration with the exactness and precision of physical and mathematical theorems, and that, owing to this fact, there are many who conclude that they have no objective value, and that each individual can do as he pleases with regard to them, according to the principle that what is convenient is good, and that what pleases is beautiful. After the failure of the attempts of certain philosophers to subject moral facts to the laws of natural causality, many thought themselves justified in being thus sceptical as to the possibility of ever reducing them to any law whatsoever. They consequently denied the possibility of any form of science outside the science of material phenomena and of mathematical abstractions, and gave up the attempt to find a positive foundation for the moral life. Whence the assertion that science does not satisfy the ideal requirements of humanity, and the declaration (made with more or less conviction and sincerity) that religion alone can fulfil this condition.[2] The only possible way of solving this much-

[1] Amongst these authors we must quote Rickert, *Die Grenzen der Natursinnenschaftlichen Begriffsbildung* and *Kulturwissenschaft und Naturwissenschaft*; Windelband, *Geschichte und Naturwissenschaft*; Gumplowicz, Stein. See my criticism upon these theories in "Psychology and History" (*The Monist*, January, 1902).

[2] Concerning the importance of the moral sciences as regards ethical life and

debated question is, first of all, to be clear concerning the meaning of the word "science." If the term be understood to mean physical science alone, there is every reason to say that its laws cannot serve alone to regulate moral life; but if it is used to indicate not only the sciences of nature but those of the mind as well, these reasons fall to the ground. Nevertheless, it is reasonable to ask whether the laws of the mind have a universally recognised value? whether, in regard to moral as in regard to physical phenomena, there exists a consensus of opinion on fundamental questions? This is a serious problem, which deserves a careful answer.

We have seen that psychological laws, whether those of "relation" or of "psychical evolution," are founded upon data obtained by contemporary Psychology. The application of the experimental method, the results of ethical Psychology and of the various moral sciences, the observation of pathological cases, all this has enabled Psychology to formulate with sufficient precision the mode of evolution of conscious processes. The experimental method has, moreover, established, by means of the law of relativity, several almost mathematically accurate relations between the various states of consciousness; and psychological synthesis and analysis have revealed themselves as facts which control the whole conscious life in all its forms. In this way conscious processes have come to be regarded as possessing a physiognomy specially their own, which prevents us from assimilating them to the phenomena of matter. This special character is briefly indicated by the term "qualitative" applied to psychical phenomena, whereas physical phenomena are "quantitative." It is impossible, therefore, to compare those two series of facts, which, though indivisible, follow their own special laws. The processes of consciousness cannot be reduced to quantitative measurements, any more than Weber's law can determine a given sensation as a standard of measurement for other sensations. If this is not possible for sensations, which are all directly produced by external impressions, it is still less possible in the case of feelings and of free and voluntary impulses, which depend in a great measure on a complexity of subjective circumstances.

The excellence of the sciences of nature consists in their "foreseeing" capacity, owing to which they are enabled to establish beforehand, and generally with mathematical precision, the

---

science in general, see Dilthey, *Einleitung in die Geisteswissenschaften*, p. 4, and Wundt, *Logik*, Vol. II., Part II., p. 53.

remotest effects of a physical cause. This is completely wanting in the case of Psychology and of the moral sciences. Thus, whereas the physical sciences can follow a "progressive" method, which consists in deducing the effects which will follow upon a given cause taken as a starting-point, Psychology and the sciences of the mind must content themselves with a "regressive" method, which consists in the contrary process of selecting effects as a starting-point whence to discover the cause.[1] Mill had perceived this "inverted" order of historical and social analysis; but his conclusion was that, when the causal nexus of events has been found by means of that process, it is easy to prove that that particular choice of cause and effect was the only possible and necessary one. This is a mistaken conclusion which was quite natural in 1843, when Mill wrote his *System of Logic*, for at that time modern psychological and moral studies were in their infancy. At the present day it is inadmissible, for enough light has been thrown upon the inner nature of the processes of consciousness to establish the fact that no psychical effect can be foretold from the causes known to be connected with it. Mill's idea had too empirical and provisional a character to form a part of any philosophic system. In accepting the inverse deductive process as the only one possible, he was guided solely by the fact that the causality of moral processes is for the present, owing to their immense complexity, extremely difficult to establish; but he did not exclude the possibility that in a distant future this might be done.[2] The existence of an essential difference can no longer be denied, nor can it be claimed that Psychology and the moral sciences will ever arrive at an exact prevision of the future effects of a psychic fact.

In the case of physical causality we have as a fundamental pre-supposition the quantitative equivalence of phenomena, whatever different forms they may assume. It is for this reason that they cannot be explained except by means of the concept of "matter"—that is, of a permanent substratum, which has no formal determination—a concept which is purely hypothetical and which finds its warrant only in the peculiar character of physical phenomena. In the case of psychical causality, on the contrary, we do not require this hypothetical conception, consciousness being sufficient in itself, insomuch as it possesses an

---

[1] It must be borne in mind, however, that induction is an essential process also in the case of natural sciences.
[2] See Mill's *Logic*, Vol. II., Bk. VI., chap. x.

actual value which has not to be referred to any psychical substance underlying the phenomenon. Consciousness, moreover, is a "qualitative" fact comparable only to facts of its own kind, and not susceptible of the same kind of measurement as physical phenomena. A qualitative, ethical, or æsthetic value can never be measured according to quantitative rules. To entertain so ingenuously materialistic a notion would be quite incompatible with the progress of science and with the modern critical spirit, which refuses to allow the assimilation of two such profoundly different species of phenomena as the natural and the moral.[1] Psychical facts exhibit a form of causality; but the "causes" we here meet with are not mechanical, but "final" causes. When there is an "end" or purpose, there is volition, consciousness, and consequently "liberty." It is therefore absolutely impossible to subject conscious processes to quantitative measurements, and still more impossible to adapt mathematical formulæ to them, except in a purely general way. The forms of "pure magnitude" cannot be applied to psychic processes except in a very limited measure, as auxiliary methods and in an entirely provisional and secondary manner; nor is it possible to build general psychological laws upon them. A great discovery appeared to have been made with Quetelet's so-called law of "large numbers." This, however, really explained nothing, seeing that social phenomena are the product of a great number of individual wills, which cannot in any sense be subjected to mathematical calculations. The "law of large numbers" reduces itself therefore, as others have already noted, to a purely statistical method, very useful in collecting data for Psychology to explain.[2] It is also in vain that the hope is entertained by some,[3] owing to a wrong interpretation of Weber's law, that Psychology will some day discover laws on a par with those of Galileo, Copernicus, Meyer, and Helmholtz, in the field of natural

---

[1] We have already seen that even by substituting the concept of "energy" for that of "matter," as some would do (for instance, Ostwald), the principle of a fixed substratum underlying the changes of phenomena remains untouched.

[2] See Rümelin's criticism of this "law" in his lecture above quoted, "Ueber den Begriff eines socialen Gesetzes" (*Reden und Aufsätze*, p. 1 foll.).

[3] Ribot, for instance, who says: "Dans ces dernières années, on s'est efforcé de soumettre les actes psychologiques au contrôle précis de la mesure. Voilà en deux mots ce qui se trouve dans des milliers de livres, mémoires, dissertations ou expériences; une masse immense de faits qui attend encore son Kepler ou son Newton" (*La psychologie anglaise contemporaine*, 3rd edit. 1901, Introduction, p. xxxiii.).

phenomena. Psychologists who refuse to resign themselves to the thought that Psychology, though possessing all the characteristics of a science, is not founded upon the principles of the natural sciences, might as well join those who are still of the opinion that the manifestations of the "soul" should not be the object of scientific study, and that to religion alone, and metaphysics, it is reserved to penetrate into those mysteries inaccessible to scientific research.[1] The conclusion is that all attempts which may be made to derive the laws of consciousness from those of the material processes which attend it are doomed to failure, owing to the essential difference between psychical and physical phenomena. This difficulty is so keenly felt that many of those who still follow materialistic methods have arrived at the conclusion that there is no causality but physical causality, and that all that belongs to the order of conscious facts is subject to no law, but is completely accidental. This is a logical deduction from materialistic principles, which, when followed to their necessary consequences, end by destroying themselves.[2]

The relative autonomy of psychological laws once established, there remains another important question to discuss. As these psychological laws refer to processes of consciousness which are closely connected with the biological processes of the psychophysical individual, what, it may be asked, is the relation between those laws and the laws of mechanical causality which biological phenomena obey?

In speaking of the reciprocal independence of mental and mechanical laws, the word independence is taken in a very relative sense. Man and all animate beings are psychophysical

[1] The impossibility of finding psychological laws of the same value as natural laws is very well shown by Simmel in his book *Ueber sociale Differenzierung*. (Leipsic, 1890, especially chap. i.), which aims at pointing out the close connection of social phenomena with processes of consciousness.

[2] The most notable philosophical attempt made in late years to give a materialistic explanation of consciousness is that of Richard Avenarius, as developed in several of his writings, the completest of which is the *Kritik der reinen Erfahrung* (2 vols., Leipsic, 1888—1890). The school he inaugurated had in Germany a certain following (mostly contributors to the *Vierteljahreschrift für wissenschaftliche Philosophie*) under the name of "Empiricokriticismus." See a criticism upon it by Wundt in the *Philosophische Studien* (Vol. XIII., 1878) in two papers which form part of a larger work, *Ueber naiven und kritischen Realismus*, already quoted. A follower of Avenarius, Petzoldt, arrives at the sceptical conclusion we have alluded to concerning the value of psychical causality in a paper "Zur Grundlegung der Sittenlehre" (*Vierteljahrschrift für wissenschaftliche Philosophie*, Vol. XVIII.).

individuals, and are the product both of material and of conscious phenomena. They live, moreover, amongst physical surroundings and are partly subject to the laws which govern the latter. The psychophysical individual is, therefore, subject both to physical and psychical laws. But whereas the external physical world goes on its way apart from the action of will, the development of individual biological forms depends partly upon the consciousness or will of a psychophysical being. Thus the function of the vital organs is a product of the will, and only by dint of long practice becomes instinctive and reflex or mechanical. We have already seen the vanity of trying to establish the priority of one or the other of these two facts—the function or the organ; it is like asking whether consciousness or the animal organism first came into existence. Consciousness and animal organism, function and organ, are correlative terms, the one of which cannot be thought of without implying the other. It is therefore certain that organic evolution is closely connected with psychological evolution; for the organ to become modified it is necessary also for the function to have become transformed. Psychological laws, however, find in this necessary co-ordination with mechanical laws a limitation to their development, just as the extension of mechanical laws finds a limitation in the will of the animate being. This limitation, however, is not to be understood in the sense that those two series of laws cease, at a given point of their evolution, to follow their respective courses in order to mingle one with the other. On the contrary, psychological laws always follow their own course, and mechanical laws theirs; in physical nature there is no place for liberty, just as in the chain of mental causality a mechanical order is inadmissible. Thus, when man wishes to influence external nature, he endeavours to apply his own ideas to it; but so far from trying to change the inner essence of physical laws, he endeavours to understand their inner workings so as to guide them to his advantage. From this it follows that the increase of mental energy is subject to the physical conditions of life. In the psychophysical individual this interdependence of the laws of volition and matter is closer than elsewhere, but its nature remains the same.[1] Briefly, in all investigations and discussions of physical and psychical facts, it must be constantly borne in mind that they are mutually dependent and connected in one all-embracing unity.

[1] See, concerning this question, Wundt, *System der Philosophie*, pp. 407 foll., 545 foll.; *Logik*, Vol. II., pp. 332, 550, and 551.

CHAPTER XII

CONCLUSION

WE have now reached the end of our survey of the more important problems which form the object of psychological discussion, so that nothing remains but to sum up the results arrived at, with some remarks as to their place in general knowledge.

The object of modern Psychology is threefold, seeing that it is related as closely to philosophy as to physiology and to the moral sciences. Its separation from philosophy was gradual, as was the case with kindred sciences, such as sociology, which, in other respects, has the greatest affinity with it. The separation of Psychology from physiology is recent, for it is only recently that the phenomena of consciousness have been recognised as essentially different from corporeal phenomena, although closely connected with them. On the other hand, Psychology is becoming always more intimately connected with the moral sciences, owing to the fact that, in spite of all attempts at confining themselves exclusively to biological methods, those sciences have had to recognise in Psychology the starting-point of all studies dealing with the various products of consciousness.

While Psychology remained dependent upon philosophy, it had to follow its ups and downs, and as there have been two principal schools of philosophy from the Renaissance down to our day—namely, the English and the German—Psychology also developed in accordance with these two different systems. English philosophy having always had a prevalently empirical character, the psychological theories connected with it naturally attributed more importance to the processes of consciousness, such as sensation and perception, which are directly caused by external impressions, and proceeded upon the assumption that the mind reproduces the sequence of external phenomena. Given this point of view, the law of the association of presentations, discovered by English psychologists, followed as a consequence, to which was attributed the same exactitude and constancy as belonged to the laws of matter. This eminently empirical character of English Psychology was the reason why it also assumed so entirely an intellectualistic character, attributing as it did exclusive importance to the processes of knowledge, such as sensations, presentations, and the association of the latter. Intellectualism and empiricism are thus the distinctive features of English Psychology.

German philosophy, on the contrary, started from different principles. Disregarding the objective and external elements of consciousness, it attached particular importance to the inner factor, which expresses, more than anything else, the inmost character of the individual consciousness. Hence the metaphysical tendency of German Psychology, and its inclination to explain the origin and connection of the mental processes by means of an evolution which takes place beyond the ken of introspection in the mysterious regions of unconsciousness. This idea of unconscious elaboration is to be found, more or less vaguely expressed, from Leibnitz down to the Herbartians, and gave birth, during the nineteenth century, to entire metaphysical systems, such as that of Hartmann.

As regards intellectualism, however, English and German philosophy and Psychology were not essentially dissimilar, except that the latter explained the formation and connection of the mental processes by means of an unconscious "synthesis" allied to inference which takes place within us, whereas the English school explained them by association after the manner of physical phenomena. It was not until the nineteenth century that Schopenhauer, in developing an idea already put forth by Kant in his *Critique of Practical Reason,* demonstrated the existence of an element, the importance of which had been too much neglected until then—viz. the "will." For Schopenhauer the intelligence was a secondary phenomenon; but, apart from this and similar exaggerations, he may be said to mark the beginning of a new era in Psychology, which, as opposed to intellectualism, we may call "volitionism," and which is the most satisfactory result of contemporary Psychology. We may even affirm that it is only with the recognition of the subjective elements of consciousness that Psychology has struck out a line of its own and taken up a position independent of the natural sciences.

It is difficult to determine the exact moment when modern Psychology begins. It is commonly said to begin with Spencer and Bain in England, Herbart, Lotze, and Fechner in Germany;

but amongst all these, Bain and Fechner alone can be styled pure psychologists, whereas the others are essentially philosophers, even when they are dealing with psychological subjects, their object always being to make their psychological principles tally with their philosophical systems. Thus, on Herbart's theory, mental phenomena were a special case of the "pluralist" system; whilst Spencer applies to them the general laws of organic evolution. To Bain and Fechner the study of the mental processes owes much of its progress, the former having placed it on an empirical basis, the latter having instituted and regulated the experimental method. The latter method is, as we have seen, a consequence of the study of physiology and physics, and of the connection which was discovered to exist between physical and physiological phenomena on the one hand, and "inner" phenomena on the other, Weber's law, formulated by Fechner, opening a new horizon to psychological research.

Yet, if Bain and Fechner play a great part in the origin and development of modern Psychology, Spencer is not far behind them. He it is who had the idea of studying the mind not only in adult individuals, but during the whole evolution of the individual and also in the species. Spencer was also the first who promoted those psychological investigations which have since proved that the primitive and fundamental laws of the mental processes are the same in elementary organisms as in man, in history and in the community as in the individual.

We cannot affirm that the true significance and importance of the experimental method, as applied to the study of the mental processes, were immediately understood. On the contrary, for a long time after Fechner it was believed that experimental Psychology, owing to the fact that it deals only with the simpler mental forms directly connected with physical and physiological phenomena, is a special form of physiology. This idea was encouraged by the materialistic school, who believed that the physiologist, who carried his study beyond the functions of the other organs of the body to the functions of the nervous system, in so doing was studying the "phenomena of consciousness." Many philosophers and psychologists, though themselves opposed to materialism, have recognised the excellence of the methods and results of the biological sciences, and desired nothing better for Psychology than that it should follow in their wake.

Modern scientific Psychology has its origin also, as we have seen, in the moral sciences. The great development of the latter, during the nineteenth century, has been the principal cause of the prevalence in modern Psychology of the belief that the phenomena of consciousness have a value of their own, and cannot be referred to any immaterial substratum, or mental substance, of which they are merely manifestations. History, Philosophy, Sociology, Political Economy are all concerned with events and facts which are nothing but products of the human consciousness. Having established certain data, they endeavour to investigate their meaning and to explain them scientifically. This empirical method could not fail to exercise an influence upon the study of the processes of consciousness, considered in their most general and typical aspects— that is to say, upon psychological science.

Inasmuch as individual Psychology, however, had no direct connection with the moral sciences, seeing that the former deals with the mental processes of the individual, considered in the abstract and in isolation from other individuals, whereas the latter study the mental productions of man as he is in reality or living in social intercourse with his kind, it was necessary to find a branch of science which should serve to connect Psychology and the moral sciences. This was achieved by the "Psychology of Peoples." Originally merely an application of the results of individual Psychology to complex historical, social, or literary phenomena, the Psychology of peoples became by degrees one of the methods of Psychology, and, in conjunction with the experimental method, one of the two principal sources of psychological knowledge.

With the appearance of the "Psychology of Peoples" we may close the first period of the history of modern Psychology, a period which it will be well to sum up with the mention of a few dates. The psychological works of Herbart were written about 1820; those of Lotze about 1852; Spencer's *Principles of Psychology* appeared in 1855; Bain's *The Senses and the Intellect* in 1856, *The Emotions and the Will* in 1859; Fechner's *Elements of Psychophysics* in 1860; and *The Life of the Soul* of Lazarus, which marks the beginning of the "Psychology of Peoples" in 1855. In 1860 Lazarus and Steinthal began the publication of the *Journal of Ethnographical Psychology and of the Science of Language*. The first period of modern Psychology may therefore be said to extend from Herbart to Lazarus; and it is distinguished by the lack of any exact notion amongst psychologists of the unity of the various psychological methods, each author following a line of his own, irrespective of other methods. Nevertheless, amongst the different systems some have more points of contact than others, there being, for instance, much greater affinity between the experimental methods of Fechner and that of Bain and of Spencer than between the two latter and the "Psychology of Peoples" as founded by Lazarus and Steinthal, in spite of the fact that they had a decided leaning towards certain semi-materialistic ideas. A still greater uncertainty reigned with regard to the ultimate object of Psychology and to its place amongst the sciences. The positivist theory was loth to admit Psychology as an autonomous science, whereas Fechner and Bain considered it in this light; and finally Lazarus and Steinthal mixed it up with certain moral and philosophical sciences, such as sociology, the history of art, and the science of language. The materialistic doctrines, on the other hand, exaggerating positivist tendencies, refused to recognise any independence whatever in mental phenomena.[1]

The second period, which may be called that of "contemporary Psychology," begins, we may say, with the first publications of Sully, Wundt, and Brentano, and comes down to the present day with the later works of the two first-named authors, and with those of Ribot, Höffding, Ladd, James, Baldwin, Külpe, Ebbinghaus, Münsterberg, Ward, Bidet, Jodl, and others whose works we have already quoted and discussed. During this period we must note, first of all, that almost all those who deal with Psychology are "psychologists" in the true sense of the word, and that it is only by way of exception that some of them have brought out a general system of philosophy or have concerned themselves at all with philosophical science. This was a natural consequence of the growing importance of Psychology and of the accumulation of psychological material, which necessitated a greater subdivision of labour.[2] We must, however, bear in mind that, apart from authors

[1] Mercier, in a recent work on *Les origines de la psychologie contemporaine* (Paris, Louvain, 1897), p. 106, etc., considers Spencer, Fouillée, and Wundt as the *maîtres* of contemporary Psychology. Granting this as regards Spencer and Wundt (although the latter belongs more properly to the second period), it does not seem to us right to place Fouillée alongside of these writers. Fouillée is a philosopher of exceeding merit, but one cannot say that his writings mark any new departure in Psychology, as is the case with Spencer, and especially with Wundt. The philosophical works of Fouillée, on the contrary, appeared under the influence of the principles of modern scientific Psychology. Nor do we think it right to leave on one side Bain and Fechner, who with Spencer and Wundt are perhaps the most original psychologists of our century.

[2] Cf. chap. ii., where we have pointed out that not a few modern psychologists (such as Wundt, Höffding, Sully, Külpe, Jodl, Baldwin, etc.) have also dealt with philosophical sciences, such as logic and ethics, and even with general philosophy.

who treat of psychological questions in general, there are some who deal exclusively with experimental research, and others who follow, with modern modifications, the psychological theories of Herbart and of Spencer. On the whole, and considered with regard to its most notable representatives, we may say that this period presents the following characteristics — freedom from philosophical prejudices and tendency towards an objective and empirical method of study.[1] It may, therefore, be called "empirical," on the ground that it only concerns itself with the description of the phenomena of consciousness as they actually exist, without reference to their ultimate causes or to the philosophical questions connected with psychological problems. This empirical and descriptive method is a direct result of positivist doctrines. As a reaction against abstract metaphysical speculations, Comte and the other positivists held that the only aim of science should be that of describing phenomena with accuracy. The greatest number of representative psychologists of this period is to be found in England and America, the English school having always been distinguished by its empirical and descriptive tendency. The Germans, on the contrary, either concern themselves solely with experimental research and the founding of psychological laboratories, or else persist in enclosing Psychology within antiquated philosophical systems. Wundt, however, in his *Lectures on Human and Animal Psychology* (1st edit. 1863; 2nd edit. 1892) adopts in Psychology a method which may rightly be termed empirical. Notwithstanding all its advantages, however, the empirical system, so well represented by Höffding, cannot be said to have satisfied all the requirements of science, the ultimate object of which is not only to *describe* but to *explain* phenomena. The biological sciences have also passed through the descriptive and explanatory stages. Old-fashioned anatomy contented itself with a minute description of the structure of the bodily organs; contemporary anatomy, on the contrary, recognising that each organ is connected with, and in part the result of, some function, studies chiefly the genesis of the organs and the conditions under which their formation is made possible.[2] Briefly, biology follows nowadays a genetic rather than a descriptive method, and physiology

---

[1] Cf. what we have said in chap. ii. on the subject of the much greater affinity that psychological studies have with philosophical studies than any of the moral sciences.

[2] See Wundt, *Logik*, Vol. II., Part I., chap. v. ("Die Logik der Biologie"), p. 514, etc.

has taken the place of anatomy as the fundamental biological science. The superior importance acquired by physiology is owing to the fact that it does not deal with fixed objects, but with changeable processes, and is, therefore, obliged to make use of experiment in order the better to understand them. Thus the experimental method has become a powerful means of observation, for an experiment which consists in the voluntary reproduction of a phenomenon can show better than anything else the manner and causes of its production, evolution, and termination.

With the help of experiment and of all the other methods which it can make use of, Psychology has established various general facts which may be considered as acquisitions to science. These facts may be reduced to the following:—

1. The mental life is not a simple unit, but, as Leibnitz had already noted, is made up of a multitude of units; it is, in fact, a continuous process of simple phenomena. The apparent simplicity of consciousness has thus been analysed into its constituents. Likewise the human mind is the product of a lengthy evolution, the progressive complexity of which is observable as well in the individual as in the species.

2. Consciousness cannot be divided into a number of "faculties"; it is a unity composed of interconnected elements. Moreover, every state of consciousness embraces, in a different measure, perceptions, feelings, and impulses. The empirical system had arrived at the same conclusion; but although it had shown the intimate connection existing between the various elements of consciousness, it had not explained sufficiently the manner with which this connection is produced, nor had it discovered the original and principal source of the complicated structure of the mental life.

3. The psychophysical notion of the individual, which has taken the place of the abstract entities of a physical and a psychical individual, and is traceable to Descartes.

4. The parallelism between the evolution of the consciousness of the individual and that of the community. The same laws and principles govern both.

5. The principle, which is a consequence of the preceding, of the reciprocal action of the social surroundings on the individual, and of the individual on his surroundings. The individual, as he is at present, has been formed by social evolution, and social evolution is the work of individuals.

From these facts important philosophical conclusions may be

drawn. Philosophically, the most important, perhaps, is connected with the concept of a psychophysical individual. Modern Psychology considers the object of Psychology and the object of the natural sciences as different aspects of the same thing. Hence Psychology and philosophy lead us to the monistic concept of a grand unity embracing the two series of physical and mental phenomena, but without sacrificing either of the two.

In spite of this, each order of facts follows a path of its own. The physical world is subject to mechanical laws; the moral world, on the contrary, is spontaneous and independent. Mental energy is continually on the increase, and is the product of a conscious activity, and not an inevitable force to which free will is foreign. History, society, art, religion, and science are the result of a continuous and incessant action which has no precise limits, and which, issuing from the untrammelled will, is the expression of the noblest and most elevated part in man. The spiritual world exists by itself, as a psychical reality, as positive and real as any material reality. Ideas, feelings, acts of willing, and even the simplest sensations are all *sui generis*, and cannot be compared to physical phenomena. If, on the other hand, we find that language makes use of terms taken from material facts to express moral ideas, the reason is to be looked for in the fact that in primitive times the faculty of observation was directed more towards the external than towards the moral world. Subsequently words have remained unchanged, though their meaning has become spiritualised. The same process has taken place in art, which finds during its first stages a sensible and plastic expression, but gradually assumes a "psychological" character, turning its attention more and more towards the inner world. All these circumstances, combined with the continual development of the moral sciences, clearly indicate that, side by side with the reality of matter, that of the mind or "spirit" has also found recognition, and promises to grow in importance with the progress of civilisation.

INDEX

"Actuality" theory, 325, 329
Affinity of psychological elements, 247
Animals, Psychology of, 48, 55, 161
Animism, Theory of, 107
Année psychologique, 55
Anthropology, Criminal, in Italy, 59
Apathy's discoveries on the nerves, 101
Apperception, 11, 214, 236, 301
Appetites, 173, 183
Ardigò, R., 56, 127
Aristotle, 92, 173
Assimilation, 243, 351
Association, 238, 290, 351
Associationist school, 24
Atomism, Psychical, 307, 336
Attention, 212, 237, 275, 301

Bailey, S. 41
Bain, etc., 39, 65, 125, 139, 192, 208, 305, 342
Baldwin, J. M., 151, 154, 171, 229, 331, 371
Beneke, F. E., 26, 136, 178, 210
Berkeley, G., 16, 316
Binet, 272
Biological determinism, 279
Bonnet, 21
Brain, Experiments on the, 97
Brentano, F., 45, 64, 134, 283
Broca, P., 96
Brown, T., 19
Büchner, 112

Cabanis, G., 27
Cardano, G., 342
Causality, 114, 346
Cerebro-spinal system, 102
Character, 180, 219, 295
Childhood, Psychology of, 48

Complication, 232, 243, 351
Comte, A., 30, 135, 321
Conception, 250, 345
Condillac, E. Bonnot, de Mably de, 19, 261
Consciousness, 258, 276, 330
Consciousness of self, 332
Contrasts, Law of, 358

Darwin, C., 42, 50, 109, 161, 192
Darwin, E., 18
De Biran, 28
Definitions of Psychology, 63, 67
Democritus, 92, 107, 314
Descartes, 8, 92, 173, 260, 281, 314, 326
Determinism, 278, 347
Discrimination, 305, 343
Dualistic conception of Psychology, 8, 93, 114

Ebbinghaus, H., 75
Elements, Mental, 271
Emotions, 191, 235
Empirica or *experimentalis* (*Psychologie*), 12, 137
Empiricists, 325
Energy, 360
Enlightment, 178
Ethnographical Psychology. *See* Psychology of Peoples
Evolution, 217, 251, 274, 282
Evolution by contrast, Law of, 369
Experimental methods, 142, 148, 158, 161

Faculties, Theory of the, 94, 174
Fechner, G. T., 35, 123, 137, 342
Feeling, 69, 182, 228, 259
Flourens, J. P., his anatomical theory, 95

394 Index

Fouillée, A., 56, 368
Functions, psychical, 173
Fusions, 231

Gall, F. J., 95, 176
Galluppi, P., 29, 57
Galton, F., and Grant Allen, 50
Genetic methods, 153
Genius, 258
Gerlach, J., his theory on the nervous system, 99
Germany, Experimental research in, 139
Golgi, C., discoveries on the nerve-cells, 100
Goltz and the Strasburg school, 98
Gradation methods, 145

Haeckel, 269
Hamilton, W., 31, 263
Hartley, D., 17, 175, 317
Hartmann, 216, 282
Hegel, 23, 135, 161, 319
Height of sensibility. *See* Upper limit of sensibility
Herbart, F., 24, 134, 177, 264, 284, 319, 328
Heterogony of ends, Law of, 366
Histology, 99
Höffding, H., 46, 67, 123, 216, 287, 343
Horwicz, A., 38, 66, 188, 204
Hume, D., 16, 175, 317, 327
Hylozoism, 268

Identity, Theory of, 123
Imitation, 254
Increase of psychic energy, Law of, 360
Infancy, Psychology of, 50, 55, 59, 154
Innate ideas, 280
Inner sense, 130
Instinct, 213, 252, 292
Intellectualism, 175, 320
Introspective method, 129, 161
Invention, 255
Italian psychologists, 57

James, W., 51, 68, 191, 228, 297, 345
Jodl, 49, 68, 331

Kant, I., 22, 106, 133, 174, 318, 327
Külpe, O., 333

La Mettrie, 20
Laboratories, Psychological, 61, 67
Ladd, G. T., 51, 345
Lange, C., 191
Language, Science of, 155, 253
Laws of Psychology, 312, 351, 373
Lazarus and Steinthal, 45, 156
Leibnitz, 11, 94, 174, 261, 281, 315, 326, 347
Lewes, G., 41, 282
Limit (upper) of sensibility, 296.
Localisation of mental functions, 97, 232
Locke, J., 10, 175, 261, 281, 316
Lotze, H., 33, 106, 111, 181, 208, 306, 329
Lubbock, J. (Lord Avebury), 43, 50, 155

Malebranche, 93, 261
Materialistic school, 9, 20, 32, 92, 111, 117
Maudsley, H., 43, 276, 282
Measurement of mental processes, 349
Mechanical theory of vital phenomena, 108
Memory, 245, 351
Mental dispositions, 286
Methods in Psychology, 128, 145
Micro-organisms, 272
Mill, J., 24, 263
Mill, J. S., 31, 263, 321
Mind, 91, 258
Minimal variations, 145
Mnemonic and associative experiments, 149
Monism, 93, 117
Moral sciences, 160
Mosso, A., 58, 191
Müller, Max, 44
Munk, H., 97
Münsterberg, 75, 152, 186, 205

Nahlowsky, 184
Naturalistic school, 50
Neo-Thomistic school, 124
Neo-vitalism, 110

Nervous stimulus, 225
Nervous system, 98

Occasionalism, Theory of, 93
Organism, 268

Pathological Psychology, 48, 161, 311
Peoples, Psychology of, 25, 43, 55, 154
Periodicals, Psychological, 61
Periods in the history of Psychology, 8
Phrenology, 95, 176
Physiological psychologists, 33, 136, 188, 282
Plato, 92, 193, 326
Play of animals, 253
Position of Psychology among the sciences, 79
Positivism, 135
Presentation, 212, 231, 281
Priestley, J., 18
Primitive naturalism, 314
Process, Nerve- and protoplasmic, 100
Psychical " substance," 327, 336
"Psychologia rationalis " (Wolff), 327
Psychology, subjective and objective, of Spencer, 66
Psychometry, 147
Psychophysical and psychometrical methods. *See* Experimental
Psychophysical materialism, 153, 1
Psychophysical parallelism, 121
Psychophysicians, 46, 70

Reality of psychical facts, 118
Recognition, 245, 354
Recurrence, Historical, 361
Reflex movement, 278, 293
Reid, T., 18, 262
Relations between physical and mental phenomena, 74, 104, 113
Relativity, Law of, 304, 341
Res cogitans and *res extensa*, 9
Resultants, Law of psychical, 352
Ribot, 54, 188, 209, 276, 301, 355
Romanticism, 178
Rosmini-Serbati, A., 29, 57, 264, 309
Rousseau, J. J., 21, 178
Rümelin, G., 323
Russian psychologists, 60

Schopenhauer, 25, 69, 119, 178, 219, 320
Seat of consciousness, 288
Sensation, 182, 225, 284
Sensationalism, 175
Sense, Inner and outer, 10
Sensibility, " Absolute," and " of difference," 144
Sentimentalism, 178
Sergi, G., 58
Span of consciousness, 148
Speech, Physiological mechanism of, 104
Spencer, H., 38, 65, 119, 125, 139, 203, 217, 267, 305, 322, 336
Spinoza, B., 9, 93, 123, 315
" Spirit," or " soul," 258, 325
Spiritualistic school, 9, 111, 117.
Stewart, D., 19, 262
Stout, G. F. 50
Strasburg school and Goltz, 97
Stream of consciousness, 297, 345
Subconsciousness, 288
" Substantiality " theory, 325
Sufficient reason, Principle of, 347
Sully, J., 49, 228, 331

Taine, H. A., 53, 322
Tarde, G., 52, 55, 371
Tetens, J. N., 14, 137, 183
Threshold of consciousness, 143, 296
Threshold of difference, 144
Threshold of space, 147
Tone of feeling, 182
Türck, L., 97

Unconscious cerebration, 282.
Unconscious psychic life, 280
" Unity of consciousness," 332
Upper limit of sensibility, 143, 296

Van Grot, N., 124
Vico, G. B., 161
Virchow, 111
Vitalism, Theory of, 107
Vogt, 120
Volitional activity, 201
Volitionism, 331

Volkmann, 181, 201
Voluntarism, 215, 320

Waitz, T., 44, 202
Ward, J., 49, 229
Weber, E. H., 34, 137
Weber's law, 138, 150, 324
Will, Importance of the, 69, 73, 178, 200, 269

Wohlwollen, Kant's principle of, 26, 179
Wolff, C. A., 12, 94, 129, 171, 262, 281, 327
Wundt, W., 36, 126, 141, 171, 210, 283, 329, 346, 368

Zanotti, F. M., 17
Ziehen, 240

The Library of Philosophy
Edited by J. H. MUIRHEAD, M.A., LL.D.
Professor of Philosophy in the University of Birmingham

THE LIBRARY OF PHILOSOPHY is in the first instance a contribution to the History of Thought. While much has been done in England in tracing the course of evolution in nature, history, religion and morality, comparatively little has been done in tracing the development of Thought upon these and kindred subjects, and yet "the evolution of opinion is part of the whole evolution."

This Library will deal mainly with Modern Philosophy, partly because Ancient Philosophy has already had a fair share of attention in this country through the labours of Grote, Ferrier, Benn, and others, and through translations from Zeller; partly because the Library does not profess to give a complete history of thought.

By the co-operation of different writers in carrying out this plan, it is hoped that a completeness and thoroughness of treatment otherwise unattainable will be secured. It is believed, also, that from writers mainly English and American fuller consideration of English Philosophy than it has hitherto received from the great German Histories of Philosophy may be looked for. In the departments of Ethics, Economics, and Politics, for instance, the contributions of English writers to the common stock of theoretic discussion have been especially valuable, and these subjects will accordingly have special prominence in this undertaking.

THE LIBRARY OF PHILOSOPHY

Another feature in the plan of the Library is its arrangement according to subjects rather than authors and dates, enabling the writers to follow out and exhibit in a way hitherto unattempted the results of the logical development of particular lines of thought.

The historical portion of the Library is divided into two sections, of which the first contains works upon the development of particular schools of Philosophy, while the second exhibits the history of theory in particular departments.

To these have been added, by way of Introduction to the whole Library, (1) an English translation of Erdmann's *History of Philosophy*, long since recognised in Germany as the best; (2) translations of standard foreign works upon Philosophy.

J. H. MUIRHEAD,
General Editor.